OUR SISTER
REPUBLICS

OUR SISTER REPUBLICS

The United States in an Age of American Revolutions

CAITLIN FITZ

LIVERIGHT PUBLISHING CORPORATION

A DIVISION OF W. W. NORTON & COMPANY

INDEPENDENT PUBLISHERS SINCE 1923

NEW YORK • LONDON

For information about permission to reproduce selections from this book,
write to Permissions, W. W. Norton & Company, Inc.,
500 Fifth Avenue, New York, NY 10110

For information about special discounts for bulk purchases, please contact
W. W. Norton Special Sales at specialsales@wwnorton.com
or 800-233-4830

Manufacturing by Berryville Graphics
Book design by Fearn Cutler de Vicq
Map by David Lindroth Inc.
Production manager: Julia Druskin

ISBN 978-0-87140-735-1

W. W. Norton & Company, Inc.
500 Fifth Avenue, New York, N.Y. 10110
www.wwnorton.com

W. W. Norton & Company Ltd.
Castle House, 75/76 Wells Street, London W1T 3QT

1 2 3 4 5 6 7 8 9 0

To Ezra, my first friend.

CANADA
(BRITISH)

Montreal • Boston
New York
Philadelphia
Baltimore
Washington,
D.C.

UNITED STATES

Lexington •

Nashville

St. Louis •

(CLAIMED BY UNITED STATES
& BRITAIN)

Baton
Rouge • New Orleans

Santa Fe •

San Antonio

Rio Grande

MEXICO

Vera Cruz

Mexico City

NORTH ATLANTIC
OCEAN

Tropic

HAIT

CUBA
(SPANISH)

JAM
(BRI

UNITE
PROVINCE
CENTRA
AMERIC

NORTH PACIFIC OCEAN

AMERICA,
CIRCA 1825

0   MILES   800

0   KM   800

Map rotated to best fit all
key geographic locations

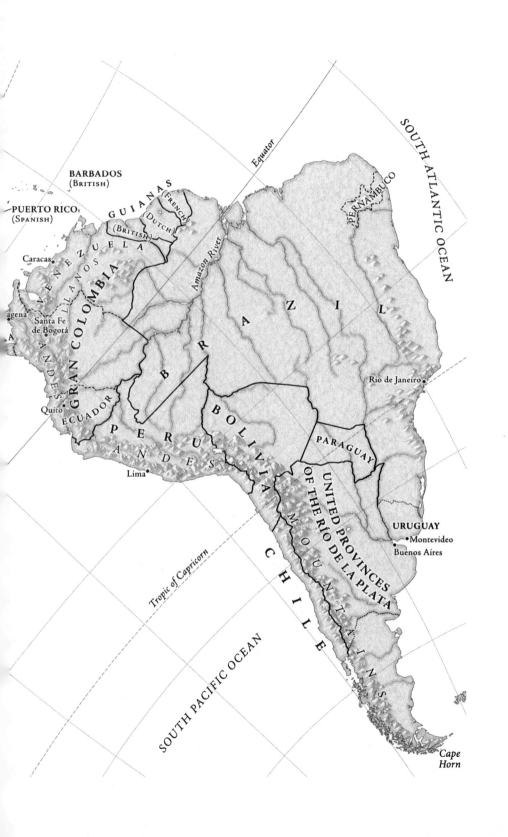

BARBADOS
(BRITISH)

PUERTO RICO
(SPANISH)

SOUTH ATLANTIC OCEAN

G U I A N A S

(FRENCH)

(DUTCH)

(BRITISH)

Equator

V E N E Z U E L A

Caracas

PERNAMBUCO

agena

GRAN COLOMBIA

L L A N O S

Santa Fe
de Bogotá

B

R

A

Z

I

L

A
N
D
E
S

Amazon River

Quito

ECUADOR

Rio de Janeiro

P

E

R

U

B O L I V I A

Lima

A
N
D
E
S

PARAGUAY

UNITED
PROVINCES
OF THE RÍO DE LA PLATA

URUGUAY

Montevideo

Buenos Aires

Tropic of Capricorn

C

H

I

L

E

M
O
U
N
T
A
I
N
S

SOUTH PACIFIC OCEAN

Cape
Horn

CONTENTS

OUR SISTER REPUBLICS

AN AGE OF
AMERICAN REVOLUTIONS

Tʜᴇ ʜᴀʟꜰ-ᴄᴇɴᴛᴜʀʏ ʙᴇᴛᴡᴇᴇɴ 1775 and 1825 was an age of American revolutions. In the United States, in Haiti, and throughout the entire Spanish-American mainland, insurgents declared independence and, improbably, obtained it, armed with tar and feathers, fire and farming implements, muskets and blood-stained bayonets. Brazil broke away too, brushing off a smattering of Portuguese forces in a single year. By the United States' fiftieth birthday, most of the Western Hemisphere was independent from Europe, and almost all of the new nations had established repub-lics, transforming subjects into citizens and breathlessly invoking equality, rights, even the pursuit of happiness. "Every thing, in fifty years, has changed, and every thing is changing," a Kentucky congressman declared in 1822. "It is the birth-day of a hemisphere redeemed," "the jubilee of nations." A new order for the New World was emerging, or so it seemed to many who lived through the tumult.[1]

From their earliest years of nationhood, U.S. audiences carefully monitored republican uprisings elsewhere in the world, proud in the belief that their own revolution had started such a magnificent trend. In reality, events south of the border owed more to specific developments within the French, Spanish, and Portuguese empires than to U.S. influence. But residents of the hemisphere's first republic had always nurtured outsized notions of their own importance. The audacity of the U.S. revolution lay not simply in the fact that thirteen disparate colonies had defied the mighty British Empire; it lay, too, in revolutionaries' conviction that the rest of the world should care. Even before the Second Continental Congress drafted the Declaration of Independence, Thomas Paine was insisting that the struggle against Britain served a higher purpose. "Freedom hath been hunted round the globe," he proclaimed in *Common Sense*, and by becoming "an asylum for mankind" the United States could save it. Sure enough, over the next several decades, that "Freedom" repeatedly attempted its international comeback. People in the United States were captivated, confident that the world's republican revolutions were earthly manifestations of the same cosmic ideals that had inspired 1776 and thus convinced that insurgents' successes abroad would strengthen the United States at home.[2]

This international enthusiasm ebbed and flowed with the Atlantic tides, but like the ocean, it was always there. It started strong in 1789, as the most storied monarchy in all of Europe started to succumb to cries for constitutional *liberté*. U.S. onlookers exulted at news from France, thrilled to think that they had inspired such a powerful country to follow in their footsteps. Precariously fresh from their own nation's revolution, clergymen bowed their heads and sang the blessings of French liberty; commoners donned tricolor cockades and sang "La Marseillaise." Eventually, however, the excitement tapered. Federalists grew especially wary as Jacobin radicals took control in Paris; Republicans grew cautious as slaves in the French colony of Saint-Domingue took up arms against the island's slaveholding masters. In 1790, that tiny third of an island (now Haiti) was the wealthiest colony in the Americas, producing half of the world's coffee and dripping, too, with the sweet juice of sugarcane and the sweat of those who planted and processed it. A year later and for the next thirteen years, it was dripping in blood, echoing with the same heady words that revolutionaries in the United States and France had sung forth—fighting words, like *liberty*, *equality*, and *freedom*. Throughout the United States, enslaved and free black people alike celebrated Haiti's founding revolutionaries; a few white people respected them, or at least hoped to profit from their business. But most white observers saw Haiti as a place of equality perverted and run amok, and the United States did not formally recognize Haitian independence until 1862.[3]

By the early nineteenth century, therefore, doubt and disillusionment had tempered the early excitement. Even erstwhile Francophiles like Thomas Jefferson (who had stocked his homes with French furniture, French servants, French wine, and *haute cuisine* cooked by his enslaved, Paris-trained chef James Hemings) cringed as Napoleon Bonaparte, a self-proclaimed emperor who only pretended that his rule was constitutional or democratic, rose to power and occupied most of western Europe. Many U.S. onlookers felt like passengers aboard a political Noah's Ark, a lonely republic bobbing alone in a churning sea of monarchy and responsible for the fate of republicanism itself. "[W]e now stand in a trying, a peculiar, and an isolated situation," one Philadelphia newspaper avowed. "We are the only free government upon earth. America is left among the nations, a solitary republic." Some historians have even said that the United States was experiencing its own Thermidorian Reaction, its own turn away from the revolutionary radicalism of Paris and Port-au-Prince. "Did not The American Revolution produce The French Revolution?" an aging John Adams asked in 1811. "And did not the French Revolution produce all the Calamities, and Desolations to the human Race and the whole Globe ever Since? I meant well however . . . I was borne by an irresistable Sense of Duty."[4]

But just as Adams penned his lament, another set of revolutions was beginning to spread, and this time across far more of the globe than before. In 1810, demanding sweeping social change, some

80,000 peasants began a march toward Mexico City and threatened to take it—the biggest metropolis in North America, nearly the size of New York and Philadelphia combined. Further south, in 1811, a Caracas *junta* declared outright independence and launched a republic; when an earthquake leveled the city one year later, some took it as a sign that God frowned on independence, or at least on republicanism. As a young Simón Bolívar pawed through the rubble hearing cries from people buried underneath and certain to die, his dusty face was (an observer later recalled) "the picture of terror and despair." But his words were defiant, and they rose above the desolate chorus of moans: "If Nature itself decides to oppose us," he screamed, "we will fight and force her to obey!" And fight they did, in Caracas and Cartagena, in Buenos Aires and Valparaíso. Over the next decade or so, the entire Spanish-American mainland would be in open revolt, and Brazil found itself racked with revolutionaries, too, men who spoke the language of republican freedom in impassioned Portuguese.[5]

Not even the listless equatorial doldrums could contain that kind of news. The trade winds and the westerlies swept it north into more temperate climes, and as they did, people throughout the United States erupted with joy, undeterred by the chaos in France and the tumult in Haiti. By the hundreds, they named their livestock, their towns, their sons, and sometimes even themselves after Spanish-speaking statesmen; by the thousands, they toasted hemispheric independence on every passing July Fourth. (And, in the first-ever episode of U.S. foreign aid, their representatives in Congress sent $50,000 worth of provisions to Caracas, "for the use of the inhabitants who have suffered by the earthquake.") The excitement was sweeping—it touched men and women, black and white, rich and poor, northerners and southerners and westerners. Most of those people took republicanism's southward spread as a compliment to themselves, seeing it as proof that their own ideals really were universal. The cause of Latin America became the cause of the United States, and to such a degree that Latin American independence helped to fuel the unprecedented torrent of nationalism that engulfed the United States after the War of 1812: between 1816 and 1825, well over half of July Fourth celebrations included toasts to the rebel movements. As one Boston editor trumpeted, Latin American independence was "flattering to our national pride."[6]

The enthusiasm went beyond mere rhetoric, and beyond patchwork disaster relief—Latin American revolutionaries sought to ensure it. Over two hundred South Americans sailed to the United States in search of aid and asylum, many of them working to transform U.S. port cities into international hubs of the American independence wars. Encouraged by these revolutionary visitors, U.S. merchants sold boatloads of arms and ammunition to the rebels (and smaller amounts to royalists), while thousands risked their lives under rebel flags as mercenaries and privateers. All the while, rebel agents variously bribed and befriended newspaper editors in an effort to rally public opinion, convinced as they were that U.S. foreign policy took shape in the smoldering crucible of democratic politics and not simply in the private recesses of Washington. Sure enough, when the United States became the first nation in the world to recognize the independence of mainland Spanish America in 1822, people throughout the country exploded in celebration, a Noah's Ark no more.[7]

*　*　*

LATIN AMERICA'S INDEPENDENCE movements resounded in the United States during this revolutionary age—an age that had great meaning in its time but has since been largely lost to history. Indeed, historians who explore the United States' early overseas connections have focused overwhelmingly on the North Atlantic, but U.S. audiences after the War of 1812 also obsessively pondered the South Atlantic, their political imaginations charting newer longitudinal axes as well as older latitudinal ones. Appalachian farmers read poetry about Andean independence; sailors wore cockades for revolutionary Montevideo; boozy partygoers sang in honor of Colombian freedom. So many people grew emotionally and personally invested in the revolutions to the south that Latin America helped to distill popular understandings of republicanism, revolution, and America itself. For as people in the United States watched other American nations grapple with the meaning of independence, they could not but grapple with their own revolutionary origins, and with what united them and defined them as a country.[8]

Those who have explored nineteenth-century U.S. relations with Latin America have generally told a different story. They have told of expansion, aggression, and war; they have also, crucially, tended to emphasize the United States' often sordid dealings with Mexico and the Caribbean. That story of conflict is important, pressing, and very real. But it is incomplete. While historians have emphasized U.S. interactions with neighboring regions, people of the time (especially those who lived away from the border) were more likely to celebrate far-off *South* America: in the early nineteenth century, songs, toasts, and baby names rarely singled out Mexico, Florida, or Cuba. And when South America was the focus, the narrative of republican brotherhood predominated over the narrative of conflict that so often defined the nation's ever-shifting borders.[9]

It was a remarkable show of hemispheric harmony, not least because the United States and its southern neighbors displayed such obvious racial and religious differences. Everyone knew that Latin America's rebels were Catholic, and the Anglophone world had a centuries-old history of antipopery. As newspapers almost universally reported, moreover, Spanish-American insurgents were collaborating with Haiti, passing gradual antislavery laws, and elevating men of color to positions of military and political authority. One could be forgiven for assuming (as several scholars have) that the cultural differences were simply too profound for white U.S. Protestants to overcome.[10]

But they weren't. U.S. observers rarely dwelled on the insurgents' Catholicism, as if republicanism's spread abroad was so exhilarating that it overshadowed concerns about religion. Still more astonishingly, most editors reacted to news of Spanish-American antislavery efforts and black leadership with casual acceptance rather than outraged alarm, and the popular celebrations continued, unabated and largely unchanged. Even white people in the Deep South were more excited about insurgents' promises to free South America than they were worried about insurgents' simultaneous promises to free the slaves. Spanish-American emancipation tended to be gradual, compensated, and ostensibly overseen by moderate white men. It resembled the model of emancipation that northern U.S. states had already begun to implement—the very model, in fact, that thousands of white southerners were still contemplating. The same country that bristled at French and Haitian radicalism in the late 1790s and early 1800s thus took Spanish-American antislavery sentiment in stride, as onlookers focused on a broader story of political independence and republican government for most of the 1810s and early 1820s. In fact, the only groups that focused consistently on race were black U.S. observers and their white antislavery allies, who contended that the Spanish-speaking rebels were fulfilling the egalitarian promise of the Americas in a way that the United States had yet to do. If white people's contemptuous responses to Haitian abolition had exposed the limits of the U.S. Revolution's universalist message, their responses to Spanish America's more gradual model demonstrated that message's persistence, and its emotional intensity.[11]

It would be easy to dismiss white observers' universalist inclinations as shallow and self-serving. The founding fathers talked of equality; they also protected property, and property in the early United States meant not just land, wagons, houses, and livestock, but also human beings. When property ran up against the egalitarian ideals, property very often won, and in much of the South, black slaves were pushed so far to the social margins that they functioned as an essential buffer upon which white men's equality rested; as the historian Edmund Morgan hauntingly argued over forty years ago, black slavery made white freedom possible in Virginia and beyond. Although northern states successively passed gradual antislavery laws beginning in the 1780s, at the federal level slaveholders more often triumphed. Despite a few scattered and partial victories—the 1787 prohibition of slavery in the Northwest Territory, for example, or the outlawing of the international slave trade to the United States some twenty years later—U.S. citizens repeatedly failed to translate egalitarian words into federal antislavery action; their lofty words must have brought little solace to enslaved southerners who lived in the aching immediacy of their own bondage. In the 1810s and 1820s—at the very time U.S. observers were feting Latin American freedom—slavery was spreading ruthlessly across the South. White people killed and expelled thousands of native people and replaced them with black slaves and sun-bleached cotton, often with support from their own elected officials. The nation's republican rhetoric sang of equality, but the reality was one of inequality.[12]

Still, the hemispheric enthusiasm mattered. Although the universalism that underlay it was often passive and perfunctory, it was also emotional and intense. It was a language of freedom and independence and equality, the very ideals that had helped good patriots explain who they were since 1776. At home, the United States was irrefutably and increasingly a white man's republic. But as those same white men (and sometimes their mothers, wives, sisters, and daughters) looked abroad to South America, whose sheer distance made it seem more like an intellectual abstraction than a pressing reality, the egalitarian and universalist narrative of 1776 prevailed. Popular celebrations of Latin American independence suggest that at a gut moral level, white U.S. observers in the early nineteenth century were more open to the abstract ideas of abolition and racial equality than many historians have recognized.

If the fifty years between 1775 and 1825 thus formed an analytically coherent period of hemispheric history, an era united by anticolonial revolutions from Boston to Buenos Aires, they also formed an analytically coherent period of U.S. history, an era defined by a widespread patriotic narrative of self-evident truths and inalienable rights that is most striking when viewed in the revolutionary context of its time. It was an age of American revolutions, in other words, not only because Latin Americans were themselves casting off colonial rule, but also because so many people in the United States saw those efforts as a continuation of 1776. For some fifty years, white people throughout the United States remained abstractly (and sometimes concretely) committed to the egalitarian principles of their own independence war, and it was precisely those principles that enabled them to knowingly and emotionally embrace a group of multiracial Catholic revolutionaries whose battles were at once anticolonial and antislavery. Despite persistent misgivings about France and Haiti, the nation's backlash against the earlier universalism had not arrived.[13]

Or at least not yet. Historians have long noted that many white southerners by the 1830s were growing skeptical of the nation's founding universalist rhetoric. Rather than seeing slavery as a necessary evil, as they had long done, they began to assert that it was a positive good—good for the South, good for the United States, good even for the slaves themselves. We need to recast that momentous shift in the international dimensions of its time, showing how the Latin American independence movements came to serve as an intellectual scaffold upon which some in the United States constructed new understandings of race and republicanism. When white southerners began to disavow the radical potential of their own Declaration—when they began to view slavery as a positive good—they did so in a world that had recently been overturned (as it seemed at the time) by antislavery revolutions. By 1825, the United States was the only American republic in which slavery was expanding rather than receding. As antislavery activists emphatically observed, the only other places that endorsed slavery's spread were monarchical Brazil and the colonial Caribbean—hardly inspiring company for U.S. onlookers, who preferred to see themselves as stalwart republican pioneers.[14]

It was in this broader geographic context that the Democratic Party—the distant ancestor of the one still with us today—first started to coalesce. In 1826, precisely fifty years after the signing of the U.S. Declaration, rising Democrats made their first-ever collective bid for power by arguing that the United States should not send delegates to an impending inter-American conference in Panama. They gave many reasons: the gathering, they said, would unduly inflate federal and executive power, embolden meddling and moralistic do-gooders, and undermine national sovereignty. To that potent mix, the incipient party's southern congressmen added another reason: slavery. The United States, rising southern Democrats suggested, was a white republic in a hemisphere full of darker-skinned radicals, the moderate exception in a hemisphere of republican pretenders who had taken the ideas of freedom and equality to mortally perilous proportions. The Democratic Party's earliest roots reached circumstantially south into Spanish America, where they tapped into a set of nations that served as convenient foils for the United States and its tightening racial hierarchy.

It was a canny political strategy. Events elsewhere in the Americas had captured voters' imaginations for the previous decade, so a debate about hemispheric policy offered a perfect opportunity for a new political coalition to announce and define itself. Moreover, emerging southern Democrats were helping to resolve a long-standing mismatch between the nation's egalitarian rhetoric and its increasingly unequal reality. They closed the gap by changing the rhetoric to fit the reality, unleashing popular prejudice in a new and politically potent direction.

Many people balked at this newly racialized depiction of Latin

America. Some publicly skewered it; others just quietly distanced themselves, or else offered other kinds of reservations about Latin American capabilities. But in voicing doubts about hemispheric brotherhood, rising southern Democrats helped to dampen the previous decade's worth of enthusiasm. As Congress's debates concluded, the public displays of hemispheric ardor measurably cooled, especially as Latin America transitioned from the heady drama of revolution to the more mundane challenge of governance. The age of American revolutions was over, partly because Latin America was turning toward a new and turbulent period of nation-building, but also because many within the United States were openly starting to question their own Declaration's soaring universalist implications. If U.S. observers in the 1810s and early 1820s had derived a sense of patriotic identity from republicanism's spread into new and largely nonwhite places, by the nation's fiftieth birthday members of a new generation were using Spanish America to define a narrower kind of nationalism, one that proclaimed the nation's uniqueness rather than its universality.

* * *

THE U.S. RESPONSE to Latin American independence recalls the ancient Greek story of Narcissus, who, having spurned his many suitors, came to a riverbank and fell in love with his own reflection. In celebrating foreign revolutions, U.S. observers were celebrating themselves, and like Narcissus, they were so riveted they could barely look away. They were blithely unaware that the object of their affection was an image, an illusion, something easily dispelled by a pebble tossed casually in the river; that was why, in 1826, the international (and, as it turned out, largely one-way) love affair so quickly faded into vanishing ripples.[15]

That narcissism is precisely what makes the international revolutionary ardor so interesting. When it came to their views about such abstract concepts as inalienable rights, self-evident truths, and equal creation, everyday citizens rarely left much of a paper trail. But when it came to their views about foreign revolutions, common white men (and sometimes women and people of color, too) repeatedly left their mark in toasts, baby names, musical selections, and sartorial flair. Some of these clues can be counted and tracked through space and across time; especially when considered alongside newspaper reports and congressional votes, they can serve as a crude measuring stick not just for popular views about foreign revolutions, but also for popular thinking about race, nationalism, equality, and territorial expansion. Ordinary people's responses to Latin American independence reveal the possibilities as well as the limits of egalitarian thinking in the early United States, and they help to show how revolutionary-era universalism found growing competition from a newer rhetoric of white U.S. exceptionalism.

Leading policymakers like James Monroe, John Quincy Adams, and Henry Clay played important roles in this inter-American revolutionary drama, their deeds at once reflecting and shaping the views of ordinary voters. If we are to understand all that Latin American independence has to reveal about the early United States, however, high-stakes diplomacy and high-rolling commerce must be placed alongside less famous (if not always less humble) actors. Actors like Elizabeth and Aylett Buckner, Kentucky farmers who named their son after a Spanish-speaking revolutionary some 2,000 miles away; Emiliano Mundrucu, a *mulato* revolutionary who fled from South America to the United States and informed the antislavery movement at a crucial moment; and James Rodgers, a headstrong New York adventurer who attacked royalist troops abroad and died at the hands of a Brazilian firing squad. Their collective stories emerge through research in Portuguese, Spanish, French, and English, and from archives throughout the hemisphere, manuscripted memorials to the inter-American horizons that shaped these people's lives.

What results is less a history of early U.S. relations with Latin

America than it is a U.S. history that uses Latin America to cast new light on the United States. Despite the work of its revolutionary agents, Latin America didn't intentionally and directly transform the United States, and the United States' influence throughout Latin America was smaller than most U.S. patriots—and some Latin Americans—had hoped it would be. As U.S. audiences crowed about rights and revolution, however, Latin America became a mirror that crystallized and clarified what was at stake. For over a decade, most U.S. patriots had looked proudly to Latin America and seen themselves: republicans, revolutionaries, Americans. In 1826, the heat of emergent party politics started to warp that international looking-glass, transforming it into something more like a funhouse mirror that reflected different images back to different people depending on where those people stood and how they carried themselves. As U.S. observers realized that they saw different reflections—as they realized that they had different understandings of revolutions both foreign and domestic—they started to conclude that they were different people with different goals and different values. That realization facilitated their division into parties, much as the French Revolution had polarized the nation into Republicans and Federalists to an even greater degree one generation before. *Mirror, mirror on the wall, who is the fairest of them all?* As some in the embryonic Democratic coalition saw it, Spanish America was fair by neither of the standard definitions: its revolutionaries were darker-skinned, and their antislavery efforts were certainly not going to bring justice to U.S. slaveholders.[16]

Support for the uprisings in Spanish America and Brazil thus turned out to follow much the same bell-curved trajectory as had responses to France several decades before, rising amid a period of heady optimism and then falling amid angry partisan warfare—although the bell curve for Latin America had a longer plateau that inspired more united support, coinciding as it did with a decade that was largely devoid of nationwide partisanship. Still, attitudes

toward Latin America diverged as soon as partisan tensions resurfaced. At once a contributor to and a casualty of partisan warfare,
support for foreign revolutions fell apart; the center did not hold,
for to define revolution was to define the United States itself.[17]

A NOTE ON TERMS

TERMINOLOGY BECOMES TRICKY when applied to the revolutionary history of America, beginning with the idea of revolution itself.
In speaking of *revolution*, I have not meant to imply that the independence movements that shook the British, French, Spanish, and
Portuguese empires from 1775 to 1825 always produced sweeping
social changes. Insurrections that were radical in some ways were
often conservative in others, with egalitarian gains for some groups
coming at the expense of others as if political rights were a zero sum
game. These are important trends, but they are not my focus here.
Nor am I concerned with the distinction between words like *revolutionary*, which carried positive connotations in the late eighteenth
and early nineteenth centuries, and words like *rebel*, which carried
negative ones. Instead, I have sought a lexical middle ground by
using these words interchangeably, as well as by using the more
neutral term *insurgent*. Meanwhile, I have used the term *republican*
in its strictest political sense, to denote a form of government in
which power resides in the people and their representatives rather
than in a monarch.

My emphasis on "ordinary people" also requires explanation.
The early-nineteenth-century United States was a nation of farmers, with small but significant numbers of craftsmen and mariners;
taken together, these are the people I have in mind. I am not referring to politicians or high-powered merchants, who had more power
to shape popular perceptions and formal policy alike. (I do, however, devote attention to their actions, precisely because these groups
wielded such influence.) My understanding of ordinary people

includes women, although most of the available evidence points to men; my understanding also includes African Americans, although most sources refer to white people. Where my claims clearly apply only to one gender or one race, I have tried to be explicit—speaking, for example, of "white men" or "black U.S. onlookers" as appropriate.

Indeed, this book operates on a largely black-white spectrum; it does not examine how U.S. onlookers understood native people and their descendants at home or abroad. U.S. audiences in the 1810s and 1820s devoted less attention to the hemisphere's historic centers of indigenous culture—Mexico and Peru—than they did to coastal Colombia, Venezuela, Brazil, and the La Plata region, where the descendants of Europeans and Africans more often predominated. As subsequent chapters will show, Mexico was underrepresented in the popular excitement in part because its rural and grassroots insurgency peaked in the early 1810s, when U.S. onlookers were distracted by their second war with Britain, and because when Mexico finally declared independence in the early 1820s, it did so as a monarchy. Peru, meanwhile, received less attention because it was the last part of mainland Spanish America to push for independence, and perhaps, too, because its most celebrated "liberators"—Simón Bolívar and José de San Martín—actually came from Venezuela and the Southern Cone. Furthermore, Spanish South America's liberating armies drew heavily (and very disproportionately) from slaves determined to win their freedom by fighting. Such men were critical to some of the era's most pivotal campaigns—in places they comprised as much as 30 percent of insurgent forces—and when the Panama debates erupted in 1826, people of African descent provoked far more attention than did people of native ancestry. When I speak of "people of color," therefore, I refer to individuals with varying degrees of African descent.[18]

The geographic implications of my terminology are equally important. I have spoken about "people in the United States" and "U.S. observers" rather than "Americans," a slippery term when used in a hemispheric history like this one. I try to reserve the term *American* to evoke the Western Hemisphere's shared and interwoven histories of colonization, forced labor, immigration, and, in many cases, revolution and independence. In referring variously to *South America* and *Spanish America*, I have chosen my words deliberately and thoughtfully, staying true to the terminology that the sources in question actually used. I have avoided the term *pan-American*, which did not appear until the late nineteenth century, but I have bowed to both conciseness and modern usage in speaking of *Latin America*, a term that only emerged when white Spanish-American intellectuals in the 1850s spoke of uniting against U.S. expansion, and when French imperialists in the 1860s sought to justify intervention in Mexico by claiming a shared historic and linguistic descent.[19]

For all that is included in this book, one part of the hemisphere is conspicuously absent: Canada. Indeed, I use the term *hemispheric* to emphasize the United States' early connections to Brazil and mainland Spanish America, and I look periodically to the Caribbean along the way; these places collectively comprise most of the hemisphere but not all of it. All I can offer in my defense is that this project had to end somewhere, and I have adopted the same broad geographic parameters of the people I study. With the exception, perhaps, of those who lived along the nation's northern border, few U.S. onlookers in the 1810s and 1820s referred to British Canada when they were talking about their so-called "Republican Hemisphere"; after all, and despite the hopes of many in the United States, Canada had no republican uprisings until back-to-back breakouts in 1837 and 1838. By then, the age of American revolutions was already slipping away—not least in the United States itself, where the earlier rhetoric of inalienable rights and self-evident truths was increasingly challenged by assertions of white superiority and U.S. exceptionalism.[20]

CHAPTER ONE

SQUINTING SOUTH

B ORN TO A PAIR of Connecticut farmers in 1754, Joel Barlow
became many things in his life: a Yale graduate, Continental
Army chaplain, honorary citizen of revolutionary France, U.S. consul in Tripoli. But above all, Barlow was a poet, a man of meter
and rhyme. His widely read *The Vision of Columbus* (1787) and epic
The Columbiad (1807) were works from the heart, written, as Barlow put it, "from the most pure and ardent desire of doing good to
my country." The *Columbiad* in particular was a "patriotic poem,"
he explained, designed "to encourage and strengthen in the rising
generation, a sense of the importance of republican institutions . . .
in the condition of human nature." In elaborate, book-length verse,
Barlow sang the glories of America.[1]

But Barlow's America did not stop at the Appalachians and
the Alleghenies. It extended all the way to the Amazon and the
Andes, forming a united "western world" of patriotic potential.
Before so much as gazing to North America, in fact, Barlow began
by invoking the sublime beauty of Quito and "the Oronoque." That
sweeping geographic vision perfectly befitted a pair of poems written in honor of Christopher Columbus, a man with special cultural
appeal for U.S. patriots who yearned to distinguish themselves
from Great Britain. Although Columbus had never set foot in

North America, he enabled people to identify with an era of colonization that predated the journeys of Englishmen like the great sirs Raleigh and Drake, and so he came to personify the nation's independent spirit. Poets like Phillis Wheatley employed the allegory of Columbia in the 1770s and 1780s; King's College became Columbia College in 1784, and in 1800, the District of Columbia became the nation's capital city, a republican political nucleus named not only for the United States' first president but also, indirectly, for a Genoese Catholic who sailed for Spain.[2]

These early allusions to a liberty-loving Columbia derived from little more than a feeble sense of shared historical geography. Aside from those who lived near the United States' southern borders (where Creeks, Seminoles, and other native people far outnumbered whites), Spanish and Portuguese America remained blurry stereotypes in the minds of most U.S. onlookers—equal parts El Dorado and Hernán Cortés, military rivals and imperial foils more than political or cultural peers. The Iberian empires had minimized foreign commerce for centuries, and although smuggling flourished anyway, contacts between North and South Americans remained muffled and subdued. Interactions multiplied as the French Revolution and the rise of Napoleon plunged Europe into a quarter century of war, leaving Americans North and South to trade with each other relatively undisturbed. But it was not until the early 1810s, when independence movements erupted across mainland Spanish America, that people throughout the United States began to develop genuine affinities for their southern neighbors.[3]

In fits and starts, the United States thus awakened to the world that stretched south of its borders, from Texas and Florida to Tierra del Fuego. If Barlow's expansive definition of America functioned primarily as poetic metaphor in the 1780s, by the early 1810s the idea of a cohesive Western Hemisphere was bolstered by a growing web of political, economic, and cultural realities.

* * *

IN THE BEGINNING, there was trade. Ships cut doggedly through the Atlantic, their sails dotting the otherwise monotonous oceanic horizon. Spain tried to stop them from crossing imperial lines, determined that the fabled wealth of the Indies should stay in Spanish hands rather than bleeding out to the godforsaken English or, eventually, their conniving U.S. progeny. But the thirst for profit knows few national bounds. Where money was to be made, men in all empires sidestepped regulations; commercial restrictions slowed the trade but couldn't stop it. As one Connecticut merchant put it, men learned to do business "in the Smuggling way," while pirates and sea dogs, with their booty and their bluster, did business in the violent way. Goods and people trickled stealthily between empires: grains, fish, and other edibles from North America; sugar, coffee, cacao, and precious metals from Spanish America; African slaves all around. When the United States arrived on the scene, its traders also became eager reexporters of European manufactures, spreading foreign-made goods around the Atlantic rim and, increasingly, beyond.[4]

Occasionally, trade between the Anglophone and Iberian worlds operated more openly. In times of war, Spain periodically bowed to necessity by opening its American ports to neutral traders, fearing that its colonists might otherwise perish (or revolt out of starving desperation). By 1797, Spain had grown so embroiled in European conflicts that it intermittently tolerated neutral trade for the better part of a decade. U.S. merchants happily offered their services, and within just five years of the new policy's implementation, trade with Spanish America had multiplied by a factor of four. Business quickened to such a degree that the modern U.S. dollar sign ($) seems to have evolved in this period out of the shorthand for *peso* (*p*ˢ, which looked increasingly like today's dollar sign as merchants began to superimpose the *p* and the *s*).[5]

Most of that growing trade was with nearby Cuba, where sugar, coffee, and slavery were symbiotically booming after the slave rebellion in Saint-Domingue slowed production in what had so recently been the world's leading producer. U.S. consumers wanted sweets and U.S. merchants wanted gold and silver specie, while Cubans depended on U.S. flour and other foodstuffs lest they starve to death amid their sprawling fields of coffee and cane. (Cubans also imported New England ice and snow, boatloads of the harrowing northern winter shoveled south to mitigate Cuba's endless summer.) Meanwhile, despite state and federal laws that forbade U.S. citizens from trafficking in enslaved Africans outside the United States, U.S. merchants—most of them from the North and Mid-Atlantic—did exactly that. In the first decade of the nineteenth century, U.S. citizens delivered some 25,000 Africans to stoke Cuba's surging economy. It was sordid, but it was lucrative, enough to inure men to the ugliness of the enterprise. Taken together, in fact, the Cuba trade buoyed the U.S. economy at a formative moment. Spanish-American specie monetized U.S. banks at home and balanced out trade deficits abroad, and all the while merchants and traders reinvested their winnings in domestic industry, banks, and infrastructure, a massive economic multiplier effect rooted in offshore chattel slavery.[6]

Cuba was never the sole Spanish-American destination for U.S. ships, however, and by the early nineteenth century, traders and sailors were venturing further afield. Some looked across the Caribbean to Venezuela, contracting with Spanish colonial officials to supply food, weapons, and other supplies that helped to sustain the empire at a time of disorder and scarcity. Others looked to regions still more remote, sailing around Brazil and Cape Horn to the Pacific coast of Chile. There they killed blubbery mammals on an astonishing scale, harpooning whales and sea elephants until the water and rocks turned red. They killed seals, too, hundreds at a time, forcing the helpless creatures to run the gauntlet between men lined up in rows and armed with five-foot clubs. U.S. participation in the transatlantic slave trade reached these distant climes as well: half of the twenty-two U.S. ships that arrived in Montevideo in 1805 carried enslaved Africans; by 1807, the number had grown to twenty of thirty.[7]

Coincident with the growing commercial interest was a rising expansionist chatter among high-level policymakers, who sought to extend U.S. power in North America and beyond. "[W]e ought certainly to look to the possession of the Floridas & Louisiana," Alexander Hamilton advised a colleague in 1799, "and we ought to squint at South America." In 1801, Hamilton's nemesis Thomas Jefferson "look[ed] forward to distant times, when our rapid multiplication will expand itself beyond those [current U.S.] limits, & cover the whole Northern, if not the Southern continent." Such talk represented a real threat to nearby Spanish territory; the United States bought Louisiana from France (which had itself just acquired the territory from Spain) in 1803, added Florida by 1821, and took half of Mexico less than three decades later. The bluster about expansion into *South* America remained the stuff of daydreams, something easily imagined for "distant times" but much harder to implement as long as national ambition outweighed national power.[8]

∗　∗　∗

CULTURAL CONNECTIONS BETWEEN the United States and Latin America were also deepening in the late eighteenth and early nineteenth centuries, though the awareness usually remained superficial. Colonial British Americans had long relied more on fusty stereotypes about their southern neighbors than on actual experience. Only a few institutions and individuals owned many books on Latin America—the insatiably curious Thomas Jefferson had dozens of relevant volumes in his personal library at Monticello, and East Coast erudites at the New-York Historical Society, Harvard College, and Philadelphia's American Philosophical Society had collected literary and scientific information about Latin America throughout the eighteenth century. But these groups imported most of their titles from abroad; colonial printers issued few if any books on Latin America, perhaps because they expected few if any people to buy them.[9]

At his college graduation in late September of 1771, the loud and husky Hugh Henry Brackenridge unintentionally summarized what most late colonial onlookers thought about Latin America— if they thought about it at all. Cloaked and capped in a black gown and square hat, he joined the president and trustees of the College of New Jersey as their feet crunched along the gravel walkway and up the stairs into stately Nassau Hall, the cupola bells pealing in happy celebration. Aaron Burr, a precocious fifteen-year-old junior who had won prizes in English, Latin, and Greek oratory one day before, was in attendance; graduating senior James Madison was out sick. Meanwhile, ladies and gentlemen from Philadelphia to New York had descended on Princeton for the day, eager to witness the spectacle.[10]

After a series of formal debates, orations, and songs, Brackenridge rose to speak. He and his friend Philip Freneau, a New Jersey farm boy who would later become one of the most influential Republican newspaper editors in the country, had written an effusive celebration of colonial potential entitled "The Rising Glory of America." For some reason Freneau—Madison's roommate— couldn't attend the ceremony. So Brackenridge read the whole poem himself, his Scots burr surely commanding the hall and encapsulating widespread attitudes about Latin America along the way. For the first two or three minutes, he lyrically urged listeners to gaze "no more" upon classical antiquity or old Europe. He turned south: eight lines of gauzy rhetoric about "this western world" of the Americas, four lines of praise for "the hero" Columbus. Then came the corpses and the blood.

But why, thus hap'ly found, should we resume
The tale of Cortez, furious chief, ordain'd
With Indian blood to dye the sands, and choak
Fam'd Amazonia's stream with dead! . . .
Better these northern realms deserve our song . . .
Undeluged with seas of Indian blood,
Which cruel Spain on southern regions spilt.

Why dampen the day's buoyant spirits? Latin America's colonial history was too gloomy to dwell upon, Brackenridge maintained; better to focus on Britain's more promising colonies. The audience seemed to agree, because when Brackenridge finished a half-hour or so later, the building's beige sandstone walls echoed with applause.[11]

Brackenridge's vision was rooted in centuries-old stereotypes of Iberian depravity later to be known as the "Black Legend." That narrative was so persistent that it flourished even after Spain aided the United States in the fight against Britain, and New Haven resident Jedidiah Morse was part of the reason. In 1784, the twenty-three-year-old first published his *Geography Made Easy*, "[c]alculated," as he explained, "particularly for the Use and Improvement of SCHOOLS," and dedicated to "the Young Gentlemen and Ladies, Throughout the United States." The text cut like a razor. "[T]heir character is nothing more than a grave, specious insignificance," Morse wrote of Spanish-American elites; "their whole business is amour and intrigue." Worse, Morse charged, Spanish-American cruelty had transformed many native people into "a dejected, timorous and miserable race of mortals." Although many indigenous South Americans had converted to Catholicism, Morse dryly judged the "exchange not much for the better." (No surprise that Morse's son, the future painter and telegraph inventor Samuel Finley Breese Morse, would become famous for his anti-Catholic xenophobia.) Morse's text spawned several related titles, and his collective opus became a runaway hit. Over the next several decades, sales in at least some places exceeded those of all other texts with the exception of Noah Webster's spellers, Isaac Watts's psalms, and the Bible itself.[12]

The widening commercial horizons that followed Spain's 1797 neutral trade decree stirred cultural interest. Almost immediately, in 1798, a New York editor published a U.S. edition of the Scotsman William Robertson's volume on Latin America. The usual stock figures made their appearances—rapacious conquistadors, licentious priests, dying Incas. But a flurry of translated texts from Spanish America itself offered other perspectives. In 1801, a Salem editor announced that if 500 subscribers could be found, he would print Bernal Díaz del Castillo's *Historia verdadera de la conquista de la Nueva España* in translation. Apparently, he got the response he was looking for: in 1803, the *True History* appeared in its first U.S. edition. One year later, a Philadelphia publisher issued Francisco Javier Clavijero's *History of Mexico*; so, too, did a Richmond printer in 1806, the same year that Washington Irving translated a history of Venezuela from French into English. Even tiny Middletown, Connecticut, contributed to the flow of information, when, in 1808, a local editor published the Jesuit missionary Giovanni Ignazio Molina's *Geographical, Natural and Civil History of Chili*. The mere fact that these texts existed suggests that U.S. readers were growing more interested in Latin America, and some of the books may even have fed early nationalist pride: Clavijero and Molina had both celebrated the Western Hemisphere's potential, openly refuting European critics who said that the Americas and the things that lived there were impotent shadows of their Old World counterparts. But aside from Robertson's *History of America*, which U.S. newspapers excerpted for decades, it was unclear whether any of the titles had very wide circulations, and none were written by U.S. authors or for U.S. audiences.[13]

More information did not always mean more affection. Take the controversial Venezuelan visitor Francisco de Miranda, who arrived in the United States late in 1805 determined to win support for his life's mission: liberating Venezuela from Spain. Miranda had spent the previous two decades in Europe scheming for support, in Britain most of all. In 1805, he finally gave up and turned to the North American republic. Fifty-five years old, with a powdered grey ponytail and fidgety hands and feet, Miranda was old for an aspiring revolutionary general, but that didn't stop him; he had always been more of a dreamer than a pragmatist. From federal warehouses in Springfield, New York City, and West Point, he stockpiled pikes, cannonballs, and mortars; elsewhere, he obtained firearms, powder, and uniforms, and even inspired John Adams's grandson to drop out of college and enlist as an aide-de-camp. (The former president was horrified when he found out, but it was too late; as he later wrote, "I gave up my grandson as lost forever.")[14]

Most merchants refused to back Miranda; they were already profiting from trade with loyal Spanish officials in Venezuela and beyond. Newspaper editors, who had less to lose, were more encouraging. The "United States of South America like the United States of the North, will represent to admiring Europe another republic independent, confederated, and happy," the *Richmond Enquirer* predicted after Miranda and his roughly 200 recruits finally disembarked early in 1806. Newark, New Jersey's *Centinel of Freedom* professed itself "among those who wish him success, and who would gladly echo his triumphs." Manhattan, where Miranda did most of his recruiting, produced the loudest buzz of all, and when the Republican governor accused several prominent Federalists of having violated federal neutrality laws by supporting Miranda's scheme, a jury quickly acquitted them.[15]

The attention grew more critical as Miranda made his way south. Recruits complained of harsh treatment aboard ship and even mutinied unsuccessfully (a Saint Patrick's Day celebration gone awry, they later tried to explain). Worse, when Spanish *guardacostas* intercepted the expedition off the coast of Venezuela,

Miranda fled, abandoning two ships and about one-third of his men. Those unfortunate sailors were bound back to back, loaded with heavy chains, and deposited in humid subterranean dungeons, where, greasy, hairy, and increasingly emaciated, they sat in their own feces awaiting trial. Ten were eventually hanged and publicly decapitated "with a chopping knife," one survivor grimly recalled. Those who managed to escape over the next several years returned to the United States with stories that reflected as poorly on Spain as they did on the man who had tried to overthrow it. Three recruits lashed out in tell-all books, and editors, who published over 450 discrete articles about the Miranda expedition, denounced the would-be liberator as a megalomaniac fraud. It was a bumbling debacle, and it discredited early advocates of Spanish-American independence before a nation of readers.[16]

Among U.S. onlookers, therefore, Spain's neutral trade decree of 1797 had triggered a desultory swell of commercial and cultural interest in Latin America. Much of the attention was critical, and there is little other evidence that ordinary people knew or cared much about what was happening south of their borders. As late as 1810, editors were still struggling to explain the difference between Venezuela and Caracas, and headlines suggested that readers' New World geography was minimal: "*FROM CARACAS (S. America),*" one attentive editor saw fit to explain. Another author, his words reprinted from Salem to Richmond, mourned the "scanty geographical knowledge hitherto in our possession respecting these countries"; then, perhaps seeking to expand awareness, he declared that "[i]mmense regions are inhabited only by monkies." "We have," confessed the *Baltimore Whig*, "no accurate account of the whole population." As Jefferson lamented in 1809, even nearby Mexico had been "almost locked up from the knolege [*sic*] of man hitherto." It would take something else to kindle and then sustain popular excitement about Latin America. Much like Spain's 1797 trade declaration, that something would originate in a catastrophically violent and war-torn Europe.[17]

* * *

IN 1807 AND 1808, NAPOLEON unleashed his wrath on Iberia. As if Europe were his chessboard, the French emperor invaded Portugal and then kidnapped the Spanish monarchs, setting in motion a volatile string of events that, over the next decade and a half, gradually resulted in declarations of independence throughout Latin America—as well as in growing curiosity from people in the United States.

Napoleon's Iberian offensive began late in 1807. Earlier that year, in violation of France's Continental System, the Portuguese monarchy had refused to entirely sever the nation's longstanding commercial ties with Britain. France's response was swift and merciless: Napoleon ordered his famed Grande Armée to march on Lisbon. Rather than fight, Portugal's leaders chose flight, slipping away to Rio de Janeiro aboard a fleet of British ships just hours before French armies stormed into the capital. Seven hundred carts rattled frantically to the waterfront, accompanied by more ladies and gentlemen than could possibly fit aboard the sloppily outfitted fleet; outraged locals, trembling at the prospect of French occupation, pelted the fugitives with stones; the prince regent, Dom João VI, was reportedly reduced to tears and so panicked he could scarcely walk. They left in such a hurry that nobody noticed the Church's silver and the Royal Library's cherished books, all left stranded in crates along the quay.[18]

Though born of desperation, it was also, for those inclined to silver linings, a moment of excitement and expectation. For decades, a handful of prominent intellectuals and statesmen had wondered whether moving the imperial capital from Lisbon to Brazil might be just the thing needed to resuscitate Portugal's once-commanding global empire. *Carpe diem*, then; now was their chance. In over three hundred years of colonization, no European sovereign had so much as visited an American colony. Now the Portuguese royals and over 10,000 courtiers were making a home there, settling down amid the monkeys and mango trees. As Boston's *Columbian Centinel* explained, Brazil's "government has been colonial; it will now be metropolitan." Almost overnight, Rio became an imperial city, linchpin of a global empire that stretched from Angola and Mozambique to Goa and Macau. It didn't exactly ignite a wholesale Portuguese renaissance as some had hoped, but the monarchy's transatlantic relocation did endow nineteenth-century Brazil with a measure of dynastic stability and geographic coherence that other parts of the Americas lacked. Of all the European empires that rose up in the New World, from the British and French to the Spanish and Portuguese, Brazil alone would remain in one piece following independence.[19]

Back in the United States, few seemed to panic at the thought of a sovereign monarchy establishing itself in the Americas. President Thomas Jefferson immediately welcomed his "GREAT & GOOD FRIEND" Dom João to America, "that great Continent which the Genius of Columbus has given to the world." With similar positivity, a New York editor reasoned that "[i]t is in vain to talk of free governments being formed by the subjects of the old absolute monarchies—by people who know nothing about government but to obey." A stable, enlightened monarchy like Brazil's would be "much better," and "the Portuguese Kingdom . . . may in time become, if not the first, at least the second great nation in America."[20]

* * *

EVENTS IN THE SPANISH empire followed a bloodier course. While the Portuguese monarchs clung to sovereignty by alighting on America, Spain's royal family lost all semblance of power. Promising to help the Spanish monarchs resolve a dynastic dispute, Napoleon lured them to France, captured them, and then forcibly imposed his brother Joseph on the Spanish throne in 1808, replac-

ing the House of Bourbon with the House of Bonaparte. Few Spaniards were prepared to accept this outside pretender. Throughout
the country, men and women rose in support of their kidnapped
King Fernando VII, forming an armed and largely grassroots resistance that gave rise to the English word *guerrilla*. Napoleon was
stunned. After one particularly bad defeat, he kept confusedly
asking one of his generals to repeat what had happened, unable to
comprehend the loss. But he was too proud to retreat, and so the
chaos deepened, the rapes, plunder, and mass executions a somber
testament to what the Spanish painter Francisco de Goya simply
called *Los Estragos de la guerra*—The Ravages of War. A quarter- or
even a half-million people died in the Peninsular War, and the rest
were left to pick up the pieces.[21]

Amid such shocking pandemonium, most U.S. newspapers
emphasized events in Europe rather than speculating about the
fate of Spain's American colonies. Headlines were as startling as
they were succinct: "*SPAIN IN AN UPROAR!*" "[T]he attention
of all," a New York editor explained, "is drawn towards Spain,
whilst the world is contemplating with rapture her spirited efforts
to resist and defeat the nefarious designs of Bonaparte." Few editors seriously contemplated what the European tumult meant for
Spanish America itself. Among those who did ponder the colonies' future, however, one idea prevailed. The provinces of Spanish America, New York's *Evening Post* reflected in 1808, "are now
without a king. . . . What a glorious time for the South Americans
to make themselves independent." As Boston's *Columbian Centinel*
reasoned, Spanish Americans would "declare themselves independent until *Ferdinand* [Fernando] is restored to his throne."[22]

These writers had identified the central dilemma that confronted Spain and its American colonies. With Fernando VII
wallowing in captivity and Joseph Bonaparte clashing with the
popular guerrillas, a power vacuum emerged. Nobody was in control. In Spain itself, local governing committees (or juntas) and a

nationwide Central Junta sprang to fill the void, claiming to rule in Fernando's absence. With similar logic, Spanish Americans established their own juntas, and, in some cases, ousted local imperial officials—first in the Andean highlands in 1809, and then, the following year, in such places as Caracas, Buenos Aires, Santiago de Chile, Cartagena, and Santa Fe de Bogotá.[23]

Spanish America's juntas all professed to act in the name of Fernando VII. They were simply taking over, they said, until the rightful king resumed his throne. Such claims raised more questions than they answered. What did it mean to pledge allegiance to someone who was effectively powerless? Without a functioning monarch, were colonies simply planets without a sun, lurching and launching out of orbit into new and unpredictable paths of their own? Indeed, by swearing adherence to the captured Fernando rather than to Spain's acting Central Junta, Spanish Americans suggested that their loyalty to the king did not extend to Spain itself. Sure enough, in 1810, a full-fledged popular rebellion had erupted in rural Mexico. A year later, Venezuelan radicals declared outright independence and wrote a republican constitution; other provinces seemed on the verge of doing the same. Trying to prevent and then stop the bleeding, Spain's Central Junta had invited Spanish Americans to send elected representatives to an imperial congress, or Cortes, held in Cádiz between 1810 and 1814. But Spanish delegates—struggling as they were under the ferocious rule of the brothers Bonaparte—refused to treat Spanish Americans as equals, which only turned Spanish Americans against Spain in greater numbers. The "ravages of war" that Goya had chronicled in Spain spread grimly across the Atlantic, where the struggle for independence raged through 1825.[24]

There were many differences between Spanish-American and U.S. independence. U.S. revolutionaries had been responding to an assertion of power on the part of Britain's Parliament and monarchy; Spanish Americans were responding to the absence of power in Spain. George III had been a victimizer in the eyes of many mainland colonists; Fernando VII was a victim. Unlike Spanish America, British America had a long (if hard-fought) history of religious pluralism, local representative government, and high white literacy rates. In part due to its vast territorial reach from the Atlantic to the Pacific and from California to Cape Horn, finally, Spanish-American independence emerged on a regional basis, without a singular, overarching institution. In contrast, Britain's thirteen insurgent colonies, at one-tenth the collective size of their Spanish-American counterparts, managed to unite under one "Continental" Army, one Continental Congress, and, eventually, one constitution—albeit with much difficulty, and only after having failed to persuade Canada and the British Caribbean to join in.[25]

Still, the similarities—rebels who called themselves Americans and who were, in some cases, starting to invoke republican principles—raised eyebrows in the United States. Curiosity mounted late in 1809 and early in 1810, when news of unrest in Quito appeared in every state. Even after royal authorities in Lima regained control, political upheaval over the following year continued to fuel U.S. interest. In the summer of 1810, news arrived that Caracas's city council had ousted the region's presiding captain-general in the name of the exiled king. But because Fernando was, in the words of one New York newspaperman, "a mere political non-entity," most editors interpreted events in South America as a preliminary sort of independence. "Though loyalty to Ferdinand VII was professed," the *Boston Patriot* reasoned, "an absolute and perpetual independence of Old Spain was understood to be the real design." New York's *Evening Post* hoped that "the whole system of South America will be emancipated." From New England and New Jersey to Maryland and Virginia, other editors happily agreed that "[t]he people of this country [Caracas] appear to have begun their business rightly; and much is to be hoped from their exertions."[26]

Even as scattered local governments throughout Spanish America began to declare full-blown independence, however, many U.S. observers remained skeptical. Merchants (as Miranda had already learned) were especially chary. The same violence that mangled Napoleonic Europe had brought giddy prosperity to the United States, an avowedly neutral nation whose merchants were free to trade with belligerents on all sides. Mostly, though, they traded with Spain, nourishing the ravaged guerrillas (and their British backers) with Pennsylvania wheat and Virginia corn. By the early 1810s, U.S. producers were sustaining Spain's fight against Napoleon far more than they were sustaining Spanish Americans' incipient rebellion. People who coveted capital seldom took their eyes off of the main chance, after all, and people who struggled to survive couldn't easily afford to. Even those who might have preferred to trade with like-minded political allies could have justified their actions without much difficulty. The line between oppressors and freedom fighters was blurry; the same Spaniards who held the Americas in colonial chains looked more sympathetic in their struggle against Napoleon. As far as Spanish America's rebels were concerned, however, U.S. merchants in the early 1810s traded overwhelmingly with the enemy.[27]

Editors, too, expressed doubts, their dreams perhaps still haunted with images of Venezuelan dungeons and dismembered corpses in the wake of the Miranda expedition. News from Venezuela "augurs well," a Baltimore journalist conceded, but "we fear they are not yet capable of republican government." "The dawn of Liberty is but just breaking in upon the people of this country," explained an article that reappeared throughout New England, "and though many of the natives are men of intelligence and genius ... they know not how to act." New Orleans's *Louisiana Gazette* acknowledged that Venezuela's assertion of independence "breathes a spirit of liberty far above any thing that can be expected to exist among ... people long habitated ... under a bigoted viceroy and church government," but the editor remained skeptical. "[I]t still appears to us," he said, "that the great essentials for freedom are wanting ... ignorance and democracy will as inevitably produce despotism, as saltpeter, sulphur, and charcoal, will gunpowder."[28]

Several observers joined the *Louisiana Gazette* in identifying Catholicism as the central problem. Could Catholics really establish republics, polities ostensibly founded on reason and civic virtue? For many, the answer was doubtful. "[W]e are sorry to observe," a Baltimore editor wrote in 1812, "the finger of the *priesthood*; at all times, and in all countries (where *established* religions exist) the inveterate enemies of reason, justice, and truth." New York's *Evening Post* agreed that "the clergy and religion in all seem to be too much concerned ... for any good to result." And St. Louis's *Gazette* confessed itself "not very sanguine about the establishment of liberty on the s[i]te of despotism and darkness. The clergy of Spanish America, whose influence is every thing, cannot be friendly to equal rights."[29]

That speculative inflection—*cannot*—was suggestive. Like so many U.S. observers who wrote about Latin America in the early 1810s, the Missouri editor could not claim to know his facts with certainty (and indeed, his claim was incorrect, since clergymen were prominent in many of the insurgencies, with some advocating greater social equality). Instead, the editor asserted his skepticism based on a stereotypical understanding that he assumed to be grounded in reality. Schooled in Jedidiah Morse's *Geography Made Easy* and other such texts, editors in the early 1810s were full of uncertainty.

Even the intransigent revolutionary Thomas Jefferson, who had observed in 1793 that he "would have seen half the earth desolated" if it meant the success of revolutionary France, wasn't sure what to make of it. "I fear the degrading ignorance into which their priests and kings have sunk them, has disqualified them from the maintenance or even knowledge of their rights," he wrote in 1811;

"how much liberty can they bear without intoxication?" Then again, Jefferson had said much the same thing of Louisianans, who, unschooled in Anglo civic traditions, had been under Spanish and French rule until his own administration's 1803 Louisiana Purchase. The "representative system is an enigma that at present bewilders them," the then-president confessed in 1804; "our new fellow citizens are as yet as incapable of self government as children." By 1812, though, Louisianans had advanced to republican statehood, and perhaps it seemed reasonable to hope that Spanish Americans could follow a similar path. As Jefferson cautiously suggested to John Adams in 1818, the new republics might obtain "freedom by degrees only." It wasn't very inspiring. But freedom by degrees could eventuate in freedom all the same, so Jefferson's longer-term view was often more optimistic: "And behold!" he told an ally in 1811. "Another example of man rising in his might and bursting the chains of his oppressor, and in the same hemisphere. The insurgents are triumphant in many of the States, and will be so in all." Perhaps the cosmopolitan revolutionary of 1793 hadn't entirely disappeared.[30]

Perhaps the cosmopolitan revolutionary ardor of the country's newspapermen hadn't entirely disappeared, either. Born outside Philadelphia in 1777 just weeks after the nearby Battle of Brandywine, Hezekiah Niles was a son of revolution through and through. By 1811, the young Quaker was living in Baltimore and busily seeking subscribers for his new newspaper, the *Weekly Register*, soon to become one of the most influential periodicals of its time. But the paper's reputation was still uncertain when, in his second-ever issue, Niles devoted the first five of sixteen pages entirely to Venezuelan independence (as well as two and a half pages each to Mexico and Napoleon's Iberian invasion). It wasn't a rave, exactly: Niles prided himself on being a voice of moderation, and he confessed that his "joy was much dampened by the appearance of a decree for '*regulating the liberty of the press.*'" But he urged his countrymen to give Spanish Americans the benefit of the doubt. "We must," he argued, "make great allowances for this new people, among whom the rights of self government cannot be considered as more than a theory not yet practically understood." Great allowances, indeed: Niles confidently predicted that Spanish Americans would "cast off all the shreds of slavery, and put on the whole garment of freedom, pure and undefiled, in a short space of time." New York's *Commercial Advertiser* also looked, just a bit more hesitantly, on the bright side. "[T]he South Americans," its editor wrote, "are not running quite so wild as might have been expected."[31]

Jefferson and Niles were both Republicans, leaders of the party that had sympathized with revolutionary France in the 1790s, the party that claimed to speak for ordinary white men, small and decentralized government, and agricultural interests. Their guarded optimism was revealing: over the next few years, Republicans grew more enthusiastic about Latin America than did their Federalist counterparts, who stood for law and order at home and (usually) abroad. Prioritizing social stability and deference to authority, Federalists championed the British model of centralized political and economic power, and they argued that the American Revolution was complete. Republicans countered that the Revolution was a work in progress, to be fulfilled by further egalitarian gains for ordinary white men, so Niles and Jefferson's cautious hopes about Spanish America were not especially surprising. Still, the partisan differences between 1808 and 1810 remained as muddled and muted as the references to Latin America more generally. Of the newspapers referenced above, hope and hesitation intermingled on both sides of the party divide, and journalists remained overwhelmingly focused on war-ravaged Europe. Editors and other informed observers therefore responded to the upheaval in Latin America along a spectrum that ranged from cautious optimism to cynicism and indifference. Steeped as they were in tales of Iberian backwardness, and lacking much information to the contrary, few voiced the kind of buoyant exuberance that newspapermen later in the 1810s would go on to express. Ordinary readers would show less restraint.[32]

*   *   *

FOR WHITE MEN throughout the young United States, one day of the year inspired more conscious and widespread reflection about Spanish-American independence than did any other. That occasion was the Fourth of July, a day that stirred people's patriotism by stimulating their senses. From tiny hamlets to throbbing cities, people awoke at dawn to the pealing of bells and the thunderous gut-rattling of ceremonial cannon fire. They took extra time to dress themselves, men in their brass and buttons, women in their festive frippery. Ladies and gentlemen, pickpockets and prostitutes, gamblers and hucksters and street performers streamed into town centers even as mercury in the nation's thermometers swelled to torpor-inducing heights. Smoke from barbecue pits and militia musters suffused the air; mouths watered for holiday delicacies like turtle soup and ice cream. Aside from the Sabbath, it was one of the first days that white men in the United States got off from work, a day to see and be seen. People gathered by the hundreds at taverns and picnics and fireworks displays, transforming the day into what one Virginia editor called "a talisman" for remembering the nation's revolutionary past.[33]

After crowding into churches for midday public orations, in which local luminaries preached the civic gospel of republican freedom, many people retreated to private dinner parties, held variously in taverns, hotels, and open-air tents. As they ate and imbibed, the white men in attendance offered long lists of toasts to public authorities and patriotic ideals, cheering and carousing all the while. Black people weren't usually allowed to participate, as their mere presence increasingly struck white people as threatening on a day meant to celebrate freedom; white women, meanwhile, were seldom more than servers and spectators, their mere presence endowing the male-dominated (and often zealously partisan) celebrations with claims to disinterested virtue. For white men, though, dinner toasts offered a very public way to voice support for the people and principles that mattered most, and newspapermen regularly reprinted toasts for readers to admire the nation over, exhibiting them as what one editor called "barometers of the national sentiment."[34]

The first toasts at most parties were predictable enough, punctuated by ritualistic gunfire, cheers, and gulps of foamy cider. Guns and grog were not the safest of companions, as the accidental fires, explosions, injuries, and deaths attested, but year after year, the merrymaking continued, and so did the toasts. To the United States! To the heroes of the Revolution! To the army, the navy, the militia, the people! Some toasts became so popular that their inclusion seemed formulaic: partygoers often reserved their last toast for white women, the so-called "American fair." ("Though last in our remembrance, first in our esteem," men avowed in Bethlehem, Pennsylvania.) But with partygoers vying to outdo each other in patriotic wit, there was plenty of room for innovation and distinction, especially in response to current events, and partygoers routinely toasted their favored public officials and political principles.[35]

It was all a giant spectacle, meticulously calibrated to cultivate and celebrate national ardor (and, by the mid-1790s, partisan loyalty). But the Fourth had never just been about national affairs. The whole point of the holiday was, at least ostensibly, to celebrate the signing of the Declaration, a document that had invoked "the Course of human Events," "the Powers of the Earth," "the Opinions of Mankind," and "a candid World." People in the early United States used the holiday to reflect not only on who they were at home, but also on how their political ideals were faring abroad.[36]

July Fourth thus presented itself as a national forum for those who wanted to proclaim support for the hemisphere's latest declarations of independence. Among the first were the devoutly democratic members of Manhattan's Tammany Society, who gathered in a notoriously scruffy tavern on a "burning" but thankfully overcast afternoon on July 4, 1810. Lifting his language from the U.S. Declaration, the group's leader—the "Grand Sachem," dressed like the others in stereotypically Indian face paint, feathers, and bearskins—stood at the head of the table, raised his glass, and, to a chorus of tipsy huzzahs, toasted *"The People of South America— Embarked in the cause of liberty, for the support of which, like the congress of '76, they have pledged their lives, their fortunes, and sacred honor."* It was the same sweeping inter-American vision that had inspired Joel Barlow a generation before, but now the sentiment had a stronger political and ideological underpinning.[37]

The Tammany men were not alone. On that very same day, patriotic tipplers throughout the country were anointing Spanish America's insurgents as spiritual heirs of 1776. Between 1808 and 1812, Boston's *Columbian Centinel* and *Patriot*, Philadelphia's *Aurora*, and Richmond's *Enquirer*—collectively among the nation's most influential newspapers—printed transcripts of 175 "National Anniversary" parties throughout Massachusetts, Pennsylvania, and Virginia. The reports were striking. In 1808 and 1809, toasts to hemispheric independence were virtually nonexistent, a fact that reflects the low degree of attention paid to Latin America as well as the overall lack of revolutionary agitation there. But in 1810, just weeks after news had arrived about the "REVOLUTION AT THE CARRACAS," nearly one-fifth of sampled gatherings (or 18 percent) responded with holiday toasts in support of the insurgents. In 1811, that figure dropped to 3 percent; news about the rebels' outright declarations of independence in early July of 1811 would not begin to arrive for another month, so there was little recent news to be excited about. Sure enough, however, when the next July Fourth came in 1812, approximately 18 percent of gatherings offered toasts to Latin America. Partygoers' confidence had rebounded (see the Appendix).[38]

Such toasts offered only a rough-hewn indicator of what white men actually believed. There was no guarantee that every guest would agree with the toasts or even care about their message; a foreign observer at one party in 1814 noted that the revelers were too busy "eating, . . . talking and laughing and . . . sauntering about" to pay attention to what was being said. Furthermore, toast transcripts did not function like modern-day opinion polls. Aware that their comments might reappear in newspapers nationwide, July Fourth guests routinely used toasts to advance some causes and criticize others. Editors were in on the game, and they could easily refuse to publish toasts that distracted or diverged from their own political (and often partisan) priorities. The toasts that appeared in print, therefore, were not scientific cross-sections of popular sentiment but well-coiffed accounts designed to generate the kind of sentiment they purported to describe.[39]

Still, Fourth of July toasts mattered because they reflected as well as generated political discussions among ordinary voters. At most gatherings, planning committees wrote the first list of toasts in advance, and since men who disapproved of a toast would traditionally decline to drink or cheer for it, committee members carefully discussed their communities' values before finalizing the lists; catalogues of toasts that survive in archives are covered in insertions, excisions, and other alterations, their authors having strained to identify the most inspiring issues, the perfect words, the sharpest puns. Under such circumstances, Spanish America's growing inclusion suggests that people saw the fledgling insurgents' welfare as exciting, important, and, for guests at any given party, generally unobjectionable. Furthermore, individual guests who found the committee toasts wanting could still offer additional "volunteer" toasts. Even if they lacked the prestige, desire, or connections to participate on July Fourth planning committees, white men could still sometimes shape the newspaper reports that resulted, spreading awareness of Spanish America far and wide.[40]

The caveats, therefore, do not change the trend. If July Fourth festivals were political performances, then participants were beginning to view Latin American independence as a cause worth advocating. If the toasts that ended up in print were not accurate samples of those that people actually made, then editors were still opting to print the southward-looking salutes in strikingly high numbers. And if some guests were too intoxicated to pay attention to what was being said, others wove Latin American independence into the jollity itself—as did one group of Virginians, who, having neglected to prepare their toasts in advance, merrily succumbed to the "effusions of the moment" and raised their glasses to "*The Spanish Patriots in South America*—success to the noble cause in which they are waged." Printed toasts enabled everyday revelers to draw attention to causes that they cared about. Increasingly, those revelers took time to celebrate America as a hemispheric whole.[41]

*   *   *

THE 18 PERCENT OF JULY FOURTH gatherings that toasted Spanish America in 1812 did not exactly represent a universal showing, but those toasts were remarkable for one critical reason: they came less than three weeks after the United States declared war on Britain. Scrounging to mobilize every possible resource on behalf of its total war with France, Britain had spent the last several years impressing thousands of U.S. sailors on the high seas, abducting them from their ships and forcing them to serve instead in the notoriously severe Royal Navy. Along the Canadian border, Britain reached out to native people, who were themselves growing increasingly antagonistic toward their aggressively land-hungry republican neighbors. At first, the United States responded to these affronts with diplomatic prodding and economic coercion—most famously in the form of Thomas Jefferson's unilateral embargo against foreign trade in 1807 and 1808. But Europe was so consumed by its own violent tragedies that these efforts were like a skunk on Britain's battlefield—annoying, perhaps, but not worth confronting except for an occasional, dismissive scowl. In 1812, therefore, a bitterly divided Congress responded with a move of ostensibly last resort. Determined to prove its sovereignty once and for all, the United States declared war on Britain.[42]

As the United States began what many were calling a "2ND WAR—FOR INDEPENDENCE," therefore, Spanish Americans were embarking on their first. That simmering convergence of conflicts imbued many in the United States with a growing sense of inter-American solidarity, a heartening belief that the New World was a happily independent republican family at a time when Europe seemed to be crumbling under the weight of dynastic alliances and monarchical tyranny. "When independence is the cause, South and North America have but one cause," a Baltimore editor exclaimed; "let us act then with one heart, one hand!" Men in Norfolk invoked "The Lamp of Liberty—May it shed its benignant rays over the whole Western Hemisphere." From New Hampshire to Philadelphia, meanwhile, southward-looking newspapermen anticipated the day "when *all* the people of the American continent shall be independent of European Government and of European politics."[43]

Because the War of 1812 was so acrimoniously partisan—Republicans pushed the country into war, while New England Federalists traded with the enemy, refused to muster their militias, and sometimes even whispered of secession—responses to Spanish-American independence grew more partisan, too. (All of the ebullient inter-American remarks in the previous paragraph came from staunch Republicans.) It was Republican "war hawks" who argued that the War of 1812 was an anticolonial struggle against would-be British recolonizers; it was therefore Republican war hawks who identified most strongly with anticolonial Spanish Americans. Federalists seldom explained their lack of enthusiasm for Latin America, as if to disapprove through disregard; they seemed ambivalent rather than openly antagonistic (and at least some bipartisan July Fourth planning committees deemed toasts to Spanish America ecumenical enough to be included even as strictly Federalist gatherings usually declined to offer them). Historically, though, New England Federalists had doubted the capacities of foreigners and other outsiders, save perhaps the English-men from whom they descended in such large numbers. The French Revolution only sharpened those nativistic impulses, as Federalists worried that radical "Jacobin" principles would stream into the United States and overturn its precarious social order. ("We have our Rob-ertspierres and Marats," John Adams warned his wife Abigail in 1793.) Worried that revolutionary instability would lead to violence, chaos, and the erosion of civil society, Federalists had long doubted radical social change at home or abroad, and those doubts must have colored their reactions to what was unfolding in Latin America.[44]

Republicans were more inclined to cast off some of their earlier reservations and emphasize Spanish-American potential. Perhaps Latin Americans were products of Iberian despotism, a contrib-utor to Philadelphia's *Democratic Press* reasoned in 1812, but were they not proving themselves in the very act of revolution? After all, Spain wasn't really "the mother country of Cuba, Mexico, Chili, Peru, &c. . . . As well might it be said, that Great Britain was the mother country of . . . the millions of people whom she has subju-gated, in India!" Meanwhile, few toasts in the early 1810s referred to Spanish Americans' Catholicism, and those that did were optimis-tic. "May their noble exertions to emancipate their country from the shackles of *despotism* and *superstition*," a group of Philadelphia Republicans declared, "be crowned with complete success." In throwing off the Catholic Spaniards, Catholic Spanish Americans could redeem themselves.[45]

*   *   *

AS THE AMERICAS went to war with Europe, people in the United States were starting to find spiritual allies to the south—*far* to the south. Between 1810 and 1815, Fourth of July toastmasters were about twice as likely to speak of South America (which did not usually include Mexico and Florida) as they were of Spanish America (which did). Part of that probably resulted from people's avowedly loose grasp on hemispheric geography, and in any case the pool of data is too small to say for sure. But the cartography was clear: on maps, in travel accounts, and in Jedidiah Morse's bestselling geography primers, South America referred to the conical bulge of land that began where Panama tapered off into Colombia. It did not usually mean *America south of the United States*. There were always exceptions, but most informed observers seemed to consider Mexico as part of "SPANISH NORTH AMERICA" (as several editors put it). That was why, in 1816, Hezekiah Niles dedicated an entire volume of his already wildly successful *Weekly Register* "to the patriots of Mexico and South-America"; one place was not the same as the other, and those who talked about both often referred to both individually.[46]

Indeed, of the 225 July Fourth celebrations sampled through 1815, toasts that referred directly to Spanish Florida and Mexico were almost nonexistent. (The exception was an 1811 toast to the region surrounding Baton Rouge—then known as "West Florida"—which U.S. agents had wrested from Spain a year before, though even that toast drew no connection to Spanish-American independence.) Revelers' reluctance to single out Mexico was especially striking, because unlike Florida, Mexico experienced major popular uprisings throughout the early 1810s: indigenous and mestizo peasants, many of them armed only with farming equipment and carrying looted chairs and livestock, pressed over hills and across valleys by the thousands, collectively advocating republican independence and sweeping social change. And yet U.S. observers (at least those who lived further from the border) seemed to look beyond their closest revolutionary neighbors, skipping over Mexico in favor of "the Southern hemisphere," as Shenandoah Valley revelers proclaimed in 1812.[47]

One reason for that geographic predilection was that trade with Mexico lagged behind trade with the Spanish Caribbean and South America. When the United States first started sending commercial agents to Spanish America, it targeted New Orleans and Havana (in 1797), Santiago de Cuba (in 1798), and the Venezuelan port of La Guaira (in 1800). Mexico was not a priority, and that early disparity persisted for at least a decade. In 1807, only seven ships arrived in Philadelphia from Mexico's premier Atlantic port of Vera Cruz, compared with 138 from Cuba, 18 from Puerto Rico, and 29 from La Guaira. (Only two arrived from the La Plata region that year, but back-to-back British invasions of Buenos Aires and Montevideo in 1806 and 1807 had rendered the number unusually low.) Just as important, less trade with Mexico meant less news from Mexico, since the same ships that carried commercial cargo also carried letters, foreign newspapers, and eyewitnesses. Especially given that Mexico's rebellions were overwhelmingly rural, the political coups in rollicking commercial ports like Caracas and Buenos Aires received more attention—and more excitement—in the United States. Mexico wasn't totally ignored: editors devoted more space to it than July Fourth toastmasters apparently did, reporting favorably on what one Nashville newspaper called "these republicans, our neighbors, born to be our allies." Comparatively speaking, though, it generated less excitement. Mexico looked close on maps, but it was remote in people's minds.[48]

As war with Britain dragged on, however, even the toasts to South America dried up. Between 1813 and 1815, not one July Fourth gathering in the entire sample offered a toast to hemispheric independence. As U.S. troops marched boldly into Canada and then, ignominiously, retreated—and as British troops invaded Washington, tit for tat, and set the capital city afire—people in the United States grew too consumed with their own disheartening battles to pay much attention to what was happening south of the border. Spanish America dropped from popular attention; so did metropolitan Brazil. Hemispheric interest had not disappeared, however. It had simply gone dormant.

* * *

HEZEKIAH NILES WANTED to know more about Latin America, and he wanted his readers to know more, too. The growing stream of information that had appeared in the last two decades still wasn't enough to sustain people's interest or even really indulge their curiosity. "It is astonishing," the celebrated Baltimorean reflected in 1815, "how indifferent the great body of the people of the United States appear as to the events in these extensive regions. This may partly arise from our ignorance of their real situation and of what is going on." Not even Niles himself could find much information, beyond the "very slight" details offered in Robertson's *History of America*. "[I]t has," he lamented, "been the constant policy of Spain to keep from the world every thing relative [to] her colonies. . . . Hence our want of knowledge." As Jefferson put it in 1813, "we have little knolege [*sic*] of them, to be depended on."[49]

But knowledge of Latin America would proliferate after 1815 amid a backdrop of dramatic worldwide change. Napoleon's first fall from power in 1814 (and his second fall the next year at Waterloo) led to an Atlantic-wide shake-up. Bourbon monarchs resumed the thrones of France and Spain, while international royalty at the Congress of Vienna redrew the map of Europe to create a more stable balance of power. Britain called a truce with the United States on Christmas Eve of 1814, and the erstwhile king of Spain Joseph Bonaparte, suddenly a pariah in Europe, fled to asylum in New Jersey, where he took up gardening and landscaping. Peace had returned to the North Atlantic. But in the South Atlantic, it was more elusive than ever, as Spain's restored King Fernando spent ten more years trying to force his wayward colonies back into submission. Reports of the insurgencies would flood the United States like never before, shaping the ways in which U.S. onlookers defined themselves and their nation for over a decade.[50]

CHAPTER TWO

AGENTS OF REVOLUTION

T HEY BROUGHT THEIR REVOLUTIONS to the United States. Poets and politicians, outcasts and emissaries, sergeants and servants and secretaries, they left their war-torn homes and pursued political support as well as personal security in the sprawling northern republic. Speaking Spanish and Portuguese, French and indigenous Aymara, they were the descendants of Africans, Europeans, and native people. They hailed from the skyscraping peaks of the Andes to the grassy lowlands of the River Plate, from sun-baked and rain-washed sugar plantations to mines studded with silver and glistening with gold. Vowing support for different sovereigns, they came variously as refugees and exiles, diplomats and merchants, republicans and occasionally royalists. Most of all, they carried tales of their travails, working to transform their host cities into international hubs of the American independence wars.

The South Americans who came to the United States in the 1810s and 1820s were a small and disparate bunch. Numbering at best in the low hundreds, they were no match for the tens of thousands of rebels and refugees who had arrived from France and Haiti beginning in the 1790s. But South Americans mattered beyond their numbers for one simple reason: they told their stories, and to an eager and inviting audience. Then, they convinced editors and writers to replicate those stories for curious readers the nation over, framing and fueling the tales that U.S. onlookers were beginning to tell *themselves* about the wave of revolutions that churned the southern part of the globe.[1]

Rebels' emphasis on storytelling was not simply a way to allay homesickness or entertain listeners. It was, in many cases, part of a coordinated diplomatic strategy, predicated on a belief that U.S. foreign policy emerged in the messy world of democratic politics rather than in isolated chambers of Washington. By swaying the people through the press, agents hoped for nothing less than to sway the government itself. These tactics turned out to be only partly effective in shaping federal policy, but they inspired U.S. audiences along the way, reinforcing popular notions of republican mission and national greatness. If U.S. audiences narcissistically believed that the United States was responsible for everything good that seemed to happen elsewhere in the Americas, rebel agents—hoping that flattery would inspire support—encouraged the egotism. While U.S. observers displayed arrogance, insurgent leaders displayed agency, working hard to control their image in the United States and persuading their hosts that the latest American revolutions were a glorious tropical reprise of 1776.

* * *

SOUTH AMERICANS WHO CAME to the United States left exceedingly sparse documentary records—as well as exceedingly scattered ones whose fragments remain strewn across countries and continents. From such things as names scrawled on the back of envelopes, correspondence of rebel juntas, confidential letters that referred to people by false aliases, and gossip overheard by the Spanish and Portuguese ministers, historians must struggle to reconstruct even the most fundamental events of expatriates' lives. Eventually, from that haphazard composite of sources, broad outlines emerge.

Manuel Torres was one of the more visible expatriates, and one of the biggest thorns in the side of the Spanish minister. Exiled from what is now Colombia after conspiring against the Crown in the 1790s, the Spanish-born renegade fled to a home on Philadelphia's red-bricked and cobblestoned Spruce Street, a few blocks southeast of the mansion where Presidents George Washington and John Adams lived amid the sounds and smells of late-eighteenth-century urban life: clattering carts, clopping horses, putrefying urine, and smashed manure. Nephew of a powerful archbishop and viceroy, Torres lived the high life until enterprising locals conned him out of over $100,000 in fortune. Instead of getting downhearted, Torres got to work. He translated, he taught, and, when the first sustained waves of rebellion swept over Spanish America in the early 1810s, he made a home from the hubbub, throwing his doors open to an unending stream of revolutionary visitors. His hallways echoed with boisterous Spanish, as agitators from throughout the Americas socialized, plotted, and huddled around newspapers, anxiously scanning the headlines for news from home and debating what it all meant for the cause of human freedom.[2]

Such men gained strength by sticking together, strangers-turned-friends owing to sheer revolutionary necessity. Torres was an expert at hastening the conversion, a genteel, middle-aged revolutionary doing exactly the kind of thing that had gotten him evicted from South America in the first place. As early as 1811, Torres was connecting agents from Venezuela to new arrivals from Buenos Aires, men who knew next to nothing about each other's home provinces and yet quickly agreed to pool their meager financial resources in an effort to supply both regions with weapons, gunpowder, and credit. It was typical Torres: generous in making introductions, he convinced near-strangers to bind together their fates, their reputations, and their pocketbooks, persuading them to cover for each other if either party defaulted on a loan. As one agent put it, Torres "deserves and enjoys the confidence of everyone."[3]

Between 1810 and 1826, as their independence wars flared, over two hundred of these South American visitors descended on the United States, many of them passing in and out of Torres's ever-welcoming parlor. Their ships—salty, windy, lurching with the waves—dropped anchor in places like Baltimore and New York as sailors heaved on ropes and passengers lined the decks to breathe what one optimistic Colombian called the "air of liberty!" Most came from Colombia, Venezuela, and rebellion-prone parts of Brazil, but several dozen arrived from the Río de la Plata, and a few hardy souls made their way across the Andes or via the Pacific, sailing in from Chile, Peru, and Ecuador. Himself a magnet for revolutionary visitors, Torres, who lived in Philadelphia and its environs for over a quarter century, was relatively sedentary. Most expatriates lived itinerant lives even after they arrived in the busy northern republic, hopping restlessly amid the constellation of port cities that illuminated the East Coast: Washington and Baltimore, New York and the City of Brotherly Love itself. In the process, they spun a sprawling, underground web of agitators, one in which Torres's house and other like-minded gathering places—dockyards, freethinking taverns, sympathetic printing shops—became pulsing centers of revolution. (Still more visitors, disproportionately from nearby Mexico and the Caribbean, congregated along the Gulf Coast, developing an overlapping but distinct web of contacts and focusing more consistently on privateering and territorial raids.)[4]

The most influential of these visitors were, predictably enough, the most intentional: the agents and emissaries, men sworn to procure loans, weapons, ships, and diplomatic recognition. Some agents went further, testing the bounds of federal neutrality law by enlisting mercenaries and privateers and trying to use the United States as a launching pad for military expeditions onto Spanish and Portuguese territory. Still others—probably a plurality— came as victims of circumstance, angry exiles and tattered fugitives who had fled their homes as rebellions collapsed and rival political leaders rose to power. Having arrived "half-naked," "sick," and still aching with bullet wounds, as one demoralized exile later recalled, many of these outcasts focused more on their lives and loved ones back in South America than on events in the United States. Like Torres himself, though, several exiles became political activists in their own right, joining the agents and emissaries in a combined effort to hasten Latin American independence from afar.[5]

Though they spoke different dialects, ate different foods, and came for different reasons, new arrivals often found common ground when they disembarked in the United States, similarity overshadowing difference the moment they became foreigners in a sea of English-speaking Yankee Protestants. Most—perhaps 90 or 95 percent—had been considered white in South America. Most were men—only a handful seem to have come with their wives and children. Even where ancestry differed, many found unity in their genteel education, high social status, and prior military and political leadership. Take Vicente Pazos Kanki, born partly of Aymara Indian heritage in what is now Bolivia; he spoke Aymara, French, Spanish, a little Latin, and a lot of Quechua, which he taught as a university professor. At ease in the world of high-minded revolutionary ideals—he had recently translated Thomas Paine's *Common Sense* from French to Spanish—Pazos traveled to Buenos Aires as a young man, started an opposition newspaper, and soon faced exile along with roughly ten other prominent dissidents. When he finally arrived in the United States in 1817, he seemed inclined to emphasize the things that he had in common with other expatriates rather than the ancestry that made him unique. He didn't mention his ancestry in his published U.S. writings, nor did he add the Aymara "Kanki" to his public name until the mid-1820s. Newspapers and personal correspondents rarely if ever referred to his native descent, perhaps further suggesting that he rarely if ever mentioned it. Instead, Pazos seemed to relate to other expatriates (and to U.S. audiences more generally) on the basis of schooling and politics rather than on the basis of ancestry.[6]

Sometimes, of course, the differences became overwhelming, even insurmountable. There were strategic quarrels: some rebel visitors wanted to act more assertively on behalf of South America, vigorously pressing the U.S. government for diplomatic recognition and other privileges, while others, like Torres, urged restraint. There were political differences, too, even treachery. In 1816, one of Torres's erstwhile Mexican allies became a spy for the Spanish minister, foiling a rebel plot to take over a Mexican port. Such conflicts only multiplied as the wars dragged on and supporters of rival Latin American governments—centralists, federalists, liberals, conservatives, royalists, republicans, sometimes with competing commercial interests—converged in the United States.[7]

Even in the face of such disagreements and betrayals, however, expatriates often sensed a common fate. For although South Americans perceived distinctions among themselves, it wasn't always clear that ordinary U.S. onlookers did. That was largely why, in letters to rebel leaders back in Colombia, Torres repeatedly framed Spanish America's interests as intertwined. "[T]he recognition of our Independence," he surmised in 1820, would happen "if the Chilean expedition against Peru has a favorable outcome and if things change in Buenos Aires." Even approaching death, frail and weakened by asthma, Torres was still urging expatriates to find strength amid diversity, embracing the wisdom of e pluribus unum for a new generation of American revolutionaries. In Torres's house, the 1822 obituary read, rebel visitors "found . . . divisions quieted or averted; enmities subdued; the jealousies incident to revolutions frustrated; and a common sentiment . . . of their common interests spread over South America."[8]

The author of that obituary was one of Torres's closest friends; he may well have been exaggerating. But others agreed that Latin Americans in the United States would sink or swim together. What "hurts us very much," a Buenos Aires agent told his superiors in 1817, was "the news of the fall of Venezuela, Cartagena, and Santa Fe [de Bogotá]." Perhaps it was no surprise that Mexicans, Venezuelans, Colombians, and Brazilians marched solemnly alongside domestic military and civic leaders at Torres's four-hour funeral procession, joined spontaneously along the way by thousands of U.S. citizens who accompanied the corpse straight to Philadelphia's Catholic burial ground.[9]

* * *

AS TORRES LAY on his deathbed, wheezing but characteristically cheerful, one of the people comforting him and helping him settle his affairs was William Duane, outgoing editor of the storied *Philadelphia Aurora* (and author of the affectionate obituary). Hours after easing his friend toward death, Duane privately confessed that the experience had been "painful," and he mourned the loss not only of a great public servant and patriot but also of a "long and close friendship."[10]

Torres's relationship with Duane was neither coincidental nor unusual, different from other editorial-expatriate relationships more in degree than in kind. Rebel agents repeatedly insisted that if they could ingratiate editors and, thence, the electorate, they might win over the government, and a host of advantages would follow. Empowered by their journalistic allies, rebel agents turned themselves into key links between what happened in South America and what U.S. audiences read about South America. Like merchants, sea captains, and other international men of motion in the early nineteenth century, agents were well positioned to spread news about South America through the nation's papers. What made them collectively distinct was the degree to which they so often dedicated themselves to the task, and the credibility that their South American citizenship seemed to bestow.

Torres's influence was sweeping, but it is not always easy to pin down. How many of his revolutionary visitors did he escort to Duane's friendly printing office? How many offhand comments splashed across his dinner table and into Duane's columns? Torres did write, translate, and otherwise inform countless *Philadelphia Aurora* articles, but so did many of the expatriates whom he steered to Duane's shop, and Duane rarely specified who was behind any given piece. Oddly enough, it is easier to trace the editorial influence of agents from Brazil, which experienced fewer republican uprisings than Spanish America and which had an accordingly smaller cast of rebel characters. That smaller cast makes it possible to track the movement of people and information with greater precision, and to watch as specific Brazilian agents shaped the news that circulated through the United States—often with help from Spanish Americans like Vicente Pazos and Manuel Torres themselves.[11]

Early-nineteenth-century Brazil was not exactly a fuming hotbed of revolution. Rio de Janeiro was, almost literally, a cornerstone of empire: when the royal court arrived there in 1808, roads were paved, streetlamps installed, palaces built, the residents scurrying to transform their city into a modern and magisterial hub of Portugal's sprawling global empire. Compared to what Portuguese nobles had enjoyed back in Europe, Rio was a dirty and disgusting place. Even the best houses were crawling with rats, and because the water table was too high for septic tanks to function, enslaved men had to carry leaky barrels of human waste to the ocean each morning on their backs, dumping them right into Guanabara Bay. But compared to elsewhere in Brazil, Rio was opulent, prosperous, a playground for the lords and ladies of Lisbon.[12]

That newfound splendor, such as it was, irritated people elsewhere in Brazil—most of all in the steamy northeastern province of Pernambuco, a few degrees south of the equator and a thousand miles north of Rio's shining new cityscape. Pernambuco had a storied past. Its early sugar plantations had helped drive Portugal's imperial growth in the sixteenth and seventeenth centuries, the white (and sometimes brown) gold transformed into actual gold through a million routine acts of economic alchemy. In 1654, Pernambucans had famously banded together to expel their fourteen-year Dutch occupiers (whose policy of religious tolerance had attracted several hundred Jews to the region; with the Dutch gone, 23 of the sojourners fled to New Amsterdam, the first Jews to settle in what is now New York City). By the early nineteenth century, however, Pernambuco was the Ozymandias of the empire, its sugar plantations long since eclipsed by Caribbean competitors and by Brazil's own gold and diamond districts farther south.[13]

Pernambuco's celebrated history made Rio's imperial makeover all the harder to bear; it is crueler to sink into mediocrity than to sustain it, especially when your neighbors are playing host to European royals and your own taxes are funding the party. The more Rio basked in its newfound glory, the more residents of Pernambuco chafed, until by 1817, plagued by economic stagnation and paralyzing droughts, they had had enough. When royal officials tried to arrest several Pernambuco military officers who were also Freemasons, local elites shot back by arresting the royal governor himself and declaring Pernambuco an autonomous republic. Buoyed by slaves, small farmers, and artisans, who sensed an opportunity to promote their own interests, the revolt blazed its way through the parched Northeast, threatening the very foundations of Portuguese rule in Brazil. From his throne in Rio, Dom João VI—an inbred and melancholy monarch who feared storms and shellfish, and who had already been accused of cowardice for fleeing Napoleon—told his advisers to show no mercy.[14]

★ ★ ★

REBEL LEADERS KNEW they couldn't overthrow João on their own. Just six days into the uprising, they addressed a letter to their "Dear Brother" President James Monroe asking for help, invoking "the example of patriotism that you gave to the whole world in your brilliant revolution which we seek to imitate." Indeed, although Brazilian royalists derided the rebels as simple "Imitators of English America," many rebels announced their ideological inspiration with pride. One assumed a new name, George "Wasthon," while others pored over translated copies of the U.S. federal and state constitutions.[15]

For the most part, however, U.S. influence in Pernambuco (like U.S. influence in much of Spanish America) operated at the level of abstract ideology rather than that of day-to-day implementation. In the piles of written documents that the revolt stirred up in its wake, the United States played merely a bit part, assuming center stage only when insurgent leaders were asking for support. It was a canny strategy, and one that rebel agents would repeatedly employ: flatter U.S. audiences, tell them you wanted nothing more than to be just like them, and then ask for help. It was not a lie, really; it was just an exaggeration. Pernambuco leaders did admire the model of 1776, but by praising the U.S. revolution they were also consciously pandering to U.S. pride. On the very same day that they wrote to Monroe, in fact, rebel leaders used equally deferential tactics in a letter to Britain's foreign minister—but this time, they catered to British sensibilities. "Milord," the provisional government wrote (using a standard, phonetically derived term of address for wealthy Englishmen), "an oppressed people have a right to compassion from the Sovereign of the most respected Nation in the World." In an effort to get what they wanted, Pernambuco's rebels shrewdly indulged their audiences' respective nationalistic conceits.[16]

Monroe and the British foreign minister remained unmoved, reluctant as they both were to jeopardize relations with Portugal. But direct appeals to government officials were only one part of rebels' U.S. engagement strategy. The other part was an outreach effort to ordinary citizens, one that was all the more striking because it began in the first few days of what had, after all, been a largely impromptu uprising. As insurgents scrambled to appoint leaders, rally followers, gather money, and stockpile weapons—as they worked to secure, in other words, the most basic necessities of revolutionary authority—they also made time to target U.S. readers.

They accomplished that feat with help from two men (or perhaps one man with two names), sympathetic globetrotters determined to cultivate the insurgents' image abroad. First was an English merchant named Charles Bowen, a longtime Pernambuco resident who evidently agreed to spread the word in the United States before he returned home to Britain. Bowen scooped the story for U.S. audiences when he sailed into Norfolk, and the resulting headlines—"HIGHLY IMPORTANT! *REVOLUTION IN BRAZIL*"—screamed with breathless urgency. In an exaggerated but not wholly unfounded account that appeared in at least fourteen states as well as in Maine and the federal capital, Bowen portrayed the revolt as orderly, popular, and nearly bloodless. Lest white readers associate the revolt with smoldering cane fields in Haiti or severed heads in Paris, Bowen emphasized that "perfect harmony and tranquility prevailed"; lest readers fear that Pernambucans would veer toward Britain's model of constitutional monarchy, he—Briton by birth, cosmopolitan by choice—vowed that they would "choose . . . the United States for their model."[17]

The second early link between Brazilian revolutionaries and U.S. readers was one "Mr. Seebohm," a former Pernambuco resident then in Baltimore. (He may in fact have been Charles Bowen himself—no "Seebohm" appears in the 1820 census, or in reports from Pernambuco, or even in reports from the Portuguese minister, and the name could have been a clumsy contraction of Charles Bowen's first initial and last name.) In the heady early days of the revolt, an unnamed insurgent addressed a bundle of documents to "Seebohm" along with a note: "By request of this [rebel] government," the letter read, "I now forward despatches from it to the United States, and a few documents for publication, with which you are requested to do the needful without delay." The emphasis on timeliness—on acting *without delay*—showed that rebel leaders were determined to present their version of the revolt to U.S. audiences before anyone else did (and, presumably, before their own revolutionary momentum began to stall at home). Sure enough, when Seebohm arrived at the *Baltimore Patriot* office and unfurled the manuscripts, perhaps adding a few words of praise for his old Pernambuco friends, the editor immediately published them, followed by newspapers in at least fourteen states as well as in Maine and the District of Columbia; in early May, William Duane's *Weekly Aurora* devoted its entire front page to them. Like Charles Bowen's earlier account, the documents presented the uprising as moderate, unanimous, and—most of all—inspired by the United States. "There was but little opposition," one report said, "and few lives lost; order and regularity now prevail, and the [U.S.] Americans are hailed as brothers."[18]

★ ★ ★

PORTUGAL'S MINISTER IN the United States, a sixty-seven-year-old former abbot named José Corrêa da Serra, thought it was all ridiculous. At the beginning of 1817, the abbé Corrêa (as everyone called him) was one of Washington's most beloved personalities, a self-styled Enlightenment polymath whose liberal ideas had sent him wandering from Lisbon to London to Paris before he finally fled Napoleon in 1811. Like his friend Thomas Jefferson, the abbé was known as much for his sparkling wit as for his startlingly casual taste in clothes; he "dressed like ourselves," the admiring Secretary of State John Quincy Adams wrote, "not in the full Court Suit" favored by other foreign dignitaries. On the unending circuit of parties that defined Washington political life, people flocked to the abbé's company, for (as the famously stiff Adams observed) he was "as lively as if he were but twenty five."[19]

When Pernambuco revolted, however, Corrêa da Serra attacked the rebels with an acerbity that surprised and deterred some of his closest admirers. As President Monroe said after one particularly tense encounter, "He partakes strongly of the antirevolutionary feeling on this subject, more than is strictly consistent with his liberal and philanthropical character." "So much for reaching the summit of our wishes!" a former friend wrote. "All his philosophy vanished before the reasons of state."[20]

Corrêa da Serra especially loathed the rebels' public outreach efforts. Pernambuco leaders, he said in a stream of letters back to Rio, had "suborned" and "won over the gazettes, through which [they] inten[d] to influence the public opinion which, in a land such as this, means very much." "This may seem strange or even ridiculous to Your Excellency," he wrote, "but thank God you do not have to deal with a democratic republic. If you saw this up close, you would see that there is no better way" to sway the public, "nor anything as good." Editorial influence, he continued, "accomplishes much in a nation that spends its life reading its voluminous newspapers, and in which those newspapers are the primary mode of governance." In a republic, Corrêa da Serra stewed, newspapers were foreign agents' strongest weapons, their pages scraping away at Portuguese authority with the accumulated force of a thousand paper cuts.[21]

He was determined to stop it, even, as it turned out, at the expense of his good name. Although Seebohm seems to have retired from his informal revolutionary service after delivering his parcel of documents to the press, Charles Bowen orbited the Chesapeake for several more weeks to stir up support before he finally sailed home to England (further evidence, perhaps, that Seebohm and Bowen were one and the same). Energetic as ever, the abbé Corrêa quietly followed him, aware that the rebels' combined efforts to spread good news about Pernambuco would simultaneously facilitate their efforts to purchase armaments, recruit privateers, and win over federal officials. The abbé went "skulking about the docks" and "pushing about our shipyards," the *Baltimore Patriot* fumed after a similar incident one year later, extracting tips from liberty-loving tars who noted his informal attire and never suspected that the amiable grey-haired man with the endearing nasal accent might actually be His Excellency, the minister plenipotentiary for Dom João VI.[22]

*   *   *

BOWEN AND SEEBOHM were unofficial and *ad hoc* agents, volunteers who agreed to help Pernambuco's government during the first, inherently confusing days of the uprising. But within another week or two, rebel leaders managed to dispatch an official representative to the United States, and that man became the third and most important link between Pernambuco insurgents and U.S. audiences. Antônio Gonçalves da Cruz was in his early forties, a wealthy and well-traveled Pernambucan and every bit a match for the increasingly cranky abbé. Heir to a vast personal fortune— his family owned slaves, jewels, and gold, and sent the boy to visit Europe at age eleven—Cruz was polished and charming, his demeanor unfailingly "affable and pleasant." A lifelong bachelor, he was also just unorthodox enough to be interesting. His main residence, what one friend called a three-story "palace" in the heart of Pernambuco's capital, moonlighted as a swinging, high-stakes gambling den. It was also a center of underground Masonic intrigue and political dissent, complete with portraits of French revolutionaries and a library full of subversive books. On the night of March 5, 1817, rebel leaders met at Cruz's house; the rebellion erupted on March 6.[23]

Cruz, who had been planning a trip to the United States anyway, was an obvious pick for ambassador. Later that month, he stuffed his bags with $800,000, boarded a ship, and watched for some six weeks as Pernambuco's emerald waters gave way to the darker greys and blues of the North Atlantic. By the time Boston's skyline finally grew on the horizon in mid-May, he was ready for action, determined to charm the United States like he had charmed his Pernambuco houseguests, in a stream of handshakes, smiles, and expensive liquors. It wasn't going to be easy:

Cruz had never been to the United States, and he relied at least partly on translators. But he found plenty of eager help. As the abbé Corrêa angrily told Portuguese authorities, "the Spanish rebels of all denominations immediately entered into intimate and active correspondence with him."[24]

Cruz was a swarthy man, described like this in one of his earlier Pernambuco passports: "white, single, native to this town, ordinary stature, thin, black hair, dark-complexioned, small forehead and narrow eyes, thin black eyebrows, brown eyes, thin nose, small mouth, slender lips." White, but also dark-complexioned—*cor morena*, the passport said. Other Brazilian documents describe Cruz as *mulato*, and indeed, some among his parents and grandparents were enslaved. But wealth whitened his skin—*o dinheiro embranquece*, as Brazilians say—and Cruz was able to pass for white when he wanted to. As Pernambuco's governor explained in 1815, "the only people who see him as *pardo* [mulatto] are those who knew his parents and grandparents." Sure enough, U.S. audiences seemed to assume that Cruz was white; nobody made any printed remarks to the contrary. If Cruz told anyone about his African ancestry, they kept quiet, leaving the nation's adoring white legions to welcome Cruz into their ports and their homes without so much as a shrug, inadvertent testimony to race's socially constructed slipperiness and to its very real consequences.[25]

Keeping his secret to himself, Cruz went on to implement a sort of revolutionary triage when he first arrived, chasing the concrete and immediate support necessary to sustain his Pernambuco countrymen. Clad in a crisp new military uniform and flanked by two secretaries, he traveled up and down the coast seeking out prominent public figures, pressing them for trading privileges, loans, and diplomatic recognition. Having secured the first of those—U.S. ports were open to all rebels and all royalists, or, better, to their money—Cruz proceeded to his second task, the purchase of guns and gunpowder. Before long he was flouting federal neutrality law, working alongside Spanish Americans to outfit privateers and even entice former Napoleonic officers in the United States to go to Brazil and fight.[26]

But much of the work was softer, more personal, more indirect, a question of cultivating public sympathy in order to ensure the Republic of Pernambuco's longer-term survival. "You surely know," rebel leaders instructed Cruz, "how much affability leads to the success of negotiations, and it is therefore your duty to make yourself popular, and accepted by the People wherever you reside." Cruz didn't need the reminder. Pledging to win "the affection of the Government and of the People," he worked to cultivate "a certain external splendor," the better to demonstrate Pernambuco's wealth, stability, and creditworthiness. Spending freely and playing the gentleman was part of the job, after all, as long as you didn't overdo it: a revolutionary agent in the United States might benefit from looking rich, but he also had to be unfailingly modest. When people respectfully called him His Excellency the Ambassador, therefore, Cruz humbly corrected them. Please, just call me *patriot*, he said, for "all titles of nobility had been abolished."[27]

Cruz was only one person, of course, his secretaries only two. But with help from the press, they set out to charm the entire electorate. Almost every time they arrived in a new city, Cruz and his secretaries made their way to local newspaper offices and repeated their dual message of moderation and emulation. Sometimes, like Seebohm, they provided editors with official documents and proclamations to print; more commonly, they wrote their own, anonymous news accounts and handed them over for publication, or else they let editors write the copy themselves. Cruz, for his part, preferred to meet with newspapermen face-to-face—charisma works best in person, after all. When he wanted coverage in cities that he could not immediately visit, however, he rallied Spanish Americans to act as his surrogates. As the *New-York Columbian* reported, Colombia's "Mr. REVENGA called at the office of the Columbian, with articles for insertion relative to Pernambuco, which he stated as coming from Mr. *Da Cruz*, of Philadelphia." Before long, Cruz and his allies had become such desirable founts of patriotic principles that newspapermen started to approach them and ask for more. Cruz, of course, unfailingly obliged.[28]

It worked, at least as far as newspapers were concerned. Having witnessed Cruz's magnetism firsthand—and, possibly, having been loosened by his money—writers were eager to tell their readers precisely how virtuous, how moderate, and how cultured he was, and one after another they vouched for his cause. Within a day or so of arriving in the United States, Cruz and his secretaries walked into the *Boston Patriot* office to sing the praises of republican government and revolutionary restraint. It is easy enough to imagine: on one side, Cruz, looking dapper as always in his freshly pressed uniform, nodding approvingly as the translator rendered his words into English; on the other, the editor, journeymen, and apprentice boys, wiping their inky hands on their aprons as they went to shake Cruz's hand, honored to be in the presence of this Portuguese-speaking "Adams or Hancock" (as they wrote in the ensuing report). When Cruz finally left, they described him as "gentlemanly, affable, intelligent, and dignified" and ascribed "wisdom, humanity, moderation and unanimity" to his countrymen.[29]

The *Boston Patriot* was the first to gush, but it was hardly the last. Cruz's efforts led directly to the publication of perhaps seventeen original articles about the Pernambuco revolt, as well as to scores of responses and reprintings in at least thirteen states as well as in Washington. Such editorial dexterity was remarkable, especially since Cruz couldn't have had much experience in newspaper publicity. Wary of empowering would-be malcontents, the Portuguese monarchy had outlawed printing presses in colonial Brazil; the first one arrived in Rio along with the royal court in 1808, and Pernambuco had no newspaper of its own until 1821, four years after the revolt. Perhaps Cruz sensed the power of the press during his earlier travels in Europe; surely, too, Spanish Americans like Torres taught him "which doors to knock on," as the abbé Corrêa grumbled. Whatever the reason, Cruz had a flair for publicity when he arrived in the United States, and it was no coincidence that positive press tended to follow him where he went.[30]

Once rebel agents had seeded it, the news took on a life of its own as printers far and wide republished it for the nation to behold. In a sample of 169 newspapers throughout the country, nearly 80 percent of the titles carried at least one story on the Pernambuco uprising, and most published repeated updates. Because newspapers of the era tended to enjoy circulations between 500 and 2,000 copies, even a conservative estimate would indicate that tens of thousands of people in the United States had access to news of Pernambuco, and probably hundreds of thousands. In fact, it is possible that people in the United States were more informed about Pernambuco's plight than were people anywhere outside of Brazil itself. With its high literacy rates and burgeoning political excitement, the United States boasted more newspaper readers than anywhere else on the globe, and those newspapers provided audiences with unparalleled opportunities to learn about foreign and faraway places. From southern county seats to remote trans-Appalachian hamlets, most of these readers had access to news of Pernambuco.[31]

Rebel leaders had not produced this burst of publicity single-handedly. Dozens of reports from Pernambuco floated into U.S. ports independently of rebel efforts, courtesy of roaming sea captains, curious merchants, foreign newspapers, and overseas observers. Sure enough, these updates tended to follow the same storyline as did reports from Bowen, Cruz, and rebel leaders. "[T]he struggle only lasted a few hours, and with less loss of human life than could possibly have been expected," an unidentified Pernambuco resident wrote in a letter that appeared from Cooperstown to Carolina. A similar note from a "French gentleman at Pernambuco" appeared throughout New England, calling the revolt "very moderate" and emphasizing that the insurgents enjoyed full military support. Indeed, people in the United States may have been inclined to applaud the revolt even if agents had not actively framed the story to Pernambuco's advantage; certainly, U.S. onlookers a generation before had welcomed the early French Revolution with the same kind of zeal. But Pernambuco's agents had a distinctive and decisive impact as writers and readers began to react to the good news.[32]

* * *

JOHN ADAMS HADN'T seen it coming. The former president had always been something of a reluctant revolutionary, uneasy with the violence of the American Revolution that he had helped to wage, more comfortable with monarchical Britain than with Jacobin France. He believed in law and order, hierarchy and deference, at least more than his Republican rivals did; once, as vice president, he told an astounded Senate that had he foreseen the degree to which his countrymen would cast off Britain's example, "he would never have drawn his sword." Of Latin America he was especially cynical. "The People of South America," he told a correspondent in 1815, "are the most ignorant the most biggoted the most Superstitious of all the Roman Catholicks in Christendom," "abjectly devoted to their Priests" and terrified of the Inquisition. Such people could hardly sustain a "free Government," he wrote; it "appeared to me as absurd as Similar plans would be to establish Democracies among the Beasts Birds or Fishes."[33]

Then Antônio Gonçalves da Cruz showed up at the eighty-one-year-old's grey-and-black Georgian abode just south of Boston, on a late May day in 1817, flowers blooming in the garden, the orchard trees finally approaching the dark, mature greens of summer. Something warmed the old revolutionary's heart, and Adams soon found himself recalling his own days as a revolutionary abroad, when he had pled what sometimes seemed an impossible case to people whose language he scarcely spoke. Adams wrote about it a few days later, in a letter to Thomas Jefferson. "The Pernambuco Ambassador his Secretary of Legation and Private Secretary, respectable People, have made me a Visit," Adams said. "Having been Some Year or two in a Similar Situation, I could not but Sympathize with him." As the *Boston Patriot* affirmed in its next issue, the encounter "forcibly recalled to the mind of the venerable sage the events of our own revolution," and "the difficulties, the toils and dangers which were endured . . . and the recollection, revived in so interesting a manner, sensibly affected him."[34]

Adams was not alone in his sympathies. Journalists and readers responded to the rebels' two-pronged message of moderation and emulation with one consistent refrain: what excellent taste the Pernambucans had, choosing the United States as their role model. Residents of Massachusetts, pleased to be Cruz's first U.S. hosts, were especially moved. "*Boston*, illustrious place of nativity of FRANKLIN, HANCOCK, ADAMS, WARREN, OTIS, and other immortal statesmen and heroes," one *Patriot* contributor wrote, "your example has already been imitated in most of the regions of South-America, and now is followed by Pernambuco." An anonymous reader was even moved to verse:

Hail, Chief of Pernambuco, dear!
Hail, friend of freedom's sacred laws!
Hail, friend of man! with hearts sincere,
We hail thee first in freedom's cause.

The enthusiasm was contagious. When the *Boston Patriot* declared that Pernambuco's "revolution" had "a character of brilliancy far superior to any which has yet taken place in South America," the commentary reappeared in at least eight states, from North Carolina to Ohio. The poem resurfaced in newspapers as far south as Virginia, and a New York publisher included it in a book of "Songs and Recitations."[35]

Boston's *Yankee* launched into the most rhapsodic praise of all.

"The republican citizens of this country," its editor wrote, "cannot fail to feel gratified by the arrival of a Minister from the new republic of *Pernambuco*." It was "flattering," he explained, to see "the ambassadors of freedom from every quarter of the earth, congregating round our national capitol, like satellites round their parent orb, and proclaiming the genius of our country the centre of the great system which contains them." Gazing at the revolutions in South America was like gazing at the night sky—the "influence of the [U.S.] American revolution on the moral destinies of mankind," the editor waxed, "is a subject too vast to be comprehended by the most enlightened statesmen." Arrogant, yes; self-congratulatory, no question—but the conceit did not grow from within the United States alone. Cruz was there the entire time, telling his listeners precisely how inspiring they were, pleased to inflate their visions of international and even celestial importance.[36]

The adulation continued even when reports referred to the rebels' Catholicism, as if Pernambucans were redeeming themselves in the very act of rebellion. Pernambuco's "clergy are represented as being very patriotic, singing *Te Deum* and animating the people as our clergy did in 1775 to resist tyranny and establish liberty and independence," the *Boston Patriot* wrote, its words reprinted as far away as small-town Tennessee. Only scattered reports suggested that anything was inherently amiss with Pernambuco Catholicism, and even those hailed the uprising for chipping away at papist obsolescence. "The news of the revolution in Pernambuco," mused Boston's *Columbian Centinel*, showed that "liberty [was] . . . dissipating the clouds of ignorance and superstition which have long enveloped in monkish darkness one of the fairest portions of the world." It was a more unanimous response than Spanish America's Catholic insurgents had received earlier in the 1810s; perhaps the collective endurance of South America's rebellions had inspired more confidence seven years in. Whatever the reason, editors by 1817 seemed so eager to embrace their calling as republican role models that they happily gave Pernambuco's Catholic rebels the benefit of the doubt. They offered no explanation; they did not seem to think that they needed one. For those who wanted to support republicanism's spread abroad, neither religion nor Iberian heritage would stand in the way.[37]

Although the glowing news coverage had not arisen wholly from the work of rebel envoys like Bowen, Seebohm, and Cruz, Pernambuco's representatives had a unique and identifiable impact. Take Boston, for example, the city which had first welcomed Cruz to the United States, and the one that most consistently dished out exuberant Pernambuco praise. That kind of enthusiasm was unusual for Boston's newspapermen, several of whom remained doubtful of *Spanish* America's insurgents. The difference seems to have been that few Spanish-American agents regularly ventured north of New York. It could hardly have been coincidental that the one rebel government to dispatch agents to Boston was the one rebel government to receive unilaterally high praise from that city's newspapers. Cruz and his secretaries had transformed countless New Englanders—including the querulous John Adams himself—from skeptics into supporters. Indeed, Cruz's physical presence may further explain the diminished concerns about Pernambucan Catholicism, his own personal magnetism having perhaps dissipated the abstract stereotypes. It was one thing to criticize Catholic rebels who lived thousands of miles away in a dark and hazy netherworld; it was another thing to criticize Catholic rebels who showed up admiringly on your doorstep, poised, genteel, paragons of republican virtue.[38]

* * *

THERE WERE QUESTIONS, of course. The uprising struck some as makeshift and impromptu, lacking a strong ideological or political foundation. Rebel leaders were "greatly overrated," the *Albany Argus* said; the revolution, Washington's *National Intelligencer* agreed, was "too sudden to be permanent." But even these editors remained sympathetic, or at least agnostic. Just one day later, the *National Intelligencer* reprinted a Savannah article promising that Pernambucans and other South Americans would be "multiplying in the rear, and becoming victors in turn." "The news of the revolution in Pernambuco," the Albany editor agreed, ". . . while it is altogether unexpected, tends in a measure to strengthen the hope, that the work of political reform will eventually pervade the whole western continent." If not all newspapermen were convinced that the rebels would triumph, most of them wanted to be, and the positive articles far outnumbered the more ambivalent ones.[39]

The skeptics should have held their ground, at least if they valued accuracy over advocacy. Although Cruz couldn't have known it yet, the Republic of Pernambuco was unraveling just as he disembarked in Boston. Dom João's armies invaded Pernambuco from the south; his royal navy blockaded the sea. Cruz was racing against time: in order to save his countrymen, he had to discredit the increasingly damning news reports that the abbé Corrêa was diligently spreading, and he had to do it fast enough to get aid to his gasping Pernambuco countrymen. For all his criticisms of newspaper diplomacy, the abbé was not above it, and he fought fire with fire, print with print. As he told his superiors in Rio, he took "the irregular step of having published in several newspapers . . . an official notification of the blockade of Pernambuco," even though he hadn't yet received word that a blockade existed and even though he hadn't informed federal officials. It was an "illiberal and impolitic . . . aberration" for an ambassador to publicly announce a blockade before notifying the administration, former President James Madison crossly told interim Secretary of State Richard Rush, himself equally exasperated. By the time the administration, the press, and Cruz himself had set the record straight, it was too late: merchants, bankers, and insurers had closed their purse strings, and in any case João had successfully crushed the rebellion.[40]

The mission, in short, was doomed from the start, and for once, Cruz came up short. Though he successfully cultivated popular enthusiasm, the popular enthusiasm did not sway the Monroe administration—even though Cruz had taken his message of moderation and emulation to Washington itself. ("[W]e imitate our Polar Star," he told the interim Secretary of State, *notre Étoile du Nord.*") It wasn't that rebel leaders had miscalculated, and that popular enthusiasm held no sway over public officials; indeed, the enthusiasm would arguably help persuade federal policymakers to recognize the independence of *Spanish* America's more permanent nations five years later. The problem for Cruz was that the revolt collapsed within weeks, well before Monroe and Rush would ever have considered recognition. No amount of public support could have secured the measure in time.[41]

Sure enough, although Cruz failed to win federal support, he and his countrymen had captured the imaginations of countless ordinary onlookers along the way; his story shows just how quickly U.S. audiences could seize on foreign revolutions as well as how effectively rebel agents could stir up support. Even as reports of the revolt's collapse began to arrive in the summer of 1817, July Fourth revelers remained buoyant, toasting Pernambuco from New York and Philadelphia to Washington and Kentucky. In fact, the sweeping coverage of Pernambuco may even have spurred a quantifiable geographic shift in the way that ordinary white men understood their revolutionary age. In a sample of 130 Fourth of July toasts offered to hemispheric independence between 1810 and 1820, toasts to South America outnumbered toasts to Spanish America every single year. But toasts to Spanish America grew even less common after Pernambuco's revolt. They were over five times as likely to occur in the years before 1817 as they were in the following three— after which point Mexico veered toward monarchy and toasts to Spanish America disappeared almost entirely. Though the data is too spotty to say for sure, perhaps Pernambuco's insurgency helped convince U.S. onlookers that republicanism in Latin America transcended Spanish-speaking territories. After 1817, Brazil seemed to be bursting with republican potential. As Boston's *North American Review* reported, Brazil's "anomalous independence" as a monarchy was ". . . of course a temporary state of things. The atmosphere of America is not one, which can ever be breathed freely by kings and emperors." Spurred partly by Pernambuco's agents, popular faith in a republican Brazil endured.[42]

*　*　*

CRUZ INTERACTED SO regularly with Spanish-American agents, and on so many levels, that he can hardly be seen as anomalous. Once it became indisputably clear that the Pernambuco revolt had failed, Venezuelan agent Juan Germán Roscio defended the rebels' attempt in a pamphlet; shortly thereafter, Cruz returned the favor by accompanying Roscio and other Spanish Americans to lobby for support in Washington. Meanwhile, when a bobbing band of some ten Pernambuco refugees began to wash up in the revolt's wake, Cruz diligently welcomed them into the rebel community. Much like his by-then associate Manuel Torres, Cruz hosted elaborate dinner parties for Spanish Americans, Pernambucans, and their U.S. allies; the abbé Corrêa, whose moles had burrowed into rebel communities up and down the coast, said that the guests offered toasts, "with all the pomp of public festivals, 1st to the liberty of all meridional America, 2nd to the perseverance in the good cause, 3rd to the vengeance of the martyrs of liberty in Pernambuco, 4th to the extinction of tyrants, and 5th to the confusion and ruin of their satellites everywhere." When some of those Pernambuco refugees then sailed off to fight in Colombia, Cruz was at the dockyard seeing them off, along with the brother of famed Venezuelan rebel Juan Bautista Arismendi.[43]

Cruz's vigilant public outreach efforts also typified the broader community of revolutionary agents. "Take particular care to refute all the slanders that are spread or divulged in the public papers or in any other forum," the Buenos Aires government advised its consul general in the United States in 1818. That same year, Buenos Aires leaders sent a bundle of governing documents to still another agent, urging him to "circulate them in those States in the best way you see fit" and publish them "in some of the newspapers of that Country." In 1824, Buenos Aires's supreme director instructed his U.S. emissary to "employ all means" to reach both "the Wasingthon [sic] Government and the generality of the said Nation." Like Cruz, Spanish-American agents spent their lives scribbling—writing articles, contacting printers, and translating foreign news clips into English for publication. As a Colombian agent put it, "I occupy myself exclusively with . . . [buying weapons and] restoring public opinion."[44]

Much as Cruz and Bowen had done, these Spanish Americans insisted that their countrymen were emulating the United States. The very first official emissaries, a set of Caracas delegates who arrived in 1810, repeatedly told newspapermen of "the strong affection which their countrymen felt for the U.S.," as one report put it. Of the three rebel expatriates who published English-language books in the United States, two portrayed the American revolutions as ideologically linked; the third, Colombia's Manuel Palacio Fajardo, did so not in his book (which was, after all, published simultaneously in London), but in a pamphlet that appeared one year after. "North Americans! remember the story of your fathers," he implored; South Americans fought for "the same glorious cause." Imitation was flattery, after all; what better way to win sympathy than to tell people that you aspired to *be* them?[45]

Other Spanish Americans persuaded well-connected U.S. allies to spread the news for them. Chilean General José Miguel Carrera had fought for political independence throughout the early 1810s, and he pursued support in the United States in 1816, after José de San Martín and Bernardo O'Higgins forced him out of power. Carrera spoke almost no English, but he sought out allies who did, including Baltimore postmaster John Stuart Skinner. "I have been incessantly writing" newspaper articles, Skinner assured Carrera, ". . . endeavoring to arouse the feelings of the nation & to animate the Government in behalf of your Country"; Skinner and his friends had even "proposed the establishment of a society for collecting & distributing information in regard to South America." As Naval Commissioner David Porter, himself an ally of Skinner and Carrera, argued in 1817: "We want to make it appear [in the newspapers] that . . . we are the Natural allies of S America that unless we aid them they will throw themselves into the hands of our worst Enemy [England] . . . that no time is to be lost."[46]

Not everyone wanted so much publicity. Especially in the early and mid-1810s, many agents worried more about buying weapons than they did about swaying voters; some, wary of attracting attention from the Spanish minister, even aspired to anonymity by traveling under fictitious names. Because determined individuals like Cruz could markedly influence news coverage, however, the rebel expatriates who did seek to shape printed reports had an impact beyond their numbers. Befriending sympathetic journalists, publishing rebel proclamations, writing books, and emphasizing the rebels' similarity to the United States all the while, agents of all nationalities actively worked to frame the narratives that U.S. audiences consumed. Cruz's story, in short, was the story of Spanish-American agents, too. With such collaboration across national and linguistic lines, it is little wonder that toasts to a combined South America proliferated.[47]

* * *

IN 1824, PERNAMBUCANS took up arms once again. This time, they rose against the newly independent *Brazilian* monarchy in Rio, established in 1822 by João's son Pedro after liberal reformers back in Portugal demanded João's return. But when the young Brazilian emperor veered toward centralist absolutism, Pernambucans revolted. Having just won independence from Portugal, they would be no colony of Rio de Janeiro.[48]

One of the insurgent leaders in 1824 was an elite *pardo* (or mulatto) major named Emiliano Felipe Benício Mundrucu, who commanded Pernambuco's *pardo* battalion; his name suggests that he may also have had ancestors among the Amazonian Munduruku Indians. Although the 1824 rebellion was collectively ambivalent on questions of slavery and racial equality, Mundrucu was clear as day. He wanted to make Pernambuco into a new Haiti, and he had copies of a verse printed and plastered throughout the insurgent capital:[49]

I imitate [Henri] Christophe
That immortal Haitian,
Yes! Imitate his people,
Oh my sovereign people!

With his newly independent nation on the line, Dom Pedro couldn't allow it. Once again, royalist forces overwhelmed Pernambuco resistance, and once again, the revolt collapsed just weeks after it had begun. Mundrucu had little choice but to flee, or die trying; in 1817, royal armies had beheaded rebel leaders and then dragged their corpses Achilles-style through city streets. Now, seven years later, Mundrucu had no reason to expect anything less. But how to escape, when the city was swarming with royal sentries? As an outraged official later explained, "it is known that on the day of the Shrovetide" festival, a U.S. merchant "gave flight to Major Emiliano, embarking him on an American Vessel . . . in a mask, taking advantage of this means on an occasion, on which this was tolerated." In other words, Mundrucu had gone incognito, donning a costume and parading to the harbor unnoticed, making his way among the discarded bayonets and cartouche boxes that still littered the streets. There he boarded a ship bound for Boston, where, he later recalled, he "was very well received."[50]

A man of color, very well received in the northern white republic? Mundrucu's use of the passive voice obscures who, exactly, offered such a warm welcome. He probably collaborated with some of the other forty or fifty Pernambuco refugees who had turned up in the United States by the spring of 1825 (about 20 percent of whom were people of color). Perhaps he crossed paths with Boston's antislavery community, too; somehow, after all, he managed to depart for Haiti shortly after his arrival, evidently in an effort to find work in the place that had done so much to inspire his egalitarian vision. Apparently unsuccessful, though, he quickly returned to Boston and colluded with his Spanish-speaking counterparts. By 1826, he had joined at least seven other Pernambucans who left the United States and proceeded to Colombia, where he enlisted in the patriot army—evidently so committed to Spanish-American independence that he was willing to die for it. (Still other Pernambuco refugees, meanwhile, made their way to Lima, Buenos Aires, and Mexico.)[51]

A denizen of the revolutionary Americas if ever there was one, Mundrucu was bold, tireless, and darker-complexioned than Cruz, unable to pass for white and probably unwilling to in any case. When the revolt in his native country failed, he carried his cause elsewhere rather than abandon it, and he soon helped to inform the United States' antislavery movement at a pivotal moment. Indeed, Mundrucu eventually lost faith in Bolívar and was back in Boston by late 1827 or early 1828, when he rented space from a Haitian woman, opened a clothing store, and continued to spread his revolutionary vision—and his affiliated crusade against racial prejudice. He had a soft spot for fellow freedom fighters: he once gave free clothes to a destitute revolutionary exile from Poland (which had risen up against Russian rule late in 1830). Shortly thereafter, the battle became even more personal, when Mundrucu tried to head to Nantucket on business along with his infant and sick wife ("a very good-looking respectable mulatto," a British traveler said). After the Pernambuco veteran had paid the fare and watched the stevedores muscle his horse and gig onto the steamboat, the captain told Mundrucu's wife that she couldn't go into the ladies' cabin despite the cold November downpour. ("Your wife a'n't a lady; she is a nigger.") Mundrucu responded with an unfavorable comparison to the Russian tsar. "You Americans talk about the Poles!" he protested; "You are a great deal more Russian than the Russians." One thing led to another, and soon the entire family—husband, wife, baby "at her breast"—found themselves back on shore, preferring to be stranded and sick rather than accept inferior accommodations and the inferior humanity they implied.[52]

This story survives because Emiliano Mundrucu (and probably his wife) kept talking about it, including to the rising young antislavery activist Lydia Maria Child and her husband David, a fiery journalist who (as the United States' former secretary of legation in Lisbon) spoke fluent Portuguese, became one of Mundrucu's friends, and periodically accompanied him through the streets of Boston. Mundrucu affirmed and enriched their antislavery thinking, strengthening their case that (as David put it) U.S. slaveholders were "THE WORST IN THE WORLD." David sang Mundrucu's praises and decried his ill treatment, openly referencing him in an 1833 speech to the recently formed New England Anti-Slavery Society (for which Mundrucu was himself a modest financial donor). Lydia devoted several pages to Mundrucu's story that same year in a groundbreaking antislavery book whose comprehensive vehemence surprised even her like-minded friends. "[I]f a person of refinement from Hayti, Brazil, or other countries . . . should visit us," she observed, "the very boys of this republic would dog his footsteps with the vulgar outcry of 'Nigger! Nigger!'" Indeed, she added, "it has been my good fortune to be acquainted with many highly intelligent South Americans, who were divested of this prejudice, and much surprised at its existence here." Mundrucu gave a similar impression to David Child, as well as to the British abolitionist Edward Abdy, who visited Boston and discussed the Pernambuco expatriate at length in an ensuing 1835 travel account. Prejudice in Boston was "unequalled by any thing in his own country," Mundrucu evidently told Abdy; as David Child reported, "colored men" in Brazil "occupy the highest stations; they command armies, plead causes, heal the sick, and minister at the altar." Mundrucu had clearly been talking about race and racism in a comparative context, and Abdy and the Childs drew on his insights to inform and embolden their own antislavery efforts (albeit perhaps too optimistically when they described South America as an egalitarian paradise).[53]

The Childs were fixtures of Boston's antislavery community, small though it was at a time when racial equality remained an alarmingly radical proposition as far as most white people were concerned. If Mundrucu knew them, perhaps he knew yet another of the city's abolitionist stewards: David Walker, a North Carolina native whose explosive 1829 *Appeal to the Coloured Citizens of the World* numbered among the first radical abolitionist works of the antebellum era. Walker and Mundrucu both came to Boston in the mid-1820s (though the precise dates are unclear). Both were highly educated free men of color. Both were about the same age—Walker was around thirty when he arrived in Boston, and Mundrucu was about five years older. Both went into business selling clothes, both carved out respectable livings for themselves, and, most of all, both were willing to make assertive public demands for racial equality. Indeed, Walker alluded twice to people "of North and of South America" in his *Appeal*. He charged that whites wanted people of color to "dig their mines and work their farms"—the former evidently a reference to the mines of Spanish America and especially Brazil, where African slaves and their American descendants continued to chisel and wash wealth out of the ground to that very day. He railed against "Bartholomew Las Casas, that very very notoriously avaricious Catholic priest" and "pretended preacher of the gospel" who had "proposed to his countrymen, the Spaniards in Hispaniola to import the Africans from the Portuguese settlement in Africa, to dig up gold and silver, and work their plantations for them." Thus began a "period of three hundred and twenty-six years," Walker calculated, since "our wretchedness first commenced in America." Only a hemispheric and diasporic outlook could have enabled Walker to reference *our wretchedness* when he was talking more immediately about enslaved Latin Americans.[54]

Walker must have absorbed these sweeping perspectives in part from reading the papers; he was a Boston agent for the first black-owned-and-operated newspaper in U.S. history, a New York–based weekly whose editors closely monitored Latin American race relations. Given the similarities between his life and Mundrucu's, it also seems possible that Walker developed his capacious geographic approach to slavery and abolition in conversations with the equally outspoken revolutionary from Brazil. As a firsthand witness to slavery's metastasized contagion, after all, Mundrucu could have put a human face on Walker's geographically expansive interests. Both men called vociferously for racial equality and sometimes even racial rebellion at a time when doing so was exceptionally dangerous. Mundrucu evaded early death with a mask. Walker died suddenly in 1830—most likely of consumption, which had taken the life of his infant daughter just days before. But some wondered if he had been murdered: black men had been killed for saying far less, and Walker knew it. Perhaps the two men emboldened each other; it is not quite as terrifying to stare death in the face, after all, if others are staring with you.[55]

* * *

THROUGH PERSONAL ENCOUNTERS and through print, Pernambuco expatriates worked to shape the views of people in the United States. Emiliano Mundrucu informed David Child, Lydia

Maria Child, Edward Abdy, and possibly David Walker. Antônio Gonçalves da Cruz, having convinced editors that Pernambucans lionized the United States, produced a reciprocal wave of adoration that inflamed popular visions of global importance and national greatness. South American insurgents vigorously managed their image in the United States; they were not just a group of passive objects for people in the United States to examine. As Cruz's experiences suggest, that outreach was both qualitatively and quantitatively significant, and it had a lasting impact even when revolts collapsed and royalist armies regained control.

Although Cruz and Mundrucu both made a habit out of hemispheric storytelling, Mundrucu's tales differed dramatically from the ones that Cruz told. Mundrucu spent his life saying things about slavery and equality that made people uncomfortable. Cruz, in contrast, wanted to be liked, and he seemed to avoid the subject of slavery almost entirely. In a sense, his chameleonic adaptability—his ability to pass for white where he wanted—well befitted the story that he shared with U.S. readers. Amid all his talk of moderation and emulation, he left questions of slavery and race implicit, unanswered, and even unasked.

U.S. audiences continued to look south for the entire decade that followed the War of 1812. As they did, it quickly became clear that Cruz's flattering story of moderation and imitation was coming to overshadow Mundrucu's more challenging call for equality. Indeed, Pernambuco's other agents in 1817 referred to race and slavery only perfunctorily: Bowen's early report on the rebellion passingly noted that Pernambuco's army was "as various in its character as its color," and one of Seebohm's documents noted that rebel leaders had noncommittally gestured toward the "slow, regular, and legal" abolition of slavery in the abstract future even while they simultaneously disavowed abolition "by force." Editors scarely flinched at these cursory references to race, even in Virginia and South Carolina; only one account cited the rebels' racial ancestries as problematic, and that was only in retrospect, after the revolt had failed. Pernambuco race relations formed a peripheral part of newspapers' overall coverage, subordinated instead to a broader emphasis on shared republican principles. That emphasis had immense staying power, and it endured even as rebels throughout Spanish America began to embark on a mission that the United States and Brazil had yet to embrace: the abolition of slavery.[56]

CHAPTER THREE

THE NEWS, IN
BLACK AND WHITE

PROFESSIONALLY AND MATERIALLY, Seaton Grantland and his brother Fleming were consumed by the news. Editors of Milledgeville's *Georgia Journal*, they sat at their desks each day surrounded by scissors and pens, inkwells and article clippings. The "exchanges"—complimentary newspapers that journalists throughout the country sent each other, free of postage, in order to stay informed—spread across their work surface, piling up and threatening to overtake the brothers in an avalanche of paper. (At roughly two feet square when opened, early U.S. newspapers could get unwieldy fast.) And so the brothers stacked and they sorted, they sleuthed and they spliced, digging their way out of the muddle as they decided which articles to reprint from the exchanges, which ones to excerpt, and which ones to call readers' attention to.[1]

Printers were men of elegant words and big ideas. They were also manual laborers, apron-sheathed and ink-stained workers who crawled into bed at night with aching backs and sprained shoulders. Every letter, every space, every punctuation mark that appeared in their papers had to be pulled without looking from an upright typecase and then arranged into words, sentences, and paragraphs. For a standard four-page paper like the *Georgia Journal*, this process took about sixteen hours, a flurry of fingers and

type. Then the Grantlands or one of their assistants would lug the
rows of cumbersome metal type over to the press and lower them
into place. By pulling a heavy lever, the printer pushed the inky
type against the paper; in between tugs, his partner would remove
the finished sheet of paper, moisten a new one, lower it into the
press, and beat the type with ink to prepare for the next impression. Working together in that delicately coordinated dance, two
brawny men and their prized machine could print 240 sheets of
paper in an hour—but then they would still have to print the other
side of each sheet, and stack and fold everything into newspaper
form. Once a week, whenever they were about to release a new
issue, the Grantlands or their assistants were likely to stay up late
into the night, finishing the job just before Milledgeville's readers
awoke hungry for news. Then, bags under their eyes and hands
blackened with ink, they started all over again.[2]

At least the bulletins that streamed into the *Georgia Journal*'s
office during the summer of 1816 seemed worth the effort to report.
As the exchange papers piled up in the shop—just a stone's throw
from the state capitol, and not far from the local whorehouses and
public commodes—what began as a startling rumor became a
confirmed fact: Haiti's mulatto president, Alexandre Pétion, had
bestowed military and financial aid upon a young white rebel Venezuelan named Bolívar, who was in the Caribbean plotting an assault
on the Spanish Main. In other words, an international, interracial,
revolutionary alliance was mobilizing just south of Georgia.[3]

The Grantland brothers worked vigilantly to spread the word.
Slaveholders themselves, and central arbiters between what happened elsewhere in the world and what people in central Georgia
knew about it, they parsed the exchange papers, meticulously set
type, furiously churned their press. (Maybe their slaves helped:
printing was dirty work, from the boiled varnish and soot used
in manufacturing ink to the urine-soaked goat hides used in
applying ink to type.) Over the month of July, the Grantlands'

once-a-week newspaper carried eleven articles about Bolívar's expedition, five of which mentioned Haiti. But the two brothers were not reporting out of fear and disgust. Rather, they reported out of excitement and empathy, and by late July they had concluded that the Spanish-American rebels were republican allies, joined with the United States in a cosmic battle against colonial tyranny. "The progress of the Revolution in South America . . . resembles so much our own [nation's] struggle for freedom," the brothers wrote, that readers needed to learn more about the conflict and support the rebels more actively. This, even though in the very next paragraph the Grantlands matter-of-factly reminded readers "that Gen Bolivar . . . [had] retired with many of his followers to the island of St. Domingo [Haiti], where he organized a new expedition." Instead of faulting Bolívar for relying on support from abolitionist Haiti, they emphasized the righteousness of his anticolonial cause and portrayed South American independence as a return to the principles of 1776.[4]

Other men in Milledgeville—population 2,000, or about half that if you left out the slaves—seemed to agree with the Grantlands' supportive assessment. Just one day after the Grantlands had first called attention to Bolívar's Haitian ties, white men across Georgia celebrated the Fourth of July, and they used the occasion to applaud the latest American revolutionaries. From rural Eatonton to the capital itself, inebriated inhabitants drank to "the Patriots of South America" and seconded the sentiment with ceremonial gunshots. As for the editor Seaton Grantland, readers seemed altogether satisfied: he went on to serve as mayor as well as U.S. representative.[5]

White Georgians' nonchalance toward Bolívar's Haitian alliance was, as it turned out, perfectly ordinary. The articles that the Grantlands ran in the *Georgia Journal* were among the most popular of their time; from Charleston, South Carolina and Charles Town, western Virginia, to Williamsburg, Ohio and Washington, Kentucky, burly newspapermen were heaving and ho-ing their presses in unison, pumping out precisely the same accounts. Indeed, candid and accepting references to Spanish-American race relations blanketed the nation during the 1810s and early 1820s, presenting readers with stories about how the latest American revolutionaries were grappling with questions of slavery and equality. Even as most of the new Spanish-American states went on to enact gradual antislavery laws and promote leading men of color to military and political office, journalists throughout the United States looked on without voicing alarm. Those who, like the slaveholding Grantlands, might have been expected to oppose rebel antislavery efforts tended to look beyond slavery toward what they instead saw as a broader story about the Americas' republican triumph over European imperialism.[6]

Such casually accommodating reports may seem surprising given the often contemptuous responses of white U.S. citizens to Haitian abolition a generation before. But Spanish America was no Haiti; Bolívar, no Louverture. Haitian independence in 1804 had ultimately been a means to rebels' long-cherished end of abolition; the reverse was true for Spanish America's white leaders, whose antislavery deeds stemmed more from military and political necessity than from humanitarian conviction. In most of insurgent Spanish America, antislavery efforts turned out to be painstakingly moderate; slavery waned but did not finally die for another generation, and real equality was still more elusive. If Haiti occupied the resolutely antislavery end of the Western Hemisphere's revolutionary spectrum, and if the United States, with its growing slave population, occupied the other, then mainland Spanish America lay somewhere in the middle. And yet white U.S. observers were open-minded enough to consider it a republican ally—or at least they were not so close-minded that they immediately ruled it out. In their apparent view, Haiti had gone too far, but Spanish America hadn't.[7]

Beneath newspapers' easygoing acceptance of Spanish Americans' antislavery tactics lay an idea, and an identity. Insurgent Spanish America was far enough away that it looked more like an abstraction than a reality. Its insurgents seemed to be pursuing abolition on their own terms, not at the pushy insistence of the kind of organized movement that might someday (like the one underway in Britain) turn its attention to the United States. As far as most U.S. observers were concerned, therefore, Spanish-American emancipation was playing out in a less threatening, more hypothetical world. And in that hypothetical world, even slaveholding editors like the Grantlands instinctively accepted that all men should be free—at least someday, somewhere. That universalist impulse may have offered little consolation to people already enslaved, men and women and children who toiled unremittingly in their own adverse present. But it was meaningful nonetheless, since it was language about liberty and equality and freedom, the very ideals that had helped people throughout the country define and explain themselves ever since their own revolution. That national self-image persisted for the nation's first fifty years, even as slavery spread at home and racial inequality deepened, and it primed white people throughout the country to welcome Spanish America's strategically antislavery republics as fellow passengers aboard the tumultuous ship of republican revolution.

There were exceptions, of course, arresting patterns that exposed the ultimately fragile underpinnings of universalist and egalitarian thinking in the early United States. But for the most part, Spanish-American antislavery appeared in the U.S. press as a subject of moderate curiosity rather than as an all-consuming obsession, and writers routinely envisioned rebels of color as courageous soldiers and virtuous republicans. In the process, they promoted a perfunctory but sincere kind of universalism, one in which commitment to political independence and republican principles mattered more than race. As editors from Haverhill, Massachu-

setts, to Leesburg, Virginia, put it in 1817, "every people are suscep-
tible of the blessings of a republic."[8]

*   *   *

BLACK HAITIANS LIBERATING all shades of Spanish Americans?
Baptis Irvine, coeditor of the *New-York Columbian*, was fasci-
nated. "Who could have foreseen, some years ago," he asked his
readers, "that a few regiments of West-Indian free negroes should
co-operate in giving liberty to the whites and blacks of the southern continent?" It was a remarkable world in 1816, the Irish-born
journalist mused—and it was becoming more remarkable every
day. For as Irvine correctly surmised, Haiti had offered its support
on one critical condition: that Bolívar end slavery in all the regions
he clawed away from Spain. This was fine with Irvine, who noted
that Bolívar's recent victory was itself destined to have "a great and
auspicious influence on the liberation of all South-America." In
Irvine's moral calculus, the anticolonial end unambiguously and
self-evidently justified the antislavery means.[9]

There was no mistake about it—Baptis Irvine was a revolutionary and a fighter. He saw the United States' independence war as
the opening salvo in an ongoing international struggle for republican liberty. As the staid Secretary of State John Quincy Adams
put it a few years later, Irvine "thinks of liberty as a blessing to be
acquired, and never as a blessing to be enjoyed." Sure enough, over
the next few years Irvine worked to hasten Spanish-American
independence. He advocated it in his columns. He abetted South
Americans who came to the United States. He traveled to Venezuela as a special agent for the Monroe administration in 1818, and in
1822, he even tried to revolutionize Puerto Rico.[10]

Irvine was exceptional in the *scope* of his commitment to
Spanish-American independence, but his sympathies were widespread. In a sample of 128 nationwide newspapers, over 90 percent
would report on Bolívar's 1816 alliance with Haiti or else on the

emancipation proclamations that followed. Sure enough, most editors reacted like Irvine and the Grantlands, either republishing the reports without comment or else matter-of-factly praising Bolívar's broader anticolonial conduct. In the U.S. press, Bolívar was antislavery by anticolonial necessity, fighting for republican principles so holy as to outweigh concerns about the radicalism of his Haitian associates. Irvine's enthralled commentary itself was reprinted not just in mostly free states like Ohio, Connecticut, and New Jersey, but also in slaveholding Virginia and border-state Maryland. A similar report that spread from New England to the Upper South described Bolívar's Haitian alliance, then called the general "an able and brave man." A five-minute stroll from Baptis Irvine's lower Manhattan office, the Irish-American *Shamrock* liltingly noted that Bolívar's victory against Spain—Haitian support and all—would "cheer the drooping spirits" of readers. Far from a curiosity, Irvine was "one of the men with whom this age abounds," Adams sighed, "a fanatic of liberty for the whole human race."[11]

Over the next few months, once news of Bolívar's Haitian sojourn had sunk in, editors turned more specifically to consider his ensuing antislavery influence. In truth, Bolívar's antislavery proclamations of June and July 1816 were not especially groundbreaking. They extended freedom only to slaves who enlisted as well as to their families, and they echoed measures that rebels and royalists alike had already been implementing at particular times and places; Bolívar's action, driven by a need to win over the region's large population of color, was simply more expansive. Few slaves rallied to the general's cause, at least at first; many continued to enlist with Spain, doubting, perhaps, the motives of slaveholding rebels who spoke of republican freedom. Bolívar himself owned over a hundred people, whom he did not free for another five years, and his early emancipation decrees were more important for their rhetorical power than for their real impact.[12]

But in the United States, that rhetorical power resonated. Phil-

adelphia's *Democratic Press* had Bolívar's antislavery decree "hast-
ily translated," then printed for circulation throughout the nation.
"The unhappy portion of our brethren, who have groaned under
the calamities of slavery, are hereby set free," Bolívar had proclaimed. "Nature, justice, and policy, demand the emancipation of
the slave; henceforward there shall be known in Venezuela only one
class of men—all shall be citizens." From his harried Manhattan
office, Baptis Irvine immediately reprinted the entire document
verbatim. So did the Grantlands, outnumbered by slaves in their
tiny Georgia town and even in their own households. In fact, so
many printers reproduced Bolívar's words that it is possible more
people read them in the United States than in Venezuela itself:
the proclamation appeared from Georgia to Maine and every state
in between with the potential exception of North Carolina, and
most of those reports also joined the *Democratic Press* in referring
to Bolívar's broader efforts against Spain as "astonishing successful
[*sic*]." Meanwhile, a separate account of Bolívar's other antislavery
proclamation appeared in at least fourteen states; from Charleston
to Chillicothe, this report concluded by hailing Bolívar's military
offensive as a "complete success." The cause of personal independence from slavery was merely incidental to the cause of political
independence from Europe, newspapers implied, and if Spanish Americans had to end slavery in order to end colonialism, the
trade-off was worth it.[13]

A similar pattern emerged in the topics that editors chose to
cover, with articles about republican revolts gaining more attention
than did articles about slave revolts. In 1816, for example, enslaved
people on the British island of Barbados rose up against their masters for four days before colonial authorities regained control. Some
twenty-two separate reports on that rebellion appeared in the
United States—far fewer than the scores that had appeared on, say,
Pernambuco's republican revolt, which occurred one year later and
which had almost no antislavery undertones. While newspapers

covered the Barbados rebels for an average news cycle of twenty-six days, they spent an average of over two hundred days covering the Pernambuco rebels. To be sure, the Pernambuco uprising had lasted six weeks, the Barbados revolt less than one. But the crackdown in Barbados endured, and even if we subtract six weeks from Pernambuco's coverage, the figure would still easily outweigh that for Barbados. So why did Barbados get less attention? Perhaps editors hesitated to publicize it for fear of creating the kind of alarmed buzz that might have spread to people of color in the United States. Still, anxiety was probably not the only reason for the disparity, since even northern editors (who had less immediate reason to fear slave rebellions) published far more on Pernambuco; apparently, they judged it to be more newsworthy. North or South, therefore, the primary story that appeared before readers was about the battle over republican government, not the battle over chattel slavery.[14]

* * *

FROM THE UPCOUNTRY trading town of Camden, South Carolina, William Langley monitored this news with special interest. Riding the white-tipped wave of cotton that overtook the early-nineteenth-century South, Camden had grown rapidly over the past few years, its black population most of all. By 1816, over half of the people who lived there were enslaved. To Camden's residents, black as well as white, slavery was no abstraction; it surrounded them and saturated their lives.[15]

So when Langley, a town councilman and editor of the newly-minted *Camden Gazette*, mined the exchanges and learned that Bolívar was striking against slavery in Venezuela, he took note. He ensured that others would, too, calling attention to Bolívar's antislavery proclamation with supersized fonts, front-page commentary, and one succinct headline: "IMPORTANT." Clearly, Langley thought emancipation newsworthy. But then, without so much as flinching at the antislavery proclamation, he proceeded to focus on Venezuela's emancipation from Spain. Bolívar was "every where successful," Langley wrote, "beloved by his soldiers and the South Americans generally. We wish him all the success the cause of liberty deserves."[16]

William Langley was no fool. Like any southerner, he knew that Carolina race relations were on the constant verge of boiling over. Just two months earlier, a group of Camden slaves had allegedly conspired to rise up and kill their owners on July Fourth; as white men grew tipsy and sang of freedom, black men would make good on the Declaration's promises, sealing them even with blood. Planters crushed the rumored rebellion before it began, but panic and "great confusion" gripped the region's white people nonetheless; "VIGILANCE *should be the watch-word*," a Charleston daily exhorted. Panic must have gripped South Carolina's black people, too, as they whispered among themselves of crackdowns and reprisals; indeed, one day after white Carolinians finally celebrated their Independence Day, five black men were hanged as guilty. It is hard to imagine a more explosive crucible of terror, violence, and fear: white people going to bed at night, wondering if they would awaken at gunpoint to the determined gazes of their house slaves and field hands; black people, wondering how many of their own would be tortured in prison or dangled in the gallows as payback for a conspiracy that may never have existed.[17]

Yet it was amid that stifling terror that Langley—who, as councilman, had heard the accused slaves' testimony just weeks before—unapologetically publicized Bolívar's antislavery proclamation. He seemed to think his readers would take the news in stride, too; as editor of a new paper, Langley had a reputation and a business to build, and he couldn't afford to alienate his audience. If he worried that word of Bolívar's proclamation would reach Camden's slaves and inspire them to press further for freedom, he took the risk and published the report anyway. So did other editors throughout the South, who were so excited about Bolívar's promises to free

Venezuela that they scarcely fussed about his promises to free the slaves. As Richmond's influential *Enquirer* put it less than a year after printing one of the translated antislavery proclamations: "We should be the last people in the world to be indifferent to the cause of Venezuela and Pernambuco—and with all our souls not to wish them success."[18]

There were exceptions, of course. On one hand, some writers directly and explicitly singled out Bolívar's antislavery deeds for applause rather than viewing them as benign offshoots of a more important struggle against Spain. As the editor of Bennington's *Vermont Gazette* put it, Bolívar "will increase his armed force by his just and righteous emancipation." On the other hand, a report that appeared in Boston and rural Maine reminded readers that the residents of northern South America were "a motley mixture of whites[,] blacks, Indians, mestizos, and every intermediate shade." "From such a population," wrote the author, "our expectations, should not be very sanguine." While a few writers variously praised or criticized Bolívar's antislavery efforts, however, most avoided overt judgment and simply suggested that Bolívar's strategy was secondary to a wider struggle against Spain. These authors seemed at least passively supportive of Bolívar's efforts to liberate Venezuelans from Spain, and slaves from their masters.[19]

Like Bolívar himself, such men accepted Venezuela's antislavery struggle because they believed so strongly in the broader anticolonial one that it served, and also because that struggle seemed so abstract, so distant, and, hence, so unthreatening. But another, implied condition of journalists' acceptance was their own knee-jerk sense that ending slavery was something that good republicans might reasonably do when the time and conditions were right. Of course men like William Langley and the Grantland brothers would have insisted that that time and those conditions had *not* arrived in the U.S. South; if slavery was evil, most white southerners of the early nineteenth century insisted, it was also necessary.

But Spanish America was a different case, another place. While slavery's growth at home starkly delineates the limits of egalitarian thinking in the early United States, the widespread embrace of Spanish America's antislavery revolutionaries reveals egalitarian thinking's endurance, and its connection to widely held patriotic ideals. For in celebrating Spanish America, editors were simultaneously celebrating the United States as an advocate for worldwide republican liberty even when that liberty happened to necessitate slavery's slow and deliberate overseas downfall. *This, too, is what we stand for*, editors quietly suggested; *they are American revolutionaries no less than we.*

*   *   *

PERHAPS THE STRONGEST testament to the strength of this welcoming anticolonial narrative was that the articles that *did* criticize Bolívar's antislavery tactics often met with swift public condemnation. Late in 1817, for example, somebody sat down and penned a series of long, handwritten letters to Washington's *National Intelligencer*. Calling himself *Phocion* in order to conceal his identity, the author had watched popular reactions to Spanish-American independence tensely, even angrily. The reason? Among other things, nobody seemed to care that the "*emancipating system* of Bolivar & Co." was turning South America into "a new Hayti." U.S. slaveholders, *Phocion* sardonically observed, "having drawn their first breaths, in Virginia, the Carolinas, or Louisiana, and the kindred countries," rose "so far above the feelings of *vulgar nature*, as to say Hosanna! well done!" to the rebels. Southern whites should have loathed Bolívar, *Phocion* warned, but instead they overlooked the general's antislavery tendencies and hailed him as a republican hero.[20]

In one regard, at least, *Phocion* was right: his determined opposition to Spanish-American emancipation was indeed exceptional. Although a Washington printer published *Phocion's* columns as a pamphlet, few if any newspapers seem to have reprinted them, and, as Christmas 1817 rolled into New Year's 1818, all of the responses that did appear assailed *Phocion*'s argument as incendiary and unrepublican. The *City of Washington Gazette* accused *Phocion* of "exciting terror" about race in order to serve political ends. A contributor to William Duane's *Philadelphia Aurora* agreed, indicting *Phocion*'s attempts "to persuade the people of the southern states of North America, that the liberty of southern America must be a *bad thing*, because the South Americans have declared that negro slavery shall not exist among them after a given period!" Other correspondents likewise shook their heads at *Phocion*'s letters; the problem, they said, lay not with Bolívar's antislavery efforts but with *Phocion*'s "anti-patriot" and "anti-republican" reactions.[21]

Exceptionally well informed on developments in Latin America, *Phocion* was probably a political insider. The abbé José Corrêa da Serra, fresh from the commotion over Pernambuco, thought the author was none other than the newly installed secretary of state, John Quincy Adams, who, as an opponent of early diplomatic recognition for the rebels, had reason to generate doubts about their abilities. Poised to become the nation's most prominent skeptic of Latin American independence, Adams did echo *Phocion*'s misgivings a few weeks later, in a private letter to his father, the former President John Adams. "[B]y their internal elements of the exterminating war between black and white," the son told the father, Spanish Americans "present to us the prospect of very troublesome and dangerous associates—and still more fearful allies." More recent investigations, however, have cast strong doubt on Adams's authorship—the timing doesn't add up, and Adams's own statements indicate otherwise. A more likely author was President Monroe's son-in-law and confidant, George Hay, a well-versed skeptic of Latin American independence who used the *Phocion* pseudonym on other occasions. Although we may never know *Phocion*'s identity for sure, the uncertainty is itself revealing: the author worked hard to cover his tracks, evidently reluctant to take public credit for his views. With good reason: the attacks on Spanish Americans didn't go over well. Surely some readers agreed with *Phocion*, but few if any seemed comfortable enough (or distraught enough) to commit their views to print.[22]

Newspapermen, meanwhile, continued to accept Spanish Americans' cautiously antislavery tactics well into the 1820s, by which time the territories that now comprise Colombia, Venezuela, Ecuador, and Panama had banded together into one sweeping republic. That republic was called Colombia, and it struck its first major blow against slavery in 1821, when congressional abolitionists passed a "free womb" law under which all babies thenceforth born in Colombia would be free (though they would have to work for their mothers' owners for eighteen years as a means of compensation). The translated text of the new legislation appeared in newspapers throughout at least ten states, as journalists plucked it out of the exchanges from New England to Charleston to the rural outskirts of St. Louis; another account plastered New England and the Mid-Atlantic with further and overlapping reports. As before, most writers suggested that this latest strike against chattel slavery was only one part of a more important effort against Spain. Few if any southern newspapers openly criticized the law, and some even offered explicit praise. In the western Virginia village of Fincastle, a local headline hailed Colombian emancipation as an act of "PRACTICAL PATRIOTISM." In New Bern, North Carolina, an editor endorsed a London newspaper that described how Colombia had "adopted the Constitution of the United States as a model, and improved upon this beau ideal of legislative perfection, by the complete abolition of slavery." Looking to the abstract world embodied by far-off Spanish America, such men denounced slavery as evil and hailed insurgents' controlled efforts to end it. Even those who accepted Spanish-American antislavery more passively drew from an implied moral logic in which ending slavery was a reasonable step for determined republicans to take.[23]

What was perhaps most remarkable about these complacent

responses to Colombia's emancipation law was that they came on the heels of the most divisive debates about slavery that the United States had witnessed to date. In 1819, the Missouri Territory had petitioned to enter the union as a slave state. With the nation already precariously balanced between eleven free states and eleven slave, Missouri's request drove a latitudinal wedge through the country until legislators finally hammered out a series of compromises that permitted Missouri's entrance as a slave state, allowed Maine's entrance as a free state, and established the 36°-30' parallel as a cutoff for slavery's future westward spread. The crisis left its mark, and it led many observers to conclude that debates over slavery threatened to tear the nation apart. From his Monticello retirement, Thomas Jefferson confessed that the Missouri crisis felt like "a fire bell in the night" that "awakened and filled me with terror." It was, the former president feared, "the knell of the Union."[24]

Somehow, as talk about domestic slavery grew increasingly antagonistic and fatalistic, talk about foreign slavery continued much as it had before. Even amid the heat of the Missouri crisis, in an 1820 congressional debate on hemispheric policy, Kentucky slaveholder Henry Clay felt comfortable citing Spanish-American emancipation as evidence that the rebels were good republicans. "In some particulars," he volunteered, ". . . the people of South America were in advance of us . . . Grenada [Colombia], Venezuela, and Buenos Ayres had all emancipated their slaves." Antislavery policies in Spanish America resembled the gradualist ones that many northern states were already carrying out, and the same ones that thousands of moderate southerners like Clay still hoped someday to employ.[25]

Colombia and Venezuela dominated U.S. reports on Spanish-American slavery—partly because trade with that region easily exceeded that with the rest of Spanish South America, partly because of Bolívar's personal fame, and partly because Colombia and especially Venezuela had more people of African descent than anywhere else in insurgent Spanish America. As Clay's observation suggests, though, antislavery efforts from Chile to Buenos Aires generated similarly sanguine reactions. In fact, Spanish-American expatriates—desperate though they were to stir up U.S. support— openly praised rebel antislavery measures in books, confident that readers would remain supportive. They were right.[26]

But antislavery was only the beginning of the story. What happened next was just as important. On the eve of revolution, only around 6 percent of Venezuela and Colombia's 2.3 million people were enslaved, far fewer than the roughly 16 percent of the more populous United States (and fewer still compared to southern states in particular). If U.S. southerners were ever going to follow their northern and Spanish-American neighbors by ending slavery, they would have to do so on a whole different order of magnitude. Notwithstanding the varying paths they would have to follow, black and white people in the United States and Spanish America (as in the rest of the hemisphere) shared a similar dilemma: how to coexist *after* emancipation. For if Venezuela and Colombia had far fewer slaves, they had far more free people of African descent, or about a quarter of their combined populations. While people in the United States were starting to debate the merits of colonization—the idea, that is, of sending free blacks and former slaves to live abroad on the understanding that such people could never coexist peacefully with whites at home—U.S. audiences turned to Spanish America for their first-ever glimpse of what life in a racially diverse and guardedly antislavery republic might look like.[27]

* * *

JOSÉ ANTONIO PÁEZ was to Venezuela what Ajax was to ancient Greece, or perhaps what Davy Crockett would soon become to the young United States. As legend had it throughout North and South America alike, Páez toppled wild bulls, just for fun, simply by snapping their tails with flicks of his wrist; he swam across flooded rivers, wrestled alligators, fatally harpooned furious beasts with single fell swoops. Raised on the forbidding plains of western Venezuela—the *llanos*, as they were known even in the United States—Páez threw his support to the rebels, hammering his unruly fellow plainsmen into South America's most fearsome cavalry. Although he lacked a formal education—he could barely read, write, or use knives and forks until adulthood—he schooled himself to become one of the most important military and political figures of his generation.[28]

For over ten years, Páez and his renowned cowboy cavalry galloped through the pages of U.S. newspapers. The more famous they got, the more curious John Binns became. Editor of Philadelphia's *Democratic Press*, Binns was (like Baptis Irvine in New York) an Irish immigrant and an ardent supporter of the nascent working class; at a time when many still saw democracy as a dangerous form of mob rule, Binns celebrated it in his masthead. He was also ambitious. Having recently become Philadelphia's most prominent Republican printer, he had been the first to publish Bolívar's 1816 antislavery proclamation.[29]

By 1817, Binns—ever attuned to popular appetites—sensed that his readers wanted to know more about Venezuela's mounted superman. He set out in search of more information, scouring the city for "the best informed persons" he could find—walking through Philadelphia's humming dockyards in search of merchants and sea captains recently returned from Venezuela, perhaps, or consulting rebel and royalist expatriates. The results of these investigations gave Binns pause. As he put it in his next edition: "General Paez, who is said to command 10,000 cavalry in the province of Varinas is a BLACK MAN," and the new republican government would soon "be in the hands of Black or Coloured people."[30]

Binns was wrong; Páez passed for white in Venezuela, even

though some doubted him. Binns's informants may have confused Páez's heritage with that of his rank-and-file, most of whom were black, mulatto, and *zambo* (that is, of both African and native ancestry). People in the United States could hardly have known any better, though, and the story spread to at least nine states as well as the federal capital, including to places as far west as Chillicothe, St. Louis, and Lexington, Kentucky. As usual, most editors declined to comment, although one Bostonian grew openly critical. Páez and the other "*patriots of South America*," the writer sneered, were "as parti-coloured as their complexion, and the further they keep from our coast the better." Meanwhile, Baptis Irvine's old *New-York Columbian* jumped to Páez's defense—not by arguing for the capacity of black officers, but by insisting that Páez was "a white, born in Merida."[31]

It was not the most promising start for reports on Spanish Americans of color. But over the next few years, Páez's popularity only grew, relegating Binns's early alarm to the editorial margins. In 1819, for example, the *City of Washington Gazette* matter-of-factly stated that Páez was "commander of the cavalry composed of the free people of color and blacks of the plains, called *Llaneros*." Rather than portraying these armed equestrians as somehow tainted, the editor spoke with awe and reverence, studiously describing how they had designed an offensive so daring that even Bolívar hesitated to approve it: Páez and his loyal *llaneros* had forded a billowing river with "temerity . . . unexampled," surprised the royalist army, taunted it into a fight, and, ultimately, triumphed. When Páez and his men marched victoriously back to camp, onlookers "were electrified to admiration, or petrified to the astonishment at this achievement." The author portrayed Páez's black and mulatto troops as nothing short of heroic, braver even than Bolívar himself, and the article reappeared in places like Columbia, South Carolina; Clarksville, Tennessee; and Gettysburg, Pennsylvania. The only additional commentary was positive, like that from the two upstate New Yorkers who agreed that Páez's was "a chivalric exploit" if ever there was one. To be sure, all these writers portrayed the *llanero* cavalry as exotic and superhuman, and perhaps racial difference inclined them to do so. But even if the exoticism was implicitly racialized, writers presented it as an asset, not a liability.[32]

Páez consolidated his power over the next several years, going on to lead the Venezuelan army (and eventually the entire Venezuelan republic). U.S. coverage remained largely the same, with writers praising Páez for his actions rather than faulting him for his ancestry. According to an 1825 article that originated in Boston's *North American Review* and then reappeared throughout New England:

> Paez, so much known for his valor and the vigorous traits of his character, is a mulatto, and the troops with whom he has accomplished such feats of military prowess, are but half civilized, undisciplined, and of the same colour as himself. His influence over his soldiers is surprising; he lives with them on terms of intimacy and equality, shares in their privations, amusements, and exercises, while at the same time, by the high example of his courage, and the native power and firmness of his mind, he commands a perfect respect and obedience.

No timidity here; the author handily condemned Páez's troops as "half civilized," and (in contrast to some of the earlier authors) he implied that blackness was perhaps a liability after all. Yet if blackness was a burden, it was a burden that Páez had overcome (and a burden that his men, who partook in the "military prowess," were perhaps in the process of overcoming). Páez's skin color opened the discussion rather than closing it, and although the author erred in calling him mulatto, what mattered was the image that appeared before New England readers: Páez looked intelligent, brave, and instinctively republican, even if his followers appeared as coarse and uncouth.[33]

The ancestries of Páez and his cavalry were therefore well publicized—even if the reports were sometimes questionable. But few writers dwelled on race, and many lavished Páez with color-blind praise, as if his ancestry was irrelevant given the importance of his deeds. In 1819, for example, Norfolk's *American Beacon* called Páez "a man possessed of great military talents" and "the most undoubted courage." The following year, newspapers up and down the East Coast as well as in Frankfort, Kentucky, and the newly organized Arkansas Territory reported that Páez presided over 3,000 "excellent cavalry." In 1821, papers from New England to Richmond praised "the 1,500 native cavalry of Paez, whose extraordinary exploits appear almost a romance," while the *City of Washington Gazette* went straight for the superlative, heralding Páez as "one of the most extraordinary men of the age." The general even acquired Homer-like epithets, appearing variously as "the gallant Paez," "the immortal Paez," and "the brave Paez." While it was possible that some editors were happy not to report openly on powerful rebels of color, the overall scarcity of criticism in other references to Spanish-American race relations makes it seem unlikely that such anxieties were common.[34]

In the end, there was little evidence that newspapermen collectively agonized over South American race relations, much evidence that they did not. Widespread coverage of such topics as Colombian emancipation, Páez's cavalry of color, and Bolívar's Haitian alliance offered plenty of ammunition to anyone who wanted to condemn the rebels as egalitarian extremists. But few critics emerged. Rather than frowning at or focusing on such things, writers continued instead to emphasize battlefield maneuvers, military strategy, and republican politics. Rebels of color routinely appeared as legitimate

so long as they advanced political independence. As an anonymous contributor to Philadelphia's *Aurora* wrote in 1817, "[i]f they
[Colombians] could obtain black troops to send against the Spaniards, they ought to do it; their duty and the soundest policy would
authorise it." In reports on Latin American independence, race
and slavery were peripheral but present, and concerns about racial
difference seldom overshadowed excitement about republican government and anticolonial freedom. As the flummoxed abbé Corrêa
protested in 1818, it was "as if every person . . . was denounced as an
anti-patriot, if he be not an advocate for supporting every rebellion or insurrection . . . whether these self-styled patriots are white,
black, or yellow." Heaven help the patriot who couldn't abide Spanish-speaking black revolutionaries; his countrymen would call him
un-American while defending the foreigners.[35]

In truth, the version of Spanish-American race relations that
appeared in the U.S. press was too simplistic, and that simplicity
rendered it too sunny. When writers bothered to mention the varied ancestries of beloved insurgents like Páez and his *llaneros*, they
suggested that Venezuelans of color routinely served as virtuous
republicans and courageous generals. It would have been easy for
readers to conclude that Spanish Americans inhabited a racial
democracy, and indeed, Venezuelan and Colombian rhetoric often
suggested as much. Determined to win support from men of color,
rebel leaders had constructed an ostensibly color-blind nationalism,
one that prized racial harmony and condemned racial hierarchy.
It was a nationalism that purported to make race irrelevant, one
that claimed to reverse centuries of inequality simply by insisting
that racism could not be widespread in Colombia because it was
un-Colombian. In practice, that kind of circular reasoning stifled
egalitarian progress as much as it furthered it; racial discrimination
persisted, and people of color who dared to protest were accused of
inciting hatred against white people and placing racial identity over
national loyalty. Even Simón Bolívar had a tendency to execute men

of color who grew too powerful, consumed as he was with night-
mares of what he called *pardocracia*—rule by the nation's *pardo* (or
mulatto) masses.[36]

But U.S. editors—who, after all, got much of their information from Colombian newspapers and government documents that
espoused precisely that kind of color-blind nationalism—seldom
dwelled on such complexities. Neither attentive enough to learn
the full story nor anxious enough to worry, editors casually implied
that Spanish Americans were building increasingly free, multiracial
republics. Although historians have long emphasized the differences between racial ideology in the United States and in insurgent
Spanish America—contrasting Colombia's rhetorical endorsement
of racial equality, for example, with the United States' racialized
citizenship restrictions—the difference was more complicated. At
home, the United States was undeniably a white man's republic, one
that rewarded whiteness as a way of fostering loyalty among citizens.
But as editors reported on revolutions abroad, as they imagined
what life was like in the new and moderately antislavery American
republics, a more egalitarian narrative prevailed. One can hardly
help but wonder whether, at some level, editors glimpsed in Colombia a better and more egalitarian vision of themselves, an alternative
picture of who they might have been—and, just maybe, who they
might become.[37]

★　★　★

BENJAMIN LUNDY WAS a small-town saddler with a big idea.
The scrawny twenty-six-year-old had just opened his own work-
shop, stacking and stitching leather into tack for the horses of
St. Clairsville, Ohio. Known for his quality work and fair prices,
Lundy thrived, and he quickly made enough money to buy land
and build a house on it for himself, his wife, and his two young
daughters.[38]

Lundy could have had an easy life. But as an earnest and

soul-searching Quaker, he sat at his workbench each day only to realize that ease was not really what he wanted. He was haunted by what he had seen during his recent apprenticeship in nearby Wheeling, western Virginia: men, women, and children, bound in chains and coffled together as they marched south and west to their new masters. Through their wails and their moans, Lundy later recalled, "the iron entered my soul." As he labored in his saddle shop, his clients' horses snorting and stomping outside the door, he dedicated his life to fighting slavery.[39]

Though Lundy had been raised with just a few piecemeal months of formal education, he was a voracious reader who believed in the power of print. Ink and paper became his weapons, and in 1821 he moved to Mount Pleasant, Ohio, and produced the first issue of his newspaper, the *Genius of Universal Emancipation*. It was every bit a start-up: with no money to buy a printing press and no idea how to operate one in any case, Lundy walked twenty miles each way, newspapers slung on his back, to get a neighboring printer to publish them. After a few months, a group of Appalachian antislavery activists offered Lundy the use of their press in Greeneville, Tennessee. Accompanied by a twenty-year-old printer who agreed to teach him the trade, Lundy set out on the long and winding journey, half by water and half by foot. For a man who had outfitted horsemen for a living, Lundy spent a lot of time on his own two feet.[40]

He also spent a lot of time reading the exchange papers. Amid his news clippings in Ohio and Tennessee (and eventually Baltimore, where he set up shop in 1824), Lundy identified a distasteful pattern. Haiti. Buenos Aires. Chile. Colombia. All of them republics, all of them antislavery. And yet the "elder sister of the American republics," he charged, "who has pompously and ostentatiously styled her domain 'the cradle of liberty,' and 'an asylum for the oppressed of all nations,' appears likely to be 'last on the list' of those who practically support the genuine principle of rational liberty, which they were the *first* to profess . . . !" The United States, Lundy indignantly observed, was increasingly becoming the hemisphere's lone slaveholding republic.[41]

Forged in the heat of the Missouri crisis, Lundy's *Genius of Universal Emancipation* tirelessly proceeded to contrast slavery's gradual decline in mainland Spanish America with its rapid spread throughout the southern and western United States. The paper became a clearinghouse of information on rebel antislavery efforts, devoting space to Latin America in roughly 60 percent of its issues before 1829. In a broader sense, in fact, every issue referred to Latin America indirectly, for Lundy's masthead quoted the universalist language of what it called the *"Declaration of Independence U.S."* So many nations were declaring independence that the "U.S." apparently offered necessary clarification. That sweeping outlook quickly attracted a nationwide audience, and by the end of its first year, the *Genius* had a remarkable seventy-five agents in twenty-two states and territories. Lundy's shoestring creation was the foremost antislavery newspaper of the decade.[42]

Lundy turned to hemispheric comparisons for the same reasons that thousands of his contemporaries did—he believed passionately in republican government, and it was thrilling to watch insurgent American underdogs topple mighty European monarchs. But his geographic range also had strategic benefits. Independent Spanish America presented readers with their only contemporary example of how gradual, nationwide emancipation might unfold in a republic. While most mainstream editors saw the United States as a model for Spanish America, Lundy and his contributors saw the opposite, invoking Spanish America as a model for the United States. In 1821, for example, Lundy reprinted Colombia's emancipation law and concluded that it offered a "virtuous exampl[e] . . . for the imitation of others." "Go ask General BOLIVAR" for advice about how to rid the nation of slavery, an anonymous correspondent urged his countrymen several months later. A Tennessee reader even dedicated a poem to Colombia's antislavery leader, urging "Each virtuous patriot, by close imitation" to "Aspire at BOLIVARS' summit of fame [sic]" by fighting slavery.[43]

The comparison also served rhetorical purposes, enabling Lundy to portray U.S. slavery as unrepublican and anachronistic. "The fiend of Slavery in North America is surrounded," he proclaimed in 1822. "The free states of this Union are on the east, the north, and the west [of the slave states]—Hayti and Colombia, on the South." In reality, the Americas' enslaved population was growing thanks to slavery's dramatic expansion in Brazil, the Spanish Caribbean, and the United States. When Lundy counted the number of antislavery *nations*, though, U.S. slaveholders seemed to be swimming against the tide. Having warned that the United States was the only American republic in which slavery was expanding rather than contracting, Lundy concluded that his country was embarrassingly similar to the slaveholding *monarchy* of Brazil. The United States and "Imperial Brazil," he charged, were "TWIN-MONSTERS IN SLAVERY AND CRIME."[44]

With republican Spanish America as a positive example and monarchical Brazil as a negative one, Lundy and his correspondents relentlessly sought to shame readers into reform. In the process, Lundy became one of the only newspapermen of his time to regularly conjure dusty stereotypes of Spanish scurrility. "[I]n the performance of our duty as Republicans," he wrote in 1821, "we are *so far behind* those whom we so recently viewed as *ignorant, biggoted* [sic], KING RIDDEN AND PRIEST RIDDEN CREATURES!!!" Other antislavery advocates nodded along, and Lundy's impassioned appeal reappeared in Shelbyville, Kentucky's *Abolition Intelligencer*. If "priest ridden" Spanish-American Catholics could end slavery, surely liberty-loving U.S. Protestants could do the same.[45]

In all of this work (if not in the religious typecasting), Lundy was doing something profoundly important, something that would have lasting implications for the antislavery struggle and for

U.S. history more generally: he was helping to remake the "*Declaration of Independence U.S.*" for a new generation. In 1776, that document had served a very practical purpose: to announce to the "Powers of the Earth" that the United States was entering the international arena as an independent player. The Declaration's second sentence—the one that spoke of equality, rights, liberty, and happiness—was strictly ancillary, and contemporaries mostly ignored it. Many revolutionaries still condemned slavery, but they usually did so by pointing to the lofty egalitarian language found in state bills of rights, not the more instrumentalist Declaration.[46]

Now, with independence assured and the Declaration's original work done, nostalgic patriots throughout the country were beginning to venerate the document as a national icon. They read it aloud on July Fourth, even hung copies of it in their homes and offices. For Lundy, the timing was perfect. By turning people's attention to the part of the Declaration that remained unfulfilled, as he saw it— the part that spoke of equality—he could channel the document's newfound popularity to slaves' advantage. Could the United States finally make good on the Declaration's uplifting words? Lundy found his answer to the south. "If we permit the people of Hayti, and those of the new republic of Colombia to answer," he wrote on July Fourth of 1822, ". . . they will tell us, that if we had the *will* to do it, we might easily accomplish it." Haitian and Spanish-American independence could strengthen Lundy's reinterpretation of the Declaration; that was why he so often argued that the United States was a two-faced anomaly, talking of freedom while it sanctioned slavery. Everywhere else, anticolonial republicans were also antislavery; everywhere else, declarations of republican independence brought declarations of personal independence. Spanish America helped Lundy and his supporters argue that the United States *could* live up to the egalitarian ideals of its Declaration—and that it *had* to, lest its own revolution remain hollow and incomplete.[47]

Not everybody agreed, to say the least. In presenting the Declaration as a document about human freedom rather than simply one about political independence—and by refusing to let his countrymen continue to focus on the latter at the expense of the former—Lundy was helping to set the stage for an impending clash about nothing less than what the nation stood for, and what it should aspire to be. After all, a man who publicly called slaveholders "disgraceful whoremongers" and said they served "the prince of darkness" would find easy enemies just about anywhere he went in the early United States, where most white people preferred polite talk and averted eyes when it came to slavery, not confrontation and action. Lundy was telling slaveholders that their money was dirty, their lives and their livelihoods unethical; he told his countrymen that they were hypocrites and bad people and bad Americans, and he blamed southern whites in particular for failing to change a world that was, more or less, all they knew. He blamed them, essentially, for taking the easy way out, flinching in the face of justice, failing to exchange their own familiar comforts for a life of uncertain struggle. He paid the price in hate mail and death threats. "[B]ullies vapored around me with bludgeons" so often, he later recalled, "that the sparing of my life might seem to have been providential." (No meek soul, this scraggy Quaker.)[48]

While most mainstream newspapermen saw emancipation as a benign derivative of the Spanish-American independence wars, Lundy saw it as paramount, and he focused on it accordingly. If the rule was that editors nonchalantly emphasized anticolonial battles over antislavery ones, Benjamin Lundy and his allies were the exception.

★   ★   ★

OR, RATHER, ONE EXCEPTION. Yet another departure from editors' customary focus on republican government over racial difference was that they were only willing to allow this narrative so long as the rebels seemed to be winning. This tendency first emerged in 1816, after

Bolívar, having just received help from the Republic of Haiti, sailed to Venezuela and offered freedom to any enslaved man who enlisted. U.S. journalists had initially accepted these tactics as a form of military pragmatism. But when news began to arrive that the expedition had failed, that Bolívar had retreated ignominiously into the sea instead of pressing further inland, editors looked back on the general's antislavery proclamations with more suspicion. Their willingness to accept interracial tactics was qualified and conditional.

Sure enough, the most popular report on Bolívar's troubles in 1816 explained that the "populace throughout the country [Venezuela] were highly enraged at a proclamation which the general [Bolívar] issued, setting the slaves on the plantations free." The article, which first appeared in New York after an incoming sea captain spoke to a local editor, reported that Bolívar had thus "found himself in the midst of a most ferocious and sanguinary peasantry, who, with the royal army, fell upon him, and almost annihilated his whole force." The story was misleading: most of Bolívar's crew had splintered away before the attack even began, so there wasn't much "force" left for the royalists to annihilate. Furthermore, although Bolívar's antislavery proclamations were unpopular among white elites, many historians have blamed early rebel defeats on a lack of outreach to people of color, not an excess of it.[49]

Fair or not, the impact was the same: the article swept through the U.S. press like a tidal wave of bad news, even in papers that had not previously criticized Bolívar's expedition. William Langley republished the report in Camden, South Carolina, as residents reeled from the alleged slave conspiracy; so did the Grantland brothers in Georgia, sweating away in the summer swelter along with printers in at least thirteen other states from New England to Kentucky. A similar article in the *City of Washington Gazette* reappeared in scattered northern and mid-Atlantic newspapers, explaining that Bolívar had "contracted the mania of emancipating the slaves from Petion" and had been "happily defeated, for the ultimate good" of the rebels (who would presumably now learn from their mistakes). "By such feeble and ill judged expeditions," an editor in northwestern Massachusetts noted, "the royal government of the Spanish Maine cannot fail to be strengthened."[50]

Not everyone was so quick to turn against Bolívar's antislavery tactics. Some writers continued to praise the rebels' overall support of political independence rather than focusing on the antislavery means. Others launched into editorial combat mode, sparring over whether or not racialized language was appropriate in the first place. The *New-York Courier*, in what it later maintained was a poor attempt at a pun, cavalierly quipped that "Bolivar's army . . . , who are chiefly *negroes* from St. Domingo . . . have been *beaten* until they are nearly all *black!*" (In South Carolina, William Langley republished the quip as well, as did scattered northern printers.) But a Vermont editor took offense, arguing that the comment "might pass for wit . . . if it did not relate to a very serious and important busines [*sic*]." "Be careful, ye friends of despotic power," he warned, "how ye ridicule the exertions of the brave spirits, who are now engaged in the same holy cause in which our Washington toiled and bled." What was perhaps most remarkable about this exchange was that the New York punster quickly backed down, swearing that if his comment "had the effect of injuring the reputation, or endangering the life of a single one of the aforesaid [South American] patriots, we are heartily sorry for it." While he still insisted that the insurgents were unprepared for republicanism, he effectively withdrew race from the equation by arguing that South America was merely "as incapable of preserving a republican government . . . as *France*."[51]

Limited as it therefore was, this kind of after-the-fact criticism was telling, since most editors only questioned Bolívar's reliance on black soldiers and former slaves when those tactics seemed to have failed. Groping for explanations, editors then snapped what seemed like a tidy ideological lens onto the messy and unpredictable enterprise of military invasion. This lens erased depth and exaggerated color, and while some white observers cast it aside like a warped pair of spectacles, others picked it up as if by default. In a world reeling from revolution, race seldom served to *predict* negative outcomes but it occasionally seemed to *explain* them. Although editors quickly returned to their former praise as Bolívar met with greater success over the following years, the short-lived and retrospective criticism in 1816 offered a portent of what was to come. When the new republics of America began to struggle once again ten years later, black Spanish Americans—and the white men who had ostensibly empowered them—would face a torrent of U.S. criticism.

* * *

THE THIRD EXCEPTION to newspapers' universalist republican narrative was perhaps most revealing of all. While reports on black troops in South America had usually been neutral or even positive, reports on rebels of color who appeared along the U.S. border were scornful, even vicious. Editors were not prepared to accept interracial republican equality as an immediate reality for the United States.

Florida was the relevant hotbed, controlled by Spain until the 1819 Transcontinental Treaty took effect in 1821. To Spanish policymakers, Florida remained a backwater, marginal to the empire for centuries and especially so now that Spain was struggling to retain its more lucrative colonies in Mexico, South America, and the Caribbean. But to U.S. policymakers from John Quincy Adams to Henry Clay, Florida was critical. It was replete with agricultural and strategic potential, and the rivers that sliced it promised to link southern planters to potential buyers in the Caribbean, the Gulf of Mexico, and beyond. On the other hand, Florida presented dangers as well. Indian wars, slave revolts, and other kinds of turmoil there threatened to spill across the international border, inspiring people of color in the southern United States and offering them valuable foreign allies. The trick, as federal policymakers saw it, was for the United States to occupy Florida without unbottling some kind of race war—or, just maybe, to seize Florida on the supposed grounds of preventing that war.[52]

This explosive jumble of greed and fear blew open in 1817, when rebel agents from Mexico, Buenos Aires, and Venezuela joined forces in the United States and determined to seize a Florida island for their governments' combined use. (They had help from Vicente Pazos, the Andean-born and Aymara-descended polyglot who had just disembarked in the United States after his exile from Buenos Aires, and also, it seems, from Antônio Gonçalves da Cruz, who had found himself otherwise unemployed after the defeat of his Pernambuco countrymen.) Partnering with a Scots adventurer named Gregor MacGregor, these agents set their sights on Amelia Island, a palm-treed and Spanish-mossed landmass that lay just off of Florida's Georgia border. Having gained Amelia, the thinking went, rebels from throughout the Americas could then use the island as a privateering base, pouncing on Spanish ships en route to Cuba or Puerto Rico.[53]

Things started out well enough. MacGregor arrived in the United States with loads of military experience, puffing on cigars and vaingloriously festooned in epaulettes and medallions. Short, swarthy, and stocky, he had been a professional soldier since the age of sixteen, when he fought against Napoleon's occupation of Portugal. In 1811, he sailed for Venezuela, married Simón Bolívar's well-born cousin, and took up arms against Spain, eventually joining the same 1816 expedition from Haiti to Venezuela that had so captivated U.S. onlookers. But MacGregor's thirst for military glory remained unsatiated. Along with his wife, he traveled to the United States to build support for the mission that he hoped would finally make him famous. An affable and hard-drinking man who could carouse in several different languages, MacGregor recruited investors and enlisted sailors at parties and shipyards all the way from Philadelphia to Savannah.[54]

MacGregor's tiny but confident crew consisted mostly of poor white southerners, who disembarked at Amelia Island on a scorching June day in 1817. After a six-mile march through knee-high mud, the men captured Spain's threadbare garrison on the same day they arrived, having fired scarcely a shot. MacGregor promptly decorated each soldier's left shoulder with a large red and yellow badge that read "Vencedores de Amelia"; his own medal read DUCE MAC GREGORIO, LIBERTAS FLORIDARIUM, and, on the other side, AMALIA VENI VIDI VICI.[55]

MacGregor's Caesar-like ambition outpaced his ability, however. Toppling royal power on the margin of the margins of the beleaguered Spanish empire was one thing; building a new form of authority was an entirely different project, one at which MacGregor did not excel. He quickly lost control to a succession of other strongmen, including a former New York City sheriff, a former Pennsylvania congressman, and, eventually, a French-born adventurer named Louis Aury. The sheriff and the congressman had support from the original, white, U.S.-born invaders. But Aury enjoyed the backing of roughly four hundred black, mulatto, and white adventurers who had sailed in from Haiti, the Gulf of Mexico, and the rest of the Caribbean. As these two groups vied for power, racial tensions simmered to the surface, and the resulting instability gave the Monroe administration the chance it had been waiting for. In late 1817 and early 1818, the United States took military control of the island, pointing out that the rebels had sold slaves illegally into the United States and contending that Spain had threatened U.S. security by failing to control the region. As Secretary of State Adams put it, the Amelia insurgents were little more than "sham patriots" whose "profligacy" endangered the United States; from Nashville, Andrew Jackson approved the occupation as well, and immediately offered to take mainland Florida, too. ("[L]et it be signifyed to me through any channel . . . that the possession of the Floridas would be desirable to the United States," Jackson portentously wrote, "& in sixty days it will be accomplished.") In the years that lay ahead, Adams and Jackson would become rancorous political enemies, divided (among other things) by their conflicting visions of national development in general and hemispheric policy in particular. For now, though, they found common ground on Amelia Island.[56]

Early on, most newspapermen had supported MacGregor and his white sailors. But as word broke about Aury's polychrome and polyglot arrivals, many had second thoughts. Perhaps seeking to inform white readers while confounding people of color, printers north and south began to reduce Aury's black soldiers to strings of asterisks. "Commodore AURY, with his ***** troops," they would say, or—still less inscrutably—"a considerable disturbance took place between the whites and ******." Not every editor elided such terms, of course, and for every paper that used asterisks, another did not. Still, the divergence from other coverage was clear, since printers seldom if ever redacted words when referring to rebels of color in South America. From their Milledgeville office, just a few days from the tumultuous Florida border, the Grantland brothers themselves turned to asterisks and criticized Aury's "sable followers," even though just a year before they had nonchalantly praised Bolívar's multiracial armies further south.[57]

Armed black insurgents near the Georgia border clearly struck the Grantlands and their nationwide counterparts as more dangerous than did armed black insurgents in Cartagena and Caracas. The reason was clear, rendered unabashedly explicit in column after column. "It will be a happy thing," wrote one Georgian, "if this pernicious example [of black soldiers at Amelia] be lost on the people of their complexion in our neighborhood." Many northern editors seemed sympathetic, and when one New Yorker wrote that "the late news from Amelia Island is of a character calculated to excite serious apprehensions from the influence which a dangerous example may have on the neighboring states," his comments reappeared as far south as the Virginia towns of Charles Town and Petersburg. Other authors neglected to couch their bigotry in the language of security, instead presenting their prejudice as self-justifying logic. As one

Georgia planter put it in a letter that reappeared in newspapers as far north as New Hampshire, Aury's troops were "brigand negroes—a set of desperate bloody dogs."[58]

As always, dissenting voices emerged. "South America has no right [i.e., need] to blush for her heroes [at Amelia], though there were among them 35 *blacks*," read an article in William Duane's *Philadelphia Aurora*. Even the *Savannah Republican*, source of many of the most egregiously prejudiced articles, conceded that Aury's "motly [sic] squad have behaved with uncommon civility since the surrender of the island." Editors lifted this commentary from the exchanges and reprinted it in at least nine other states as far north as Rhode Island, often in the same newspapers that had previously printed vicious racial slights.[59]

Despite such outliers, the trend was clear. The slurs that swirled around Amelia's rebels of color were far more inflammatory than was the neutral and often positive vocabulary used to describe rebels of color in South America. This was true even though many of the rebels were coming from exactly the same place. In 1816, editors had accepted and sometimes even commended Haitian soldiers who fought under Bolívar and promoted emancipation. But when Haitian soldiers sailed to Amelia just one year later (albeit more as adventurers than as part of an organized army), the reports grew anxious, scornful, and vindictive. In the metrics of race and rebellion, proximity and fear were key variables. It was easy to apply the egalitarian rhetoric of the U.S. Revolution to South American rebels of color, for those rebels lived largely in the imagination. Only when those rebels of color arrived at nearby Amelia Island did they start to seem real. When that happened, editors' sanguine, universalist talk of republican equality wilted.[60]

* * *

FOR ALL OF THE EXCEPTIONS, printed coverage of Spanish-American slavery and race relations was remarkably consistent.

Few editors presented race as a salient factor in the South American independence movements, and when they did talk about it, they tended either to withhold judgment or else offer qualified approval of rebel antislavery tendencies. Most, like Georgia's small-town Grantland brothers, simply concluded that the rebels were fighting for republican ideals so sacred as to outweigh any concerns about racial difference. They looked abroad with an instinctive sense of universalism, one in which men of color could be virtuous republicans, gifted leaders, and courageous soldiers.

Although this collective emphasis on republicanism over race constituted a kind of universalism, it simultaneously rendered that universalism shallow. The reason that Spanish-American antislavery didn't particularly concern editors was that editors didn't think very carefully about antislavery to begin with. They described foreign emancipation but did not seriously contemplate it; they reported but did not reflect. Rather than grappling with what successful Spanish Americans of color might suggest for the United States, editors speedily moved on to a simpler part of the story, one about the Americas' supposed triumph over Europe. Most accepted Spanish Americans' tentative moves toward equality only passively, more enthusiastic about the spread of republican government than they were concerned with deeper questions of social equality. The rhetoric that resulted was unexamined, reflexive, and superficial, something that writers instinctively applied to revolutions abroad but seldom took to heart at home. That was why, when the rebels stumbled, or when they sailed close to the United States, the reaction literally and figuratively darkened.

But those cracks in the broader narrative of hemispheric republican unity remained faint—noticeable mostly in retrospect, after they had deepened and spread. For white people living in the uncertainty of their own present, republican universalism offered a happy vision of hemispheric harmony. So long as the narrative was about republicanism and not race, after all, most onlookers would feel inclined to support the rebel movements. If the excitement that resulted was perfunctory and complacent, it was also genuine and heartfelt. Drawing as it did on the United States' own founding revolutionary rhetoric, support for the rebel movements helped people in the United States explain who they were. Latin American independence went on to become one of the most popular causes of its time, as the optimistic newspaper reports inspired patriotic ardor throughout an entire nation of readers.

CHAPTER FOUR

BOLIVAR, U.S.A.

GEORGE P. MORRIS WAS A precocious young man. Lucky, too: born in Philadelphia and raised in New York, he had the connections and the wherewithal to develop his creative talents. By fifteen, the curly-brown-haired youth was publishing his poetry in a Manhattan newspaper; by twenty, he was coediting an important belles-lettres journal, having become a denizen of the nation's emerging literary scene.[1]

But at heart, Morris was a songsmith. Music flowed through his soul, perhaps even timed the pace of his steps each day as he walked among the businessmen, dandies, hucksters, and beggars of lower Manhattan. When he heard about Spain's final defeat in South America, he (and an unnamed associate) turned instinctively to verse—coloring half notes into quarter notes, sharpening and flattening and syncopating. "Rejoice, rejoice with gratitude," the young man urged his countrymen,

> "Join in the loud in the loud Huzza!"
> With blooming wreaths his brow we'll grace,
> With many with many a gem and star.
> Hail benefactor of thy race,
> Immortal, Immortal BOLIVAR.

The resulting composition, slow and stately, wound its way to the newly built Chatham Theater, where somebody sensed that Morris's hemispheric excitement could help pack the house. And it did: when a singer and a pianist jointly performed the piece sometime around 1826, the audience expressed its own enthusiasm through "unbounded applause."[2]

"BOLIVAR. *A PERUVIAN BATTLE SONG*" was one of many odes to Latin American independence published in the early United States. Though other composers' names are largely lost to history, the titles linger, like a determined procession of *forte* notes: "Gen. Bolivar's grand march & quick step," released in Baltimore in the early or mid-1820s; "General Bolivar's favourite Scotch march," printed in Philadelphia around the same time; and "General Bolivar's address to his army: suggested by the motto Vencer o' morir = Conquer or die," released in New York in 1826. It is hard to know how well this printed sheet music actually sold, harder still to know how often people actually performed the tunes; they were popular in Morris's native Philadelphia, at least, where Fourth of July revelers regularly washed down their hemispheric toasts with Bolívar songs. In any case, even this long parade of melodies failed to satiate the public's desire for music about South America. Other songs, variously dedicated to Buenos Aires, Brazil, Peru, and Chile, appeared as well, and by the mid-1820s composers had published nearly twenty odes to South America.[3]

The apparent demand for South American songs was remarkable because it suggests that ordinary people were paying attention to the newspaper reports that men like Antônio Gonçalves da Cruz and the Grantland brothers had done so much to encourage. Even more than in the early 1810s, with greater frequency and fewer reservations, expressions of hemispheric solidarity proliferated in the decade following the War of 1812. U.S. observers welcomed their new "sister republics" with open arms, undaunted by the insurgents' Catholicism and unfazed by the developing reports on Spanish-American antislavery efforts. Every July Fourth, thousands of people cheered South American independence; year-round, they named their homes and their children for Simón Bolívar. When quantified and mapped over space and time, these toasts and naming patterns demonstrate that hemispheric solidarity transcended not only region but also, under certain circumstances, gender and race. The muse that had inspired George Morris was singing to the entire country.

There were several reasons that so many people hailed the victories of far-off South American revolutionaries. Some pointed to geopolitical benefits, arguing that the United States would be safer if conflict-prone European dynasties had less influence in what many were beginning to call "the American hemisphere." Others envisioned new inter-American trade routes through which the United States could exchange manufactures and agricultural produce in return for sorely needed gold and silver specie. But as rebel agents like Cruz had intuited, something profoundly emotional was at stake, too. Latin American independence gave U.S. audiences a cause greater than themselves, made them feel that they stood at the forefront of a worldwide movement for liberty, and inflated them with visions of international grandeur.[4]

★ ★ ★

SUN BLAZED DOWN on Norfolk's old-fashioned fife and drum parade on July Fourth of 1822, but the weather deteriorated for the afternoon picnics. The region's best-connected residents—the governor, the militias, and a smattering of European consuls—had gathered at a spot shaded by majestic sycamores as well as by a soaring, umbrella-like canopy of nautical sails built for the occasion. A feast lay piled high on the tables; black men and women had probably spent weeks preparing it in dangerously sweltering kitchens. But just as the party was getting started, a dark, angry cloud shut out the sun. The rain was torrential; the wind, ferocious. Some ran for cover—hats and napkins flying, dinners half-eaten. Most shrugged, looked at the splashing, unfolding chaos, and laughed. Soaked now with rain instead of sweat, Virginia's leading citizens dined that day on soggy food, sang above the howling wind, and drank to the glory of their republic.[5]

They also drank to the glory of South America. Although a large U.S. flag was the gathering's visual centerpiece, flags from Europe and Latin America sailed above the party as well, whipping and snapping (and maybe blowing over) in the wind—the Latin American flags "according to seniority" and the European flags "in the order they stand in their acknowledgment of our Independence." That international homage continued even amid the confusion of the storm, as guests cheered for "The People of South America." "We have sympathized with them in the day of their adversity," the revelers soddenly declared; "it is now our turn to rejoice with them on their emancipation."[6]

In taverns and townhouses, at picnics and plantation homes, the sentiment was the same: delighted patriots after the War of 1812 took their South American love affair to new heights, viewing their past as prescriptive for a new generation of American revolutionaries. ("May our example excite them to imitation," exclaimed partygoers at an eastern Virginia courthouse, punctuating their toast with six hearty cheers—as opposed to three cheers apiece for the Constitution, "State rights," and fellow Virginians Jefferson, Madison, and Monroe.) Such toasts had existed in the early 1810s, but after the War of 1812 they grew utterly ordinary. As early as 1816, Washington's National Intelligencer noted that toasts to South America had become nearly "universal"; throughout the country, people "regard the contest which now exists in that quarter, with an interest, and indeed anxiety, the extent of which had not before been realized."[7]

The National Intelligencer wasn't exaggerating. That year, with news of Bolívar's Haitian sojourn just days old, two-thirds of July

Fourth parties offered hemispheric salutes, and over the ensuing decade that figure averaged around 55 percent, as if the entire nation had suddenly cranked its telescope south (see the Appendix). Based on coverage in seven different newspapers—Philadelphia's *Aurora* and *Democratic Press*, the *Richmond Enquirer*, Illinois's *Edwardsville Spectator*, Boston's *Columbian Centinel* and *Patriot*, and the *Arkansas Gazette*—this figure draws from hundreds of holiday parties throughout four states and one organized territory, and it solidly underestimates the actual number of hemispheric toasts. Chronically short on space, editors often printed just two or three toasts from any given celebration, meaning that countless toasts to Latin America were never published. Sure enough, in the decade that followed the War of 1812, editors of all political stripes agreed that southward-looking toasts numbered among the most popular in the entire nation. On their most important patriotic holiday, as they strived to define and celebrate what united them as a country, people looked abroad in order to explain who they were at home, their international and national ardor bleeding smoothly into one as they proudly took credit for South American successes.[8]

The most ardent of revolutionary evangelists occasionally bemoaned what they saw as insufficient fervor. Born in Pittsburgh, raised in Louisiana, and living in Baltimore by 1817, Henry Marie Brackenridge was among those who yearned to convince the holdouts. Perhaps it was too late to convince his father, the 1771 Princeton graduate and poet Hugh Henry Brackenridge, who had died a year earlier after a long career as a politician, judge, editor, and writer. The son, however, believed that his father's Revolution lived on in South America, and in 1817, about to depart for that continent as part of a federally sponsored fact-finding commission, he made the case in a widely read pamphlet. "Although the sentiment in favor of the Patriots, through the United States, is almost universal, and seems to become each day more earnest," he protested, "yet there are a few who pretend to advocate a cold indifference."

"On this subject" of South American independence, the *Baltimore Patriot* groused that same year, "there appear to be manifested less interest and feeling than, in our opinion, the importance of the occasion demands." But as Brackenridge's own comments anticipated, such complaints were infrequent, and they had largely faded by the early 1820s, at which point popular support for the rebels had evidently proven itself an enduring reality. For every person who lamented that the public was not supportive enough, there were others—often high-powered merchants and federal policymakers affiliated with the Monroe administration, as the next chapter will show—who complained that the public was all too excited. Meanwhile, religious differences continued to go almost entirely unaddressed: just a handful of postwar toasts mentioned the rebels' Catholicism, and those that did almost always supported the rebellions anyway.[9]

To lead, to inspire, to uplift the hemisphere—it was, evidently, a burden that the United States proudly bore. Republicanism's success abroad seemed to demonstrate the universality of U.S. ideals; it made people feel like they mattered. It was no accident that the surge in inter-American toasts coincided with the better-known surge in nationalism that followed the War of 1812. Nor was it an accident that those toasts emerged with such frequency on the country's most self-consciously patriotic of holidays, and during an era in which reminiscent citizens, their own independence finally assured, were elevating the Fourth of July into a sacrosanct national celebration. Much like Andrew Jackson's victory at New Orleans, the spread of independent republics elsewhere in the Americas seemed to confirm that the United States was divinely ordained and destined to lead. After the acrimonious war with Britain, at a time when nationalism was often sectional and splintered, Latin American independence offered a more unifying language of U.S. greatness. Celebrations of Spanish America "have produced some of the finest effusions of genuine patriotism," New York Senator

Martin Van Buren proclaimed; in Philadelphia, military men even conflated foreign freedom with that of the United States, toasting "The Patriots of South America" and then, improbably, adding, "May Freedom be ours." Nationalism soared after 1815 not just because the War of 1812 had come to a seemingly honorable close, but also because so many people found patriotic affirmation below the nation's borders.[10]

Along with the heightened interest in Latin America after 1815 came a deepened sense of hemispheric distinction. As Napoleon wasted away in his Saint Helena exile, republicanism and constitutionalism bloomed throughout the Americas but wilted in Europe. U.S. observers concluded that the United States was leading the Americas to global greatness as monarchical Europe struggled to dig out of its shattered postwar ruins. For those inclined to see themselves as central players in a cosmic battle against tyranny, the stakes could not have been higher. Absolutist powers in Europe were reacting against the French Revolution and Napoleon at that very moment, resolving to fight liberal constitutionalism across the globe. Central to that effort was a rising coalition led by Tsar Alexander I of Russia and Prince Klemens von Metternich of Austria, who called themselves a "Holy Alliance" and vowed to reestablish absolutism wherever they could. These men weren't bluffing: in the early 1820s, they helped to crush a liberal revolution in Spain. Such events led people in the independent nations of the Americas to worry that the Holy Alliance would try to reconquer parts of the Western Hemisphere as well—hence Monroe's famous "doctrine" of 1823, which declared the Americas off limits to further European incursions.

All of that transatlantic bluster and diplomatic posturing sharpened the sense of common hemispheric cause that had developed in the early 1810s. The Americas increasingly seemed like a sanctuary for liberal republics; Europe, a final, desperate bastion for absolutist monarchy. Even Secretary of State John Quincy Adams—

long a skeptic of Spanish America—sang the hemisphere's glories in 1822, shortly after the United States had formally recognized Spanish-American independence. "*The American Hemisphere, and the Declaration of Independence*," he proclaimed in a toast, offered "A new world of matter for a new world of mind."[11]

Such swagger about America's distinctiveness from Europe was common fare at Fourth of July celebrations in the early and mid-1820s, but it was exaggerated. For one thing, Europe was not entirely absolutist. Spanish and Portuguese reformers fought for liberal constitutions in the early 1820s, Greek insurgents rose against Ottoman rule throughout the decade, Irish dissidents sought greater autonomy from England, and Britain's constitutional monarchy emerged as the Holy Alliance's greatest global adversary. By the same token, America was not wholly republican; it wasn't even wholly independent. Russia claimed rights in Oregon. Brazil and Mexico declared independence as monarchies. Canada remained part of the British Empire. The new nations didn't even control much of the land that they claimed; in vast expanses of territory from Texas to the Amazon, indigenous people called the shots. And except for Haiti (which many whites denied was really independent anyway), the entire Caribbean remained under colonial sway.

Still, it was hard to deny the overall trend. The shot heard round the world ricocheted loudest in the Americas, and for a full fifty years—or so it seemed to those who had fired it. Between 1775 and 1825, all of Portuguese America, all of mainland Spanish America, much of British America, and (as antislavery activists added) the most lucrative colony in French America broke away from Europe. Most of these places established republics, and the exceptions often seemed to prove the rule: Mexico's monarchy quickly gave way to republicanism, and Pernambuco's uprisings led many U.S. observers to predict that the Brazilian court teetered on the verge of collapse. "American Emperors shoot up too fast to be of firm growth," the *Charleston Mercury* concluded, "and the drapery, which surrounds them, conceals but badly, the internal weakness of their frames." Philadelphia's *Christian Advocate* agreed, proclaiming in 1824 that "the whole American continent is likely soon to be done with royal sway of every kind." Although anticolonial republicanism and constitutionalism were inspiring outposts of admirers throughout the world, they seemed to be spreading fastest in the Americas.[12]

Such weighty geographic visions found their clearest expression in federal policy. In 1822, the United States became the first nation in the world to recognize the independence of mainland Spanish America, but it declined to do the same for Greece one year later. Likewise, the Monroe Doctrine did not just warn Europeans to stay out of America's business; it also promised them that the United States would stay out of Europe's business in return. The United States' interest in the Americas, Monroe asserted, superseded its interest in Europe.[13]

Far outside of Washington City, meanwhile, ordinary people looked around the world and reached instinctively similar conclusions, even framed them in the most personal of terms. While Greek insurgents generated enormous excitement, for example, July Fourth revelers seldom referred to them as family—something they had done when talking about Spanish Americans ever since 1810. One of the most popular hemispheric toasts, offered in such disparate places as Fredericktown, Maryland, and Manchester, Missouri, was to "Our Sister Republics of the South." In Charlestown, Massachusetts, men exuberantly saluted the "Republics of South America" as "Sisters of the new world!" Citizens of Vandalia, Illinois, welcomed Colombia "as the new born sister of the United States," while the Volunteer Corps of Harrisburg switched the gender and preserved the sentiment, toasting Colombia and "hail[ing] her patriotic citizens as brothers." In Natchez, Mississippi, men hailed "*The Independent States of S. America* . . . as new members of the Republican Family." The Greeks appeared as ideological allies, cultural icons, and descendants of an ancient civilization that had itself helped inspire the statesmen of 1776. But they rarely appeared as family. Fighting for American freedom and against European colonialism, Latin Americans—not Greeks or any other denizens of the Old World—seemed like the closest, blood heirs to the United States' own revolutionary tradition.[14]

★　★　★

WHEN THE CITIZENS of Steubenville, Ohio, gathered to commemorate their nation's fiftieth year "jubilee" on July 4, 1826, it was a ram who stole the show. The celebrity ruminant had just returned from a journey to Baltimore, where he impressed the judges at an agricultural fair and walked away with the prize cup—even though, as newspapers later reported, "he had to contend with the best merinoes and Saxons that could be produced from any part of the union." Back in Ohio, the champion ram rode atop a float in the national anniversary celebration, draped in garlands and sporting a silver trophy around one of his horns. "I *went*, I saw, I conquered," boasted a flag that rode along on the side. And so he had—Bolivar, the prizewinning sheep, was to livestock what his Venezuelan namesake purportedly was to South America, a sturdy and virile victor whose enemies quivered and collapsed at his feet.[15]

The ram's owner clearly had a sense of humor, and it was probably with a grin that he named his cud-chewing cloud of fleece after South America's most exalted general. But although countless other farmers named their livestock after Venezuela's so-called Liberator, others endowed the name Bolivar with the highest possible praise by bestowing it earnestly on their own flesh and blood.

Born in 1793, Aylett Hartswell Buckner was a case in point. When he was a boy, his family had joined the thousands of Virginians who, hoping to improve their chances in life, climbed up and over the Appalachians to start anew in Kentucky. Like many young men of his generation, Aylett first made a name for himself fighting British soldiers and native people in the War of 1812; when U.S. soldiers killed and skinned the pan-Indian leader Tecumseh at the Battle of the Thames, Private Aylett Buckner was there, his frontier education forged in blood and human scalps.[16]

When he returned to Kentucky after the war, Aylett Buckner—now in his early twenties and known for his good looks and spirited charisma—looked to settle down. In 1819, he joined the Hart County board of magistrates, and that same year he married eighteen-year-old Elizabeth Ann Morehead, another Virginia-born Kentuckian. Having acquired a plot of nearby land, the newlyweds set off together into the central Kentucky woods, carving their way through dense foliage and almost certainly battling gnats, ticks, and mud. At their new homestead, they drew on their fourteen slaves—most of them women and children—to clear the trees, fashion the logs into a home, and plant crops.[17]

When Aylett and Elizabeth's first child arrived after a year of marriage, they named the boy after a grandparent, and they did the same for a daughter who arrived the following year in 1821. But when the third child was born a year and a half later, Aylett and Elizabeth honored someone far outside the family tree. Born in 1823, Simon Bolivar Buckner numbered among the first baby Bolivars in the country.[18]

From their remote Kentucky cabin, Aylett and Elizabeth had clearly kept up on the news—perhaps by reading the Lexington newspapers or others that wound their way into the nearby hamlet of Munfordville, passed along from reader to reader until their crisp white pages grew wrinkled and worn. Clearly, too, Aylett and Elizabeth talked about events in Spanish America, but beyond that we can only wonder at their decision. Who first suggested the name? Did the other parent hesitate? Ask questions? Beam approvingly? Were the Buckners inspired by the region's history of anti-Spanish sentiment? Was Elizabeth—whose father had fought in the U.S.

war for independence and whose mother had tended to wounded revolutionaries—honoring her family history as she created her family's future, surrounded by belching infants and babbling toddlers? Was Aylett reliving his war days by naming his son after the hemisphere's greatest living military hero? (Surely Bolívar's reputation for martial valor contributed to his appeal; one can imagine it was what the war hero Andrew Jackson had in mind when, in the midst of the heated 1824 presidential election season, he named his prized "stud colt" Bolivar, after America's *other* premier general.)[19]

Whatever the answers, the Buckners' decision spoke volumes. Giving a name to one's baby is a recognition of that child's personhood, a chance to associate that new life with the people, values, and ideals that matter most. Remarkably, in the early and mid-1820s, scores of parents reached the same conclusion that the Buckners did. Manifest today in federal census reports, the Bolivar baby names enable us to track Bolívar's popularity across space and over time in a way that July Fourth toasts, which passed through editorial filters, do not. The resulting patterns poignantly reveal that support for South America was not just pervasive; it was also personal.

Through the late 1810s, Bolivar babies were almost nonexistent in the United States. That changed as Bolívar consolidated his power abroad. The first baby Bolivars were born in 1820, in Maine, Maryland, and the two Carolinas, just months after a Venezuelan congress had elected the Liberator president. Over the next few years, scattered other drooling, driveling babes joined them, including Simon Bolivar Buckner in his Kentucky log cabin. But the numbers first skyrocketed in 1825, as news arrived that Bolívar had finally expelled Spanish royalists from South America once and for all. That year, 30 couples named their sons Bolivar; in 1826, 35 more did the same, and the following year brought 32 more. By the end of 1830, about 200 baby Bolivars were crawling through the country. The parents of these children were among the nation's most enthusiastic supporters of South American independence—after all, for every parent willing to stamp his or her son with such a unique name, there were presumably others who gave their children more familiar rebel names like Simon or Martin, names whose long-standing ubiquity makes it difficult to pinpoint specific namesakes. The baby Bolivars joined a generation with even greater numbers of baby Jeffersons, Washingtons, and Lafayettes. Maybe some parents just liked the sound of the names, but many specifically sought the political connotations, as their other children's names suggested. In southeastern Illinois, the farmers James and Barbara Nabb named their first son Bolivar and their second Hamilton; in western New York, Sophia Johnson named one son Boliver and another Ypsilanta, after the leader of insurgent Greece.[20]

Coinciding as it did with Bolívar's culminating victories in South America, the 1825 Bolivar baby boom shows just how quickly editors could introduce international developments to national audiences—and how quickly those audiences could respond. Thanks to the exchange papers, parents from Mississippi to Michigan studied the same headlines at the same time, then gave their sons the same names. News flourished without any clear regard for geography, defying mountains and rapids and muddy backroads until it arrived in places like the Buckners' stump-filled Kentucky homestead. (One Transylvanian visitor gawked as his stagecoach driver systematically flung newspapers out the windows, "left and right," to remote backwoods cabins in Ohio; "No matter how poor a settler may be," the visitor wrote, "nor how far in the wilderness he may be from the civilized world, he will read a newspaper.")[21]

Nor was it always enough to simply *read* the news. More than today, when we routinely consume news stories alone and in private, people in the early nineteenth century got their news in the company of other people. Readers pooled money for subscriptions; they clipped articles and passed them around; and when they journeyed into town, they read shared copies at taverns and hotels and post offices, all of which became pulsing epicenters of news. Most of all, people liberated news from the printed page by reading it aloud, gossiping about it, and making and staking opinions. Conspicuous names like Bolivar only furthered that trend, since they surely invited questions from people who might not otherwise have known who Bolívar was. Once printers swung their presses into motion, news spread through word of mouth, from coffeehouses to courthouses to front porches, even through infants too young to speak or walk.[22]

The Bolivar baby boom was a decidedly grassroots development, and the parents who powered it were mostly farmers and craftsmen. There was Boliver Nabb (Hamilton Nabb's big brother), born on an Illinois farm around 1825 to a midwestern mother and a Maryland father. Bolivar Laughlin entered the world in Kentucky, welcomed by farming parents who themselves were Kentucky-born, while a farming couple in western New York was giving birth around the same time to little Boliver Horton. Early census returns say nothing about these families' finances, but by the time federal officials began to estimate household wealth in 1850 and 1860, the Bolivar families spanned the spectrum, from the Buckners, who owned over a dozen Kentucky slaves, to Connecticut-born Bolivar Cooper, who had no property to speak of at all. Far from silver-spooned scions of the coastal elite, Bolivar children were a cross-section of the country, a testament to the familial love and cosmopolitan excitement that inspired some four hundred parents to name their children for a Spanish-speaking statesman.[23]

★   ★   ★

WIDESPREAD THOUGH THEY WERE, the baby Bolivars were not spread evenly throughout the nation. Nor were the Fourth of July toasts. While inter-American ardor inflamed the whole country, it was strongest in the West, weakest in New England. Between 1816 and 1825, only 32 percent of July Fourth parties in Massachusetts included hemispheric toasts—barely half as many as in Virginia and Pennsylvania, where nearly 60 percent did so. The Arkansas and Illinois papers reported on July Fourth parties too infrequently to detect any reliable trends, but the Bolivar baby boom—which was unmediated by editorial bias—both fills in and confirms the pattern. Midwesterners were the most likely to name their children Bolivar, with 16 out of every 100,000 newborn white males bearing the name in the 1820s. Southwesterners and southeasterners were close behind, with 15 and 12 of every 100,000 white boys named Bolivar, respectively. Numbers dropped off somewhat for the Mid-Atlantic, where the figure was only 7 per 100,000; in New England, the numbers were just over half that, and congressional votes on hemispheric policy display the same broad patterns.[24]

Taken separately, the toasts, naming trends, and legislative ballots would be suggestive, not conclusive. But pieced together, the generalities line up. Hemispheric enthusiasm thrived throughout the country, but it thrived more consistently in western states and territories, and less so in New England. The reasons for these broad regional variations are important, for they help to explain what motivated the songs, toasts, and baby names—and what didn't.

In New England, part of the reason for the diminished ardor was surely economic. Trade with Spain and its loyal Caribbean colonies outweighed trade with the entire Spanish-American mainland, and that trade was heavily centered in the Northeast. From flour and fish to nails and spermaceti, New England exports fed, built, and illumined slave plantations throughout Cuba; some New Englanders even acquired their own personal slave plantations there, brandishing whips and chains and pistols like the most fearsome of Caribbean planters. Why should such people have risked angering some of their most important economic allies by supporting Spain's renegade colonies? Within states, too, that commercial interest occasionally correlated with international diplomacy. Philadelphians were heavily invested in the U.S. trade to Cuba, and their congressional representatives were less likely to support active engagement with the rebels than were other Pennsylvania representatives. Throughout New England and in cities that traded heavily with the loyal Spanish empire, people were more likely to see South American independence as a risk rather than a reward.[25]

New England also differed because of its disproportionately Federalist politics. It was not so much that Yankee hearts didn't beat to the tune of George P. Morris's "BOLIVAR" battle song; it was that Yankee Federalists' hearts didn't. This pattern had manifested itself ever since the early 1810s, and it continued even after the War of 1812 concluded and the national Federalist Party—disgraced now by its wartime opposition—collapsed. Take Boston's *Columbian Centinel*, edited by a stonemason's son named Benjamin Russell ever since the 1780s and one of the nation's most influential Federalist papers. Russell famously transcended partisan bitterness in 1817 by heralding James Monroe's Republican presidency as an *"ERA OF GOOD FEELINGS,"* but the paper's Federalist disposition lingered: in the postwar decade, just under a measly 10 percent of July Fourth parties that Russell chronicled included inter-American toasts. Similar skepticism manifested itself in Congress, where erstwhile Federalists voted to a man against further hemispheric engagement between 1815 and 1818. Congressional supporters of rebel engagement, meanwhile, were nearly all Republicans, and 36 percent of July Fourth accounts in the Republican *Boston Patriot* included relevant toasts. The nation's ascendant postwar Republican majority was welcoming the latest American revolutions more warmly than was the retreating Federalist minority.[26]

Federalists had the same reservations they had harbored in the early 1810s. They feared dramatic social upheavals, especially when those upheavals came at the hands of violent foreign revolutionaries; that was why they had read in horror of bloodied, broken heads toppling in the streets of Paris some two decades before. Edward Everett was certainly thinking about such atrocities; in 1821, as editor of

Boston's high-brow *North American Review*, he asked, "how can our mild and merciful people, who went through their revolution without shedding a drop of civil blood, sympathize with a people, that are hanging and shooting each other in their streets . . . ?" Nothing, the twenty-seven-year-old said, "would transform their Pueyrredons and their Artigases, into Adamses or Franklins or their Bolivars into Washingtons."[27]

More than violence, though, Everett—whose friends nicknamed him "Ever-at-it" because he never seemed to stop working—turned to culture. How, he sniffed, "can our industrious frugal yeomen sympathise with a people that sit on horseback to fish?" Unlike most observers, Everett also pointed to race, adding that no sense of national community could develop "under such heterogeneous and odious confusions of Spanish bigotry and indolence, with savage barbarity and African stupidity." Everett far preferred the revolutionary Greeks, which was hardly surprising: when he wasn't editing the *Review*, he was teaching the young men of Harvard (including his adoring student Ralph Waldo Emerson) about the glories of Greek literature from Homer to Hesiod, and by 1823 he was the nation's leading champion of Hellenic independence. Ancient Greek culture (not to mention the Federalists' beloved England) had shaped the early United States and remained a useful model, the professor reminded his countrymen, but Spanish Americans had a ruder inheritance. "We are sprung from different stocks," he wrote, ". . . we have been brought up in different social and moral schools, we have been governed by different codes of law."[28]

A similar sense of cultural superiority may have dulled some New Englanders' excitement for Latin America, but few Federalists went so far. More typical was a sixteen-year-old apprentice for Massachusetts's famously Federalist *Newburyport Herald*, who penned a series of pseudonymous essays in the summer of 1822. (With surely a hint of irony, he signed his name as "AN OLD BACHELOR.") Slipping them under the printing shop's door when nobody was looking, William Lloyd Garrison quietly exulted when the editor approvingly ordered the pieces into print, all the more so, perhaps, to typeset his own texts and muscle them through the press. It was probably the first time he saw his slow and careful cursive transformed into print.[29]

"Lloyd," as everyone called him, started by writing light and comical satires. Within a month or two, however, he addressed a weightier topic: South America. In his list of the new nations' sins, the boy pulled no punches, drawing on classically Federalist concerns about social disorder. *Indolence. Anarchy. Civil discord.* And *vice of the most notorious order.* There was, Lloyd said, a "striking contrast between those patriots who achieved *our* independence, and the patriots of South America." Yet Lloyd—who would by 1831 become the United States' most infamous white abolitionist—remained optimistic. South Americans, he conceded, had "manfully struggled for their just rights and privileges," shown a "firm and steady determination," and, ultimately, triumphed against monarchical Spain. God willing, he wrote, they would yet "take the United States as a fair and beautiful model," until "the nations of North and South America may cordially unite, and be, as it were, but one government."[30]

Blending universalist optimism with diagnostic doubt, William Lloyd Garrison's essays typified the views of postwar Federalists, who—Everett aside—usually preferred to sandwich their skepticism between professions of genuine goodwill. Few Federalists opposed Latin American republicanism per se; they simply doubted whether the revolutionaries could succeed, and they hedged their enthusiasm accordingly. "[A]lthough we are not among the number of those who are very *romantic* on the subject of South American politics," a Federalist editor in New York explained in 1816, "we wish them all success in their undertakings." While the Republican *Boston Patriot* had endorsed Pernambuco's Antônio Gonçalves da Cruz with garrulous effusion, the *Colum-*

bian Centinel was supportively concise, with a splash of cold water: Cruz was "a man of intelligence, urbanity and firmness," Benjamin Russell succinctly reflected, but unlikely to receive diplomatic recognition. Maybe Federalists voiced support in part because they did not want to look like apostates to the anticolonial principles of the U.S. revolution, especially once their opposition to the War of 1812 left them vulnerable to charges of disloyalty. Surely, too, they believed what they were saying. Just months after the United States had recognized Spanish-American independence in 1822, Russell casually reported that "the South American Republics . . . were not forgotten in any of the [July Fourth] libations."[31]

The dying Federalist Party, therefore, never mounted much vocal opposition to Latin American independence. It could hardly have accomplished much in any case—Federalists in Washington fell from a third to a fifth to a seventh of delegates in successive postwar congresses, and by 1820, even those scattered holdouts were breaking ranks on hemispheric issues. Federalist skepticism of the rebels had become a waning regional side note amid the waxing national fervor. Peaking as it did in a decade when the United States was largely without nationwide partisan animosity, Latin American independence was not nearly as polarizing as the French Revolution had been a generation before, and it inspired longer-lasting and more united support. Still, that support wasn't uniformly enthusiastic. While few Federalists opposed Latin American independence, few were eager to name their sons for the latest revolutionaries or down flasks of whiskey on the rebels' behalf. It was their ambivalence more than their opposition that dampened New England's public displays of enthusiasm.[32]

★ ★ ★

WHAT, THEN, OF THE WEST, where people like Elizabeth and Aylett Buckner eagerly embraced Latin American independence, hungrily scanning newspaper headlines out of a belief that the American nations' fates were bound somehow inextricably together? Why were such enthusiasts more common west of the Appalachians? Politics once again offers part of the answer: at their strongest in New England, Federalists were weakest in the West. Another part of the answer was economic: unlike the influential merchants of the East, westerners had perhaps less to directly lose if trade with Spain and Cuba collapsed, and some thought midwestern farmers might even profit by selling their wheat and other grains to satiate rebel stomachs. Little ventured, something gained—it was an appealing proposition. As a Louisiana newspaper correspondent put it, Spanish Americans' "success would open a source of trade to us more important than any we have with the old world." Yet a third, interwoven explanation lay in the anti-Spanish sentiment that had marked western regions for decades, especially given Spain's history of trying to sever U.S. access to the Mississippi—the central artery of westerners' economic livelihood. ("I hate the Dons," the characteristically pugnacious Andrew Jackson declared from his log Tennessee farmhouse in 1806.) By favoring Spanish Americans, U.S. observers could spite Spain.[33]

But for southwesterners above all, another, more palpable factor joined the equation: territorial expansion. One of the most basic facts of the early United States, white people's hunger for land shaped both federal policy and family decisions alike. In pursuit of a widespread and deeply embedded dream—a chunk of soft, rich earth and the wherewithal to grow a living from it, perhaps with help from slaves depending on what you wanted to plant—white settlers moved onto native people's lands, to Spanish lands, to Mexican lands. As often as not, the federal government defended their claims with laws, treaties, guns, wars. The irony was intense. Even as the United States envisioned itself as the anticolonial leader of an anticolonial hemisphere, its people and its government were reaching into nearby territories and grasping for land, for wealth, for power; they were anticolonial and imperialistic, all in one.[34]

The dual imperatives of inter-American brotherhood and territorial expansion could be mutually reinforcing, especially in the Southwest. Take John Hamilton Robinson, a St. Louis doctor whose baby-faced looks belied his brazen, aggressive gall. Robinson was a filibuster, as his kind would be known by the 1850s—a private citizen who invaded foreign territories with which the United States was ostensibly at peace. Robinson risked his life traveling to Mexico and promoting its independence during the War of 1812 and its aftermath; it was all, as he saw it, part of one glorious hemispheric crusade against European imperialism. (It was also illegal, and the Madison administration tried to stop him.) But if Robinson yearned to set Mexico free, he also yearned to subjugate it. In 1819, his armed escapades having fizzled out despite guarded support from Mexican insurgents, he published an enormous five-foot-square map that cavalierly showed the United States as the rightful owner of Spanish Texas, all the way to the Rio Grande. There was no contradiction in Robinson's mind: the northern republic liberated in the very act of conquering. For Robinson, Spanish-American independence thrilled and inspired partly because it held out the possibility that the territories in question might one day be annexed to the United States.[35]

Many who lived near the nation's southern borders agreed: territorial acquisition and republicanism's southward spread were reciprocal and symbiotic. Mexican independence would be a blessing for humankind, Nashville's *Clarion* exclaimed, only to add that if Mexico then fell into the hands of Britain or France, an "American army would then be marched into that rich and beautiful country, and the dominions of Montazuma [sic] would swell the territories of the American republic." This appealing mix of professed altruism and palpable interest helps explain why white southwesterners were among the most likely to define the cause of Latin America as the cause of the United States.[36]

★ ★ ★

THE FLIP SIDE OF that pattern is just as important. In the rest of the country, among people who lived farther from the nation's ever-disputed borders and had accordingly less to gain, dreams of continental expansion did less to inflame the hemispheric ardor.

Consider the filibusters. If territorial expansion had been a major nationwide engine of inter-American enthusiasm, one would expect to see Robinson and his fellow filibusters hailed as popular heroes throughout the country, especially when they claimed to act in the name of Spanish-American independence. But that was not the case. Of the hundreds of sampled July Fourth celebrations, over fifty referred to South American leaders like Bolívar, but not one referred overtly to southbound filibusters—even in places like Arkansas and southern Illinois. A few toasts gestured approvingly toward other kinds of expansionist and ostensibly anticolonial enterprises in Spanish territory, but those toasts remained sparse and indirect at best. Many onlookers supported filibusters anyway, of course, especially in the Southwest, and there were certainly exceptions in which writers connected Spanish-American independence to U.S. expansion. In the early stages of Gregor MacGregor's 1817 expedition, for example, the *Richmond Enquirer* approvingly noted that the rebels "may be disposed to resign" Amelia Island "to us, after it has served them to assist the flame of revolution in Mexico or Venezuela." If July Fourth was any indication, though, most people were prouder of republicanism's spread in South America. When they dreamed of hemispheric liberation, it was Simón Bolívar they pictured, not John Hamilton Robinson or even General MacGregor.[37]

Filibusters like Robinson were also geographically exceptional. Their dreams of republicanism's spread centered on nearby regions like Florida and Texas, and with good reason: for those who wanted to annex new land to the United States, it made sense to start close to home. Most inter-American enthusiasts, meanwhile, focused on far-off *South* America, a pattern that holds even if we set aside the sometimes blurry terminological distinction between South America and Spanish America. Mugs clinked, sloshed, and emptied not just for Simón Bolívar, who single-handedly received dozens of the sampled toasts, but also for José de San Martín, who expelled the Spanish from Chile and Peru; José Gervasio Artigas, who led Montevideo against its triple rivals of Spain, Brazil, and Buenos Aires; Antonio José de Sucre, who helped found Bolivia; and José Antonio Páez, who had famously rallied western Venezuela's black, mulatto, and white plainsmen against Spain.[38]

In fact, while 85 percent of sampled inter-American toasts cited South America and its nations, generals, and statesmen, not one specifically praised Mexican generals or statesmen, and only 4 percent singled out Mexico more broadly, where the popular republican uprising of the early 1810s had reached a gloomy nadir by the time U.S. onlookers turned decisively south in 1816. Ever the optimists, U.S. audiences focused instead on South America's more inspiring struggles, a pattern that hardened still further when Mexico declared independence as a monarchy in 1821 and 1822 (and, for that matter, a pattern that had existed since the early 1810s, when Mexico's rural rebellion went overshadowed by the revolts in South America's bustling port cities). For all of the songs that people like George P. Morris dedicated to South America, just one seems to have celebrated Mexico. While around two hundred sets of parents named their sons Bolivar, only a scattered few named their sons after Mexican leaders. There isn't much reason to think that ordinary readers avowedly disliked Mexico; there just isn't much reason to think that they were avowedly inspired by it, either. Newspapers continued to welcome the prospect of Mexican independence, but Mexico's gasping republican movement simply couldn't compete with the more active rebellions underway farther south, and by the time Mexico became a republic in 1823 and 1824, the geographic pattern had already set.[39]

In short, when they celebrated Latin American independence,

white men outside of the Southwest rarely looked to Mexico, Cuba, and Florida—or to the filibusters who illegally invaded such places. Although territorial conflict within North America was central to the United States' development, hemispheric enthusiasts were more likely to think about faraway South America, where republicanism's spread seemed more promising. When they did, the language of republican kinship overshadowed the language of conflict that had long helped to demarcate the nation's contested boundaries.

Among those who yearned for new lands in the South and West, in fact, it was not even clear whether Spanish-American independence would help or hurt—despite what filibusters' grand visions often implied. Secretary of State John Quincy Adams was one of the nation's leading territorial expansionists, known for tenaciously working to annex Spanish Florida as well as insistently pursuing a strengthened claim to what is now the Pacific Northwest. Adams worried that popular inter-American enthusiasm was "flaunting in such gorgeous colours in this Country" (as he acerbically wrote) that it actually *threatened* territorial expansion by angering Spain and jeopardizing the acquisition of Florida. In Adams's careful calculus, the Spanish empire needed to remain intact long enough for it to cede Florida to the United States. Territorial expansion may have fueled some people's inter-American enthusiasm, but it dampened that of others; the expansion and the enthusiasm were not one-to-one.[40]

★ ★ ★

TO THE EXTENT that people in the 1810s and 1820s drew on self-interest when celebrating an independent Spanish America, in fact, they spoke less of land and more of money. Even the nation's premier continental expansionists turned more to trade than to territory when they endorsed hemispheric cooperation. By 1823, for example, John Quincy Adams himself was observing that "as navigators and manufacturers, *we* are already so far advanced in a career upon which *they* are yet to enter, that we may for many years . . . maintain with them a commercial intercourse."[41]

House Speaker Henry Clay—another leading expansionist—agreed. Latin American independence, the tall and tow-haired Kentuckian said, presented the most important foreign policy question the United States had ever decided, and probably ever would decide; it "concerned our politics, our commerce, our navigation." Not *our territory*. As Clay saw it, commerce with South America would encourage domestic manufacturing as well as the lucrative "carrying trade," through which U.S. ships shuttled foreign goods around the globe. ("In relation to South America," Clay bluntly explained, "the people of the United States will occupy the same position as the people of New England do to the rest of the United States.") In fact, Clay's famous "American System" did not just denote the efficiently reciprocal web of protective tariffs, a national bank, and federally funded roads and canals that history books usually describe. It also sought to place the United States at the head of a thriving, inter-American trade zone, one in which tariffs, infrastructure, and a national bank would form the domestic roots of an economy whose branches extended throughout the hemisphere. As Clay's fellow Kentuckian David Trimble proclaimed on the floor of Congress in 1822, "[t]he American system is free government and free trade; monarchy and monopoly is that of Europe."[42]

To many observers, Clay's hemispheric American System literally gleamed with possibility—silver, gold, and other precious metals sparkled in Latin American mines. Those metals were incredibly valuable in the young United States; they were central to foreign trade and even to the nation's entire monetary system, in which the paper bank notes that people used to buy and sell were theoretically backed by cold, hard specie. But specie was scarce, leaving some observers to hope that if Latin Americans separated from Spain and Portugal, the new governments would open their ports to U.S.

traders, who might then sell their wares and their crops in return for gold and silver coinage. As Washington's *National Register* predicted in a front-page story, "the independence of South-America would be invaluably beneficial to the United States. The surplus produce of this country would always find a market there . . . while the facility of obtaining metalic medium would contribute to the preservation of our credit at home and abroad."[43]

Perhaps the white men of Hatchie, Tennessee, read this kind of commentary as they hitched their hopes for Latin America to hopes for their own commercial success. These were ambitious souls, slaveholders and aspiring cotton barons who dreamed of carving a canal some seventy miles west to the Mississippi. Such a project, if only they could pay for it, would enable them to "attain considerable importance," as one observer put it, by positioning them "on the great thoroughfare from East Tennessee and Upper Alabama to New Orleans." It was the mid-1820s, and the time certainly seemed right; after 1815, the U.S. South embarked on a journey of dramatic economic and social transformation, one in which white cotton—planted and picked by black slaves—began to blanket the South like warm-weather snow.[44]

Hatchie's citizens wanted to speed up that transformation, and to profit from it. As they dreamed of remaking their tiny town into a regional mecca for cotton and chattel, they decided that they needed a new name, one more suited to their tastes and aspirations. In 1825, they convinced the state legislature to officially rechristen the community as *Bolivar*.[45]

The Bolivar canal never materialized, but the name stuck, forever memorializing the cosmopolitan excitement, attachments, and interests of the town's founders. Such qualities were common in the years that followed the War of 1812, when at least four other communities—in western Virginia, New York, Ohio, and Pennsylvania—all named themselves after South America's premier general. These Bolivar towns seem mostly to have emerged in 1825, the same year that baby Bolivars first surged and, in fact, the same year that July Fourth toasts specifically targeting the Liberator grew popular; Bolívar had finally expelled Spain from its last mainland stronghold, and people throughout the United States sought to share in the victory. But if Bolivar babies revealed the depth of individual passion for Latin America, Bolivar towns revealed the scope of that passion, and its unifying power. Naming a town was a delicate task: you had to choose something popular, something that virtually all citizens could accept as the basis of a necessarily fragile new civic identity. Bolivar, U.S.A., then—in 1825, the name boasted precisely that kind of collective and patriotic appeal.[46]

Beyond the simultaneity of their foundings, the Bolivar towns shared another quality, one that perhaps symbolically attested to residents' commercial aspirations. As in Hatchie, white men were inflamed by canal fever in all of the Bolivar towns. In Ohio, for example, villagers initially tried to name their new community after the canal commissioner from the next county over. When that label fell through—the commissioner, it seems, was too modest— they turned to Bolívar, as did aspiring canal towns in Virginia and Pennsylvania. In southwestern New York, residents of Bolivar were perhaps too far from the newly built Erie Canal to feel its immediate effects, but people throughout the county were already petitioning the state to build a nearby branch canal. Nor did the canal craze simply inspire town names; Albany resident Harvey Cobb, who could hardly have hoped to rename the state's centuries-old capital city, named his ship *Bolivar* as he shuttled whiskey, salt, lumber, and other goods across the state's waterways.[47]

Perhaps some of these townspeople expected to profit personally from inter-American trade, but the connection between trade and hemispheric independence was also more conceptual. If canals meant commerce, after all, they also meant cosmopolitanism. For rural farmers and small-town residents throughout the inland

United States, it was through canals that the outside world beckoned. In 1825, one of the most inspiring residents of that broader world was Simón Bolívar.

In the end, though, economic interest only goes partway in explaining the hemispheric ardor. Hard as it was to identify a decisive territorial motive in the inter-American enthusiasm, it was also hard to identify a clear economic one. While Henry Clay kept insisting that the nation could continue its money-spinning trade to Cuba and simultaneously tap new markets on the mainland, others worried that Spanish America's revolutions—and U.S. support for them—would disrupt commerce with Cuba and the rest of the remaining Spanish Empire. Moreover, for each person who envisioned the United States and independent Latin America as eager trading partners, others, noting that the regions produced similar staples like cotton and tobacco, argued that the United States and its southern neighbors would become competitors. Having surveyed the agricultural economies of insurgent Spanish America, one Philadelphia merchant maintained in an anonymous 1818 pamphlet that "we find but little to strengthen our hopes, or excite our cupidity. . . . no demand for a large portion of our productions, but an alarming threat of eventual rivalry in the remainder." The commentary, which fueled debates from newspaper offices to the halls of Congress, contributed to the overall confusion about how Spanish-American independence would affect U.S. trade. Help or hindrance—it was hard to say. Sure enough, although congressmen and newspapermen regularly pointed to potential profits as a reason to hope for rebel victories, most ordinary hemispheric boosters preferred to frame their excitement in terms of inter-American unity and republican mission: not one sampled July Fourth toast referred to territorial gain when praising the rebel movements, and only one referred to commercial profit.[48]

That the idealistic rhetoric was often self-serving did not render it disingenuous. For people like Elizabeth and Aylett

Buckner, inter-American ardor was not primarily about the money, nor was it about the land. When new parents named their sons for Spanish-speaking statesmen, it is hard to imagine that economic and territorial interests entered very far into their calculations. Even those who did look south to dream of new land and pudgier pocketbooks must have taken pleasure in thinking (along with the filibuster John Hamilton Robinson) that they were simultaneously serving the cause of republican freedom and celebrating the United States' ostensibly trendsetting example. Interest helps to explain the broad regional variations in hemispheric enthusiasm, in other words, but it does not single-handedly explain the emotional intensity.

★   ★   ★

SO FAR, MOST OF the discussion has centered on white men, not white women—the Aylett Buckners, not the Elizabeths. The Ayletts of the country chattered tirelessly about Latin America, after all, and in ways that left a paper trail. They sang about it, wrote about it, sometimes even got drunk and fired guns in its honor. The Elizabeths of the country left fewer archival tracks. But they talked, too, in their kitchens, parlors, farmhouses, and town squares. If we cast our nets widely enough, it is possible to hear echoes of what some of them said.

Daniel Griswold loved his young and very pregnant wife; really, he did, "as warmly as man can feel for woman," he confessed in 1816. But the youthful New Yorker loved Chile more. "All the endearments of country home and woman I would gladly barter for a military reputation" forged on the battle lines of South America, he told José Miguel Carrera, a rebel expatriate who was in Manhattan raising money and men for an expedition to liberate Chile.[49]

Only one thing stood in the way of Griswold's international military glory: his father. His "wishes are in direct opposition to my own," the young man wrote in frustration, "and he appears resolved to turn every obstacle in the way of my intentions," starting with finances. Although a lawyer, Daniel Griswold owed people money, and without his father's help, he couldn't pay off his debts before he embarked.[50]

When Carrera's Chile expedition sailed, Daniel Griswold remained in port, full of "anxiety," "pain," and disappointment, still yearning for a life of saltwater and saltpeter. He quickly hatched another plan: he would move his wife to Buenos Aires and work in the new government there, perhaps launch a mercantile business. This time, it was his father-in-law who evidently raised the objections, all of them exasperatingly practical. *How will you find a place to live? What if South Americans don't like U.S. visitors, or appreciate their talents? What if you don't like them?* And: *What of your young wife and forthcoming child? How will you provide for them when you can't even discharge your debts here?*[51]

Those questions must have irked Griswold, and the last one in particular may especially have irked his wife. Mrs. Griswold (whose first name never appears in the correspondence, and whose identity remains unclear in census reports) evidently wanted to travel to South America as well. She had met Carrera and she, too, fell under his spell, "truly proud to rank you amongst the most valuable and esteemed of her friends," Daniel Griswold told Carrera in a letter. By October, Mrs. Griswold had even penned a song in Carrera's honor—the "Grand Chilean Victory March," which her husband delivered to Carrera in person. Were "the little lady" not large with child—"*a confinement*," as Daniel Griswold put it—she would have joined the mission herself, "gladly aton[ing] for the crime of taking your first recruit by offering to share in the expedition with me but you must be aware of the madness of such a proceeding in the present state of things." As it was, a name would have to suffice. "She has consented to name the first son 'José Miguel' after a little persuasion," Daniel Griswold drolly told Carrera.[52]

Mrs. Griswold's thoughts on Latin America come to us only indirectly, through her husband. While it is certainly possible that Daniel Griswold was exaggerating his wife's admiration for Carrera, there is little reason to think he was lying. (For starters, Mrs. Griswold really did write a song in honor of Chile; the general passingly noted it in his diary, so that fact, at least, checks out.) Although Mrs. Griswold left neither her own writings nor even her first name in the documentary record, the outlines of her personality emerge. Idealistic. Feisty. Determined. Like her husband, inspired by what was happening in South America. (Perhaps outspoken, too—in a letter, Daniel Griswold playfully told Carrera that "Mrs. Griswold commands me to offer to you her good wishes.")[53]

In many ways, Mrs. Griswold was an outlier, even compared to the roughly two hundred other mothers who named their sons after South-American statesmen. She lived near a major port city, she knew her baby's possible namesake personally, and she was apparently willing to travel to South America with little José Junior in tote (or *Josefa*, perhaps, if it was a girl?). Her pluckiness stands out, too. Yet it seems reasonable to assume that the other mothers who decided (or, like Mrs. Griswold, agreed) to name their sons Bolívar would at least have learned about the Liberator; perhaps they openly admired him.

And why not? According to some early-nineteenth-century standards, white women were supposed to play the role of republican mothers and wives, coaxing their husbands to lead lives of virtue and raising their children to be productively patriotic members of society. Women who took their assignment seriously may well have found inspiration in the new republics that were emerging in South America. Editors seemed to expect as much, anyway: in New York City, the *Ladies' Weekly Museum, or Polite Repository of Amusement and Instruction* reported regularly on South America, distilling and reprinting stories from mainstream newspapers. In

1817, the editor called reports on Pernambuco's republican uprising "[t]he most important news this week"; one year later, borrowing from a Pittsburgh paper, the *Ladies' Weekly Museum* proclaimed that "South-America affords, at this time, the most interesting subject for the speculation of the world, and . . . its inhabitants are engaged in a struggle, in which we must have our sympathies particularly concerned." The articles suggested that white women should hail Bolívar and his allies, and for much the same reasons that white men seemed to: Venezuela's so-called Liberator embodied civic virtue, patriotic sacrifice, strength of character, and military prowess.[54]

Mainstream newspapers also sometimes seemed to target female readers with these reports. In 1819, for example, an article borrowed from London newspapers and entitled *"Female patriots"* chronicled the military exploits of Andean women. South American women, the article read, "are animated with a republican devotion to the cause of independence, the sole guarantee of private happiness." One general's wife accompanied her husband into battle and bravely seized a Spanish flag (much as the Griswolds had imagined doing); other women "were stationed to defend a post" in battle. Printers republished the story in at least twelve states, including in such far-flung places as Claiborne, Alabama; Washington, Pennsylvania; Georgetown, South Carolina; Rochester, New York; and St. Louis, Missouri. Men surely comprised much of the readership, but the article's popularity—not to mention its eventual appearance in the *Ladies' Museum*—suggests that the Bolivar mothers were not wholly anomalous. It also suggests again that white women welcomed South American independence for much the same reasons that white men did, since the article celebrated rebel patriotism, virtue, and bravery.[55]

By 1823 and 1824, that kind of inter-American interest had helped inspire a new fashion trend. From Boston and Albany to Chillicothe and Savannah, merchants advertised "Bolivar hats" in an assortment of colors as well as in "ladies" and "girls" sizes; in Hartford and Nor-wich, Connecticut, female shopkeepers themselves took the initiative to advertise and stock them. Maybe some mothers and daughters just liked the style—ornamental, broad brimmed, lots of feathers—but the name struck at least some sellers as an effective marketing tool. A week before Independence Day in 1825, one New York business-man prominently advertised the hats in multiple Manhattan papers, urging readers to don their patriotic headgear for the approaching festivities and implying that they could chasten European tyrants in the process. As he put it, the Holy Alliance's "hearts must quake . . . at the noble elevation of the illustrious BOLIVAR." If he was right, "civil Liberty on this blessed continent"—by which he meant the whole Western Hemisphere—was a cause that women would pay to associate themselves with.[56]

Whether buying Bolivar hats for their daughters or nam-ing their sons for Spanish-speaking luminaries, many women embraced South American independence with personal interest and patriotic intent. If Mrs. Griswold never ultimately made it to South America, it is easy enough to imagine her setting her future son on her knee, regaling him with stories about his namesake, and imbuing him with the virtues she most cherished as she dreamed of the life they almost had.

★   ★   ★

IF LATIN AMERICAN INDEPENDENCE meant roughly the same thing to the white men and women who sang the rebels' praises, its meanings diverged for people of color. White observers, for their part, tended to look south and see political independence and republican government, with armed black rebels and gradual abolition incidental to that larger story. After all, it was probably not Simón Bolívar's antislavery sympathies that the aspiring cot-ton barons of Hatchie had in mind when they renamed their tiny Tennessee town. Nor did July Fourth revelers openly devote much thought to Spanish-American antislavery efforts: not one toast in the entire sample referred to rebel race relations.

Even at parties full of antislavery sympathizers, white people declined to mention Spanish Americans' gradual moves toward abolition. Fourth of July guests in Lancaster called slavery a "curse and a blot on the fair fame of our country," but when they toasted Spanish America, they simply wished the rebels "the means to establish their independence" and "the wisdom to model their governments on the republican form." From northern Connecticut to southern Pennsylvania, from eastern Ohio to western Illinois, much of the same: men who openly denounced domestic slavery quietly neglected its gradual end in mainland Spanish America, as if antislavery efforts at home and abroad were unrelated. Even William Lloyd Garrison, the teenaged Newburyport apprentice and future abolitionist, spent the 1820s seeing Spanish-American antislavery as secondary to a broader struggle against monarchy and absolutism. Except for the *Genius of Universal Emancipation*'s Benjamin Lundy (who helped enlist Garrison in the antislavery cause when the two first met in 1828), white people rarely placed race, slavery, and abolition at the center of their hemispheric understandings, whether slaveholding southerners or antislavery northerners.[57]

People of color saw it differently, and Baltimore—home to the country's largest black community—was a case in point. In 1825, France had moved toward recognizing the independence of its former colony in Haiti (albeit indirectly, and on the condition that Haiti pay massive, even crippling, reparations to compensate for France's loss). U.S. lawmakers refused to make the same concession to reality until the Civil War, recoiling as they did at the thought of welcoming black ambassadors to Washington. The "respectable colored people" who gathered in Baltimore one Thursday in August, however, were determined not to let France's begrudging gesture go unnoticed. One after another, the men stood up, raised their glasses, and cheered for Haiti as well as for the French monarch who had finally recognized its independence. They also applauded the antislavery cause more generally:

The American Eagle.—Its head and tail unsullied white, its body resplendent black—virtue is not designated by colors.

Our Wives and Children.—May they and their posterity be free.

The Emancipation Societies in the United States.—Glorious and shining lights in a country still enveloped in the fogs of prejudice and slavery.

In fact, virtually every toast at the gathering invoked abolition or racial equality. It is not therefore hard to imagine that the dinner guests had the same themes in mind when they offered their very first toast of the occasion. "Washington, Toussaint, and Bolivar," the men exclaimed; "Unequalled in fame—the friends of man kind—the glorious advocates of Liberty."[58]

Exactly what that toast meant is unclear. Were the dinner guests *praising* the United States' antislavery traditions? Maybe the toast was meant to reference George Washington's will, which had provided for the emancipation of his slaves. Or maybe the revelers were *criticizing* the United States' comparatively weak antislavery traditions by positioning abolitionist Haiti and moderately anti-slavery Colombia as implicit foils for the United States—the lone American republic to sanction slavery's spread.

Either way, one thing was clear; by including Haiti in their cat-alog of new American nations—which white hemispheric enthusi-asts almost never did—these men were pushing readers to consider slavery's role in the revolutionary Americas (a fact confirmed by the "Emancipation Societies" toast, which went on to note that antislavery sentiment was "penetrating the gloom of our southern hemisphere"). When these black Baltimoreans thought of Spanish America, they thought of slavery, of abolition, of racial equality: not just freedom from European tyrants, but freedom from domestic tyrants, too. For that was something they knew personally; though most of these celebrants were probably free, some may have been formerly enslaved, and surely all had beloved friends and family who remained in bondage—thus the toast to the freedom of their wives and children. Among black men who knew slavery so inti- mately, it was hard to speak of Latin American independence with- out seeing slavery and abolition as central to what was happening. These men were universalists, too, but not because they saw race as secondary. They were universalists who saw race as central.

John Russwurm had seen much of the world, and he agreed. Born in 1799 to a white merchant and a black woman in the Jamai- can tropics, he traveled to wintry Montreal for boarding school at the age of eight, and when his doting father died, the teenaged Russwurm saved money for college by teaching black schoolchil- dren in Philadelphia, New York, and Boston. In 1824, he enrolled at Bowdoin; two years later, he delivered the college's commencement address, a glowing ten-minute discourse about "The Condition and Prospects of Hayti." (Though he began his speech nervously as he looked out at the sea of curious white faces, Russwurm composed himself and finished to waves of applause; "I do declare," an old woman in attendance reportedly exclaimed, "the negro has done the best of them all.")[59]

One of the first black people in the country to earn a college degree, the conquering graduate quickly undertook another first. He traveled to New York, joined forces with a Delaware-born minister named Samuel Cornish, and co-launched the nation's first-ever black- owned-and-edited newspaper. From the very first column of its very first issue, that paper—*Freedom's Journal*—heralded emancipation throughout the Americas. "[H]as the Eternal decree gone forth," Cornish and Russwurm asked, "that our race alone, are to remain in this state [of subjugation], while knowledge and civilization are shedding their enlivening rays over the rest of the human family?" Did not "the establishment of the republic of Hayti after years of sanguinary warfare ... and the advancement of liberal ideas in South America, where despotism has given place to free governments, and where many of our brethren now fill important civil and military stations, prove the contrary"? People of color in the United States suffered discrimination and enslavement, the editors wrote, but the strides of men in South America and Haiti as well as in Africa itself offered hope for things at home.[60]

Cornish and Russwurm grappled regularly with what it meant to be African American in an inter-American world. In their newspaper's first calendar year of 1827, they devoted space to Latin America in over half of their issues, and in such detail that it seems almost certain they and their correspondents had been following the Latin American news all along. The editors devoted still more attention to Haiti, perhaps because its more radical antislavery model and its wholly black and mulatto leadership held greater appeal than did Spanish America's painstaking gradualism. There was a personal connection, too: Haiti's government had actively recruited black people to emigrate from the United States, and in the mid-1820s, as many as 13,000 men, women, and children did precisely that. (Most of them eventually returned, frustrated by the cultural differences and reeling from the harrowing agricultural labor that Haitian leaders expected from them.) But Cornish and Russwurm—like the black Baltimoreans—didn't delve into comparisons. They portrayed efforts in Spanish America and Haiti as complementary, and they moved easily between the two regions as they used developments abroad in order to demand change at home. "In South America and Haiti," Cornish and Russwurm wrote, "where the Man of Colour is seen in all the dignity of man, freed from the prejudices, and endowed with the rights, and enjoying all the privileges of citizenship, we behold him not a whit inferior to any of his fairer brethren." Black people's diminished scholastic and professional achievement in the United States, they insisted, was due to bigotry and not biology.[61]

It wasn't just educated black urbanites who turned south for inspiration. Of the approximately two hundred Bolivar boys born in the 1820s, at least 5 percent were black. Most of these babies were enslaved. Like little Bolliver Hawkins in North Carolina and Bolivar Harris in Maryland, they labored as slaves right through the Civil War, after which they began to appear in federal census reports as illiterate farmhands.[62]

Many enslaved parents lacked the freedom to name their children, so perhaps it was slaveholders who named these little boys Bolivar. A slave named after a conqueror? Or after a freedom-fighting liberator? It was from precisely that dissonance that such names derived their meaning; indeed, many slaves bore grandiose names, like Caesar or Pompey, that contradicted their own deficit of power. To enslaved children and their parents, the name Bolivar may have seemed a malicious joke—after all, Bolivar was a popular name for livestock, too. But it also seems logical to imagine that enslaved parents, if left with any choice in the matter, might have had their own, competing reasons to name their sons Bolivar, especially if they had heard stories of Simón Bolívar's antislavery sympathies. It is easy enough to envisage: a woman silently serving dinner to guests in her master's plantation home might overhear a discussion of Colombian independence, then pass the news along to her friends and family back in the slave quarters. A man traveling to Baltimore on his master's business might learn of Venezuelan antislavery efforts as he haggled with black vendors in the harbor. Through such mundane interactions, information could spread exponentially to entire plantations, neighborhoods, and regions.[63]

Some black Bolivar parents were evidently free, and their choices spoke volumes. Sometime around 1827, somewhere in Pennsylvania, a baby boy named Simeon entered the world. His first name, biblical as it was, would not itself have been particularly notable. But the boy's last name was Boliver, and his parents were black. These parents, their first names lost to history, were probably free: Pennsylvania's gradual emancipation law had been in effect for nearly five decades, and only about 1 percent of the state's black population remained enslaved. Most likely, the Boliver parents had won their freedom in the last decade or so, and they had chosen their last name as a way to inaugurate their lives as free people; indeed, because there were only a tiny handful of Bolivar surnames anywhere in the United States at the time, it seems doubtful that the Boliver family simply inherited its name from someone else. In any case, Simeon Boliver's parents had evidently heard of Bolívar's exploits in South America, and they evidently approved.[64]

Born in central North Carolina in the mid-1820s, Nicholas and George Bolivar entered the world under similarly cloudy circumstances. By 1850, these two men (brothers, it seems, or perhaps cousins) were living as free men in Philadelphia, where census records classified them as "M"—mulatto. When Nicholas, a tailor and a sailor, paid a local notary to fill out a passport-like seaman's "protection certificate" for him, the notary described the short young man's complexion as "Dark," then crossed it out and wrote "Sambo," noting his black hair and hazel eyes. Like baby Simeon's parents, Nicholas and George Bolivar (or perhaps their parents) seem to have chosen the family name rather than inheriting it. For aside from one "Bolevar" family that appeared in the 1790 census and nowhere else, no other people of that name appear to have lived in North Carolina for decades to come. Most likely, George and Nicholas Bolivar—or their parents—had been born into slavery, and they chose the name Bolivar to mark their rebirth as free men.[65]

We cannot ultimately know what these men and women had in mind when they named their sons and evidently themselves after Spanish America's leading liberator. The most basic facts of their lives remain obscure; the logic behind their most personal of decisions, even more so. But each black Bolivar was one part of a broader whole—one parent, one son, one friend, one fellow laborer in a far-reaching community of people who lived and talked and loved, people who, we can imagine, asked the Bolivars how they got their unusual names and why. Though themselves few in number, the black Bolivars suggest that hundreds, and possibly thousands, of black people in the United States were talking about Spanish America. If Russwurm, Cornish, and the black Baltimoreans were any indication, slavery and race loomed large in the conversation.

★ ★ ★

IN THE TEN YEARS that followed the War of 1812, a shared language of republican universalism inspired people throughout the country. Black and white, men and women, northerners and southerners and westerners—they raised their sons to emulate Bolívar, called the rebels *brothers* and *countrymen* and *Americans*, and literally rejoiced at patriot successes.

Although black and white onlookers showed their support for South America in superficially similar ways, the logic that underlay those shared displays of support was different. Many black people had hailed Spanish-American republicanism while simultaneously emphasizing the new governments' antislavery credentials. White observers, in contrast, tended to tell a more sanguine story about political independence and republican government. Theirs was a story that seemed to confirm the universality of the United States' founding ideals, a story that inflamed U.S. nationalism by appealing to U.S. internationalism. Drawing from events abroad, white onlookers' breezy narrative framework seemed to cultivate national unity at home, enabling a superficial but convenient consensus that marginalized the divisive issue of slavery. That consensus would not last forever, and it simultaneously concealed deeper divisions about liberty, who was entitled to it, and how exactly the United States should seek to spread it.

CHAPTER FIVE

A GENUINE
AMERICAN POLICY

AT SIXTY-FIVE, JAMES MONROE looked like a relic, and he rather liked it that way. His hair greying, his face rutted with wrinkles from a lifetime of public service, the Virginia-born president proudly and pointedly wore the outmoded wardrobe of the bygone eighteenth century: shoe buckles, tricorner hat, knee breeches, hose. Years ago, as a young man, he had crossed the Delaware with Washington and then nearly died of gunshot wounds while storming the snow-covered Hessian garrison at Trenton; later, in the 1790s, he served as U.S. minister in Paris until his former comrade, President Washington, recalled him for overzealously embracing the French cause. Now, in 1823, he looked every bit the aging revolutionary, wizened and weathered and dressed for the 1770s.[1]

Monroe was known more for his integrity than for his intellect. (He had "a mind neither rapid nor rich," one observer wrote sympathetically—much to Monroe's chagrin.) But if Monroe was not the brightest of his generation, he was among the most discerning. "[W]hen called on to decide an important point," John C. Calhoun later recalled, Monroe would "hold the subject immovably fixed under his attention, until he had mastered it in all of its relations." So sat Monroe in Washington's crisp autumn, holding foreign policy in his thoughts like a jeweler appraising a diamond, turning it around, inspecting it from all sides. At stake was nothing less than freedom itself, or so it seemed in the tension of the moment. The Holy Alliance of Russia, Prussia, and Austria had recently persuaded France to crush a constitutionalist uprising in Spain, leaving Spain's absolutist monarchs poised to reconquer their former American colonies. Meanwhile, Tsar Alexander I had declared much of the North Pacific off limits to other powers, a move that boldly asserted Russia's claim to Oregon at the expense of the United States' own ambitions. The United States aspired to be a transcontinental and hemispheric power—an "empire for liberty," as Thomas Jefferson had memorably put it. But if Tsar Alexander and his Holy Allies had their way, that republican empire might never control the Pacific coast, and its southern neighbors might become the puppets of Europe's most formidable tyrants, prone to drag the United States into war and all that accompanied it.[2]

Enter George Canning, the balding and brilliant foreign secretary of Britain. Would the United States, Canning asked, be interested in issuing a joint statement warning the Holy Allies to back off? A constitutional monarchy, Britain chafed at the Holy Allies' absolutism. Like the United States, Britain had its sights on Oregon, and its merchants hungered to trade with an independent Latin America. Although Anglos and Americans had been at war just a decade before, Canning insisted, they might now come boldly together in a marriage of convenience.[3]

It was a flattering—and tempting—proposal. Britain was a global powerhouse; the United States, a second-ring show in the high-strung Atlantic circus. By accepting Canning's offer, Monroe could bring Britain's "mighty weight into the scale of free government," Jefferson advised; "with her on our side we need not fear the whole world." James Madison energetically agreed; so did Secretary of War Calhoun, and, in fact, nearly everyone Monroe asked for advice.[4]

Only one man objected: the aloof New Englander John Quincy Adams, who argued (correctly, we now know) that the threat from the Holy Allies was exaggerated. ("I no more believe that the holy Allies, will restore the Spanish Dominion, upon the American continents," the Secretary of State wrote in his diary, "than that the Chimborazzo will sink beneath the Ocean.") Less threat, less reason to ally, Adams argued; why tether the nation unnecessarily to Britain, which was as much a competitor in the Western Hemisphere as it was a friend? Instead of accepting Canning's offer, Adams contended, the United States should issue its own unilateral declaration against European meddling in the Americas. That way, the United States might get credit for its diplomatic bluster rather than looking like a mere "Cock-boat in the wake of the British man of war." If Adams was somehow wrong—if the Holy Alliance *did* invade the Western Hemisphere—Britain would probably intervene anyway, the bite behind America's bark.[5]

Adams was notoriously stiff, calculating, and severe, his disposition as stony and cold as a Massachusetts winter. But he was also persuasive, and in early December of 1823, President Monroe issued the unilateral declaration that Adams had hoped for. In three short paragraphs toward the end of his annual message to Congress— what we now call the State of the Union—Monroe announced the three principles of foreign policy that subsequent generations would come to know as the Monroe Doctrine: noncolonization (in which the Western Hemisphere was to be free from further European incursions), abstention from European affairs (in which the United States would stay out of strictly European conflicts), and an assertion of the nation's unique interest in its southern neighbors (according to which the United States would consider any European action against the independent nations to be an affront to the United States itself). Explicitly anticolonial and implicitly imperial, Monroe's message challenged European colonialism even as it claimed the Western Hemisphere as the United States' special turf.[6]

Adams and Alexander, Calhoun and Canning—their bluffs, power plays, and intrigue have been pored over by some of history's best historians. With good reason: statecraft mattered. Protracted wars, or even just threatening foreign neighbors, could mean a standing army, higher taxes, bigger government—really, a different kind of nation. Implement those changes, and people might rebel; international turmoil could foment domestic divisions in a heartbeat.[7]

But if high-level statesmen like Monroe and Adams therefore set the stage for much of what unfolded in the early nineteenth century, we know far less about what might be called low-level diplomacy—the ways in which ordinary people understood and influenced foreign relations. That influence mattered, if not always in a straightforward or obvious way. As the historian Ernest May has shown, the Monroe Doctrine took shape as it did partly because all the major players on the U.S. side (apart from Monroe himself) were trying to position themselves for the 1824 presidential election. To a man, they all took positions that corresponded with their own electoral interests. A New Englander and a former member of the anglophilic Federalist Party, for example, Adams could hone his nationalist and Republican credentials by playing tough with Britain; conversely, Calhoun would look good if Adams looked bad, and as secretary of war he might gain special consideration if the nation accepted Canning's offer and voters began to fear a transatlantic showdown. The statesmen of 1823, in other words, were also politicians, acutely aware that voters might make decisions based at least partly on foreign policy.[8]

Where inter-American relations were concerned, in fact, popular opinion influenced far more than the Monroe Doctrine, and it did not operate only through the ballot box. In the late 1810s and early 1820s, public opinion informed congressional debates about whether to extend diplomatic recognition to the new would-be nations of Spanish America—an issue that ordinary voters saw as more important than Monroe's unilateral declaration, and, for that matter, an issue that itself paved the way for the 1823 doctrine. Meanwhile, and farther from Washington, popular hemispheric ardor helped inspire thousands of U.S. adventurers to take up arms for Latin American independence, while U.S. merchants became one of the rebels' main suppliers of arms and ammunition. Foreign relations therefore took shape not just in the State Department, the President's House, and the halls of Congress, but also in barnacled and brackish harbors and the manure-covered heartland. The Monroe Doctrine was just the beginning.

★ ★ ★

DIEGO DE SAAVEDRA and Juan Pedro de Aguirre were not who they said they were. According to the passports that they carried with them to the United States in 1811, their names were José Cabrera and Pedro López; according to their conversations with curious inquisitors, they were visiting the United States on strictly personal business.[9]

The deceit served a higher purpose. Saavedra (whose father led Buenos Aires's governing junta) and Aguirre (a Buenos Aires merchant) were on a mission to defend the liberty of their homeland. Although Buenos Aires's junta still professed loyalty to Fernando VII, by 1811 those claims were increasingly insincere; many leaders were quietly working for outright independence. For that purpose, Buenos Aires would need weapons, and lots of them. "Two thousand pairs of Pistols of one ounce caliber," the junta ordered Saavedra and Aguirre to buy. "Four thousand Carbines, or else short cavalry arms with bayonets. . . . Eight thousand Swords, or Sabers. . . . Ten thousand Guns with their cartridges . . . one million Flints." And, if possible, an additional 30,000 firearms. The junta was essentially asking its agents to box up and send an entire arsenal.[10]

Saavedra and Aguirre—or, rather, Cabrera and López—

disembarked in New York, but it wasn't until they got to Washington several weeks later that they revealed their true identities, in a meeting with then–Secretary of State James Monroe. Perhaps they were taken aback by what a later observer called Monroe's "plain, homely" appearance. (Monroe's neckcloth was "small, ropy, and carelessly tied; his frill matted"; his countenance "dull, sleepy, and insignificant.") But Monroe greeted the visitors so courteously that they could scarcely contain their enthusiasm. He "received us with the most flattering displays of friendship," they told an ally from Venezuela, and assured them on President Madison's behalf "that the United States saw with pleasure the efforts, that the South Americans made to imitate their brothers of the North." Monroe "told us . . . we could run about the whole country," the agents breathlessly reported back to Buenos Aires, "and freely contract the succors, that we pleased, that this [executive] branch of government, desiring to help us, would for its part dissemble its knowledge of the goods contracted therein." The agents were free to stock their arsenal.[11]

It was a message that rebel visitors heard repeatedly over the next decade and beyond. Although Spanish and Portuguese representatives tenaciously pressed the United States to restrict the weapons trade, federal officials (who were always looking to expand the country's commercial opportunities) refused. In private and off-the-record meetings, they assured rebel visitors that the United States would not turn rebel buyers over to royalist officials; under international and federal law alike, after all, it was perfectly legal for private citizens of a neutral power to sell weapons abroad, and there was little reason for the commercially minded United States to veer from that tradition. "This Government," an agent jointly representing Buenos Aires and Chile informed his superiors in 1817, "says that it is not in its interest to compromise itself in a war with Spain, and that the only thing it can do: is let me do as I will." Pernambuco's Antônio Gonçalves da Cruz got a similar impression that same year, and as late as 1824, Buenos Aires's minister said that Monroe (by then the president) "had received repeated complaints from Spain" about weapons shipments but "had found honest and reasonable ways to equivocate."[12]

For over a decade, moneyed men in the United States thus proceeded to sell boatloads of equipment to South America with "weapons as ballast," as Pernambuco's vexed royal governor wrote. Many of these shipments came at the specific request of rebel agents, men who, like Saavedra and Aguirre, trawled the United States and Britain for supplies. Other consignments left U.S. ports at the request of self-appointed emissaries who claimed, often dubiously, to represent their home governments. Still more goods seem to have shipped out without any clear invitation at all, courtesy of merchants who, on the basis of newspaper reports and commercial hearsay, cast their goods into rebel ports and hoped that buyers would await. Whatever the setup, the weapons trade was extraordinarily risky business. According to international practice, ships laden with munitions and destined for rebel troops were fair game for Spanish and Portuguese royalists, who could seize entire cargoes on the high seas. Even if such cargoes evaded confiscation, merchants took the chance that rebel governments, oft-changing and cash-strapped, would refuse to pay for whatever firearms finally arrived.[13]

Despite the hazards, the weapons trade to insurgent Latin America began in 1810, when agents from Venezuela sent an unidentified quantity of arms to compatriots back home. Over the next few years, men like Saavedra and Aguirre edged into the trade as well, but their timing was poor: when the United States declared war on Britain in 1812, its woefully unprepared military needed all the supplies it could get, and sales to Latin America plummeted. As Simón Bolívar observed, "[t]he United States of North America, which . . . could have supplied us with munitions, did not do so because of her war with Great Britain." "Otherwise," he reflected,

"Venezuela could have triumphed on her own," and without further assistance. (Sure enough, Saavedra and Aguirre returned home in 1812 with just 1,000 bayoneted muskets and 362,050 flints—a far cry from the mountains of smoothly chiseled and hot-forged matériel they had hoped for.) If rebels felt undersupplied in the early 1810s, though, Spain felt differently. According to the frustrated Spanish minister, rebels in Cartagena had only been able to withstand a royalist siege for as long as they did because of supplies purchased from the United States.[14]

The trickle of weapons that dripped southward from the United States before 1815 turned into something more of a stream following the peace with Britain, just as public excitement began to crest as well. Even the federal Ordnance Department got involved, freeing itself of surplus postwar gunpowder by selling some to Venezuela on credit in 1816. The loan was an aberration, since the federal government had elsewhere made a point of refusing similar transactions in the name of neutrality. Merchants, however, were free to do as they pleased, and even a conservative estimate would indicate that U.S. businessmen shipped at least 150,000 firearms to rebel governments in South America, as well as more than a million flints, hundreds of tons of gunpowder and bullets, and untold piles of swords, bayonets, uniforms, knapsacks, and canteens, all packed carefully into crates and stowed aboard ships—and those figures do not even count the thriving commerce with nearby Mexico. Some of these supplies were reexports from Europe, and some never actually ended up in rebel hands, confiscated as they were by royalist navies and port authorities. But of the equipment that shipped out, a plurality seems to have been destined for Venezuela and Colombia, with substantial cargoes also headed to Buenos Aires, Chile, and Pernambuco. In contrast, firearm sales to Spanish and Portuguese royalists seem to have been smaller, perhaps numbering in the low tens of thousands.[15]

The United States formed only one spoke in the water-churning wheel of Atlantic trade, of course, and it was not the only country that sent supplies south. Britain, too, was drowning in weapons after the Napoleonic Wars, and its merchants sold probably hundreds of thousands of those leftover firearms to Latin America—more than U.S. merchants did (although U.S. merchants seem to have served routinely as partners and middlemen). The exact scope of the trade from either nation is impossible to determine because weapons traders, loath to attract attention from Spanish and Portuguese officials, were quiet and clandestine as a matter of commercial survival; those who supplied European royalists may have kept quiet, too, for fear of being known to serve an unpopular cause. If they dared to leave written tracks at all, men who trafficked in munitions sometimes wrote in secret code or, like Saavedra and Aguirre, they operated under fake names.[16]

Although secrecy was central to the business, one thing seems clear. U.S. merchants were one of the rebels' primary suppliers of armaments, and the magnitude of the sales sometimes proved decisive in an era when rebel armies routinely numbered in merely the hundreds or low thousands. As one Venezuelan admiral confessed in 1820, "[o]ur savior has been the arrival of a Boston brig full of provisions and sundry necessary articles for our navy, at a time when we were beginning to perish." Or, as the celebrated Colombian expatriate Manuel Torres told his superiors, 1820 marked "the most critical situation that has ever confronted our revolution"; the aspiring nation's only hope was to "pu[t] 50,000 rifles and the corresponding amount of powder, munitions, etc., in the hands of Colombian territory." "Where will we be able to get this?" Torres asked. "From the United States and maybe Holland."[17]

For their part, Saavedra and Aguirre set their sights high when they arrived in the United States. At Torres's suggestion, they quickly approached one of the wealthiest men in the country: Stephen Girard, a Bordeaux-born Philadelphia banker known as much for his philanthropy as for his breathtakingly risky commercial ven-

Before the Latin American independence wars gained momentum, the so-called "Black Legend" of Iberian iniquity shaped U.S. thinking about Latin Americans. This engraving shows the fatal outcome of Francisco de Miranda's 1806 effort to liberate his native Venezuela from Spain with help from about 200 U.S. recruits. Ten of those recruits were publicly hanged and decapitated; those who managed to escape over the next several years returned to the United States with stories of Spain's brutality and Miranda's ineptitude.

Francisco de Goya's haunting depictions of the Spanish Peninsular War famously and unflinchingly addressed the human capacity for violence. The chaos in Spain was a critical precondition of Spanish America's independence wars, which witnessed similar levels of destruction.

Painted originally by an unidentified Haitian artist, this portrait (shown here in a reproduction by Alfredo Rodríguez) depicts Simón Bolívar during his 1816 refuge in the Republic of Haiti. With Haitian support, Bolívar would go on to become a leading figure in Spanish-American independence, and U.S. audiences called him the "Washington of South America."

The Republic of Haiti's president, Alexandre Pétion, was the only head of state to give direct military and financial assistance to Spanish America's insurgents. In return, Bolívar promised to end slavery in all the regions he clawed away from Spain. U.S. editors reported widely on Bolívar's time in Haiti, with overwhelmingly sanguine reactions.

With its high white literacy rates and burgeoning political excitement, the United States boasted more newspaper readers than any other country by the early 1820s. From pulsing port cities to rural hamlets, printers used presses like this one (now on display in Old Salem, North Carolina) to pump out a flood of news on Latin America after 1815.

José Antonio Páez and his fearsome *llanero* cavalry galloped through the pages of U.S. news-papers in the 1810s and early 1820s. North and South, editors widely noted that the Venezu-elan's troops were "composed of the free people of color and blacks of the plains," and they remained overwhelmingly supportive, heralding Páez as "gallant," "brave," "immortal," and "one of the most extraordinary men of the age."

As House Speaker for much of the 1810s and early 1820s, Henry Clay was the nation's premier advocate of Latin American independence. In this portrait, the lanky Kentucky lawyer holds a copy of an 1821 House resolution declaring that "the House of Representatives participates with the people of the United States" in its enthusiasm for Latin Americans' success.

This 1819 July Fourth celebration in Philadelphia included all the hallmarks of the holiday: military parades, music, alcohol, explosives. In the decade that followed the War of 1812, most parties also included toasts to Latin American independence.

Slave markets like the one pictured here would surely have been familiar to Emiliano Mundrucu, the *pardo* (or mulatto) revolutionary who urged his countrymen to build a new Haiti in Brazil during Pernambuco's 1824 uprising against the independent Brazilian monarchy. Perhaps Pernambuco's slave markets were also familiar to James Rodgers, the young New York adventurer who was executed here in 1825 after commanding a ship in the rebellion.

A leader of the rising abolitionist movement, Lydia Maria Francis Child looked south of the border to explore other approaches to slavery and freedom. She and her husband David were friends with Emiliano Mundrucu, who fled to Boston in the wake of Pernambuco's failed 1824 uprising. "[I]t has been my good fortune to be acquainted with many highly intelligent South Americans," she reflected in a trailblazing 1833 book, "who were divested of this [racial] prejudice, and much surprised at its existence here."

In his long-running newspaper, the *Genius of Universal Emancipation*, Benjamin Lundy repeatedly positioned Spanish-American antislavery efforts as a model for the United States, noting that the United States was the only American republic in which slavery was spreading rather than receding.

Born in the Jamaican tropics, raised in wintry Montreal, and educated at Bowdoin, John Brown Russwurm was coeditor of *Freedom's Journal*, the first black-owned-and-edited newspaper in the United States. Like Lundy's *Genius of Universal Emancipation*, the paper paid close attention to antislavery developments in Spanish America. (By the time he sat for this portrait around 1850, Russwurm was a governor in Liberia.)

As secretary of state under President James Monroe, John Quincy Adams was the nation's leading skeptic of Latin American abilities, supporting the insurgents in principle but worrying that U.S. involvement would jeopardize the acquisition of Spanish Florida. In 1822, he finally came out in support of diplomatic recognition; one year later, he masterminded the Monroe Doctrine.

In the early- and mid-1820s, musicians and lyricists published nearly twenty odes to South American independence, including this one, written by New York's George P. Morris.

Samuel F. B. Morse's 1822 painting of the House of Representatives evoked the drama of the Missouri crisis and foreshadowed the drama of the Panama debates.

When he sat for this portrait in 1811, Virginia Representative John Randolph was known for riding his horse around Washington each morning and then tardily ambling into Congress, whip snapping in his hand and hounds snarling at his feet. Randolph would play a central role in the 1826 Panama debates, when he disavowed the Declaration of Independence's egalitarian rhetoric and cast the United States as a white republic in a hemisphere of darker-skinned radicals.

tures and the enormous profits he so often reaped from them. If the U.S. government quietly advanced the agents weapons from its own supplies, Saavedra and Aguirre wondered, would Girard be willing to restock the federal arsenals as more weapons became available? Time was of the essence, after all, and the U.S. government was the agents' most promising and immediate source of firepower. Girard had already extended modest credit to rebel agents from Caracas. Let the United States help Buenos Aires, then; Girard could replenish the federal arsenals later, for a pretty penny.[18]

Blind in one eye, partly deaf in one ear, and still bearing a heavy French accent, the temperamentally austere Girard heard the agents' appeals and professed himself "disposed to be serviceable." The Madison administration was disposed to be serviceable, too, and it agreed to the plan—or so Monroe apparently insinuated to a euphoric Saavedra and Aguirre. When pressed, however, the secretary of state declined to give explicit, written approval; doing so would have implicated the government in a potentially embarrassing situation, one that probably didn't befit a neutral power like the United States. Lacking overt permission from Monroe, Girard demurred, and the deal fell through. Instead, Saavedra and Aguirre ended up buying their small stash of weapons from a pair of modest Philadelphia speculators.[19]

Saavedra and Aguirre's experience of seeking out high-profile commercial partners—and contracting with lower-profile ones— was not unusual. Over the next decade and a half, Latin American agents approached some of the most famous men of their time for help: John Jacob Astor, the German-born fur magnate; Éleuthère Irénée du Pont de Nemours, the French chemist who fled his own country's revolution, moved to Delaware, and established the DuPont powder manufactory; even Eli Whitney, the Connecticut Yankee who, after inventing the cotton gin, built a firearms factory just outside of New Haven. These men met repeatedly with rebel agents, but none followed through with much sustained assistance.

Evidently deciding that such deals were too risky, they left rebel buyers to less conspicuous suppliers.[20]

Famous or not, sellers pursued profit as well as principle. As a Boston merchant informed an ally in Calcutta, "we have many ships gone there [South America] to supply the Republicans with Rations, and relieve them of their Dollars." "We hope they [Spanish Americans] may finally succeed, both for the sake of humanity and political freedom, and for the benefit of trade," he told another associate; "15 millions of consumers who would require supplies from England, and from this Country, would put a great deal of labor in motion and reward it well." A U.S. citizen in Venezuela appealed to the same mix of money and morality when, in 1820, he urged his countrymen to sell their guns southward. In a letter that first appeared in Charleston's *City Gazette* and then spread to newspapers in at least twelve states and as far west as Nashville, the writer appealed to people "animated with the spirit of independence and generosity, who can be induced to dispatch 10 or 15000 muskets for the shores of South Columbia, receive his Spanish milled dollars for them, and put into the hands of his compatriots of the southern continent of his sister America, the weapons of retributive justice."[21]

Henry Hill, for one, guardedly agreed. An earnest twenty-two-year-old New York evangelical who bestowed Bibles upon any sailor who would accept one, Hill voyaged to Chile in 1817 as supercargo of the brig *Savage*, his cabin lined in fine-grained mahogany and luxurious carpet. His task: selling weapons to Chile's insurgents. But the rebel leader with whom Hill's business partners back in Baltimore had contracted had been banished by the time the *Savage* arrived in Chile, so Hill struggled to find buyers. Speaking mediocre Spanish and better French, Hill met repeatedly with Chile's founding fathers: Supreme Director Bernardo O'Higgins and the formidable but opium-addicted General José de San Martín, both of whom dragged their feet in hopes of lower prices. ("Every thing is done here poco á poco," Hill despaired.) Worried that failure would destroy his fledgling reputation, the young man confessed himself to be nearly sick with "heart-ache" and "dread." "I am . . . hanging on by the eye-lids," he told his ship's captain; "my hands and feet are completely tied."[22]

Why did he bother? Reading his despondent and anxiety-ridden letters, one gets the sense that Hill would probably not have undertaken the voyage had he known how it would unfold; far from a revolutionary ideologue, he seemed to care more about spreading God's word than about spreading republicanism. (Although, whether because of language barriers, time constraints, concerns about the legality of proselytizing, or a belief that Chilean Catholics were already set in their ways, evangelizing seemed to occupy little of his time once he arrived in port.)

Yet even Hill found comfort in the cause he served. The young man took pride in selling "implements for repelling the [Spanish] foe, and for defending its [Chile's] liberty," and he saw nothing wrong with soliciting "some small privileges . . . in consequence of having risked liberty and life in addition to property." Although rebel leaders suspected him of seeking royalist buyers in Peru, Hill maintained his innocence to the end. "I have never had the slightest idea of undermining this country's efforts," he told General O'Higgins, "by putting arms in the hands of its enemies, so that they can fight against the men who fight for their liberty, and the defense of their rights." Such statements of idealistic commitment were unquestionably self-serving, but they also appeared genuine; in the scores of confidential letters that Hill sent to allies and investors, the only alternate buyers that he discussed were in China and the Columbia River basin, thousands of miles from the South American imperial meltdown. Hill eventually sold his wares to San Martín and O'Higgins, and for a lower price than the original contract had stipulated. Then, he stayed in Chile for several more years, importing weapons and outfitting privateers.[23]

Hill's main career ambition was money, of course: no profits, no weapons trade. Merchants were professional opportunists; their job was ostensibly to make money, not help the brotherhood of man. Aside from the market in weapons, most U.S. merchants followed their purse strings straight to Spain and Cuba, where they sold the grain and other supplies that helped to sustain the struggling Spanish empire, not revolutionize it. David Curtis DeForest, the tall and paunchy U.S. consul in Havana, even worked to undercut Francisco de Miranda's 1806 expedition to free Venezuela, utterly unwilling to imperil his windfall by supporting the already controversial mission. DeForest's pursuit of fame and fortune bordered on the obsessive; as he once told his brother, "Time is Cash, Credit is Cash, Knowledge of Business is Cash." But when circumstances changed and DeForest saw a chance to make his Cash by serving revolution, he moved to Buenos Aires, outfitted privateers, even became a dual citizen. A former Connecticut stable boy, he returned to the United States a millionaire (at least as his proud young wife told it). When he finally settled back down in New Haven, in an exorbitant custom-made mansion overlooking the town green, he hosted a blowout party every year on the anniversary of Buenos Aires's independence. He even insisted that future residents do the same: "greeting," read a marble tablet in his cellar, "[I] assisted in establishing" the United Provinces of the Río de la Plata, and "I demand: that you assemble your friends together on every 25th day of May in honor of the Independence of South America." It was classic DeForest, burnishing South America's reputation and his own in a single imperious stroke.[24]

Merchants continued to trade overwhelmingly with Cuba, of course, and DeForest probably would have too, if he thought he could have made more money that way. But if republican idealism seldom overrode commercial profit, the two imperatives formed a prouder and more potent mix when they coincided: had DeForest made his primary fortune in Cuba, it is hard to imagine him gathering his friends to publicly commemorate continued colonialism there (much less strong-arming future homeowners to do the same). When republican principles underlay the financial principal, it was a pleasing alignment, and men like DeForest and Hill had no reason to choose between the two. In this sense, men who proudly sold supplies to the rebels were one more manifestation of the same hemispheric interest that inspired the songs, toasts, and baby names. They simply brought that interest into their business, doing well for themselves by doing good for Latin America.

★　★　★

MEN WERE CONSTANTLY knocking on William Duane's office door. Eager to work but unable to find jobs, they came most days of the week to ask for help getting employment. In a better economy, they might have toiled in manufacturing, shipbuilding, or the merchant marine. Many were veterans of the War of 1812, men who knew how to fight, how to sail, how to command, and how to obey. Lacking other options, they set their vocational sights on the armed conflicts of Latin America, asking Duane to recommend them for service in rebel militaries as well as in privateering and filibustering expeditions. The Philadelphia journalist confessed that their requests—243 of them in 1817 alone—became "a most vexatious tax upon the business hours and even the hours of refreshment" of his printing shop. With so many supplicants, it was hard to work and hard to relax.[25]

Duane wanted to help; he felt irritated that he couldn't do more. A pugnacious supporter of Latin American independence, the Irish-educated editor knew many rebel expatriates personally (including Torres and Cruz), and his correspondents numbered among the country's most outspoken defenders of rebel antislavery efforts and multiracial armies. But as his sooty printing office became a way station for men looking to enlist under Latin American flags, Duane feared that some of his visitors were spies employed by the Spanish minister, who might be trying to entrap would-be rebel recruits. When the visitors asked for help, Duane demurred. (Or so he told readers, although the fact that he kept such careful count suggests that he took the solicitations seriously.)[26]

Duane or no Duane, the men continued to search for jobs; what else could they do? In Philadelphia, in Baltimore, in Charleston and New Orleans and New York, peace with Britain had left thousands of mariners and dockworkers underemployed. As Naval Commissioner David Porter observed at war's end, "[m]any valuable officers will be thrown out of Employment . . . and most of them have turned their thoughts toward South America," where seafaring traditions were few and rebel navies often relied on foreign expertise. As Duane put it, "hundreds of men accustomed to military life without resources or occupation" had begun to hope that "employment in the military service of South America could be obtained."[27]

The subsequent surge in foreign enlistment and privateering drove the Spanish and Portuguese ministers crazy. How, these officials complained, could the United States seriously claim to be a neutral power while letting its citizens prey on royalist forces? The privateers in particular—men who, with the blessings of rebel governments, sated themselves on Iberian sail—grew so numerous that opponents described them as arthropodic pests who "swarmed" in "nests" around port cities like Baltimore, itself a "new Algiers." Rotating their way through the State Department and the presidency, Madison, Monroe, and Adams successively implored Congress to crack down against all the armed adventuring, determined as they were to avoid a war (or, presumably, bruised commercial relations) with Spain, Portugal, and other colonial powers.[28]

The Neutrality Act of 1817—"a bill for making peace between His Catholic Majesty and the town of Baltimore," as supporters nicknamed it—failed to immediately deter U.S. citizens from casting their lots with South America. In cities where men and women wrested their livelihoods from the sea, customs officers hesitated to enforce the new law, and as late as 1819, Baltimoreans were still decorating their hats and lapels with the red, white, and blue insignia of Montevideo privateers. Even when officials dared to press charges, sympathetic juries routinely acquitted accused privateers "with great applause from the audience," Portugal's José Corrêa da Serra griped, their cheers erupting from the courthouses and spilling into the streets.[29]

In some ways, Monroe and Adams were opposites: Monroe, the phlegmatic Virginia farmer born into the lowest echelons of the colonial gentry and a longtime supporter of foreign revolutions; Adams, the fractious Harvard grad, son of a president, and a skeptic of Latin American capabilities. ("Their governments are Chinese Shadows," he wrote several years later; "they rise upon the Stage, and pass off like the images of Banquos descendants in Macbeth.") But from their perch in Washington, the two men agreed that individual citizens could not be permitted to drag the nation into transatlantic war. Despite protests from House Speaker Henry Clay and his allies—and despite Thomas Jefferson's sense that the crackdown had already gone "against the very general sentiment of our country"—Monroe and Adams convinced Congress to pass a growing string of neutrality and antipiracy laws. By the early 1820s, privateering from the United States had virtually ceased.[30]

Still, armed adventurers had left their mark. In the six years that followed the War of 1812, over 3,000 privateersmen sailed from the United States under the flags of Buenos Aires, Montevideo, Caracas, Cartagena, and Mexico; hundreds more enlisted in rebel navies, with dozens gaining officer commissions. As with the weapons trade, U.S. contributions were complemented and ultimately outweighed by those of Britain, which did not ban foreign enlistment until 1819, and which saw over 5,000 men leave for the South American service. While the United States went on to reject the informal alliance that Canning would propose in 1823, individual

Anglos and Americans had already converged for years in fighting for Latin American independence on the ground—and, more often, at sea.[31]

* * *

THE FACT THAT privateering and foreign enlistment soared during an era of underemployment indicates financial motives, and countless privateers pursued subsistence above all. But what was true for weapons traders was true for adventurers: other incentives were at work, too. Take James Rodgers, a twenty-four-year-old New Yorker who sailed to Brazil in search of republican glory. In 1824, the young man disembarked in Pernambuco's capital city, a tropical Venice spliced by rivers and built so close to sea level that one British observer said it had "the appearance of being built in the water." Surrounded by ornate baroque churches and breezy palm trees, Rodgers immediately found himself amid a bustle of foreign sights and sounds. Free men and women of color peddled their wares in melodic, emotive Portuguese, white ladies rode to church in elegant sedan chairs carried on the shoulders of black men, and merchants counted and weighed their slave-grown goods for export: cotton to feed England's textile mills, sugar to sweeten North Americans' tea and coffee.[32]

Rodgers hardly had time to take it in. At that very moment, Pernambuco—led by men like the *mulato* republican Emiliano Mundrucu—was in the midst of its armed rebellion against the newly independent Rio monarchy. As headstrong as he was hapless, Rodgers threw himself wholeheartedly into the rebel cause. He commanded a ship and used it to fire on royal troops. He signed his name to a public document that repudiated the Rio monarchy's claims to sovereignty over Pernambuco. According to his enemies, he hurled explosives at imperial troops; others swore that at one point he raised a gore-splattered coat above his head and boasted that the blood came from dead Europeans.[33]

Rodgers's ship was called the *Independência ou Morte*—Independence or Death. At some level, Rodgers must have thought about what that meant as he pushed himself to the front lines of another country's revolution. Perhaps he also thought about it as he faced the firing squad several months later, draped in a white gown, freshly converted to Catholicism, and ready to die. Informed that the emperor himself had denied Rodgers's pleas for a pardon, the executioners aimed first at the young man's abdomen and groin, then his heart, and finally his head. A Philadelphia editor declared that Rodgers "died nobly, professing the same love of freedom and abhorrence of tyranny, that had ever marked his short, but gallant life." A Maine newspaper compared him to Lafayette; a Pernambuco priest, to Jesus.[34]

During his trial, Rodgers swore that he had only been in it for the money. It was the best defense someone in his situation could have mustered, but it didn't add up. As Brazilian authorities put it, "he says that he did it for want of subsistence, yet he chose to take a very active part in the rebellion." Even if money helped to explain how Rodgers ended up in Brazil, it didn't explain the passion with which he subsequently fought, nor did it explain the defiant ten-minute speech he made minutes before his execution, in which he urged Pernambucans to continue the fight. The U.S. consul later reported that Rodgers had come from a well-respected family, the son of a doctor. If money was all he wanted, he could have stayed in New York. Rather, the willful young man embraced Pernambuco's cause with a zeal that suggests other, more emotional impulses: military glory, adventure, a belief in the righteousness of Pernambuco's cause. Perhaps, in his fleeting moments of combat as in his posthumous heroization, he achieved the first two, even as Pernambuco's star faded and men like the masked Mundrucu slipped away to seek refuge in the United States.[35]

Rodgers may have been uniquely impassioned. Yet even many of lesser means—men who didn't have the option of relying on their well-connected New York families—genuinely believed in the cause they served. "You will probably ask what are my motives in leaving a fine [U.S.] Ship & applying for a command under your Flag," one mariner bluntly informed Brazilian authorities. "I answer, 1st my own promotion & 2d The pleasing hope of seeing the whole continent of America perfectly Independent of the Tyranny of all Europe." As one recruiter explained, armed adventurers were men "without occupation & full of ardour for the enterprize of the South." There was no shame in getting paid for doing good, the *City of Washington Gazette* explained; "That these volunteers do not serve from mere 'sympathy,' is no disparagement of the cause in which they adventure. You do not find them in the *royal* ranks of Spain.... If they volunteer abroad at all, they fly to the armies of freedom." To be fair, Spain was drawing on centuries of seafaring lore and had less need to rely on foreign sailors than its rebellious colonists did. Still, there was little reason to doubt the stated motives of men who made their livings by making independence.[36]

★ ★ ★

MEN LIKE JAMES RODGERS and Henry Hill—gun-toting and gun-peddling rebel partners who risked their lives and their fortunes on behalf of hemispheric liberation—actively shaped Latin America's independence wars, or tried to. The vast majority of hemispheric enthusiasts never got so directly involved. Too far from the coastlines to consider privateering and too undercapitalized to think about high-rolling international commerce, most simply continued to throw parties, offer toasts, and name people, places, and things after Simón Bolívar. That kind of breezy enthusiasm didn't easily translate into a clear set of policy mandates. But Henry Clay was convinced that it should.

By 1817, Clay had had nearly enough of Washington. In rare moments of quiet, the thirty-nine-year-old House Speaker thought about retiring from Congress and heading home to Ashland, his Kentucky hemp plantation. James Monroe had just been elected president, and Clay had wanted desperately to become his secretary of state—a position powerful in its own right and an unofficial stepping-stone to the presidency. Instead, Monroe chose the sober New Englander John Quincy Adams, leaving Clay equal parts embarrassed and irate. The ordinarily fun-loving, hard-partying Kentucky statesman— known for flirting, fiddling, drinking, dueling, gambling, and, during one especially raucous dinner party, dancing down the full length of a food-filled sixty-foot banquet table—resorted to petty snubs: conspicuously absenting himself from Monroe's inauguration, refusing to let the Senate bring its plush red leather chairs into the more demure House chamber for the event. (The House's furniture, "such as it is, was very much at their service," Clay tartly retorted.)[37]

Clay ultimately decided to stay in Washington for the new congressional session, and for one reason above all. Like so many of his countrymen, he believed that the United States was leading a global struggle for human freedom. As he leafed through his oversized stack of newspapers to learn what was unfolding in Latin America, he felt compelled to act. It helped, too, that there were political points to be scored: Monroe and his darling secretary of state were offering the rebels moral but not much material support—thus their crackdown on privateering and foreign enlistment. By arguing on behalf of the rebels, therefore, Clay could publicly challenge his newfound political enemies. The administration had wounded him; now, a vengeful Kentucky Achilles, he would return the favor.

As he presided over the House—a temporary, second-floor chamber hurriedly built after the British torched Washington's first capitol in 1814—Speaker Clay channeled his political fury and his republican idealism to become the nation's leading congressional advocate of Latin American independence. For the next decade, he relentlessly urged the United States to become a "rallying point" for freedom fighters across the globe, starting with Latin

America. Standing before hushed and packed House galleries, the lanky lawyer implored his nation to be for Latin America what France had been for the insurgent United States, or something like it. Beginning in 1817, he had resisted Monroe and Adams's suppression of privateering and armed adventuring. The following year, he began to urge diplomatic recognition. All the while he advocated for his "American System" of domestic economic development coupled with hemispheric trade. Clay spoke not just with his sonorous baritone but with his whole body, shrugging, smirking, raising his arms, every contortion revealing "the uncontrolled expression of violent feelings," as a disapproving New Hampshire congressman told his father.[38]

Proceed with caution, countered Monroe and his newly installed secretary of state; *send well-wishes, not warriors*. Tirelessly urging restraint, the administration supported Latin American independence in theory throughout the 1810s but worried that precipitous action would anger Spain, jeopardizing trade with Cuba as well as U.S. territorial ambitions in Spanish Florida and the Columbia River basin; moreover, the administration argued, further U.S. involvement might actually hurt the insurgents by provoking a harsher reaction from Spain. Where Monroe and Adams sought to lead mostly by example, Clay aspired to actively push the revolutions along with greater commercial and diplomatic support. Where Monroe and Adams took a wait-and-see approach to diplomatic recognition, Clay supported it early, when it was still an unlikely cause. With the angry partisan divisions of the previous quarter century dissipating after the Federalists' post-1815 downfall, congressmen who debated hemispheric policy over the following decade usually lined up behind these two fluid coalitions according to personal attachment and diplomatic and political logic, rather than according to any kind of newfound partisan infrastructure.[39]

As the battle lines took shape in Washington, however, they

remained hazy elsewhere. Although the popular celebrations showed that U.S. citizens wanted the nation to support Latin America, it was seldom clear what that support was supposed to look like as a matter of policy. Of the hundreds of toasts raised to Latin American independence and sampled in the last chapter, only a tiny handful gestured toward the government's role in promoting such an end, and even those offered few specifics. Privateering? Neutrality? Diplomatic recognition? On these pressing questions of policy, toastmasters abstained. Their inattention was striking, since men in the early United States regularly used toasts to champion particular candidates, platforms, and policies, from tariffs and gradual emancipation to banks, states' rights, and "internal improvements" (what we call infrastructure). When they invoked South America, though, they were seldom so specific. They talked a lot about hemispheric independence, but relatively little about how the United States might formally help to bring it about.[40]

Some even suggested that diplomacy was irrelevant, as if South America was destined to be independent regardless of how it got there. Take an 1813 July Fourth gathering in New Jersey: "Our South American brethren," guests proclaimed, ". . . We have shewn the world that to be free is only to will it." Or William Lloyd Garrison in 1822: "There never can be much doubt of the result of a contest between those who fight for freedom and independence, and those who oppose them, however unequal the combat may be." And one year later, from a party at Mount Vernon: "The South American Republics; men must, who dare, be free." If these observers were correct, the United States had little reason to concern itself with policy; it could simply sit back and watch independence spread inexorably over the earth.[41]

There were exceptions, of course, ones that must have given Clay hope. Although very few July Fourth revelers endorsed specific hemispheric policies, those who did often endorsed Clay himself. In the summer of 1825, for example, thousands of people descended upon Lancaster, Ohio, where ground was to be broken for a new canal. ("On the day previous," one newspaper reported, "all the roads leading to the point selected for the celebration, were crowded with people on foot, on horseback, and in every description of vehicle.") At the ceremony, the governors of Ohio and New York drove their spades into the dark, damp soil, the first shovelfuls of millions. Spectators thanked God Almighty, their roars of approval even louder than the ceremonial artillery; they also thanked Henry Clay, whose famed American System endorsed not just federal support for canals but also hemispheric trade. As guests at an ensuing dinner party approvingly put it, Clay was "the early advocate for the recognition of South American Independence, and the firm and eloquent supporter of internal improvement."[42]

It wasn't just men who felt that way. The "ladies of Lawrence-burgh," Indiana, reached the same conclusion, their Ohio River town pulsing with flatboatmen and farmers. "[P]ermit us, Sir: with pride to acknowledge our profound respect & gratitude for your distinguished Services," they wrote to Clay after a formal gathering in 1825, "in advocating the interest of the West. The independence of South America & of clasic [sic] Greece, The principle of Internal improvement, Domestic Manufacture and Agriculture, And for your eloquent and Successful exertions in every thing that could add to the happiness and Glory of our country." The leading signatories were a well-connected bunch: Mary Lane was a former schoolteacher, wife of a former state congressman; Mary Skipwith Randolph had been married to one of Thomas Jefferson's cousins, a Virginia state legislator who died in the 1811 Battle of Tippecanoe; Sarah Wardell was likely married to a local lawyer; and Lucy Dennis was soon to marry a local editor. The letter was unusual partly because it was written by women, a fact which—like the mothers who named their sons Bolivar and dressed their daughters in Bolivar hats—suggests that at least some white women joined their husbands, fathers, brothers, and sons in celebrating

Latin American independence. It was also unusual because so few people of either gender bothered to express opinions on formal questions of hemispheric policy, even in this roundabout and retrospective way.[43]

In Virginia, New York, and Clay's own Kentucky, scattered Fourth of July patriots made the same connection, commending Clay and Latin America in the same bated breaths. Indeed, it is possible that many enthusiasts would, if pressed, have similarly inclined toward Clay's policy of recognition and engagement, as opposed to Monroe and Adams's more laissez-faire approach. But because so few enthusiasts openly made the connection (and because only one of the hundreds of sampled toasts did so), it is hard to be sure, and plenty of hemispheric toasts came from gatherings that also toasted Clay's political enemies. Hemispheric enthusiasts specialized in abstract ideals, not in the nitty-gritty particulars of high-level diplomacy. Those who thought much about policy might have leaned toward Clay, in other words, but not very many *did* think about it, at least in ways that left a written record. Nevertheless, that ambivalence helped set the stage for a political showdown, one in which Clay sought to politicize the excitement while the administration battled to keep it at bay.[44]

★ ★ ★

VOTERS' APPARENT AMBIVALENCE toward inter-American diplomacy did not stop Henry Clay—canny politician that he was—from claiming a popular mandate. The public fervor provided him with political cannon fodder, evidence he could marshal to make a strong and urgent case that the good people of America supported recognition. Monroe and especially Adams quietly ceded the point, privately calling the popular enthusiasm a "Tragi-Comedy of passion" and speaking of the need to rein it in. Clay, in contrast, openly gave it voice. "Every where an interest is excited in behalf of our Southern brethren," he told an ally in 1818, "and I have seen, with great satis-

faction, the most abundant evidence of this interest in the recent celebrations of the fourth of July." Even the wrinkly and white-haired
House chaplain, himself a veteran of the U.S. revolution, had led
Congress in prayer for Latin America, the Speaker reminded listeners; indeed, "the whole nation looked forward to the recognition"
of Latin American independence ". . . as the policy which the Government ought to pursue." Vague and nondescript though it was,
the popular enthusiasm created a political climate that empowered
Latin America's most vocal advocates. It made Clay's momentum
possible, and it defied the administration's inertia.[45]

Clay quickly put the administration and its supporters on the
defensive, suggesting that anyone who opposed him was defying
the will of the people and the welfare of the nation. "Let us become
real and true Americans," Clay urged his fellow congressmen
while pushing for diplomatic recognition in 1820. His was a "genuine American policy," he insisted several weeks later; as he told
supporters in his home town of Lexington, "*his* desire had been to
pursue a course exclusively American." By playing with that term—
American—Clay maintained that his platform would benefit not
just the nation but the entire hemisphere, too.[46]

It was a potent charge, because nobody wanted to look un-
American in either sense of the term, hostile to America's first revolutionaries or to its latest. One after another, Clay's opponents—
Monroe's supporters—stood before Congress to swear that they
loved Latin America as much as anyone; they simply didn't want
to risk war with Spain and its European allies, or jeopardize the
lucrative trade to Cuba that such a conflict might imperil. Hugh
Nelson, a fifty-year-old Virginian whose girth had grown with
the years, even praised the rebels until his vocal chords betrayed
him, "his broken voice rendering him unable to proceed," as one
witness noted. With congressmen and gallery observers straining
to hear, Nelson opposed diplomatic recognition for Buenos Aires
even as he insisted that everyone in the country supported South

America in spirit. "Do we essentially differ in our avowed objects?" he asked, his whisper of a voice dwarfed by the sonorous House chamber. "Not at all. . . . Are we unwilling that the people of South America should shake off the yoke of Spain? No, we are not." It simply made no sense to go out on a limb for South America, Nelson argued, when doing so might endanger the nation's security. Though "scarcely competent to make himself heard" on the floor of Congress, Nelson was determined to make himself heard among Virginia's voters, carefully presenting himself in the congressional record as a devoted supporter of international republican liberty.[47]

Even the standoffish John Quincy Adams felt the popular pressure, disparaging the rebel movements in private but shrewdly toning down his verbal assaults in public. "I had seen and yet see no prospect that they would establish free or liberal Institutions of Government," he scribbled in his diary. ". . . Arbitrary Power, military and ecclesiastical was stamped upon their education, upon their habits, and upon all their Institutions." (Like father, like son; the elder Adams had said much the same thing in 1815, before meeting with the Pernambuco charmer Antônio Gonçalves da Cruz, and he voiced those doubts to his son several months after Pernambuco's rebellion imploded. South Americans "will be independent, no doubt. But will they be free?") In a letter to his brother, Adams derisively ventriloquized Clay's supporters: "eighty-eight degrees of Latitude!—eighteen millions of virtuous Patriots!—Spanish tyranny and oppression!— Atlantic and Pacific Oceans!—Mountains and Rivers!" The nation teemed with such men, Adams mordantly remarked, "fanatic" and reckless crusaders determined to spread liberty to everyone, everywhere. But Adams was more charitable when addressing voters. "The United States goes not abroad, in search of monsters to destroy," he famously proclaimed in an 1821 public address, standing at the congressional rostrum and cloaked in his Harvard professor's gown. "She is the well-wisher to the freedom and independence of all. She is the champion and vindicator only of her own." The sentiment was the same—Adams still urged caution—but the message was packaged in respectful and generous language.[48]

Owing, perhaps, to similarly political calculations, few congressmen in the 1810s and early 1820s ever came close to disavowing Latin American independence on principle. Georgia's John Forsyth was one of the few who did. A blond-haired and blue-eyed Princeton graduate who lowered his voice for emphasis rather than roaring and gesticulating as Clay did, Forsyth acknowledged that "[s]ympathy for the people of the South was universally felt," but he saw a major difference between South American revolutionaries and their U.S. counterparts. "We asserted, vindicated, maintained, and improved our rights," Forsyth said; South Americans, in reacting to Napoleon's Iberian usurpation, found "independence . . . cast upon them" by "accident." "The time has been," the thirty-eight-year-old continued, "when my young heart swelled with emotion at the *sound* of liberty. But these days of youthful delusion have passed, I hope, forever." International revolutionary ardor as a form of delusion? Few congressmen went so far. In fact, Forsyth himself rarely went so far. Just a year before, he had "professed the best wishes" for "the success of the patriots." The difference, he warned, was that sympathy alone should not inspire actual policy.[49]

Even if voters were not especially interested in the details of foreign relations, their raw passion helped to shape the way elected officials talked about revolution, as federal policymakers bent over backward to publicly praise the rebels. Whether that passion also influenced the way men like Adams, Monroe, and their congressional colleagues acted toward revolution was another question—and, ultimately, a more important one.

★ ★ ★

CLAY HAD WANTED to be secretary of state, yes. But more than that, he wanted to be president, and everyone in Washington knew it. In scornful, sideways glances and in brash, open insults, the House Speaker badmouthed Monroe and Adams at dinner parties and political encounters throughout the capital city, sometimes while "warm with wine" (as Adams reported) and taking the Lord's name in vain. With his explosive temper and his fondness for drink, Clay couldn't have hidden his ambition even if he'd wanted to.[50]

As he mapped out his path to the presidency—the better to humiliate Monroe and Adams—Clay chose Latin American independence as his first cudgel against the administration, and he wielded that weapon for the better part of a decade. It was a telling strategy, because there were other weapons from which to choose. Territorial expansion, military appropriations, commercial development—all were likely to be divisive issues for the new Congress, and Clay, a famously hard worker known for toiling by candlelight deep into the night when he wasn't out roistering, could easily have busied himself with them. Latin American independence, in contrast, and particularly diplomatic recognition, didn't have to be such a major issue. According to federal precedent, recognition had proceeded through the president, but Clay spent years doggedly trying to link recognition to Congress (which, as he was quick to point out, had the power to fund the ambassadorial missions that accompanied formal relations).[51]

Clay was genuinely committed to the rebel cause; his statements on behalf of Latin American independence far predated Monroe's State Department slight. Still, it seems unlikely that the notoriously ambitious Speaker would have made such a concentrated effort had he not also expected voters to reward him. As one of Clay's critics reflected in 1826, Spanish-American independence "has been Mr. Clay's darling—he has hugged it to his bosom for years, as the sure hobby that one day or other was to elevate him to [presidential] office." Clay was not just claiming a popular mandate as a matter of political convenience, in other words. He actually believed that he had one, and he saw Latin America as a winning issue—for his own political fortunes and for the cause of human freedom, too.[52]

Monroe and Adams winced at Clay's audacity. The secretary of state recorded every slight in his persnickety diary, not simply because those slights represented personal rebukes but because they seemed to endanger one of the most important items on the administration's foreign policy agenda: Spanish Florida. Peninsula and panhandle, the stakes there were incredibly high. If white U.S. settlers and their government could kill or expel native people and replace them with black slaves, Florida's loamy and alluvial soils could be converted into cotton fields, fallow for the planting and ripe for the picking. Georgia's planters would no longer have to worry about slaves escaping to freedom south of the border. Places like Amelia Island would no longer serve as offshore hubs for multiracial revolutionary renegades. Because Florida's Gulf Coast was the endpoint for rivers that began in Mississippi, Alabama, and western Georgia, the acquisition of Florida would enable planters throughout the region to float their goods into the Gulf and, thence, the world. Three birds, one stone: a takeover of Florida would bring more slaves, more cotton, more capital to vast stretches of the South.[53]

Monroe and Adams were not willing to risk all of that for Latin American independence. As they saw it, congressmen who supported recognition were jeopardizing expansion into an area that was critical for national security. If the United States angered Spain by recognizing Spanish-American independence, then Spain might reciprocate by refusing to cede Florida, or even by declaring war. (One Spanish diplomat had apparently said as much in a private conversation with Adams: through knowing nods, raised eyebrows, and "much show of mysterious meaning," Adams wrote, the Spanish diplomat "meant me to understand him as saying . . . that Spain would cede to us the Florida's," but only if the United States would "satisfy Spain about the South American insurgents" by declining recognition.) Clay, himself a truculent expansionist, insisted that Monroe and Adams were setting up a false choice; the United States could have it all, he insisted, Florida *and* recognition. But as the administration guardedly saw it, Florida (and the rest of the nation's western boundary with Spain) had to come first.[54]

Only a few dared to disagree. To do so was to line up as an opponent of the president, flouting federal precedent regarding recognition and testing the administration's carefully laid plans for territorial expansion. In 1818, when Clay first proposed recognition by urging the House to fund a minister to Buenos Aires, the measure failed by a vote of 45 to 115 (a decision understood to be so important that some congressmen reportedly rose from their sickbeds to speak). Enthusiasts' relative silence on policymaking specifics enabled politicians to bow to stronger strategic, political, and economic forces—concerns about the Florida treaty, a reluctance to oppose the president, and a desire to prioritize trade with Cuba—while paying inter-American lip service in debate. For the risk-averse, caution therefore prevailed, and most congressmen fell in line behind Monroe and Adams's circumspect path.[55]

Those who sided with Clay did so at their peril. Years after having endorsed Clay's hemispheric vision, Louisiana Representative Thomas Robertson recalled that Monroe "never forgave" him. Even New York Senator Rufus King, such a strong supporter of Latin American independence that he had been an early (if ultimately fairweather) ally of Francisco de Miranda, demurred. "So far as I can fathom the system of the Executive they mean to act with caution," the aging Federalist stalwart told an ally in 1818. "Such indeed are my own views.... You will not suppose that I have changed any of my former opinions ... but it is a serious question, and I shd. regard it as an unfortunate decision of it, that we shd.... plunge into a war for the deliverance of these Colonies."[56]

King was one of the most engaged rebel supporters of the previous twenty years, though he, too, saw fit to bide his time and side with the administration. That was how high the political and strategic hurdles were when it came to supporting Henry Clay. Over the next few years, those hurdles would topple. As they did, more and more policymakers would, like Clay, give diplomatic heft to the public's glib enthusiasm.

★   ★   ★

THE HEMISPHERIC EXCITEMENT clearly swayed Henry Clay, who believed that it could help propel him into the White House. There were also signs that the excitement swayed Clay's colleagues. None of the signs would have been single-handedly convincing, but taken together, they paint a compelling picture, one in which the toasts, the parties, and the poems—vague though they were—gradually prodded Washington's leading men into action.

To begin with, congressional votes correlated with public displays of inter-American passion. Baby Bolivars were most likely to be born in the Midwest and the Southwest, followed by the Southeast, the Mid-Atlantic, and New England. This geographic ordering mirrored that of legislators who sided with Henry Clay: midwestern and southwestern congressmen voted with the Kentucky congressman on hemispheric policy issues 76 percent of the time, followed by their colleagues from the Mid-Atlantic (56%), the Southeast (39%), and, finally, New England (25%). The order was nearly identical. It indicates correlation, not causation; most of the Bolivars were born in 1825 and 1826, several years after the major hemispheric policy votes had been cast. Still, it suggests that Clay's Latin American agenda enjoyed the most support in regions where popular enthusiasm burned brightest.[57]

The chronology lines up, too. Inter-American fervor had begun as a grassroots groundswell, instigated not by Washington politicians but by editors, rebel agents, and readers throughout the country. The hemispheric toasts began their decade-long plateau in 1816, a full year before Clay provoked Congress's first major debates on South American policy. Legislative deliberations could not have provided the initial spark for the popular festivities, therefore, but the popular festivities could have informed the first legislative debates. Congress's rhetoric may thereafter have fueled the fervor, but that influence was implicit at best, and it was not the first engine of excitement.[58]

The popular enthusiasm touched the executive branch, too. Ensconced at the White House and the State Department—the former still smelling of paint and plaster after its postwar repairs, the latter crammed into a two-story building shared with the Navy and War departments—Monroe and Adams confessed that public opinion weighed on their minds and shaped their deeds, an incessant and often irksome background noise that amplified on every passing July Fourth and whenever major hemispheric policy decisions arose. As Adams later recalled, Monroe had confessed himself "well disposed to go further" and consider recognition when Clay first raised the issue in 1818, "if such were the feeling of the nation and of Congress." But the "angry acrimonious course pursued by Mr. Clay" had left Monroe reluctant to compromise, and so the administration demurred.[59]

By 1820, Adams was convinced that the popular enthusiasm *was* skewing Monroe's actions, and for the worse. Monroe—who had long been more optimistic about Latin Americans' prospects than his instinctively cynical secretary of state—had urged the monarchies of Europe to join the United States in a combined act of diplomatic recognition; he had praised the rebels in his public writings; he had appointed a prominent rebel sympathizer to serve as a district judge in Baltimore. "[T]hese measures . . . have been compliances to popular sentiment in favor of the South Americans," Adams wrote; "compliances perhaps politic, to counteract the invidious misrepresentations of Clay and his partizans, of the President's partiality against the Revolutionists." As Buenos Aires's minister later told his superiors, Monroe had privately confessed that "the public opinion of this country . . . is currently completely favorable to the new [South American] States, and . . . if it changed it would make it impossible for the government to deploy its . . . aid." What the people demanded, Monroe apparently suggested, the government must eventually do.[60]

Adams—by now much relieved to have moved into a bigger office building with Ionic columns and stately, arched windows—had particular reason to heed that advice. He, too, coveted the presidency, even if—unlike Clay—he was loath to admit it. (He was of good Puritan stock, wary of untoward ambition.) Since so many people associated Latin American independence with Clay, Adams had a strong incentive to neutralize the issue by coming out, finally, in favor of recognition as well. Sure enough, in 1822, Adams did exactly that. Many factors contributed to his decision: a series of convincing rebel victories throughout Spanish America, a newly found confidence that European monarchs would not retaliate against U.S. recognition, and a desire to cultivate Latin Americans' political affections (and their commercial proclivities) by extending recognition before anyone else did. Most of all, Spain had reluctantly approved the Transcontinental Treaty late in 1820, its hand forced in part by Andrew Jackson's refractory 1818 invasion of Florida. Through that agreement, Spain ceded Florida and gave the United States a stronger claim to what is now the Pacific Northwest. With Florida finally in hand and the western borders better defined, Spain's feelings no longer had to be spared; the United States could kick Spain while it was down by acknowledging the erstwhile colonies' independence. Those newfound circumstances all help explain Adams's endorsement of recognition. But, with the 1824 presidential election looming in electrifyingly plain sight, Adams surely also realized that his announcement would coincide handily with his political interests.[61]

★ ★ ★

THE HURDLES, THEN, had toppled. Florida was safely netted; the administration had backed recognition. With the pendulum of public opinion (and politics) ostensibly behind them, congressmen like Rufus King latched on and swung into action. The United States became the first nation in the world to welcome a new set of republics onto the world stage as equal and independent players: Peru, Chile, the United Provinces of the Río de la Plata, and Colombia, which itself included modern-day Colombia as well as Venezuela, Ecuador, and Panama. Policymakers also recognized monarchical Mexico, much as they would do two years later for Brazil (which did not declare independence until later in 1822); better, they figured, to be an American monarchy than the colony of a European one. Only one representative and three senators voted nay on recognition, and of those, at least one got expelled from office based partly (as critics charged) on this resistance; another gained open notoriety at home. With the practical barriers out of the way, the rest of the nation's congressmen greeted Latin Americans onto the world stage. Their near-unanimity was perhaps one final sign of hemispheric enthusiasts' policymaking power. Latin American independence was a feel-good issue, and once political and strategic expediency allowed, legislators seemed eager to act. Nudged along by ordinary observers who refused to let the dream of hemispheric independence die, Congress became Latin America's champion, or purported to.[62]

As news of recognition spread in the spring and summer of 1822, the nation erupted with unprecedented applause. In the sticky heat of Norfolk, in the wavy and crop-lined hills of Lancaster, Pennsylvania, in rainy Little Rock, and near the ancient Mississippian temple mounds of Cahokia, Illinois, white men joyfully welcomed their new sister republics to the international arena. The number of July Fourth celebrations that toasted hemispheric independence surged to at least 75 percent, easily a record (see the Appendix). By comparison, only 34 percent of toasts saluted Latin America after the following year's Monroe Doctrine, and the difference was logical enough. Monroe's message to Congress was a high-level diplomatic statement of the sort that onlookers habitually disregarded; although the Doctrine hadn't been wholly top-down, average citizens hadn't seen it coming, either. Recognition, in contrast, was an outcome, the capstone and consummation of the American independence wars. It lent an official (if misleading) sense of finality to the vision of hemispheric independence that people had been trumpeting for over a decade. (And indeed, that sense of finality also helps to explain why hemispheric toasts fell by half in 1823, and still further in 1824—having been ostensibly achieved, the cause of independence may have seemed less urgent.)[63]

On one hand, Congress's vote in favor of recognition had caused the surge in excitement by giving people something to celebrate. On the other, the sustained enthusiasm of the previous seven years had slowly helped spur policymakers into action. Clay yearned for electoral rewards. Monroe and Adams were themselves sensitive to public pressure. Others supported recognition as practical concerns dissolved, evidently prepared to translate the public's abstract ardor into concrete action. Popular opinion was their tailwind, and Clay was right out front, riding the gale of excitement straight into the White House—or so he hoped.

By helping to sway federal policymakers, the hemispheric enthusiasm shaped formal diplomacy; by helping to inspire adventurers and arms dealers, the enthusiasm directly affected Latin America's insurgencies. But the inter-American excitement would not last forever. Few saw that change coming—few, that is, except for a South Carolina senator named William Smith.

★ ★ ★

IN 1822, WILLIAM SMITH lost his Senate seat. An impassioned defender of small government and states' rights, Smith had represented South Carolina in Washington for nearly six years, railing against tariffs and opposing federally funded roads and canals. When the Missouri crisis unfolded, he did not just defend slavery, as most southern whites at the time did; instead, he eagerly applauded it, arguing that "no class of laboring people in any country upon the globe" were "better clothed, better fed, or more cheerful" than slaves in the United States. Despite Smith's efforts, the South Carolina state legislature refused to appoint him to another term.[64]

There were many reasons for the defeat, most of which boiled down to Smith's very public disdain for fellow Carolinian John C. Calhoun. Critics in the newspapers pointed to additional, more specific reasons, and among those was the senator's refusal to vote for diplomatic recognition of Spanish America in 1822 (or, as Smith was quick to specify, his refusal to support the funding that would necessarily follow). In a justificatory letter that reappeared in newspapers throughout Washington, Virginia, and South Carolina, Smith laid out his reasoning. For one thing, he had feared that recognition would provoke a costly war with Spain; for another, he wasn't convinced that Spanish Americans were actually independent.[65]

Smith's logic also stemmed from unabashed prejudice. "In those provinces," the former senator wrote, "upon the first impulse of revolution, the people of color, of every description, were, in their constitution, declared free. And of these people a great part of their armies consisted." Smith then launched into lurid detail about emancipation in Venezuela and Mexico, where "blacks and mulattoes are so numerous, and so influential, that they commit the most horrid butcheries and murders, on the whites, with perfect impunity." Brazil, he continued (quoting a letter from a U.S. agent in Buenos Aires), was "in a most feverish state, and, should civil war burst forth, it would be the signal of the emancipation of a numberless horde of slaves, and most horrid scenes of blood." "I should not prefer an intimate connection with these people," Smith concluded, "until they should first have given us some proofs of a national character favourable to our southern institutions."[66]

William Smith had clearly been reading the news, which had been upfront about the rebels' racial ancestries and antislavery policies for years; as Smith put it, information on Latin American race relations had "long since been known to the public," and the resulting unease was "not confined to my breast." But although Smith insisted he was not alone, he found himself outnumbered by the men who expelled him from office based partly, as his own detractors said, on his opposition to recognition.[67]

At the national level, too, Smith was perhaps the only public official whose concerns about racial hierarchies superseded his support for Latin America's revolutionaries. His nemesis, John Calhoun, strongly backed the South American rebels throughout the early 1820s and displayed no evident concern over their antislavery policies; as secretary of war, Calhoun had even briefly argued that the government should sell weapons to Colombia on credit. In the deliberations that led to the Monroe Doctrine, neither Calhoun nor anybody else appears to have raised South American race or slavery as an issue. Only a handful of congressmen in the postwar decade so much as alluded to the rebels' varied ancestries, and those comments were desultory at best—vague and cursory gestures toward Haiti that occupied a few sentences out of hundreds of hours of debate. (In the middle of a speech supporting tighter neutrality laws in 1817, for example, Virginia Representative John Randolph cited a decade-old determination "to leave nothing undone which could possibly give to the white population in that island an ascendancy over the blacks," but he quickly moved on.) Even when discussing Amelia Island, congressmen spoke the language of neutrality, piracy, congressional procedure, and international law, not the language of race. Those who wanted to smear Gregor MacGregor, Louis Aury, Vicente Pazos, and their motley followers unsparingly condemned such men as "sea-rovers," "buccaneers, banditti, and pirates" who lacked any legitimate connection to Latin America's insurgent governments. These were fighting words, and perhaps implicitly racialized, but they lacked the overt racial fear-mongering that dominated newspaper reports on Amelia; congressmen appeared hesitant to go so far. In the debates over hemispheric relations, not one congressman ever raised South Americans' skin colors as a central policy consideration. (Smith himself never explained his views on the Senate floor because the recognition vote proceeded too quickly, he later complained.) Like the public and usually the press, congressmen portrayed events in South America as a contest over political independence and republican freedom, one in which race was incidental.[68]

But things were changing fast. New political parties were taking shape. Cotton was transforming the South. Latin America's republics were entering a period of instability. Against that backdrop, William Smith, who had looked like an unpatriotic anomaly in 1822, would soon strike many as a visionary.

CHAPTER SIX

AN IMAGINARY KINDRED

H ENRY CLAY WAS IN A BIND. For all of his presidential aspirations, he lost badly in the 1824 election, trounced by a
hotheaded philistine (Andrew Jackson), an antisocial prig (John
Quincy Adams), and an incapacitated stroke victim (outgoing
Treasury Secretary William Crawford). Jackson had shocked
political insiders by winning a plurality of the popular and Electoral College votes, but that wasn't enough for him to claim the
laurels. Because there were so many candidates in the race, the
dark horse Tennessee general lacked the majority of votes required
by the Constitution. The election went to the House, where
Speaker Clay became de facto tie breaker between Jackson and
runner-up Adams.[1]

Clay disliked Adams personally, found his starchiness tire-
some. But Jackson was an impulsive renegade, an upstart military
chieftain known (among critics like Clay) for exceeding orders and
placing himself above the law. Adams was at least predictable, trust-
worthy, cultured. He believed in the kind of vigorous government
upon which Clay's American System depended, and an alliance
with him would strengthen Clay's popularity in the Northeast.
Jackson, in contrast, would challenge Clay's status as the leading
light of the West. Strange bedfellows, then; Clay threw his weight

to Adams, Adams won the presidency, and—in an agreement that critics immediately decried as a "corrupt bargain"—Clay became secretary of state, a satisfying consolation prize on his unending path to the presidency. It was one of the most controversial elections in U.S. history. Crying foul over the seemingly undemocratic result, Adams's vanquished rivals gradually began to coalesce into what would, over the next few years, become the Democratic Party.

Adams assumed the presidency on a rainy Friday in 1825, promising (as others had before) to transcend partisanship and faction. His opponents were not so easily appeased, and in December they saw their chance to pounce. In his annual message to Congress, Adams announced that he had decided to send delegates to the first-ever conference of American nations, to be held in Panama the following year. He didn't anticipate much opposition to the measure, especially given how many other controversial topics were up for discussion: relations with native people, federal election procedures, internal improvements, and territorial expansion, to name a few. Anyway, Adams's opponents seemed unlikely to prevent the Panama mission; in a city where people weighed and tallied each other's allegiances with relentless obsession, most came to suspect, correctly, that the measure would pass. But Adams's opponents—still known as *the opposition* rather than as *Jacksonians* or *Democrats*—could use parliamentary stalling tactics to delay the mission, dilute its force. They had a broader goal in mind, too: by taking a seemingly simple proposition and turning it into a major legislative roadblock, they could publicly embarrass the new administration and show their power.[2]

They would also announce what they stood for. Indeed, it was with good reason that Adams's opponents chose the Panama mission as "the first bow, upon which . . . to bend their strength against the present administration," as one Maine editor observed; Panama offered what a pro-Adams Virginia congressman called a perfect "touch-stone of party." Because events in Latin America had enthralled voters for the previous ten years, a discussion of hemispheric policy would offer a powerful soapbox, and it would push voters to think hard about what kind of nation they wanted to be. Indeed, opposition members weren't fixated on Latin America per se. Rather, they latched onto the Panama mission because it arose at the right time and because it involved essential and defining issues of federal power and social values. As New York opposition Senator Martin Van Buren later recalled, the Panama mission was the "first tangible point for the opposition which had been anticipated and could not have been avoided without an abandonment of cherished principles."[3]

As southern opposition members saw it, the Panama mission also involved slavery. For years, antislavery activists had been urging their countrymen to grapple with the meaning of freedom in a hemisphere born of bondage, and thus with their own nation's revolutionary inheritance. Ironically, what finally ignited the nationwide soul-searching about North American slavery and South American abolition was a group of legislators—the southern wing of the rising Democratic Party—who proudly asserted that the United States was the lone success story in a hemisphere of radicals, the white republic in an America endangered by black and mulatto ones. What made the United States special and superior, southern opposition members suggested, was that it enslaved its black people rather than enfranchising them.

It was a change of focus more than a change of fortune. The earlier universalism about South American race relations had been largely passive, and that passivity rendered it vulnerable. Its limits had been exposed before—when rebels of color occupied Amelia Island, for example, and when Bolívar's troops momentarily faltered and editors retrospectively assailed his antislavery tactics. The universalism's limits had become still more glaring at home, where cotton, capital, and human bondage were remaking the southern landscape. Indeed, the United States looked different in 1826 than it had in 1810 or even 1815: more land, more states, more slaves, more cotton. When opposition southerners finally encouraged voters to view Latin America through a racial lens, they were not creating a new issue so much as they were forcing voters to confront an older and evolving one, a story of hemispheric race relations that had long been peripheral but that was becoming harder to ignore as more slaves were made to plant more seeds on more southern soil.[4]

* * *

BY THE END OF 1824, Simón Bolívar was at the height of his glory. Admired around the world, he had liberated half a continent, mastered more territory than Napoleon. He had led an army across the arid and ice-tipped Andes, dangling from ropes as he crossed mortally deep ravines. He had ridden such great distances across the punishing and rain-soaked Venezuelan *llanos* that his men called him Iron Ass. He had foregone food and sleep, endured incapacitating fevers, slept on the naked ground and awakened with his mustache covered in frost.[5]

Now, comfortably situated in an airy country home just outside of Lima, surrounded by fig trees and custard apples, he began to enjoy the pleasures of peace. Bathed, brushed, and cologned, Bolívar waltzed across Peru's dance floors, exulting in his endless throngs of admirers. He took up with his smart and free-spirited mistress, Manuela Sáenz, a cigar-smoking, cross-dressing republican who had come to serve on the general's paid staff. (When her lovestruck husband begged her to be loyal, Sáenz matter-of-factly replied: "you are a boring man.")[6]

So Bolívar spent his nights. His days he spent sitting at his desk or sprawling in his hammock, working to implement a decade-long dream: the summoning of an inter-American congress. ("How beautiful it would be," he had mused as a scrappy and outmatched revolutionary back in 1815, "if the Isthmus of Panamá could be for us what the Isthmus of Corinth was for the Greeks!") Bolívar envisioned what might eventually become a permanent hemispheric assembly, one empowered to mediate disputes between members, establish a shared means of defense in the event of foreign aggression, and streamline relations with the rest of the world as well as between member states. It would be the Western Hemisphere's answer to Europe's Holy Alliance.[7]

Interested primarily in the fate of Spanish America, however, Bolívar left the United States, Haiti, and Brazil off his guest list when he sent out invitations at the end of the year. He wanted a more homogeneous assembly, one united by history, language, and imperial origins. Indeed, for all of the love that U.S. audiences showered on Bolívar, Bolívar never really loved the United States. He begrudged a certain amount of respect to the burgeoning northern republic, admired its astonishing growth and political stability. But he thought that Spanish Americans would have to forge a different path to prosperity. "It has never for a moment entered my mind," he declared in 1819, "to compare the position and character of two states as dissimilar as the Anglo-American and the Spanish American." The United States and its colonial British antecedents, he said, had been "cradled in liberty, reared on freedom, and maintained by liberty alone"; Spanish Americans, he admonished, had no such history, and would need to find their own way. If they ever somehow had to choose between the Quran and the U.S. Constitution as the basis of their government, Bolívar wryly vowed to urge his countrymen toward the former, "although the latter is the best in the world."[8]

Not all of Spanish America's leaders wanted to exclude the United States from the upcoming assembly. Bolívar's own vice president invited the United States to attend, and Bolívar, more interested in cultivating ties with mighty Britain (which was itself sending an official observer), declined to protest. That circuitous invitation ignited a bitter political struggle in Washington; as newspapers variously put it, the Panama question was one of "the most important ever submitted to the American people," a deliberation that would "stand on record as one of the most imposing debates which ever took place in Congress." The Peace Society of Maine summoned the strongest superlative, arguing that the Panama Congress would inaugurate "the greatest epocha in the history of man, since the advent of the Savior of the world." If that last claim was overblown, the others were less so, albeit for reasons that the authors could only begin to appreciate.[9]

* * *

JOHN QUINCY ADAMS believed in power. At a time when most white people in the United States worried that the federal government would threaten individual liberties—the right to speak and worship freely, to enjoy due process, or even to own slaves—Adams boldly reversed the equation. Federal power would make people more free, not less, the new president informed the nation in his first annual message to Congress; as he bluntly put it, "liberty is power." It was not a popular view among men whose fathers had died protecting American liberties from British tyranny. But Adams was too proud, too certain of his own well-schooled views to do something solely because everyone wanted him to; part of the antisocial streak, perhaps. The dour New Englander laid out a breathtakingly expansive vision of federal initiative, insisting that the government should construct a national observatory, build a network of roads and canals, even switch to the metric system. "[T]he spirit of improvement is abroad upon the earth," he proclaimed in his rousing peroration, all part of one sweeping effort to maximize people's moral and economic potential.[10]

The Panama mission fit easily alongside that dynamic understanding of government. As Adams maintained, attendance would enable the United States to strengthen relations with Latin America and preach the trinity of republican government, commercial reciprocity, and religious tolerance. Minus the religion piece, it was what Secretary Clay, with his hemispheric American System, had been saying all along. Yes, Adams had long questioned Latin Americans' capabilities. But by 1825, those nations had proven themselves sovereign, and so Adams reached out to them in his interminable quest toward human uplift; that was how, when it came to foreign policy, he and Clay were suddenly able to coexist as allies rather than as enemies. In one graceful gesture, the president and his right-hand man suggested, federal power at Panama could enrich people who lived in the United States and even beyond it. Adams and Clay seemed to think all of that could happen, moreover, without much political fanfare: in the weeks before Adams delivered his message to Congress, he and his Cabinet vigorously debated the document's political expediency, pondering the electoral ins and outs of everything from a national university to a reorganized Executive Department. Adams recorded the discussions each night in his diary, staying up so late in the flickering candlelight that his eyes blurred and stung. Not once during those critical weeks did he bother to mention any internal debate over Panama. The opposition caught the secretaries and the president by surprise, and within weeks, administration supporters were privately referring to the ensuing political explosion as one big "Embarrassment."[11]

Indeed, all the talk of federally funded "improvement"—Adams used the word and its variants no fewer than twenty-seven times in his annual message—made the opposition cringe. Like any measure that relied upon federal power and finances, opponents contended, the Panama mission would open the way to special interests and waste while undermining the authority of individual states and citizens. And for what? The president's Panama proposal was utterly "Quixotic," opposition members charged, a foolish "scheme" reminiscent of the careless naïveté displayed by the nation's growing legions of overeager social reformers. Increasingly after the War of 1812, these busybody reformers spoke of world peace. They converted heathens to Christianity. They sent former slaves to colonize West Africa. A small few, like Benjamin Lundy, even attacked slavery itself. Washed over by the wave of evangelical fervor known as the Second Great Awakening, many believed they were doing nothing less than perfecting humankind, remaking God's kingdom on earth.[12]

As skeptics saw it, the Panama mission stemmed from the same misguided impulse. The burly Missouri Senator Thomas Hart Benton likened it to a touchy-feely Methodist camp meeting—a "Love-Feast," he called it. As Virginia Senator John Randolph argued, the Panama mission stemmed from "[t]he same meddling, obtrusive, intrusive, restless, self-dissatisfied spirit" that also appeared "in Sunday Schools, Missionary Societies, subscriptions to Colonization Societies—taking care of the Sandwich Islanders [Hawaiians], free Negroes, and God knows who"; biding his time in Nashville, Andrew Jackson called the Panama mission "one of the most dangerous, and alarming Schemes that ever entered into the brain of visionary politicians." The Panama mission enabled Adams's opponents to link their distrust of energetic government to their distrust of energetic do-gooders—especially, as it turned out, do-gooders who hinted of racial uplift. Opposition leaders therefore agreed that their foremost task, once the new session of Congress convened, was to resist the mission and everything it stood for.[13]

* * *

A MUNICIPAL PHOENIX, Washington in 1826 had literally risen from the ashes. Sacked and burned by the British just over a decade earlier, its reconstructed public buildings were bigger and brighter than before even as the rest of the city remained an underdeveloped swampland. The National Mall, muddy and lined with sheds, was an eyesore. But at the Mall's eastern boundary, construction on the glistening, neoclassical Capitol mercifully diverted attention. The celebrated Boston architect Charles Bulfinch had worked with the nation's best sculptors and artists to adorn the building, and by 1826, workers were putting the finishing touches on the stately copper dome.[14]

From the outside, the Capitol looked orderly and imposing, the pride of a nation that already had a famously high opinion of itself. Inside, it was a different story, as the Panama question ignited three months of stormy debate. In terms of congressmen's sheer volubility, the subject of neutrality dominated discussion. Adams had insisted from the beginning that U.S. ministers would participate only "so far as may be compatible with . . . neutrality." But his opponents—inspired, perhaps, by the high-handed circumstances of the late election—boldly retorted that Adams could not be trusted. Invoking George Washington's famous admonitions against foreign alliances, they also argued that the United States' mere presence would implicitly sanction whatever measures the Panama Congress adopted, potentially angering Spain or provoking a transatlantic war.[15]

Opponents of the mission made other arguments, too, ones that complemented their general disdain of idealistic improvement projects and big government. Some contended that Adams had exceeded his constitutional powers (and his flimsy electoral mandate) by accepting the invitation without prior Senate approval. Others mocked Adams's desire to encourage religious tolerance in the new nations, where such liberties didn't generally exist. Several U.S. states had religious tests for officeholders, one congressman noted; wasn't it hypocritical to urge religious freedom on others? Future president James Buchanan added that priests had led several of Latin America's revolts; Catholicism, he concluded, had been "a blessing" there. Adams had not publicly questioned Catholicism, despite what he sometimes wrote in private; his message on Panama had only questioned state-sponsored Catholicism. His opponents blurred the distinction. If Adams stood for New England's Protestant establishment, many of his challengers lined up as advocates of domestic pluralism, foreshadowing the Democratic Party's future strength among Catholic voters.[16]

Most opposition congressmen made the most of these arguments, especially the one about neutrality, but southern opposition members added another element into the mix: slavery. It wasn't merely the specter of a foreign alliance that concerned opposition southerners, though that might have been damning enough. It was also, Thomas Hart Benton warned, the kind of people with whom that alliance was supposedly to be forged, and the kind of topics that might conceivably be discussed. Expelled from the University of North Carolina after stealing from his roommates to pay tuition, Benton had moved to Tennessee in 1801 along with his widowed mother, his seven siblings, and the family slaves. There he became a protégé of Andrew Jackson, but Nashville proved too small for the two of them. In 1813, Benton shot the general in a hotel gunfight and left him slumped in a pool of blood. He absconded to St. Louis shortly thereafter, but by 1826 the two men had reconciled in the name of politics. "Who are to advise and sit in judgment . . . ?" Benton demanded. "Five nations who have already put the black man upon an equality with the white, not only in their constitutions but in real life; five nations who have at this moment (at least some of them) black Generals in their armies and mulatto Senators in their Congresses!" "I would not debate whether my slave is my property," the senator concluded, "and I would not go to Panama to 'determine the rights of . . . Africans' in these United States." The speech resonated; it reappeared in the opposition's favored newspaper and was sold separately as a pamphlet, in at least two editions.[17]

Other opposition southerners agreed: Spanish Americans were the last people in the world with whom the United States should affiliate. "If it is the policy of the [United] States not to suffer this great question [of slavery] to be touched by the Federal Government," South Carolina's Robert Hayne reasoned, "surely it must be the policy of this Federal Government . . . not to suffer foreign nations to interfere with it." *Don't talk about it* in Panama, in other words. But in making the point, Hayne did talk about it in Congress, vividly and at length, much as Benton had done. "Those Governments have proclaimed the principles of 'liberty and equality,'" he explained in a speech that reappeared in newspapers nationwide, "and have marched to victory under the banner of 'universal emancipation.' You find men of color at the head of their armies, in their Legislative Halls, and in their Executive Departments." Tennessee's Hugh Lawson White concurred. "In these new States," he said, "'. . . whoever owns a slave shall cease to be a citizen.' Is it then fit that the United States should disturb the quiet of the Southern and Western States, by a discussion and agreement with the new States [of Spanish America], upon any subject connected with slavery?" Spanish Americans had "colleagued with all colors and complexions, in the consummation of their revolution," South Carolina's James Hamilton, Jr., concluded in a sharp and prolonged passage on slavery, and now they were "destined to give us more trouble than all the rest of the world put together."[18]

Benton and his colleagues were not suggesting that the Panama Congress would dispatch antislavery militants to U.S. shores. More commonly, they pointed to the Caribbean, arguing that Spanish-American antislavery ideas would poison the United States by way of Puerto Rico and especially Cuba. Spain's last remaining strongholds in America, these sugar-and-slave islands were of enormous economic and strategic value, and by 1826, many worried that Spain might use them as a launching pad for recolonizing expeditions onto the mainland. Belligerent parties in Spanish America therefore concluded that they should jointly preempt the attack, invading Cuba before it invaded them.[19]

But any attempt to liberate the Spanish Caribbean from colonial thralldom would be risky, at least as white U.S. onlookers saw it. If Cuba won independence but then grew politically unstable, it might become a protectorate of Britain, France, or another power stronger than Spain, thereby extending European influence in the Americas and endangering the United States' own territorial and commercial aspirations. Still worse, because roughly half of Cuba's population was enslaved, imperial turmoil there might create what James Hamilton called "a second Hayti." "Marching under the banners of universal emancipation, as these [Spanish-American] Republics do," the South Carolinian reasoned, "the first means of success would be an appeal to the slaves themselves, which, in producing an internal concussion in that island, would inflict on our Southern country an example of the darkest and most perilous aspect." As Virginia Senator John Randolph ominously reminded voters: the United States "may be invaded from Cuba in rowboats."[20]

Opponents of the Panama mission also drew an unprecedentedly close link between Spanish America and Haiti. For the previous decade, U.S. onlookers had viewed Spanish America's rebels as followers of the moderate U.S. example rather than of Haiti's more radical one, despite Bolívar's well-publicized agreement with Alexandre Pétion. Now opposition legislators swung the other way, noting that the Panama Congress might discuss the possibility of extending diplomatic recognition to the black nation. In fact, Haiti remained a secondary concern at Panama; Peru, for one, forbade its delegates from so much as discussing it, and Adams assured Congress that he opposed Haitian recognition in any case. But opposition southerners remained skeptical. The Panama Congress, Benton exclaimed, could press the United States to "permit black Consuls and Ambassadors [from Haiti] to establish themselves in our cities, and to parade through our country, and to give their fellow blacks in the United States, proof in hand of the honors which await them, for a like successful effort on their part."[21]

Not all opposition members turned against the new nations

so intensely. As before, some continued to praise Latin American efforts while citing practical concerns about the mission—not least opposition delegates from Kentucky, who hedged their bets given Clay's home-state support and the inter-American ardor that accompanied it. "It is a source of mortification to me to hear harsh epithets used against our sister Republics of the South of this Western hemisphere," said James Johnson. "They are neighbors ... they have my most devout prayers." Charles Wickliffe, another Kentucky opposition member, agreed, endorsing "the success of liberty, in whatever clime or country she struggles." But now, this more accepting language was challenged by precisely the kinds of "harsh epithets" that Johnson denounced.[22]

The putative figurehead of the opposition, Andrew Jackson, likewise declined to mobilize voters' racial fears in pursuit of political gain during the debates. Nursing his electoral wounds and plotting revenge, the general watched Congress's debates unfold in the stream of letters and newspapers that flooded his Tennessee plantation home as his prized "stud colt" Bolivar grazed outside. For his part, Jackson cited mainly constitutional and diplomatic concerns about Panama. "The moment we engage in confederations, or alliances [sic] with any nation, we may from that time date the down fall of our republic," the general warned an ally; "*May this not lead to War.*" At the same time, Jackson didn't exactly distance himself from the racialized rhetoric, either. He repeatedly sent his regards to the very opposition members who employed the most sharply racialized barbs of the debate—particularly John Randolph, who, in turn, extolled Jackson from the Senate floor, and who was helping to coordinate the general's presidential campaign in Virginia by 1828.[23]

The color-blind consensus of the previous fifteen years had evaporated. Despite broad awareness of Spanish-American emancipation, no standing congressman had ever employed such racialized language against rebel engagement; few newspapermen, for that matter, had either. But in 1826, the earlier universalist narrative found a loud and unabashed competitor, even among men who had been in Washington for years and never made such freighted remarks about the rebels. Of the eight southern senators who spoke against Adams's proposed mission, five employed the same kind of racialized invective that Benton did; two others, while not raising the same level of alarm, gestured warily toward Haiti, Cuba, and Puerto Rico. The House was more restrained, but a substantial minority of southern opposition members there likewise invoked slavery and race. For the first time, congressmen were publicly and repeatedly insisting that Spanish-American emancipation imperiled the United States. Looking now to South America's Caribbean connections, Adams's southern opponents portrayed the rebels' antislavery tendencies as infectious, something to be quarantined and confined at all costs. Once tapped, that venom flowed readily.[24]

* * *

JOHN RANDOLPH WAS as controversial as he was conspicuous. Tall, emaciated, and angular, the Virginia senator had a memorably bony forefinger that he slashed at adversaries like a saber. Due to an unidentified lifelong illness, his face remained boyish and beardless; his voice, a sharp soprano. (One observer quipped that he seemed "fixed for an Italian singer"; another said his voice was as "shrill and piercing as the cry of a peacock.") But he was strong enough to ride and hunt, and before the War of 1812 he had been known for galloping around Washington each morning and then tardily ambling into Congress, whip snapping in his hand and dogs snarling at his feet. The dogs skulked menacingly around the chamber, sniffing one irritated congressman after another, but Randolph was so brashly confident that few dared object until the newly installed Speaker Clay finally called him and his dogs out of order around 1811.[25]

Randolph embraced political eccentricity, too. Years before, the

Virginia planter had angered stauncher Jeffersonians by opposing the War of 1812 on the grounds that it would lead to a swol-
len military, increased spending, and possibly slave revolts. In the
war's wake, when Republicans like Clay, Adams, and even John
C. Calhoun argued for expanded federal powers—Calhoun was a
devout nationalist before he veered toward states' rights later in the
1820s—Randolph wagged his famous finger and argued for small
government and states' rights instead. Clever, creative, and a master of debate, he had the sharpest tongue in the Senate. When he
spoke, people listened—peacock voice and all.[26]

Randolph's remarks on Panama were explosive. He opened by
sarcastically expressing hope that U.S. delegates would be willing
to take "their seat in Congress at Panama, beside the native African, their American descendants, the mixed breeds, the Indians,
and the half breeds, without any offence or scandal at so motley a
mixture." Then he carried his argument to its logical conclusions.
"These principles," he stated, "—that all men are born free and
equal—I can never assent to, for the best of all reasons, because it
is not true." Inalienable rights, self-evident truths, equal creation?
It was all just "a clinch of words," Randolph said, "a fanfaronade
of abstractions," "a most pernicious falsehood, even though I find
it in the Declaration of Independence." Randolph knew his words
were harsh—"The language I have applied to it is strong," he said
of the Declaration. But the stakes were too high to mince words.
"No rational man ever did govern himself by abstractions and uni-
versals," he said (channeling Edmund Burke), and neither should
a nation. In fact, Randolph suggested, his old rival Jefferson had
it completely backward. Inequality, not equality, was the nation's
defining self-evident truth.[27]

Randolph's address quickly became the most-talked-about
speech of the entire debate; it went reprinted and cited in at least
fourteen states as well as in Florida. As a Raleigh editor observed,
"whatever emanates from *John Randolph* is eagerly read by every

body." Randolph wasn't the only legislator to question the nation's founding universalist rhetoric, though. "Is this [Panama] Congress," Virginia's John Floyd demanded, "to tell ... all of us from the Southern States, that 'all men are free and equal ... and if you refuse to make them so, we will bring seven republics in full march to compel you[?]'" Men in the United States, Floyd recognized, were *not* all free and equal, and they shouldn't be treated as though they were.[28]

The new hemispheric narrative that men like Randolph, Floyd, and Benton offered had a major asset, one that had as much to do with their own political savvy as it did with a broader set of changes that had been sweeping the nation over the previous fifteen years. Although the U.S. Declaration proclaimed that all men were created equal, inequality was growing; the rhetoric did not match the reality. After General Jackson (with support from then–Secretary of State Adams) wrested millions of acres from native people in what is now Florida, Georgia, Alabama, and Mississippi, white residents rushed in and feverishly put their slaves to work planting and picking; wealth was grown from the ground, cotton tufts bagged like coins. Agricultural production soared; despite a major economic downturn in 1819, fortunes were dreamed of and, sometimes, made.[29]

As slavery proliferated, so did talk of abolition. A popular movement in England was demanding an end to slavery in British colonies like Barbados and Jamaica. Northern congressmen had tried to block slavery's spread in Missouri, endowing slaveholders with bitterness and mistrust that endured long after the begrudging sectional compromise. Denmark Vesey, a one-time slave who had purchased his freedom with a winning lottery ticket, allegedly plotted an 1822 rebellion to rise up and kill white Charlestonians in the name of justice. All the while, domestic activists saturated the Declaration of Independence with antislavery implications that were increasingly hard for men like Randolph to ignore; that was why Benjamin Lundy invoked the "unalienable rights" to "life, liberty, and the pursuit of happiness" in his masthead. The Declaration's main function in 1776 had been to assert national independence on a global stage, not to assert human equality (something more important to early state bills of rights). But after 1815, with national independence secure, men like Lundy increasingly emphasized the document's more abstract talk of rights, and its egalitarian potential. They called attention to the gap between rhetoric and reality, and, in the process, they widened it.[30]

Nature hates a vacuum, however, and so does politics. Indeed, the yawning gap between rhetoric and reality presented a striking political opportunity, for there were only so many ways it could be closed. Yes, the nation might remain forever half slave and half free, precariously balanced along the Mason-Dixon and 36°-30' lines. But as the fights over Missouri had already portended, it might also split into two, perhaps even descend into civil war. Or slaves could rise up, turning the United States into another Haiti. It was hard for white people to imagine more alarming prognoses. Randolph and his allies were advancing a final, and ostensibly easier option, one that none other than William Smith and scattered others had already proposed in the Missouri debates: rather than changing the reality, just change the rhetoric. Abandon the universalist language in favor of a new idiom that triumphantly advocated equality for white men alone; use the existence of slavery to argue, circularly, that all men were manifestly *not* equal. By amplifying and accentuating the earlier arguments of men like Smith (or for that matter the pseudonymous *Phocion*), opposition southerners in 1826 celebrated the unequal reality rather than imploring listeners to, as social reformers and even the president urged, "improve" it.[31]

The threat of slave uprisings and civil war would remain, of course, but the southern opposition's narrative held out the possibility of political reward. In previous debates about slavery, northern congressmen had usually been on the legislative and rhetorical attack, as when Federalists' politically motivated antislavery jabs in the 1790s and early 1800s left slaveholders with little choice but to respond. Even those southern legislators who had edged toward proslavery arguments in the Missouri debates were reacting to northern congressmen who had forced slavery onto the national agenda; in that sense, their posture remained politically defensive even as their language grew increasingly uncompromising. Like Thomas Jefferson, after all, southern whites had long looked sheepishly at their founding egalitarian rhetoric and conceded that slavery was evil—necessary, but evil all the same. Such arguments were fundamentally defensive and apologetic, prompted by northern criticism and, perhaps more broadly, by the progress of abolition from Haiti to Spanish America to Britain. They were also weak. For as long as southern whites acknowledged slavery a sin, antislavery activists could push that concession to the breaking point, leaving slaveholders with little choice but to end either slavery or their genuflections to universal male equality.[32]

What changed in 1826 was that opposition slaveholders opted publicly for the latter, and they did so in a legislative controversy of their own making. Congressmen had debated slavery off and on for decades (usually as an addendum to other topics), but seldom had slaveholders gone so vociferously and voluntarily on the attack. Few had directly and systematically disavowed the Declaration's universalist rhetoric, and few seemed eager to press the issue, especially when so little concrete gain was at stake; as most insiders came to realize, after all, the mission to Panama was likely to be approved. During the Missouri debates, in contrast, nothing short of the sectional balance of power—and the nation's continued existence—had been at stake.

The discussion of slavery in 1826 was far from gratuitous, however. First impressions mattered, and slaveholding opponents of the nonslaveholding New England president wanted to assert their coalition's southern bona fides—Benton, for one, was busily readying his speech for publication as a pamphlet in mid-May, well after Congress had approved the mission, and the opposition's primary newspaper offered similarly protracted coverage. As Adams groused early on in his diary: "The opposition aware that there is a small majority in favour" of the Panama mission "are throwing every possible obstacle in the way of a decision upon it . . . to waste time and endeavour to gain proselytes." By choosing to oppose the Panama mission in the first place, by choosing slavery as a key reason for doing so, and then by broadcasting their racialized rhetoric even after defeat was certain, rising southern Democrats forged the rudiments of a congressional proslavery attack. As they worked to rally their constituents against Adams and Clay, slavery looked a little less like a necessary evil and a little more like a positive good—the kind of issue important enough to merit igniting a nationwide political firestorm.[33]

The transition was only partial, of course; such things usually are. Some slaveholders (like William Smith) had already embraced proslavery thought and racialized nationalism before 1826; others continued to see slavery as a necessary evil long after. In 1831, in the brooding aftermath of Nat Turner's slave rebellion, John Floyd himself (by then the slaveholding governor of Virginia) would privately endorse statewide gradual emancipation, although he backed off weeks later (and in any case his aversion to slavery had more to do with the welfare of white yeomen than with the welfare of black people). John Randolph decried slavery to the day he died, when he played the paternalist by freeing his 400 slaves. But Randolph increasingly saw slavery as a national sin with a personal solution rather than a federal solution, and his eagerness to reject universalist "abstractions" on a national stage represented one important step along a dusty and forked road that led eventually to the southern fire-eaters of the 1850s—and, finally, to civil war.[34]

If the venom flowed readily in 1826, therefore, it was because the conditions were ripe. Congress's debates about Spanish America pierced to the heart of how lawmakers understood democracy, equality, and America itself, exposing sentiments that had long festered but that had seldom been uttered so publicly, so willingly, so consistently, and on such high authority. In some ways, opposition southerners were rehabilitating the centuries-old stereotypes of Iberian iniquity that men like Jedidiah Morse and Hugh Henry Brackenridge had invoked in the late eighteenth century. But the emphasis on race was new; the Black Legend had grown blacker. The Panama debates both reflected and furthered a new era in American history, a movement away from the nation's founding universalist language and toward a bold new vision of U.S. greatness. In opposition southerners' estimate, the United States became an entity separate and superior within the hemisphere: uniquely moderate, uniquely successful, and uniquely white.

*　*　*

THE PANAMA DEBATES got personal, even flared into violence. In the midst of the controversy, Randolph implied that Clay had fabricated the invitation to attend, then likened the secretary to a lying knave of a character in an eighteenth-century Henry Fielding novel. Already wounded by the corrupt-bargain charges, Clay couldn't bear it. He had renounced duels two years before, but, his passion soaring and his pride insulted, he challenged Randolph— an experienced hunter—to a contest anyway. In early April, the two men crossed the Potomac to a Virginia forest along with their seconds, their surgeons, and their mutual friend Thomas Hart Benton, many of them so jittery that they had skipped lunch. The seconds set the rules and measured ten paces; the principals aimed, fired, and missed, Randolph's bullet clogging a stump and Clay's ricocheting through the dirt. Clay insisted on another try. He pointed his pistol at the skeletal Virginia senator and fired through his flowing white coat; Randolph then shot into the air, dropped his pistol, and said, "You owe me a coat, Mr. Clay." (Clay's friend later remarked that Clay should have given Randolph "a strait jacket.")[35]

Randolph and Clay had resolved their personal dispute, but the political differences persisted, as Clay made clear at a dinner later that year in the rustic western Virginia resort town of Lewisburg. The event had been planned in Clay's honor, but some of the seventy-odd gentlemen who attended were surprisingly hostile, daring to toast Andrew Jackson right in front of Clay (who presumably had to raise his glass along with everyone else, swallowing his pride along with his liquor). The besieged secretary wasn't cowed, though. He delivered what one opposition editor called a "harangue of an *hour's* duration," lest his hemispheric American System—and his presidential berth— slip away over the mountainous and blue-ridged horizon.[36]

Clay had long admired Spanish-American antislavery efforts, even praised them on the floor of Congress in 1820. Indeed, he saw slavery as a national crime, and he talked optimistically of ending it slowly in the vague and far-off future—preferably, he maintained, by sending free black people and former slaves somewhere far, far away (somewhere like Liberia, whose capital, Monrovia, had been named after the supportive former president). Clay didn't dwell on that when he faced his audience at Lewisburg, though. Rather, the Kentucky slaveholder leaned the opposite way, insisting that the Panama mission would actually support slavery by enabling the United States to dissuade its southern neighbors from invading Cuba. His congressional allies back in Washington had made the same argument; one after another, they agreed that foreign antislavery principles were dangerous, then insisted that the Panama mission offered the best way to contain them. As one Louisiana congressman argued, white southerners' opposition to the Panama mission amounted to "suicide."[37]

It wasn't surprising that pro-Adams legislators accepted the newly racialized terms of debate. Nor was it surprising that some went further, denouncing abolitionists in the United States and Britain as "fools and fanatics." When it came to Latin America, congressmen had long resembled their constituents in emphasizing republicanism over race, and as long as race remained a marginal issue, they had little reason to veer from the universalist rhetoric. But when opposition slaveholders started to impugn the egalitarian rhetoric, Adams supporters remained too nonchalant about it to object, especially when attention turned to the Caribbean and party politics raised the stakes. Anyway, despite what opposition slaveholders liked to imply, President Adams himself was no foe of slavery, at least when it came to federal policy. As secretary of state, he had masterminded the nation's acquisition of Florida, and he had worked hard to expand trade with the harrowing sugar and coffee plantations of Cuba. When, in his official response to opposition critics, Adams intimated that he intended to *protect* slavery by sending delegates to Panama, he meant it.[38]

. So did Henry Clay. Indeed, what bothered the secretary most was not opposition southerners' racialized rhetoric per se. It was what he saw as their dangerously sectionalist appeals. "There are persons who would impress on the southern states the belief that they have just cause of apprehending danger to a certain portion of their property, from the present administration," he proclaimed in his Lewisburg address, which reappeared in at least twelve states from Augusta, Georgia, to Columbus, Ohio. Those people were opportunistic "alarmists," intent on building their own political power even at the expense of national harmony. It was a heavy charge, given that the most recent sectional dispute, the Missouri crisis, had raised talk of disunion. But others agreed. In a pro-Panama speech that reappeared in newspapers as far away as New Hampshire, Louisiana Senator Josiah Johnston insisted that "the danger of the mission has been exaggerated and aggravated"; Representative Daniel Webster, Adams's home state ally, decried "the perpetual alarm, which is kept up on the subject of negro slavery." "[A]ny thing to rouse the prejudices of the slave holding states," cried one Providence editor, "against the measures of the Administration!" From the administration's perspective, the southern opposition was appealing to racial fear over national progress, sectional pride over country-wide unity.[39]

*　*　*

THERE WAS NO DISPUTING the fact that the opposition was strongest in the South. Martin Van Buren, the calculating New York senator who led the opposition with help from John Calhoun, made no mistake about it. "Our greatest strength, in regard to talent as well as comparative numbers being in the Senate," Van Buren later recalled, "that body was selected as the principal field of contest" for the Panama debates. Why were the opposition's "comparative numbers" stronger there? Because even when southern states padded their allocations by counting 3/5 of their slaves toward representation, northern states dominated the House. In the Senate, where each state got two votes regardless of population, slaveholders had more sway. By focusing their efforts there, Van Buren and Calhoun were simply playing to their strengths. (To make matters worse for the administration, Calhoun was Adams's own vice president, having professed neutrality between the leading presidential contenders in 1824 only to come out against the president two years later.) Other opposition members were more blunt, using their coalition's southern strength as evidence of their credibility on what Thomas Hart Benton called "this black and mulatto question." The "States South of the Potomac," Benton continued, were ". . . united, sir, against this mission, solid as a wall of granite, some fissures about the edges excepted."[40]

Still, the charges of sectionalism were only partly fair. Van Buren wanted to win much more than the South; he wanted to realign the nation's entire political system around partisan allegiance rather than around sectional pride. As the fiery-haired New Yorker famously told the editor of the *Richmond Enquirer* just months after the Panama debates had subsided, he aspired to build a coalition between "the planters of the South and the plain Republicans of the North." Without such cross-regional affiliations, he warned, "prejudices between free and slave holding states will inevitably take their place." Even before the congressional session began, therefore, Van Buren and his allies plotted a combined attack. Though they sometimes differed on such critical issues as slavery, federal power, and states' rights, they worked hard to stick together. They visited each other's homes, dined with each other, and caucused together, forging common ground beyond their disdain for Adams. As the bombarded president wrote in his diary, "there have been great exertions made to combine all the Elements of opposition against this measure."[41]

It would take an expansive set of issues—ones that far transcended slavery—to build that kind of nationwide coalition. The Missouri crisis had made that terribly clear: slavery alone was too divisive to be Congress's sole focus, for it would undermine the broad partisan movement that would-be Democrats sought to build. Accordingly, when John Randolph proposed a resolution whose sole purpose was to request more information about "Negro slavery" in South America, fellow opposition southerner Robert Hayne convinced him to table the measure, saying it was a subject he was "reluctant to touch." But in his ensuing speech on the Panama mission more generally, Hayne discussed slavery at length, as one issue among many. That was precisely Panama's attraction: from religious pluralism, slavery, and small government to disdain for moralistic meddlers, the mission offered an appealing assemblage of issues that would, over the next several decades, help to cobble the Democratic faithful together across sectional lines.[42]

It certainly helped that opposition southerners' appeals to slavery could be smoothed for northern audiences, the rougher edges shaved away until the pill became easier to swallow. Van Buren's own Panama speech celebrated small government and blasted the mission as "dazzling" in scope, thereby echoing and complementing the arguments of opposition slaveholders while avoiding the same determined focus on slavery. The handful of opposition northerners who did address slavery directly, meanwhile, staked out a careful middle ground. "I believe it to be a great political, and a great moral evil," Pennsylvania congressman James Buchanan said, but it was "an evil . . . without a remedy." Citing northerners' financial interest in slavery, the future president also emphasized that the Panama mission might stifle trade—itself a striking point, since most congressmen who spoke of commerce agreed with Adams that the Panama Congress would promote it. Buchanan begged to differ. Farmers in the "Middle, or grain-growing States" depended on trade with Cuban plantations, he reasoned, and if the Panama Congress "proclaimed liberty to the slave" in Cuba, then Pennsylvania farmers would lose their livelihoods as surely as Cuban planters would lose their lives.[43]

Other opposition spokesmen made overtly two-pronged appeals, packaging slavery differently for different regional audiences. "Freemen of the North!" the *United States' Telegraph* blazed. "[A]re you prepared to join either General Bolivar or Mr. Clay in a crusade against your brethren of the South and West? And, Freemen of the South! are you prepared to clamor for a mission, when the avowed object of some of its advocates is to effect . . . a . . . plan of 'Universal Emancipation?'" The *Telegraph* had been founded in Washington early in 1826 as the opposition's primary editorial mouthpiece. Southern whites, its editor argued, would not fight for a mission that had possible antislavery connotations; northern whites would not endorse a cause that white southerners so despised, one that might ultimately require white men in the United States to support foreigners of color. Slavery for southern whites, union for northern ones, small government for all: the different regional emphases, when spun into a broader web of issues, enabled an otherwise heterogeneous opposition to cohere. Sure enough, although resistance to the mission centered in the South, opponents' efforts to build a coalition across regional lines showed results. Maine's senators both voted against the mission, as did one from New Hampshire; conversely, Louisiana's senators supported the mission, and the Mid-Atlantic divided. A wall of granite, its "fissures about the edges" offset by reinforcements farther north.[44]

Slavery, then, was never the sole focus of the Panama debates, especially in the North. According to opposition southerners, however, it was intricately connected to the other issues at hand and thus an essential star in the rising Democratic constellation. The administration's vigorous view of federal power, its strong backing from northern reformers, its willingness to send delegates to an allegedly interracial and antislavery congress in Panama—such things could be woven into a satisfyingly coherent story, one whose concluding chapter might conceivably portray the federal government striking a blow against slavery with support from the Atlantic world's growing antislavery chorus. That story had meaning everywhere, but above all in the white South. As Virginia's John Floyd asked, in a question that linked the threat of social reform to the possibility of emancipation: "Why should we ... engage in this moon-struck project, which threatens, at no distant day, ... the whole of our Southern frontier?" "*The safety of the Southern portion of this Union,*" Georgia Senator John Berrien agreed, "*must not be sacrificed to a passion for diplomacy.*" Adams, Clay, and their supporters could say all they wanted about needing to ward off the abolitionist threat through engagement rather than isolation. But they now had to defend their commitment to slavery, and especially among those who looked askance at federal power and social reform, that alone rendered them suspect—as did the fact that one of the proposed ministers to Panama was John Sergeant of Pennsylvania, a sworn enemy of slavery.[45]

The mud in 1826 splattered all around Washington's freshly whitewashed postwar buildings. But—and this was no childish technicality—Adams's southern critics threw it first. They forced the issue, seized the oratorical opportunity, crossed the line toward racialized fear more extensively, more readily, and more reliably. The opposition's own John Holmes of Maine noted the risk of that strategy. "You have already said too much against emancipation," he warned southern senators; "By provoking a discussion you increase the evil you attempt to remedy." In subsequent years, with a national party line to tow, southern Democrats would indeed hesitate to discuss slavery so supportively and so openly, loath as they were to alienate the party's northern wing (which was itself more inspired by Democrats' commitment to laissez-faire government and economic opportunity for ordinary white men). But in 1826, southern opposition members were assertively pressing the point, revealing their rhetorical commitment to the country's increasingly anomalous status as a slaveholding, white man's republic.[46]

★ ★ ★

WORDS SPOKEN IN CONGRESS quickly spread to the rest of the country. Correspondents in the House and Senate galleries took notes until their hands hurt, then sent their observations home to local newspapers. Printers swung their presses into motion and published the hours-long orations in full and in part. Congressmen themselves, proud of their handiwork, mailed transcripts of their Panama speeches far and wide ("to the manifest abuse of the franking privilege," as one Missouri observer protested). The news traveled as fast as steamboats, stagecoaches, horses, and human muscles could carry it, until the nation was humming with talk of Panama—and, as it happened, with talk of the *talk* of Panama, as editors debated the language of white U.S. exceptionalism that opposition southerners were advancing.[47]

Ordinary voters had long helped to shape the contours of hemispheric policy debates. They were the chorus that had gradually nudged congressmen to vote for diplomatic recognition, the background noise that Monroe and his Cabinet heard as they deliberated what to do about the Holy Alliance. For over a decade, their toasts, songs, and cockades had led even the most skeptical of federal officials to go on the record wishing Latin Americans well. Ordinary folk left their mark once again in 1826: when Randolph and his allies began to publicly and systematically reject the Declaration's universalist ideals, they were really just giving voice to voters' preexisting prejudices about race relations at home, closing the gap between rhetoric and reality in an attempt at political gain. All the while, in their quest to found a new and nationwide partisan movement, opposition members were proactively reshaping public debate about inter-American relations. By organizing what was already there— the intolerance that had periodically manifested itself when rebels approached U.S. shores, or when rebels struggled and white U.S. onlookers wanted something to blame—opposition southerners endowed longstanding popular prejudice with the weight of electoral force, and the gravity of political sanction.

Congressmen's role in shaping popular discussions was most evident in the way that newspaper coverage unfolded over time. Before Congress began to consider the Panama question, in fact, not one editorial opponent of the mission seems to have invoked Spanish-American antislavery efforts as a reason for concern— even though reports that linked the Panama Congress to a possible Cuban invasion had circulated for almost a year. The *Richmond Enquirer* was one of the few newspapers to oppose the mission from the beginning, and it simply invoked constitutional scruples as well as George Washington's famed 1796 call for neutrality. A handful of writers did connect the Panama Congress to U.S. slavery, but all of them seemed to *support* the mission, saying it would enable the United States to dissuade the new republics from invading Cuba.[48]

And then the new session of Congress began, the "scene of wanton obduracy, of wild uproar, and tumultuous strife" (as one observer called it) laid before the nation to behold. Only then did southern opposition newspapers start to blast Panama's implications for U.S. slavery, which suggests that they were adopting the racialized arguments that had debuted in Washington. Just weeks after Congress assembled, for example, in a statement that tied concerns about slavery to concerns about visionary reformers, a contributor to the *Richmond Enquirer* noted that the "whole country south of the Pennsylvania line, and of the River Ohio, to the Gulph of Mexico . . . is opposed to this novel, if not dangerous scheme of international Diplomacy"; another correspondent openly hailed John Randolph's Senate speech as "a spicy synopsis of men and things as they are." From Charleston to New Orleans, much of the same; opposition editors and correspondents who hadn't previously made the connection suddenly followed like-minded congressmen in suggesting that Spanish Americans were republican imposters, inferior sorts of men whose efforts at self-government were doomed by their skin color. As a contributor to Washington's *United States' Telegraph* sarcastically put it in a statement that seemed almost consciously to channel John Randolph: U.S. delegates at Panama would have "the honor of fraternizing with the 'American States,'" and of associating "with their inhabitants of every shade—white, black, yellow, copper, and brown."[49]

Journalists on all sides immediately grasped the enormity of what was happening. "[R]eaders have left all other matter to peruse" Randolph's speech, the *Baltimore Gazette* observed; ". . . he has set all around him, friends and foes, on fire with angry argument." As the opposition's *United States' Telegraph* realized, Randolph had opened the floodgates. "As well might Mr. Clay attempt to stay the flowing of the tide, as to arrest the current of popular opinion" that the Virginia senator had unleashed. For their part, Adams's journalistic supporters seemed stunned at the transformation in congressmen's language and all that it implied. As the editor of Boston's *North American Review* (and one of the nation's best-informed inter-American advocates) privately confessed: "Mr. Randolph's [speech] opens a ground of opposition, which I believe was hardly anticipated in any part of the country."[50]

Sure enough, Randolph's oration—the most widely reprinted speech of the entire controversy—horrified Adams's allies. "It was a speech of a madman," one Washington correspondent wrote to a Providence paper, his words quickly reappearing throughout New England; Randolph had "conjured up *black* and hideous phantoms, with flat noses, thick lips, and fizly hair, and then tilted at them, with desperate and relentless fury." Readers seemed equally taken aback. An editor in Salem, Massachusetts, had initially tried to conserve column space by summarizing Randolph's two-hour disquisition rather than printing it entire. But complaints flowed in from readers who were certain that the editor had exaggerated Randolph's position to the point of absurdity. The editor ended up printing the speech in full; "readers will at once perceive," he said, "that if the speech *has been* misrepresented . . . , it was in Mr. R.'s favor." Randolph's oration, he added, was "strange gallimaufry," "erratic," "a sort of Ostrich race over the field of politics, a half-running, half-flying course." Even Martin Van Buren's own editorial mouthpiece, the *Albany Argus*, gently distanced itself from Randolph by parenthetically noting that "his manner is not easily defended."[51]

Randolph's speech surprised several southern newspapermen as well. A "crude, [distra?]cted talk," an administration editor in central North Carolina called it; "[w]e [have be?]en astonished that the enlightened [men] of Virginia should send a man of his [charact?]er to represent her." Newspapers in Kentucky and Mississippi—the former inclined toward the administration, the latter otherwise against it— concurred that Randolph was "a mere grumbletonian and a snarling misanthrope." In border-state Baltimore, Hezekiah Niles (who supported the mission but purported to remain above the partisan fray) asked whether the United States was ready to "arrest the march of millions in the south to freedom? Does any one wish it, because some of the people are of 'mixed blood' . . . ?"[52]

Older, universalist talk of equality died hard, to be sure. For fifty years, it had helped people throughout the country explain who they were; it was not the kind of thing that could be easily discarded. But in 1826, the universalist language suffered a blow. A decade before, the scattered writers who had publicly criticized South American race relations were themselves criticized; now, at least in slave states, the racialized barbs were just as likely to meet with proud acclamation. Whatever their stance, newspapermen understood that the Panama debates probed at the core of U.S. identity, raising a question that had emerged periodically before but seldom at the behest of congressional slaveholders themselves: toward what ideals would people in the United States aspire? Would they strive toward freedom and equality for all men, or just for white men? The Panama dispute, according to Benjamin Lundy, had proven that opposition slaveholders were interested primarily in the latter. "Not being able to reconcile the assertion in our declaration of independence, 'that man is created free,' with the existence of slavery here, and elsewhere," Lundy charged in his *Genius of Universal Emancipation*, men like Randolph "boldly den[y] the truth of the maxim itself." "Such is the republicanism of slavites!" Lundy wrote a month later. "They are not only opposed to the personal liberty of all people but themselves, but they are also opposed to political liberty [in Cuba], whenever that political liberty is likely to promote the personal liberty of the blacks." Much the same could have been said of the administration, of course, but the opposition "slavites" had started it. They had provoked and then pushed the racialized line of debate, presumably because they intended to be its main beneficiaries. Lundy—who surely also noted their disdain for idealistic reformers like himself—held them ensuingly accountable.[53]

The *Genius* had been something of an outlier in the early 1820s, when few other periodicals dwelled on what Spanish-American antislavery efforts might suggest for the United States. As Congress's growing partisanship forced editors to grapple more seriously with such questions, though, many came out on Lundy's side. By ending slavery, New York's *Observer* remarked, Spanish Americans "have gone beyond us. They have acted upon principles which we only profess. Under these circumstances the people of the North will never consent that our government should treat their offers of amity [at Panama] with cold disdain." Using similar logic, Providence's pro-administration *Literary Cadet* questioned the republican credentials of Adams's opponents. "Professing to be the champion of liberty, and the advocate of universal emancipation," the editor wrote, Thomas Hart Benton "has by the course pursued in opposition to the Congress of Panama proved his previous declarations and professions insincere, and himself unworthy of the confidence of all that are truly republican in their principles." Questions about hemispheric engagement, as these writers saw it, had exposed opposition members' flawed republicanism.[54]

Although Adams's legislative allies declined to challenge the new terms of debate, his editorial allies displayed less caution— especially in the North. Meanwhile, and above all in southern states, opposition editors often accepted and even began to endorse the racialized rhetoric. Whatever stance they took, newspapers were spreading that rhetoric all over the country, and news arriving from South America over the next several months would only seem to confirm the opposition's skepticism.

★ ★ ★

ASIDE FROM ADAMS, Clay, and Bolívar himself, few people had higher hopes for the Panama Congress than Jared Sparks, and few were more cultured or better connected. Handsome and hirsute, with big brown eyes and a Roman nose, the thirty-seven-year-old Sparks embodied high-brow Boston. He was a Harvard graduate, a Unitarian minister, former chaplain to the House of Representatives, and, since 1823, editor of the nation's premier literary magazine, the prestigious *North American Review*.[55]

Sparks's predecessor at the *Review*, the Federalist philhellene

Edward Everett, had been skeptical of Latin Americans' abilities. Sparks was more optimistic, and he made it his personal mission to encourage hemispheric brotherhood through the pages of the *Review*. Proficient in Spanish, he corresponded with some of Latin America's leading lights, and he predicted in a letter to Colombia's foreign minister that the "Congress of Panamá is the greatest event in history, it should be hailed with enthusiasm by Americans in every clime, & unite them in a bond of sympathy and action, which no power of time or of accident shall dissolve." Henry Clay couldn't have said it better himself.[56]

Then the bad news started to arrive, unremittingly and, eventually, incontrovertibly, floating into Boston Harbor throughout the second half of 1826. The first blow was the Panama Congress itself, a fiasco for nearly everyone involved. Although the Senate finally approved a watered-down version of the mission in early May, the opposition's stalling tactics had effectively delayed the final vote until Central America's so-called "sickly season" had begun. One of the ministers, Richard Anderson of Kentucky (who also served as the U.S. envoy to Colombia), caught a fever en route while his steamboat sat beached on a Colombian sandbar; he passed away in Cartagena, before he ever made it to the Isthmus. The other minister, antislavery champion John Sergeant, waited for the season to pass. By that time, the Panama Congress had already adjourned, having lasted just three weeks instead of the anticipated two months. Bolivia's delegates didn't make it on time either; Argentina and Chile didn't even bother to try (nor did Brazil, which had been invited despite Bolívar's original Hispanophone vision). The men who did show up were worried about illness and riven by mutual distrust, their anxiety and irritation heightened by the oppressive tropical heat. They left the monastery meeting place as soon as they could, with very little achieved.[57]

Taken alone, what happened in Panama could theoretically have confirmed either the administration or the opposition. Adams and

Clay might have noted that Britain's observer at Panama managed to promote British commercial interests at the direct expense of the United States. The nation had missed an opportunity to counter British influence in the Americas, partly because opposition southerners had wanted to defend U.S. slavery from what turned out to be a minimal threat: the Panama Congress hadn't even come close to invading Cuba or recognizing Haiti. For their part, opposition members could point to the Panama Congress's overall incompetence. It wasn't just that the delegates declined to invade Cuba; it was that (other than consorting with Britain's observer) they didn't accomplish much of anything. Bolívar himself was the first to admit failure, grumbling that the Congress's "power will be a shadow and its decrees mere advice, no more." Sparks's heart sank when he heard. Far from "the greatest event in history," he now declared the Panama Congress "a miserable farce unworthy of a line in history." "Freedom will one day sit quietly down in South America and rule the land in peace," he sighed, "but I fear that day is more distant than I once thought." Sparks was a minister, a man predisposed to cultivate hope, but even he was losing faith.[58]

Sparks's high hopes for the Panama Congress looked about as misplaced as John Randolph's fears over how the Congress would threaten U.S. slavery. But the news reports didn't stop at Panama, and they gradually seemed to reinforce Randolph's account of Latin American ineptitude and otherness. Over the past year, while plans for the Panama Congress were still underway, Bolívar had poured his heart and soul into writing a constitution for the new nation of Bolivia. The result was shocking, not just to people in the United States but to many in Spanish America, too. The new nation would bear far more than Bolívar's name: it would bear his heavy political imprint. Bolivia's presidents would serve for life, with the right to handpick their successors. Worse still, Bolívar wanted all of northern South America to adopt similarly centralized constitutions; elections, he declared, were the "great scourge of republics."[59]

In the meantime, just as Bolívar was preaching the virtues of centralization, centrifugal forces were threatening to tear Colombia apart. On April 30 of 1826, José Antonio Páez, erstwhile leader of the famous *pardo* plainsmen and recently the supreme chief of all Venezuela, effectively declared Venezuela to be in rebellion against the Colombian union of which it had been a part. Bolívar tried to allay the conflict by offering amnesty to the rebels early in 1827. That only drew attacks from the other direction, as supporters of the government in Bogotá argued that the Venezuelan conspirators needed to be punished. Bolívar could not contain the separatism. By 1830, Ecuador and Venezuela had permanently severed ties with Colombia, and Bolívar's sprawling republic fell to pieces before his very eyes. "America is ungovernable," an unreservedly morose Bolívar rasped from his deathbed that year; "he who serves a revolution plows the sea."[60]

U.S. newspapers closely monitored all of these disillusioning events, not to mention nearly simultaneous emergencies in Chile and the Río de la Plata basin. For a U.S. audience that prided itself on stability, prosperity, and peaceful transfers of executive power, none of the news did much to buoy Latin Americans' reputations, especially after the Panama debacle (which hadn't caused the ensuing political turmoil abroad but which certainly added to a growing sense of disenchantment at home). That Bolívar "should be left to yield to temptation and sacrifice his true and lasting glory at the idol of power is not unnatural," editors in Maine resignedly reflected; a "continued exercise of power begets a love of it." "The South American Washington," Philadelphia's *National Gazette* mordantly remarked, "... is expressly recognized as a *Dictator*."[61]

The new nations' woes were not just highly publicized in the United States; they were also highly politicized. The Adams administration had so closely associated itself with Bolívar and the Panama mission that the bad news was a major political liability. Opposition newspapers responded with one common refrain: *we told you so*. As a Louisiana critic smugly noted, the "unsettled state of the South American governments has always operated with us, as a powerful argument against the Panama Mission."[62]

Worse still for Adams and Clay, Bolívar had passingly cited the United States as one of his models for the most controversial clause of the Bolivian constitution—the one that empowered presidents to choose their own successors. As Bolívar pointed out, U.S. presidents had the authority to appoint secretaries of state, whose posts had traditionally functioned as presidential stepping-stones. Desperate to create a strong executive who could hold Bolivia together, Bolívar rather liked the idea. So he took the unwritten U.S. precedent and enshrined it in Bolivian constitutional law. Adams must have winced when he learned it, given his hugely controversial appointment of Henry Clay. Sure enough, opposition newspapers were happy to make the connection. "Mr. Clay may admire this reasoning of the Liberator," the *Richmond Enquirer* scoffed, "but . . . to suffer a Chief Magistrate to dictate his successor, is one of those *legitimate* ideas, against which the theory of a Republic revolts."[63]

Adams supporters countered that the opposition was politicizing South America's sorry struggles in an attempt to profit. "[I]t forms a part of the first object of the opposition," one Providence editor wrote, "to raise a hue and cry against BOLIVAR and every thing that relates to South-America, and if they can bring the Panama Mission into disrepute, with the people, they are well assured that an incision will be made into the main artery of the administration." The editor vehemently denied what he termed "the grossest falsehoods," the "thousand silly and contemptible tales" spread about Bolívar in recent months—that he had personally authored the Bolivian constitution, and that he was involved with a married woman in Peru. Once the charges were proven true, they reflected poorly not only on Bolívar, but also on U.S. onlookers who had put their faith in him. Spanish-American politics were U.S. politics, too. As legislators and journalists fought over the meaning of that hemispheric political interplay, so did ordinary people throughout the country, who read and talked and gossiped about the scenes that were unfolding around them.[64]

* * *

IN MID-MARCH OF 1826, someone in Kentucky sent a letter to Washington's *United States' Telegraph*. "I have not conversed with five intelligent persons," the anonymous correspondent said, "in the whole range of my acquaintance, who do not decidedly condemn the proposition" on Panama. "[E]ven . . . the ordinary farmers," he added, seemed to understand that the mission imperiled the nation's historic neutrality, and, what was more: "Mr. Randolph's views in relation to Cuba, universal emancipation, the variously and sable-shaded Guatemaleans, &c. &c. have excited no little interest." The letter was clearly biased, meant to serve as evidence that the good people of Kentucky—Clay's own constituents, even!—opposed the administration. Still, it raises a critical question. What did ordinary voters think about the Panama mission—and, more important, what did they think about the revised national narrative that opposition southerners were promoting?[65]

One of the first things to change amid the Panama uproar was that ordinary people started paying attention to formal matters of inter-American diplomacy. Fourth of July toasts that explicitly addressed hemispheric policy questions had been almost nonexistent over the previous decade, but as soon as diplomacy got tangled up in partisan politics—and thus in broader issues of federal power, religion, race, and social reform—voters snapped to attention. Even in the tiniest of villages, where everyone knew everyone, the Panama mission became a topic of angry confrontation. When, in the wake of Congress's debates, Adams supporters in Harlingen, New Jersey, organized a public meeting in support of the mission, local Jackson supporters responded with an anti-Panama meeting. But Panama supporters flooded that gathering as well and forced through a series of resolutions on

behalf of Adams. That local drama played out almost simultaneously at July Fourth festivities throughout the country in 1826,
as people variously praised or condemned the mission; in the
pages of the *Richmond Enquirer*, over a quarter of Virginia celebrations included toasts against it. Meanwhile, and for the rest
of the year, newspapermen from New Orleans and Richmond to
New Hampshire and Newport used Panama as a political litmus
test, urging voters to pick candidates who had taken one stance or
another on U.S. attendance there. Opposition leaders were right:
the Panama mission was a first-rate political wedge.[66]

Along with the surge in popular diplomatic interest came a slip
in hemispheric excitement. From 1816 to 1825, about 55 percent of
July Fourth parties had included toasts to Latin America; in 1825,
the figure stood at 58 percent. On the next Fourth, two months
after the Panama debates ended, the number of toasts to Latin
American independence fell just slightly, to 54 percent (see the
Appendix). But if the enthusiasm hadn't disappeared, the harmony
had. Where previous toasts regarding Latin America had been
almost uniformly positive, more toasts in 1826 were ambivalent,
even critical. Baltimoreans raised their glasses to protest Páez's
rebellion against Colombia; Virginians said that South Americans,
having defeated Spain, still had to "conquer *themselves*, and establish the freedom of faith and of opinions." Over the next few years,
that ambivalence sank into apathy. In 1827, only 18 percent of parties
included toasts to Latin America; in 1828, only 9 percent did; and
by 1829, there was just one southward-looking toast in the entire
set. The year 1826, in short, marked the beginning of the end for
the popular enthusiasm, an inflection point, the close of a decade of
near-consensus on behalf of Latin America's insurgents.[67]

Naming practices changed, too. The Bolivar baby boom of the
mid-1820s turned out to be more of a peak than a plateau, as use of
the name crested in 1826 and then markedly dwindled; by 1830, the
number of Bolivar newborns had diminished by 34 percent. The

baby names declined more gradually than the toasts did, perhaps because parents who named their sons Bolivar were uniquely ardent supporters whose commitment was slower to erode. In any case, the evidence seems to fit together. By politicizing Latin America, opposition members had introduced unprecedented levels of controversy to a topic that had previously enjoyed widespread popular accord. The excitement might have endured anyway if subsequent developments in Latin America had seemed more promising; it wasn't until 1827 that the toasts and baby names really plummeted, after all. If the tumult in Congress rendered the enthusiasm vulnerable, however, the tumult in Latin America buried it. People in the United States were beginning to see their southern neighbors less as family than as foreigners; as Virginia Representative William Rives put it, Latin Americans were simply "an imaginary kindred." It was what Bolívar had been saying all along.[68]

As a perfect storm of bad publicity for Latin America rained down on the United States, therefore, the Panama debates combined with South American instability to dampen the popular fervor. But the rain fell to different effect in different places. In the decade that preceded the Panama debates, 56 percent of white Bolivar babies were born in slave states. Given that newspapers and legislative debates in this period usually emphasized republican principles over racial differences, Bolívar's southern appeal was not especially remarkable. But in the years following the Panama debates, the pattern subtly reversed itself. From 1827 to 1830, a majority of white Bolivar babies—56 percent—were born in free states. Only 44 percent came from slave states. Although Bolívar's reputation suffered everywhere, with white Bolivar babies increasingly rare throughout the country, white southerners seemed more unsettled. While the data set is too small to say for sure, that tentative regional shift might indicate an additional, more political explanation for the disillusionment, one that goes beyond South America's volatility, and beyond the fact that South

Americans were turning from the poetic ardor of revolution to the more prosaic process of nation-building. Such things were probably primary factors in subduing the enthusiasm nationwide, but the Panama debates in particular may have seeded doubts that found especially fertile ground in the South. Latin America's ensuing woes would then have helped those doubts germinate and take root.[69]

While the small number of Bolivar babies renders these findings suggestive rather than conclusive, a similar, corroborative transformation was simultaneously emerging in July Fourth reports. Hemispheric toasts in Virginia fell by 30 percent in 1826, at least as the *Richmond Enquirer* recorded them, but they showed negligible change in Pennsylvania, and they ticked upward in Adams's own Massachusetts. Much of that transition stemmed from editorial bias—the *Enquirer* was a leader of the opposition and printed mainly opposition toasts, while the Pennsylvania and Massachusetts papers were overwhelmingly administration supporters. The pattern probably also reflected a real difference in partisan support from region to region, as electoral politics and congressional voting patterns attested most of all. Opposition members had used the Panama mission to create a tangled web of issues that stretched throughout the nation but which seemed to hold special appeal in slave states. Perhaps because preventing the Panama mission had come to concern opposition leaders less than articulating their coalition's "cherished principles," men like Van Buren seemed pleased enough with the results. Democrats continued to employ a potent and regionally inflected blend of small government, racialized nationalism, and disdain for social reform throughout the antebellum era and beyond (even as they gradually added other, economic issues into the mix to attract working white men in the North).[70]

There are several caveats to issue here. As in Congress, the move toward racialized exceptionalism remained gradual and partial, a subtle shift rather than an immediate transformation; indeed, none of the 1826 anti-Panama toasts overtly echoed the opposition's racial-ized attacks. For years, white southerners continued to name their babies and raise their glasses in honor of Latin American freedom. Racial politics remained complicated and contested even within the South, and Randolph himself never commanded anything close to unanimity. In 1827, Virginia's legislature refused him another term by the narrowest of margins, swayed as it was by administration allies and by opposition members who found his conduct erratic and unseemly. ("The Senate of the United States," a Shenandoah Valley representative said, "had been the most august and dignified body in the world until Mr. Randolph was elected to it.")[71]

Still, the pattern seems clear enough. Reinforced by develop-ments abroad, the Panama debates helped to end over a decade of widespread accord on behalf of Latin America. That accord shat-tered nationwide, but perhaps more quickly in the South, and the opposition's racialized narrative helps to explain why. Sure enough, just months after Virginia legislators excused Randolph from the Senate, voters elected him to the House in a landslide. Of the other opposition southerners who deployed the racialized rhetoric and subsequently stood for midterm reelection, most and perhaps all won, including Thomas Hart Benton, James Hamilton, and John Floyd. Opposition leaders who hoped to pull white southerners into a broader political movement were slowly gaining ground.[72]

Randolph, Benton, and their allies had not created the racialized strain of nationalism out of thin air. They didn't single-handedly slay the inter-American ardor, which persisted for months and even years, and they certainly didn't slay the universalism, which found enduring and often fierce advocates over ensuing decades. In bringing slavery from the background of inter-American relations to the foreground, however, they brought a new level of acrimony to a cause that had long commanded sweeping support. Rather than feeling guilty about questioning the nation's founding ideals, slaveholders could feel increasingly justified in their exalted status; the newer standard glorified the prejudices that many had felt all along. As slavery swept into the Southwest, and as antislavery activists simultaneously insisted that the nation's founding rhetoric carried an abolitionist imperative, that rhetoric was increasingly hard for white southerners to make practical sense of. Something had to give, and—as had happened passingly before when Spanish-American antislavery took center stage—the rhetoric gave way first. In their congressmen's speeches, many white southerners found a more affirming reflection of themselves, a more reassuring assertion of their interests—especially when the racialized narrative was fused with partisan warnings about big government and social "improvement."

There was, to be sure, a gap between rhetoric and reality in northern states as well, one that was in many ways growing. Increasingly after 1815, northern mills wove southern cotton into clothes for southern slaves, and the ensuing profits paid for roads and schools and factories across New England and beyond; so did profits from the Cuba trade, which had grown so enormous that the two region's economies were (as Congressman Buchanan said) effectively interdependent by the mid-1820s. All the while, northern states were chipping systematically away at free black people's civic and political rights, and the opposition's rhetoric may have helped white northerners explain and justify these trends; in subsequent decades, that was often what happened, as immigrants and wage laborers (who flocked disproportionately to the Democrats) claimed whiteness as a way of asserting superiority over black people. In 1826, however, opposition northerners' emphasis on other aspects of the Panama mission—combined with the rough data on toasts and baby names, as well as with the opposition's sustained strength in slaveholding states—suggests that northern voters' need for such an explanation remained less urgent than southerners'. "No alarm is expressed," a pro-administration Cincinnati editor reassured Henry Clay; "none is felt—no mischief or danger is apprehended—The tocksin is sounded in vain."[73]

Although the rhetoric of white U.S. superiority in 1826 emerged first among opposition southerners, it had national implications. Over the next several years, opposition southerners became Democratic southerners, core members of a party that dominated federal politics for much of the antebellum era. Their argument about Latin American emancipation—that the United States was the white, moderate, and prosperous exception to a hemisphere bursting with incompetent, aggressive, antislavery radicals—at once asserted and tightened the already-growing link between whiteness and political power at home, and it seemed to strike a chord.

★ ★ ★

FOR A WHILE, black observers' hemispherically inflected activism continued apace. John Russwurm—the black Bowdoin graduate and cofounder of *Freedom's Journal*—reported on Latin America in a majority of the paper's issues during its founding year of 1827, and David Walker's electrifying *Appeal to the Coloured Citizens of the World* looked to similarly hemispheric vistas two years later. But *Freedom's Journal* folded in 1829, and Walker died abruptly in 1830, still a young man of thirty-four.

By the 1830s, black observers' interest in independent Latin America was waning even as their universalist convictions persisted. In an 1832 speech to the African American Female Intelligence Society of America, Boston abolitionist Maria Stewart urged listeners to find patriotic and virtuous role models in "the suffering Greeks," "the French in the late [1830] revolution," "the Haytians," "the Poles," and "even the wild Indians of the forest." She said nothing about Latin Americans—she was urging her listeners to solidarity, after all, and Latin America in the early 1830s was riddled with political and social strife.[74]

Martin Delany was the exception who proved the rule. Young, upwardly mobile, and, as one acquaintance wrote, "black as jet," Delany didn't lose faith in Spanish America. But by 1835, he was starting to question his faith in the United States. Delany had walked from small-town Pennsylvania to a new home in Pittsburgh four years earlier, determined to make a name for himself in the three-river iron city. A doer and a joiner, he packed his days with a medical apprenticeship and a crowded schedule of literary and social reform meetings. Delany never entirely gave up on his native country—he admired its ideals, spent countless hours working so that the nation might live up to them. But as the doors of opportunity for black people slammed shut in the 1830s with growing force and frequency, he couldn't help but conclude that the United States was giving up on him.[75]

Delany was hardly the first to wonder about leaving. Over the past two decades, several thousand black people (including Russwurm himself) had sailed for Liberia; even more tried their luck in Haiti. Delany had a different destination in mind, and in 1835 he encouraged the other young black men in his literary society to consider "the subject," he later recalled, "of Mexican, California, and South American Emigration." It didn't go well. The others "hooted at" him; it was too far, too hot, they protested. Above all, most black people of the time agreed, the United States was home, and it was better to fight for the nation's ideals than to leave, whether the destination was Spanish America or Liberia or anywhere else. Delany stood firm, and some stood with him; by 1852, he approvingly reported that "in almost every town, where there is any intelligence among them, there are some *colored persons* of both sexes, who are studying the Spanish language" in hopes of moving. The project never really took off, though, and by 1858 even Delany had turned his emigrationist energies to West Africa's Niger Valley.[76]

William Lloyd Garrison's inter-American ardor was also diminishing. In 1831, radicalized by conversations with black associates, he moved into a spartanly furnished Boston office with what family and friends later described as "dingy walls," ink-splattered windows, and a cuddly stray cat, all in order to start his own abolitionist newspaper. Though operated on a shoestring—Garrison and his partners used secondhand type and subsisted "chiefly upon bread and milk" from a bakery across the street—the *Liberator* quickly became the nation's most influential antislavery newspaper, its uncompromisingly immediatist approach to abolition attracting even more attention (and even more infamy) than Lundy's more gradualist *Genius of Universal Emancipation*. In contrast to his earlier writings as a teenaged Newburyport apprentice, Garrison's columns of the 1830s and beyond devoted only sporadic attention to Latin America, aside from a growing stream of articles on Texas and Mexico. Even Lundy published fewer articles on South America as the 1830s wore on.[77]

Still, abolitionists never entirely forgot Latin America's promise as an argument for change. In her trailblazing 1833 book, Lydia Maria Child—inspired partly by conversations with the *pardo* Brazilian revolutionary Emiliano Mundrucu—reasoned that if South Americans were really as backward as everybody then seemed to believe, "it is a still greater disgrace to us to be outdone in liberality and consistent republicanism by men so much less enlightened than ourselves." Even amid the turmoil of the Civil War, as Americans came to fight over whether the United States would be a free, multiracial republic, no less a luminary than Frederick Douglass found proof and inspiration far to the south. "[I]n Mexico, Central America and South America," he optimistically reminded his readers, "many distinct races live peaceably together in the enjoyment of equal rights." All the while, the black Bolivar babies of the mid-1820s grew into men, their names perhaps remaining as enduring glimpses of what an American nation might be—or yet become.[78]

★ ★ ★

THE TIMING OF THE Panama debates stemmed strictly from military and political circumstances in Spanish America. It was a fitting coincidence that the dispute unfolded in precisely the same year that the United States was celebrating its "national jubilee"—the fiftieth anniversary, in other words, of the signing of the Declaration. People throughout the nation were self-consciously reflecting on what they interpreted as the eclipse of an era, one most movingly embodied in the simultaneous passing of Thomas Jefferson and the elder John Adams on July Fourth of that very year. The men who had launched the first American revolution were moving on, leaving their quarreling descendants to chart an unknown future.[79]

Perhaps that national ethos of revolutionary soul-searching offers a further explanation of why U.S. audiences were so taken with the Panama debates. A half-century after white U.S. rebels had audaciously asserted the universal rights of man, many of their children and grandchildren began to recast that narrative while using Latin Americans as blackened and radicalized foils. By redefining the other American revolutions, rising southern Democrats sought to redefine the United States. Although the narrative of white U.S. superiority that resulted did not take hold everywhere, it did gain a powerful foothold, one that grew over subsequent decades and never quite disappeared.

DESTINED BY PROVIDENCE

M ANUEL DE MIER Y TERÁN killed himself on July 3, 1832. Arising early, he donned his finest military uniform, walked to an old, roofless church in eastern Mexico, and threw his body into his sword. He was only forty-three.

A famed intellectual, engineer, and brigadier general, Mier y Terán had been seen as a future Mexican presidential contender, and he pointed to Texas as his greatest source of anguish. It was a place that had haunted him for years, ever since he had traveled there to ensure that the region remained in Mexico's possession. His reports home read like an endless cascade of warnings and, increasingly, despair. In 1828: "the incoming stream of new settlers is unceasing"; "Texas could throw the whole nation [of Mexico] into revolution." In 1829: The United States was "the most avid nation in the world. The North Americans have conquered whatever territory adjoins them." In 1831: "There is no physical force that can stop the entrance of the norteamericanos." And then, in the very last line of his suicide note: *¿En qué parará Texas?* What will become of Texas? He repeated the question three other times throughout the letter. The next morning, he woke up and walked deliberately to his own death.[1]

Had Mier y Terán survived his own despair, Texas's fate would

only have deepened his sorrows. In 1836, Texas declared independence from the rest of Mexico. Nine years later, it became part of
the United States, to be followed in 1848 by much of present-day
New Mexico, California, Arizona, Nevada, Utah, and parts of Col-
orado and Wyoming. Such a swift and sweeping transfer of territory had seemed like a far-fetched idea in the 1810s and early 1820s,
a figment of policymakers' and squatters' wildest imaginations. But
by 1832, Mier y Terán saw the loss of Texas, at least, as imminent.

To understand what happened, it is necessary to begin with the
age of American revolutions, when few hemispheric enthusiasts
thought very much about Mexico at all, except for those who lived
nearby. Newspapers episodically hailed Mexico's multiracial rebels
with much the same kind of optimism that they used in describing
South Americans, but the rural republicans who struggled immediately south of the border seemed less inspiring than their more
victorious counterparts farther south. People almost never toasted
Mexico at July Fourth celebrations; musicians rarely wrote odes in
its honor; parents seldom named their sons for its generals. Texas,
a frontier province on the margins of Mexico's independence struggle, received still less attention in the popular festivities, its 2,500
white and mestizo residents overwhelmed by the broader region's
roughly 25,000 Comanches and other native people.[2]

The popular ambivalence found its parallel in federal policy,
when, in the Transcontinental Treaty vote of 1819, U.S. senators
unanimously abandoned claims to Texas in return for Florida and
a strengthened claim to what is now the Pacific Northwest. In 1821,
after Spain had finally approved the agreement as well, the Senate
re-ratified the treaty with just four dissenting votes; because the
issue arose around the same time as the Missouri crisis, most policymakers were reluctant to acquire any more would-be slave states.
"[T]he further acquisition, of territory, to the West & South,
involves difficulties, of an internal nature, which menace the union
itself," President Monroe ominously warned Thomas Jefferson in

1820. ". . . Having securd [sic] the Mississippi, . . . and erected States there, ought we not to be satisfied . . . ?" Although House Speaker Henry Clay protested the treaty's geographic renunciation, a vast majority of legislators agreed that Texas was not the nation's most pressing concern; it could, the aye votes suggested, be attended to in time.[3]

That time, as it turned out, came quickly, triggered in 1821 by an event so seemingly innocuous that its importance became obvious only years later, when it seemed too late to stop what was already happening. Hoping that foreign settlers might strengthen Texas's stagnant economy and fend off the government's Comanche, Apache, and other native rivals, Spanish officials granted a substantial tract of eastern Texas land to a U.S. citizen named Moses Austin, who promised to bring 300 families along with him. Austin died shortly thereafter, just as Mexico was declaring independence from Spain, but his son Stephen inherited the title and went on to become the era's most successful *empresario*, or immigration agent. As other *empresarios* joined in, migration soared. By 1830, more than 7,000 white U.S. settlers had moved to Texas. Six years later, nearly 35,000 white U.S. immigrants and black U.S. slaves lived there, outnumbering native-born *tejanos* by a factor of ten. Nor was Texas alone: during the 1820s, trade along the Santa Fe Trail (which ran between Missouri and New Mexico) doubled every few years. So much specie streamed into the United States that by the early 1830s, the Mexican silver peso had become Missouri's de facto currency.[4]

This was not what authorities in Mexico City had wanted. Moderate, guided development had been the goal, but exponential growth rates were politically uncontrollable and culturally overpowering. Although some newcomers married local *tejano* women and partnered with *tejano* businessmen, most declined to assimilate. They did not learn Spanish. They did not embrace Catholicism. They brought their slaves, thousands of them, even though Mexican laws frowned upon slavery, and even though U.S. laws forbade citizens from exporting slaves abroad. "[T]he colonists in Texas will not be Mexicans more than in name," Mexico's minister in the United States feared. Fully aware of the United States' expansionist history in Florida, Baton Rouge, and elsewhere, Mexico City officials worried that the influx of U.S. immigrants imperiled the republic. "Where others send invading armies," Mexico's secretary of state warned around 1830, ". . . [the North Americans] send their colonists." Although Mexico tried periodically to slow and even halt U.S. immigration, it could not reverse the trend. As Stephen Austin saw it, U.S. immigration was an unstoppable force of nature. Trying "to dam out the North Americans," the bilingual bachelor remarked, would be like "trying to stop the Mississippi with a dam of straw."[5]

In one decade, Texas had gone from a remote periphery of the Spanish Empire to a central concern for people throughout Mexico and the United States alike. The change happened so fast that it was hard to make sense of. "Our citizens are incessent [sic] in their applications to me for information as to the propriety and advantage of settling upon the grant [in Texas]," Tennessee's governor told the U.S. minister to Mexico, Joel Roberts Poinsett, in 1825. "But not having any correct knowledge on the subject I am unable to satisfy their enquiries." In other words, interest in Texas surged quickly in southwestern states like Tennessee, but the region remained unfamiliar, even among those who most wanted to learn more. As the newly founded *Texas Gazette* put it in 1830: "Texas, which was hitherto unknown, even to the Mexicans themselves, is beginning to assume its proper station [in the] geography of America."[6]

Indeed, the "geography of America" really *was* changing as Texas stormed onto the scene, at least as many in the United States saw it. While South America had dominated hemispheric excitement in the 1810s and early 1820s, by the 1830s Texas's astonishing growth placed that region front and center. Even the Monroe Doctrine began to look different as U.S. immigrants piled up in Mexico and along the border. When, in 1845, President James K. Polk invoked Monroe's famous 1823 Message to Congress, he spoke "especially in reference to North America" rather than referring to both "American continents," as Monroe had done. "No future European colony or dominion," Polk announced with an eye on Mexico, "shall with our consent be planted or established on any part of the North American continent." South America's independence struggles had faded into history, one manifestation of an age of revolutions that, as U.S. onlookers increasingly saw it, had yielded two divergent Americas rather than one united hemisphere. The trend was especially stark in gazetteers and atlases. While U.S. mapmakers of the 1810s and 1820s had usually referred to the Western Hemisphere as one American continent, antebellum mapmakers increasingly portrayed the Western Hemisphere as two separate continents, North and South.[7]

Crucially, those narrowing geographic horizons brought new thematic concerns. While border conflicts between the United States and Spanish America had always simmered (and periodically boiled over), excitement about South American republicanism had overshadowed those disputes for well over a decade in popular nationalist discourse. But in the late 1820s, the rush into Texas suggested a different storyline, one that was less about the spread of republicanism to all men in all nations than it was about westward expansion and democratic equality for U.S. slaveholders. As population pressures mounted along the border, concrete confrontations over territory came to overwhelm the earlier and more abstract language of universalism.[8]

The expansionist crusade would have been powerful on its own. Coupled with the rhetoric of white U.S. superiority that the 1826 Panama debates had helped inflame, it created an explosive state of affairs. Democrats, sustained by many of their Whig opponents, continued to portray the United States as separate and superior, a happy anomaly in a hemisphere full of darker-skinned pretenders. Such language was only one step removed from the kind of full-blown national chauvinism that marked antebellum and expansionist appeals to "manifest destiny." In other words: because the United States was supposedly whiter, smarter, and more successful, its people could invade Mexico and take whatever they liked. The nation's extraordinary political, demographic, and economic successes (as most whites perceived them) came to serve as *prima facie* evidence of U.S. virtue. It was not so much that might made right; it was that right made right, with the country seemingly vindicated by its own apparent greatness. Many in the United States saw their nation in such self-justifying terms that territorial bounds no longer seemed to apply.[9]

The first major upheaval came in 1835 and 1836. Vowing to preserve their autonomy from a new, centralist government that had assumed power in Mexico City, white *anglos* in Texas—along with their native-born *tejano* allies, themselves frustrated at the lack of federal protection from Comanche raids—declared independence under a proslavery constitution. Then, their enslaved population increasing even faster than their free population, Texans expressed interest in joining the United States. The U.S. Senate resoundingly refused, concerned (among other things) that annexation would provoke Mexico and aggravate sectional tensions. But in 1845, expansionist and proslavery southern Democrats devised a new and Machiavellian strategy: they would annex Texas through a joint congressional resolution (which required only a simple majority in each house) rather than through a treaty (which would have required approval by two-thirds of the Senate). As John Quincy Adams—now an elderly U.S. congressman with trembling hands and sparse white hair—saw it, Democrats had turned the Constitution into "a menstruous rag." The resolution squeaked through, and within months, newly elected President James K. Polk provocatively dispatched U.S. troops to the Rio Grande—an area, everyone knew, that Mexico still claimed. War came in 1846, and in less than two years Mexico had formally ceded half of its territory to the United States. Polk was disappointed. He had wanted more.[10]

Simón Bolívar, who had passed away in 1830, had seen it coming. "There is at the head of this great continent," he warned his countrymen in 1822, "a very powerful country, very rich, very warlike, and capable of anything." For all their universalist rhetoric, white people in the United States had always wanted land, and they had usually been willing to fight for it—they invaded Canada, they fought native people, they strong-armed Spain and Mexico. That they did so even as they imagined themselves at the forefront of an international movement for freedom was not lost on Spanish-American onlookers, least of all Bolívar. The United States, Venezuela's Liberator famously warned, was "destined by Providence to plague America with miseries in the name of Liberty."[11]

Ironically, Bolívar's language—*destined by Providence*—foreshadowed expansionist talk of manifest destiny in the 1840s and 1850s. Perhaps we can locate seeds of antebellum territorial aggression in the casual arrogance displayed by U.S. onlookers of the 1810s and 1820s, individuals who blithely assumed that their own revolution was responsible for everything good that seemed to be happening overseas, and who concluded that what worked for the United States would work for everybody else. Maybe it was no coincidence that the nation's next major surge of international republican fervor arose in 1848, when self-styled "Young America" Democrats sang the glories of European revolutionaries while simultaneously advocating expansion into Mexico and Cuba. Republican revolutions in far-off countries seemed to fuel nationalist arrogance closer to home, and perhaps that arrogance helped to pave the way for antebellum conquest.[12]

Antebellum conquest, in turn, paved the way for still further war, as conflicts over the fate of the new West magnified controversies between North and South. The United States might swallow

Mexico, Ralph Waldo Emerson prophesied, "but it will be as the man swallows the arsenic, which brings him down in turn. Mexico will poison us." Once again, the United States' relationship with its southern neighbors was helping to crystallize debates over slavery and equality at home, though the immediate reality of territorial expansion increasingly dwarfed the more abstract and often imagined inter-American relationship of the early nineteenth century, and talk of kinship quieted. Some U.S. southerners started to identify with the slaveholders of colonial Cuba and monarchical Brazil, fancying themselves at the forefront of an inter-American master class. But even that was a sea change from the revolutionary age, when people throughout the nation had emphasized solidarity in republican rebellion rather than solidarity in slavery.[13]

That earlier age had raised questions about human equality in potent and lasting ways, as a hemisphere rooted in bondage resonated with cries for political and personal freedom. The cries persisted long after the revolutionary age had faded, so much so that when the Confederate states declared their independence from the United States in 1860 and 1861, their new vice president, Alexander Stephens, felt compelled to address the issue of equality head-on. Thomas Jefferson was wrong, the ninety-pound Georgian told a packed indoor audience one early spring evening in Savannah, as part of an attempt to rally voters around the new Confederate Constitution. "The prevailing ideas entertained by him and most of the leading statesmen at the time . . . were that the enslavement of the African was in violation of the laws of nature; that it was wrong in *principle*, socially, morally, and politically." The Confederacy, Stephens said, was finally getting it right. "Our . . . corner-stone rests," he proclaimed to waves of applause, "upon the great truth, that the negro is not equal to the white man; that slavery—subordination to the superior race—is his natural and normal condition," and those who still disagreed were "fanatics." As Confederate President Jefferson Davis told a crowd in Atlanta that same year, "For the future, we are to be embraced in the same moral category as Cuba and Brazil."[14]

It was a profound change from the universalist rhetoric of the earlier revolutionary era, as Stephens himself observed, though perhaps not a total one. Early-nineteenth-century observers who had emphasized republicanism over race were simultaneously downplaying race's importance, minimizing the scope of the sin, and glossing over the depth of the solutions that would be necessary for change. From Amelia Island to Panama, that universalist talk often proved passive and brittle, and that frailty made it easier for men like John Randolph and eventually Alexander Stephens to push further on behalf of bondage and inequity.

But if revolutionary-era ambivalence about race sowed seeds of antebellum discord, and if popular arrogance about U.S. greatness sowed seeds of antebellum expansion, those seeds could not have sprouted and grown without a specific combination of environmental factors that still had uncertain futures by the nation's fiftieth anniversary in 1826: domestic partisanship, Texas slavery, Indian removal, Comanche raids, Mexican and U.S. immigration, and sheer electoral contingency, to name but a few. When people in the United States celebrated their nation's virtues in the 1810s and early 1820s, they focused more on republicanism's spread to far-off corners of the Americas than on territorial aggrandizement closer to home. They toasted South America, not Mexico; they cheered Simón Bolívar, not filibusters; they focused on republicanism, not race. Before the storm over Panama, before the stream into Texas, and before expansion into Latin America helped spark the Civil War, the idea of a united republican hemisphere prevailed with such force that people in the United States welcomed their multiracial and Catholic neighbors as sister republics.

July Fourth Toasts to Hemispheric Independence, 1808–1830
Sum of all sampled celebrations (N = 895)

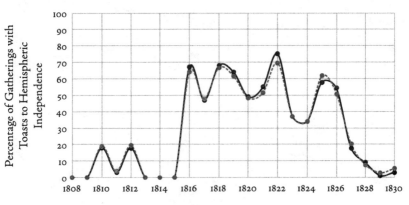

━●━ Annual Statistics (weighted for each state's adult white male population)
····●···· Annual Statistics (raw percentages, not weighted for population)

Sources: *Columbian Centinel* (Boston, 1808–1830); *Boston Patriot* (1809–1815); *Boston Patriot and Morning Advertiser* (1816); *Independent Chronicle and Boston Patriot* (1817); *Boston Patriot and Daily Chronicle* (1818); *Boston Patriot and Daily Mercantile Advertiser* (1819–1824); *Boston Patriot and Mercantile Advertiser* (1825–1829); *Aurora General Advertiser* (Philadelphia, 1808–1824); *Aurora and Franklin Gazette* (Philadelphia, 1825–1827); *Aurora and Pennsylvania Gazette* (Philadelphia, 1828–1829); *Democratic Press* (Philadelphia, 1823–1829); *Arkansas Gazette* (Arkansas Post and Little Rock, 1820–1830); *Edwardsville Spectator* (Illinois, 1819–1826); *Richmond Enquirer* (1808–1830); U.S. Department of State, *Census for 1820* (Washington, 1821).

ACKNOWLEDGMENTS

W RITING THIS BOOK has been a labor of love, not least
because I have been able to draw on such a supportive
and generous community of scholars, colleagues, and friends as I
researched and wrote it. As a graduate student at Yale, I was surrounded by faculty and students whose contagious enthusiasm for
history filled my six years in New Haven with the excitement of
discovery. John Demos, my coadviser, has been a model of how to
treat other people, whether seventeenth-century Massachusetts
farmers or twenty-first-century students. He encouraged me (and so
many others) to find my narrative voice. My other coadviser, Joanne
Freeman, nurtured this project from its earliest stages, pushing me
to think about big ideas and challenging me to consider the many
forms that political power can assume. Johnny Faragher welcomed
me into the westerners' lunch crowd even though I was always looking south. If Stuart Schwartz hadn't nudged me into his research
seminar on colonial Brazil, I would never have realized that the early
United States and South America were connected enough to merit
a full-length study; his thoughtfulness smoothed my way on trips to
Brazil and beyond. David Blight, Ed Rugemer, and, more recently,
Marcela Echeverri and Alejandra Dubcovsky served as critical inter-
locutors and readers; Seth Fein, Jay Gitlin, Gil Joseph, George Miles,

and Alyssa Mt. Pleasant, in their ways, helped me find my own way. Iris Kantor, visiting from the Universidade de São Paulo, informed my work on Pernambuco; the late Michael Kammen, visiting from Cornell, eagerly encouraged my interest in inter-American relations and spearheaded a spontaneous road trip to Vermont, complete with snacks for the ride. He is missed. I am also grateful for the camaraderie and insights of my fellow graduate students, not least Carmen Cordick de Cubero and Haydon Cherry (now my colleague at Northwestern), who both read an early draft of the dissertation.

After graduate school, I had the extraordinary good fortune to spend a postdoctoral fellowship year at the McNeil Center for Early American Studies, a hive of intellectual and interdisciplinary activity that proved timely and transformational as I began to turn my dissertation into a book. I am especially and eternally grateful to Dan Richter, whose early kindness enabled me to accept my dream job at Northwestern. It is truly a pleasure to come to work here every day—not just because my commute is a stunning fifteen-minute bike ride along Lake Michigan, but because when I arrive on campus I am surrounded by inquisitive and energetic students, can-do staff, and brilliant, encouraging colleagues who are also mentors and friends.

In Rio de Janeiro and Recife, Evaldo Cabral de Mello and Marcos Galindo Lima welcomed me into their homes and made sure that I found everything I needed in Brazil's archives. I am likewise grateful to Connie King at the Library Company of Philadelphia and Harriet Lightman at Northwestern, and to the many others who lit my way at the American Philosophical Society, the Archivo General de la Nación in Buenos Aires, the Arquivo Histórico do Palácio Itamaraty in Rio, the Arquivo Nacional in Rio, the Arquivo Público Estadual Jordão Emerenciano in Recife, the Arquivo do Serviço de Documentação da Marinha in Rio, the Biblioteca Nacional do Brasil in Rio, the Biblioteca Nacional de la República Argentina in Buenos Aires, the Historical Society of Pennsylvania, the Houghton Library at Harvard

University, the Instituto Arqueológico, Histórico e Geográfico Pernambucano in Recife, Yale University Manuscripts and Archives, the Beinecke Library at Yale University, the Library of Congress, the Maryland Historical Society, and the Massachusetts Historical Society.

I received crucial financial support from the Fulbright Foundation, the Andrew W. Mellon Foundation, the Harvard University Atlantic History Seminar, and the Society for Historians of American Foreign Relations; the Society for Historians of the Early American Republic generously sponsored a month of research at the Library Company of Philadelphia and the Historical Society of Pennsylvania. At Yale, the Graduate School of Arts and Sciences, the Robert M. Leylan Foundation, the Howard R. Lamar Center for the Study of Frontiers and Borders, the MacMillan Center for International and Area Studies, and the Smith Richardson Foundation funded my early research and writing. A Faculty Fellowship from the American Council of Learned Societies enabled me to finish.

Countless scholars in countless forums have shared their time and thoughts along the way. Michael Allen, Zara Anishanslin, Bernard Bailyn, John Bezís-Selfa, Rafe Blaufarb, Richard Buel, Tim Breen, Celso Castilho, Margaret Chowning, Brian DeLay, Kon Dierks, Charlie Edel, Eric Hinderaker, Chris Hodson, Daniel Immerwahr, Ben Irvin, Michael LaCombe, Jane Landers, Ned Landsman, Jess Lepler, Matt Mason, Kate Masur, Brendan McConville, Michelle McDonald, Roderick McDonald, John Murrin, Ken Owen, Ben Park, Jeff Pasley, Mark Peterson, Dan Preston, Jenny Hale Pulsipher, Frank Safford, Daniel Sargent, Elena Schneider, Andy Shankman, Herb Sloan, and Ji-Yeon Yuh read chapters and excerpts, providing just the right mix of encouragement and criticism. In their conference panel commentary, John Belohlavek, Linda Colley, Alec Dun, Kathleen DuVal, Matt Guterl, Sam Haynes, Paul Mapp, Bob May, and Adam Rothman helped me see the big picture. I'm not sure I would have become a historian—and I'm certain that I wouldn't have become an early Americanist—had it not been for J. Roderick Heller III, who years ago offered me a last-minute summer job researching Felix Grundy, or had it not been for the exemplary undergraduate mentorship of Jeremy Adelman, Ken Mills, James McPherson, John Murrin, Colin Palmer, Peter Silver, and especially my adviser Sean Wilentz, who inspired my interest in early U.S. politics and society.

Few things are more valuable to an author than friends and colleagues willing to slog through an entire in-progress manuscript; for that, I owe special thanks to Henry Binford, Amy Greenberg, David Head, Dan Howe, and Sean Wilentz, all of whom offered illuminating and challenging advice. Wendy Warren has been a sounding board for all things professional and parental. She, too, read the whole manuscript and offered characteristically penetrating, pithy advice. Were it not for her chance email years ago, I would never have met my agent, Wendy Strothman; without Wendy Strothman, who had faith in this project when it was still largely an academic dissertation, I would never have met my editor, Katie Adams; and without Katie, this would have been a profoundly different book. Her vision, passion, encouragement, and flat-out smarts gave this project a whole new life for me, and inspired me to write the kind of book I always wanted to. I now know the difference an editor makes.

My parents, Earl and Julianne, have been my light and my compass, a wellspring of human compassion and midwestern humility. My brother Duncan went courageously to Afghanistan; I'm glad he's now here in Chicago, where he and the delightful Anastasia Oldham Fitz are a beloved aunt and uncle to my daughters. My brother Dylan embraces life (and unreasonably long cross-country skiing races) with a combination of adventurous individualism and lightheartedness that has found its perfect complement in Hillary Caruthers, at once unflappable and inspired.

When this project was taking shape, my older brother, Ezra, was diagnosed with a malignant brain tumor. He has awed us all ever since, from the moment he asked the surgeons to play "Gimme Shelter" as they sawed into his cranium to the moment nine years later when he published his first novel. In marrying the joyful and openhearted Alba Garcia, he was the first of my brothers to give me the gift I always wanted: a sister.

Arthur, Shelley, Nathan, Rachel, Asher, and Ellie Green live with a happiness that warms all around them, and I consider myself blessed that they have welcomed me so unconditionally into their family. Their son and brother and uncle, Seth, was my collegiate nemesis for two years, my best friend and my love for fifteen and counting. Sojourner and Lundy, now five and two, are the joy of my days and a primary reason this book took me so long to write. They have made life loud, messy, and full of everyday delights.

NOTES

INTRODUCTION: An Age of American Revolutions

1   David Trimble, *Annals of Congress*, 17th Cong., 1st sess., March 28, 1822, 1390–1392. Many in the Western Hemisphere had not acknowledged European sovereignty in the first place, of course—namely, Native Americans, who still controlled much of the trans-Mississippi West as well as vast expanses of South America. See, for example, Pekka Hämäläinen, *The Comanche Empire* (New Haven, 2008). For the timing and scale of Brazil's independence war—not to be confused with a series of regionalist proindependence uprisings in the Brazilian Northeast as described in Chapter Two—see Roderick J. Barman, *Brazil: The Forging of a Nation, 1798–1852* (Stanford, Calif., 1988), 104–107.

2   Thomas Paine, *Common Sense* (3rd ed., February 1776), in J. M. Opal, ed., *Common Sense and Other Writings: Authoritative Texts, Contexts, Interpretations* (New York, 2012), 30.

3   There is an immense literature on U.S. responses to the revolutions in Saint-Domingue and especially France. Particularly helpful are Seth Cotlar, *Tom Paine's America: The Rise and Fall of Transatlantic Radicalism in the Early Republic* (Charlottesville, 2011); Rachel Hope Cleves, *The Reign of Terror in America: Visions of Violence from Anti-Jacobinism to Antislavery* (New York, 2009); François Furstenberg, *When the United States Spoke French: Five Refugees Who Shaped a Nation* (New York, 2014); Harry Ammon, *The Genet Mission* (New York, 1973); Stanley Elkins and Eric McKitrick, *The Age of Federalism* (New York, 1993), 330–373; Susan Branson, *These Fiery Frenchified Dames: Women and Political Culture in Early National Philadelphia*

(Philadelphia, 2001); David Waldstreicher, *In the Midst of Perpetual Fetes: The Making of American Nationalism, 1776–1820* (Chapel Hill, 2004); Simon P. Newman, *Parades and the Politics of the Street: Festive Culture in the Early American Republic* (Philadelphia, 1997); Gary Nash, "The American Clergy and the French Revolution," *William and Mary Quarterly* 22.3 (July, 1965), 392–412; Jeremy D. Popkin, *A Concise History of the Haitian Revolution* (Malden, Mass., 2012), esp. 1–10; Laurent Dubois, *Avengers of the New World: The Story of the Haitian Revolution* (Cambridge, Mass., 2004), esp. 20; Donald R. Hickey, "America's Response to the Slave Revolt in Haiti, 1791–1806," *Journal of the Early Republic* 2.4 (Winter, 1982), 361–379; Edward Bartlett Rugemer, *The Problem of Emancipation: The Caribbean Roots of the American Civil War* (Baton Rouge, 2008), 42–53; Ashli White, *Encountering Revolution: Haiti and the Making of the Early Republic* (Baltimore, 2010); Charles H. Wesley, "The Struggle for the Recognition of Haiti and Liberia as Independent Republics," *Journal of Negro History* 2.4 (October, 1917), 369–383.

4   *National Advocate*, December 23, 1814 (citing the *Philadelphia Aurora*); John Adams to Benjamin Rush, August 28, 1811, Founders Online, National Archives, http://founders.archives.gov. Jefferson freed Hemings in 1796. For Jefferson, France, and Napoleon, see Annette Gordon-Reed, *The Hemingses of Monticello: An American Family* (New York, 2008), 411, 468–469; Steven Englund, *Napoleon: A Political Life* (New York, 2004); Joseph I. Shumlin, "Thomas Jefferson Views Napoleon," *Virginia Magazine of History and Biography* 60.2 (April, 1952), 288–304. For counterrevolutionary reaction, see Simon P. Newman, "American Political Culture and the French and Haitian Revolutions: Nathaniel Cutting and the Jeffersonian Republicans," in David Geggus, ed., *The Impact of the Haitian Revolution in the Atlantic World* (Columbia, S.C., 2001), 72–89; Michael Zuckerman, "The Power of Blackness: Thomas Jefferson and the Revolution in St. Domingue," in *Almost Chosen People: Oblique Biographies in the American Grain* (Berkeley and Los Angeles, 1993), 175–218; Zuckerman, "Thermidor in America: The Aftermath of Independence in the South," *Prospects* 8 (1983), 349–368; Cotlar, *Tom Paine's America*; Larry Tise, *American Counterrevolution: A Retreat from Liberty, 1783–1800* (Mechanicsburg, Pa., 1995).

5   Marie Arana, *Bolívar: American Liberator* (New York, 2013), 108 (quotation). For concise English-language overviews of Latin American independence, see John C. Chasteen, *Americanos: Latin America's Struggle for Independence* (New York, 2008); Jeremy Adelman, *Sovereignty and Revolution in the Iberian Atlantic* (Princeton, 2006); Jaime E. Rodríguez O., *The Independence of Spanish America* (New York, 1998). For Mexico City's comparative size, see Daniel Walker Howe, *What Hath God Wrought: The Transformation of America, 1815–1848* (New York, 2007), 19.

6   *Annals of Congress,* 12th Cong., 1st sess., April 29, 1812, 1351; *Boston Yankee,*
     May 30, 1817; Harold A. Bierck, Jr., "The First Instance of U.S. Foreign Aid:
     Venezuelan Relief in 1812," *Inter-American Economic Affairs* 9 (1955), 47–59
     (also noting economic motives). Seth Cotlar finds a similarly reciprocal rela-
     tionship between cosmopolitanism and nationalism in the early 1790s, though
     he shows that political changes later in the decade increasingly cast cosmopol-
     itanism and nationalism as oppositional. The 1810s and 1820s, I suggest, saw
     a renewed symbiosis of cosmopolitanism and nationalism (cf. Cotlar, *Tom
     Paine's America,* esp. 83–85, 114), though without the emphasis on Painite
     democratic equality that mattered so profoundly to Cotlar's 1790s subjects.
     See Cotlar, *Tom Paine's America,* 49–114.

7   This is not necessarily to say that the United States exerted the strongest for-
     eign influence in Latin America. Emphasizing patriot leaders' intellectual,
     political, and cultural connections, Karen Racine has argued for Britain's
     influence in Spanish America, while Sibylle Fischer has noted Haiti's influ-
     ence on Simón Bolívar's thinking in particular. As a historian of the United
     States more than a historian of Latin America, I am less concerned with com-
     parative foreign influence in Latin America than I am with how Latin Amer-
     ican independence affected the United States, and with how people in the
     United States understood their place in the hemisphere. See Karen Racine,
     "'This England and This Now': British Cultural and Intellectual Influence
     in the Spanish American Independence Era," *Hispanic American Historical
     Review* 90.3 (2010), 423–454; Sibylle Fischer, "Bolívar in Haiti: Republican-
     ism in the Revolutionary Atlantic," in Carla Calargé et al., eds., *Haiti and the
     Americas* (Jackson, Miss., 2013), 25–53.

8   For some of the most illuminating studies of the United States' early trans-
     atlantic connections, see n. 3, above. Other scholars have reached further
     afield; see, for example, Robert J. Allison, *The Crescent Obscured: The United
     States and the Muslim World, 1776–1815* (New York, 1995); Frank Lambert,
     The Barbary Wars: American Independence in the Atlantic World (New York,
     2005); Lamin Sanneh, *Abolitionists Abroad: American Blacks and the Making
     of Modern West Africa* (Cambridge, Mass., 1999). Studies of U.S. relations
     with Latin America were more common in the mid twentieth century, though
     most emphasized high-level diplomacy. I have relied especially on Charles
     Carroll Griffin, *The United States and the Disruption of the Spanish Empire,
     1810–1822* (New York, 1937); Arthur P. Whitaker, *The United States and the
     Independence of Latin America, 1800–1830* (Baltimore, 1941); Arthur P. Whita-
     ker, *The Western Hemisphere Idea: Its Rise and Decline* (Ithaca, N.Y., 1954);
     Samuel Flagg Bemis, *John Quincy Adams and the Foundations of American
     Foreign Policy* (New York, 1949); and, more recently, James E. Lewis, Jr., *The*

American Union and the Problem of Neighborhood: The United States and the Collapse of the Spanish Empire, 1783–1829 (Chapel Hill, 1998); and Jay Sexton, *The Monroe Doctrine: Empire and Nation in Nineteenth-Century America* (New York, 2011). For the few studies that do emphasize popular opinions of Latin America, see Laura Bornholdt, *Baltimore and Early Pan-Americanism: A Study in the Background of the Monroe Doctrine* (Northampton, Mass., 1949); Bruce B. Solnick, "American Opinion Concerning the Spanish American Wars of Independence, 1808–1824" (Ph.D. diss., New York University, 1960); Brendan C. McNally, "Coverage and Attitudes of the United States Press Relative to the Independence Movements in the Spanish Americas, 1810–1825" (Ph.D. diss., St. Louis University, 1949); and esp. Mark G. Jaede, "Brothers at a Distance: Race, Religion, Culture, and U.S. Views of Spanish America, 1800–1830" (Ph.D. diss., State University of New York at Buffalo, 2001). Literary scholars have produced some of the most innovative recent work on early-nineteenth-century hemispheric relations, though like historians they have focused mostly on areas proximate to the United States. See esp. Rodrigo Lazo, *Writing to Cuba: Filibustering and Cuban Exiles in the United States* (Chapel Hill, 2005); Kristin A. Dykstra, "On the Betrayal of Nations: José Alvarez de Toledo's Philadelphia *Manifesto* (1811) and *Justification* (1816)," *The New Centennial Review* 4.1 (2004), 267–305; Nicolás Kanellos, "José Alvarez de Toledo y Dubois and the Origins of Hispanic Publishing in the Early American Republic," *Early American Literature* 43.1 (2008), 83–100; Anna Brickhouse, *Transamerican Literary Relations and the Nineteenth-Century Public Sphere* (New York, 2004); Kirsten Silva Gruesz, *Ambassadors of Culture: The Transamerican Origins of Latino Writing* (Princeton, 2002); Nancy J. Vogeley, *The Bookrunner: A History of Inter-American Relations: Print, Politics, and Commerce in the United States and Mexico, 1800–1830* (Philadelphia, 2001).

9   I am not the first to note the emphasis on South America. In 1937, Charles Griffin declined to make "border rivalry," as he called it, a central part of his *United States and the Disruption of the Spanish Empire*. Four years later, Arthur Whitaker observed that, before the mid-1820s, "the [U.S.] American people knew less about this next-door neighbor [Mexico] than about almost any important country or region in the West Indies or South America." Griffin, *United States and the Disruption of the Spanish Empire*, 5; Whitaker, *United States and the Independence of Latin America*, 137–138. For early relations with Mexico, Florida, and Cuba, see esp. Frank Lawrence Owsley, Jr. and Gene A. Smith, *Filibusters and Expansionists: Jeffersonian Manifest Destiny, 1800–1821* (Tuscaloosa, Ala., 1997), 7–9; J. C. A. Stagg, *Borderlines in Borderlands: James Madison and the Spanish-American Frontier, 1776–1821* (New Haven, 2009);

William Earl Weeks, *John Quincy Adams and American Global Empire* (Lexington, Ky., 1992); and, most recently, Kathleen DuVal's elegant *Independence Lost: Lives on the Edge of the American Revolution* (New York, 2015). For powerful works of U.S.–Latin American relations later in the nineteenth century, see, for example, Robert E. May, *The Southern Dream of a Caribbean Empire, 1854–1861* (Baton Rouge, 1973); Robert E. May, *Manifest Destiny's Underworld: Filibustering in Antebellum America* (Chapel Hill, 2002); Aims McGuinness, *Path of Empire: Panama and the California Gold Rush* (Ithaca, N.Y., 2008); Amy S. Greenberg, *Manifest Manhood and the Antebellum American Empire* (New York, 2005); Amy S. Greenberg, *A Wicked War: Polk, Clay, Lincoln, and the 1846 U.S. Invasion of Mexico* (New York, 2012).

10 John J. Johnson, *A Hemisphere Apart: The Foundations of United States Policy Toward Latin America* (Baltimore, 1990), 44–77 (on racial differences); Piero Gleijeses, "The Limits of Sympathy: The United States and the Independence of Spanish America," *Journal of Latin American Studies* 24.3 (October, 1992), 481–505; Arana, *Bolívar*, 259.

11 For revolutionary-era thinking about slavery, see esp. Robert Pierce Forbes, *The Missouri Compromise and its Aftermath* (Chapel Hill, 2007); Nicholas Guyatt, "The Outskirts of Our Happiness," *Journal of American History* 95.4 (March, 2009), 986–1011; Bernard Bailyn, *The Ideological Origins of the American Revolution* (1967; enl. ed., Cambridge, Mass., 1992), 230–246; David Brion Davis, *The Problem of Slavery in Western Culture* (Ithaca, N.Y., 1966); Davis, *The Problem of Slavery in the Age of Revolution* (Ithaca, N.Y., 1975); Davis, *The Problem of Slavery in the Age of Emancipation* (New York, 2014); Ira Berlin, *Many Thousands Gone: The First Two Centuries of Slavery in North America* (Cambridge, Mass., 1998), 219–365; Gary B. Nash, *Race and Revolution* (Madison, Wis., 1990) (emphasizing the limits and transience of antislavery revolutionary thinking). By invoking the egalitarian ideals of 1776 throughout this book, I am referring not just to the Declaration of Independence, but to the broader egalitarian and universalist sensibilities of the U.S. revolutionary era, which were often more clearly expressed in state bills of rights. See Pauline Maier, *American Scripture: Making the Declaration of Independence* (New York, 1997), esp. 154–208; David Armitage, *The Declaration of Independence: A Global History* (Cambridge, Mass., 2007), 1–102.

12 Edmund S. Morgan, *American Slavery, American Freedom: The Ordeal of Colonial Virginia* (New York, 1975). For the relationship between antislavery belief and action, and for equality and property, see esp. Matthew Mason, "Necessary but Not Sufficient: Revolutionary Ideology and Antislavery Action in the Early Republic," and James Oakes, "Conflict vs. Racial Consensus in the History of Antislavery Politics," in John Craig Hammond and Matthew

Mason, eds., *Contesting Slavery: The Politics of Bondage and Freedom in the New American Nation* (Charlottesville, Va., 2011), 11–31, 291–303.

13   I am not proposing a compulsory, one-size-fits-all conceptualization of the revolutionary era. We all adopt the chronological and geographic lenses that best enable us to understand our subjects, and these lenses must necessarily differ. My goal is to show what we might gain with a geographically and chronologically broader understanding of the revolutionary era. For other important counterrevolutionary trends, see, for example, Cotlar, *Tom Paine's America*; Rosemarie Zagarri, *Revolutionary Backlash: Women and Politics in the Early American Republic* (Philadelphia, 2007); Tise, *American Counterrevolution*. This book does not purport to focus on "the" American Revolution—that is, the U.S. war for independence from Britain. Rather, I am interested in how the American Revolution fit into a broader revolutionary age for the hemisphere as a whole, and in how it helped to inform the next several decades of U.S. history. I see the age of American revolutions as a subset of the more commonly studied "age of revolutions," and as a historiographic complement rather than a competitor. Several scholars have employed a similarly extended periodization of the revolutionary age, though their work tends to be more comparative than connective. See, for example, Herbert E. Bolton's classic "Epic of Greater America," *American Historical Review* 38.3 (April, 1933), 448–474; Wim Klooster, *Revolutions in the Atlantic World: A Comparative History* (New York, 2009); Lester D. Langley, *The Americas in the Age of Revolution* (New Haven, 1997). For a work that emphasizes connections, see Peggy K. Liss, *Atlantic Empires: The Network of Trade and Revolution, 1713–1826* (Baltimore, 1983). Janet Polasky offers an illuminating, connective study of the age of revolutions, though she stops on the cusp of Latin American independence; see *Revolutions Without Borders: The Call to Liberty in the Atlantic World* (New Haven, 2015); also see R. R. Palmer's classic *The Age of the Democratic Revolution: A Political History of Europe and America, 1760–1800* (1959–1964; updated ed., Princeton, 2014). David Brion Davis offers a chronologically sweeping (and admirably concise) perspective in *Revolutions: Reflections on American Equality and Foreign Liberations* (Cambridge, Mass., 1990), esp. 3–54.

14   And in fact slavery was under siege even in part of the colonial Caribbean, thanks to Britain's mounting abolitionist movement (which targeted British colonies like Barbados and Jamaica). See esp. Christopher Leslie Brown, *Moral Capital: Foundations of British Abolitionism* (Chapel Hill, 2006).

15   Ovid, *Metamorphoses*, Book III, trans. Joseph Addison, Samuel Garth et al. (London, 1717).

16   For similar revolutionary-era mirror metaphors, see Ada Ferrer, *Freedom's Mirror: Cuba and Haiti in the Age of Revolution* (New York, 2014); Seth Cotlar, *Tom Paine's America*, 77.

17   I am paraphrasing, of course, from William Butler Yeats's "The Second Coming" (1920), in Richard J. Finneran, ed., *The Collected Poems of W. B. Yeats* (1989; rev. 2nd ed., New York, 1996), I:187.

18   Peter Blanchard, *Under the Flags of Freedom: Slave Soldiers and the Wars of Independence in Spanish South America* (Pittsburgh, 2008), esp. 3. I hope that this book will encourage others to study hemispheric discourses of indigeneity in greater detail. For a strong start, see Sarah E. Cornell, "Americans in the U.S. South and Mexico: A Transnational History of Race, Slavery, and Freedom, 1810–1910" (Ph.D. diss., New York University, 2008); Frederick B. Pike, *The United States and Latin America: Myths and Stereotypes of Civilization and Nature* (Austin, 1992); Paul D. Naish, "Safe Distance: U.S. Slavery, Latin America, and American Culture, 1826–1861" (Ph.D. diss., City University of New York, 2011), 82–148, 218–282; Eric Wertheimer, *Imagined Empires: Incas, Aztecs, and the New World of American Literature: 1771–1876* (New York, 1999).

19   John L. Phelan, "Pan-Latinism, French Intervention in Mexico (1861–1867), and the Genesis of the Idea of Latin America," in *Conciencia y autenticidad históricas*, ed. Juan A. Ortega y Medina (Mexico City, 1968), 279–298; McGuinness, *Path of Empire*, esp. 152–183.

20   Cf. the insightful work of Michel Ducharme, who extends the revolutionary era to 1838. Ducharme, *Le concept de liberté au Canada à l'époque des révolutions atlantiques, 1776–1838* (Montreal, 2010). For "Republican Hemisphere," see, for example, *Democratic Press*, July 22, 1825.

CHAPTER ONE: Squinting South

1   Joel Barlow, *The Vision of Columbus: A Poem in Nine Books* (Hartford, 1787); Barlow, *The Columbiad* (1807; London, 1809), iii, xiii–xiv; Richard Buel, *Joel Barlow: American Citizen in a Revolutionary World* (Baltimore, 2011).

2   Barlow, *The Columbiad*, 1; Barlow, *The Vision of Columbus*, 23–42; Phillis Wheatley, "To His Excellency General Washington" (1775), in *Complete Writings: Phillis Wheatley*, ed. Vincent Carretta (New York, 2001), 89–90; Philip Freneau, *American Liberty: A Poem* (New York, 1775), 3; Arthur P. Whitaker, *The Western Hemisphere Idea* (Ithaca, N.Y., 1954); and esp. Claudia L. Bushman's *America Discovers Columbus: How an Italian Explorer Became an American Hero* (Hanover, N.H., 1992), 41, 82.

3   For a similar timeline (and for El Dorado), see Arthur P. Whitaker, *The United States and the Independence of Latin America, 1800–1830* (Baltimore, 1941), esp. 95–96.

4   Benjamin Keen, *David Curtis DeForest and the Revolution of Buenos Aires* (New Haven, 1947), 21 (quotation); H. W. V. Temperley, "The Relations

of England with Spanish America, 1720–1744," *The Annual Report of the American Historical Association for the Year 1911* (Washington, 1913), I:229–237; Peggy K. Liss, *Atlantic Empires: The Network of Trade and Revolution, 1713–1826* (Baltimore, 1983), 1–47; Harry Bernstein, *Origins of Inter-American Interest, 1770–1812* (Philadelphia, 1945); Whitaker, *United States and the Independence of Latin America*, 1–38; Javier Cuenca-Esteban, "British 'Ghost' Exports, American Middlemen, and the Trade to Spanish America, 1790–1819: A Speculative Reconstruction," *William and Mary Quarterly* 71.1 (January, 2014), 63–98. For Anglo-Spanish connections in the sixteenth through eighteenth centuries, also see Eliga H. Gould, "Entangled Histories, Entangled Worlds: The English-Speaking Atlantic as a Spanish Periphery," *American Historical Review* 112.3 (June, 2007), 764–786; Paul W. Mapp, *The Elusive West and the Contest for Empire, 1713–1763* (Chapel Hill, 2011); Jorge Cañizares-Esguerra, *Puritan Conquistadors: Iberianizing the Atlantic, 1550–1700* (Stanford, Calif., 2006).

5   Whitaker, *The United States and the Independence of Latin America*, esp. 23; Bernstein, *Origins of Inter-American Interest*, 15–51; Jeremy Adelman, *Sovereignty and Revolution in the Iberian Atlantic* (Princeton, 2006), 105–117; John H. Coatsworth, "American Trade with European Colonies in the Caribbean and South America, 1790–1812," *William and Mary Quarterly* 24.2 (April, 1967), 243–266. For the dollar sign, see Florian Cajori, *A History of Mathematical Notations* (1928–1929; new ed., Mineola, N.Y., 1993), II:15–30; "The Dollar Mark and the Story of its Origin," *New York Times*, December 8, 1912, X-13.

6   I am grateful to Stephen Chambers for sharing with me his then-forthcoming *No God but Gain: The Untold Story of Cuban Slavery, the Monroe Doctrine, and the Making of the United States* (New York, 2015), on which this paragraph partly draws (incl. 37 for snow and ice). Also see Leonardo Marques, "Slave Trading in a New World: The Strategies of North American Slave Traders in the Age of Abolition," *Journal of the Early Republic* 32.2 (Summer, 2012), esp. 240–241, 254; Seth Rockman and Sven Beckert, eds., *Slavery's Capitalism* (Philadelphia, forthcoming); Matt Childs, "'A Black French General Arrived to Conquer the Island': Images of the Haitian Revolution in Cuba's 1812 Aponte Rebellion," in David Geggus, ed., *The Impact of the Haitian Revolution in the Atlantic World* (Columbia, SC, 2001), 135–156; Linda K. Salvucci, "Supply, Demand, and the Making of a Market: Philadelphia and Havana at the Beginning of the Nineteenth Century," in Franklin W. Knight and Peggy K. Liss, eds., *Atlantic Port Cities: Economy, Culture, and Society in the Atlantic World, 1650–1850* (Knoxville, 1991), 40–57; Javier Cuenca Esteban, "Trends and Cycles in U.S. Trade with Spain and the Spanish Empire, 1790–1817,"

Journal of Economic History 44.2 (June, 1984), 521–543; Edward P. Pompeian, "Spirited Enterprises: Venezuela, the United States, and the Independence of Spanish America, 1789–1823" (Ph.D. diss., The College of William and Mary, 2014). For "offshore" slavery in the seventeenth century, also see Wendy Warren, *New England Bound: Slavery and Colonization at the Edge of an Empire* (New York, 2016).

7   Whitaker, *United States and the Independence of Latin America*, 15–16; Pompeian, "Spirited Enterprises"; Keen, *David Curtis DeForest*, 14–26; Bernstein, *Origins of Inter-American Interest*, 35–49; Liss, *Atlantic Empires*, 26–113. For whales, seals, and sea elephants, see Greg Grandin's extraordinary description in *The Empire of Necessity: Slavery, Freedom, and Deception in the New World* (New York, 2014), 131–141.

8   Hamilton to James McHenry, June 27, 1799 (referencing the "Quasi-War" with France) and Jefferson to Monroe, November 24, 1801, Founders Online, National Archives, http://founders.archives.gov/.

9   Zoltán Vajda, "Thomas Jefferson on the Character of an Unfree People: The Case of Spanish America," *American Nineteenth Century History* 8.3 (September, 2007), 275; Bernstein, *Origins of Inter-American Interest*, 52–65; Whitaker, *United States and the Independence of Latin America*, 141–188.

10   For this paragraph and the next, see John Maclean, *History of the College of New Jersey, From Its Origin in 1746 to the Commencement of 1854* (Philadelphia, 1877), esp. 216, 302–313, 361–362; Philip Merrill Marsh, *Philip Freneau, Poet and Journalist* (Minneapolis, 1967), 25.

11   [Philip Freneau and Hugh Henry Brackenridge], *A Poem, on the Rising Glory of America* (Philadelphia, 1772), 4–5; Alexander Leitch, *A Princeton Companion* (Princeton, 1978), 63. For Brackenridge, Freneau, Barlow, and others viewed collectively and comparatively, see Eric Wertheimer, *Imagined Empires: Incas, Aztecs, and the New World of American Literature: 1771–1876* (New York, 1999).

12   Jedidiah Morse, *Geography Made Easy* (New Haven, 1784), esp. 3–4, 102, 134. For popularity, see William J. Gilmore, *Reading Becomes a Necessity of Life: Material and Cultural Life in Rural New England, 1780–1835* (Knoxville, 1989), 64–67. For the Black Legend, see Julián Juderías, *La Leyenda Negra* (1914; new ed., Barcelona, 1943).

13   William Spence Robertson, *The History of America* (new ed., 2 vols.; New York, 1798), esp. II:156, 186, 356–357, 387–388; Bernal Díaz del Castillo, *True History of the Conquest of Mexico*, trans. Maurice Keatinge (Salem, 1803) (for subscriptions, and for original publication in London, see Bernstein, *Origins of Inter-American Interest*, 57); Francisco Javier Clavijero, *History of Mexico*, trans. Charles Cullen (Philadelphia, 1804; Richmond, 1806); Abbe Don J.

Ignatius Molina [Giovanni Ignazio Molina], trans. Richard Alsop, *Geographical, Natural and Civil History of Chili* (Middletown, Conn., 1808); François R. J. Depons, *Voyage to the Eastern Part of Terra Firma, or the Spanish Main, in South-America*, trans. "by an American gentleman" (3 vols.; New York, 1806). For Irving as translator, and for reprintings and translations more generally, see Whitaker, *United States and the Independence of Latin America*, 142–144.

14 Karen Racine, *Francisco de Miranda: A Transatlantic Life in the Age of Revolution* (Wilmington, Del., 2003), esp. 44, 158; [James Biggs], *History of Don Francisco de Miranda's Attempt to Effect a Revolution in South America* (2nd ed., Boston, 1812), 288–291 (physical description).

15 *Richmond Enquirer*, April 8, 1806, and Baltimore's *Federal Gazette*, June 30, 1806 (quoting the *Centinel of Freedom*); for these quotations, and for the expedition generally, see William Spence Robertson, *Francisco de Miranda and the Revolutionizing of Spanish America* (Washington, 1909), 361–398 (quotations, 375); Racine, *Francisco de Miranda*, 141–172. For merchants, see Pompeian, "Spirited Enterprises," 223–272. For New York, see Lindsay Schakenbach, "Schemers, Dreamers, and a Revolutionary Foreign Policy: New York City in the Era of Second Independence, 1805–1815," *New York History* 94 (Summer/Fall, 2013), 267–282. Some recruits knew the true nature of the expedition; others claimed to have been deceived.

16 Moses Smith, *History of the Adventures and Sufferings of Moses Smith* (Brooklyn, 1812), esp. 28–32, 52; [Biggs], *History of Don Francisco de Miranda's Attempt*; John H. Sherman, *General Account of Miranda's Expedition* (New York, 1808); Racine, *Francisco de Miranda*, 162. For "462 unique news pieces," see Pompeian, "Spirited Enterprises," 223; for sample reports, see, for example, New York's *Public Advertiser*, April 28, 1807; Randolph, Vermont's *Weekly Wanderer*, May 18, 1807; Baltimore's *North American and Mercantile Daily Advertiser*, September 13, 1808.

17 *Providence Gazette*, July 7, 1810; *Richmond Enquirer*, July 27, 1810 (reprinting Salem's *Essex Register*); Poughkeepsie's *Political Barometer*, June 6, 1810 (on Caracas; reprinting the *Whig*); Jefferson to Alexander von Humboldt, March 6, 1809, Founders Online, National Archives, http://founders.archives.gov/.

18 See Laurentino Gomes's remarkable account in *1808: The Flight of the Emperor*, trans. Andrew Nevins (2007; English ed., Guilford, Conn., 2013), esp. 3–39; John C. Chasteen, *Americanos: Latin America's Struggle for Independence* (New York, 2008), 42–44.

19 Boston's *Columbian Centinel*, February 10, 1808; Gomes, *1808*; Kirsten Schultz, *Tropical Versailles: Empire, Monarchy, and the Portuguese Royal Court in Rio de Janeiro, 1808–1821* (New York, 2001). Brazil officially lost its colonial status in 1815, when João declared it an equal part of the empire.

20 Jefferson to João Maria José Luis, May 5, 1808, Founders Online, National Archives, http://founders.archives.gov; *New-York Spectator*, May 28, 1808.

21 Charles Esdaile, *The Peninsular War* (New York, 2003), esp. 501; Chasteen, *Americanos*, 44–58; Ronald Fraser, *Napoleon's Cursed War* (New York, 2008), esp. 513–521. For incomprehension, see also Alan Schom, *Napoleon Bonaparte* (New York, 1997), 468–469.

22 *Fredericktown Republican Advocate*, August 11, 1808; *New-York Commercial Advertiser*, August 5, 1808; *Newburyport Herald*, August 2, 1808 (reprinting the *New-York Evening Post*); *Columbian Centinel*, February 11, 1809; Bruce B. Solnick, "American Opinion Concerning the Spanish American Wars of Independence, 1808–1824" (Ph.D. diss., New York University, 1960), 21–30. Napoleon's Iberian usurpation also fueled partisan debates at home; see, for example, Baltimore's *North American and Mercantile Daily Advertiser*, July 11, 1808; Norwich, N.Y.'s *Olive Branch*, September 10, 1808 (citing New York's *American Citizen*).

23 This paragraph and the next draw from Chasteen, *Americanos*, 34–122; Jeremy Adelman, *Sovereignty and Revolution in the Iberian Atlantic* (Princeton, 2006), 175–219; Jaime E. Rodríguez O., *The Independence of Spanish America* (New York, 1998); John H. Elliott, *Empires of the Atlantic World: Britain and Spain in America, 1492–1830* (New Haven, 2006), 369–402; Marixa Lasso, *Myths of Harmony: Race and Republicanism During the Age of Revolution, Colombia, 1795–1831* (Pittsburgh, 2007).

24 For planet-and-sun language, also see Richard White, *The Middle Ground: Indians, Empires, and Republics in the Great Lakes Region, 1650–1815* (New York, 1991), 274.

25 For concise comparisons, see Elliott, *Empires of the Atlantic World*, 374–375, 382, 396–397; Adelman, *Sovereignty and Revolution*, 1–12, 171, 369, 394–397; Rodríguez, *Independence of Spanish America*, 238–246; Lasso, *Myths of Harmony*, 151–159. For comparative size, see Herbert E. Bolton, "The Epic of Greater America," *American Historical Review* 38.3 (April, 1933), 459.

26 New York's *American Citizen*, June 6, 1810; Providence's *Columbian Phenix*, September 1, 1810 (reprinting the *Boston Patriot*); *New-York Evening Post*, June 9, 1810; Hartford's *Connecticut Courant*, June 13, 1810 (reprinting Baltimore's *Evening Post*, and also appearing in Trenton's *True American*, June 11, 1810, and Richmond's *Virginia Patriot*, June 15, 1810). For Quito, see Plattsburgh, N.Y.'s *American Monitor*, December 16, 1809 (citing the *Mercantile Advertiser*); Chillicothe's *Supporter*, December 2, 1809; Charles Town, Va.'s *Farmer's Repository*, December 1, 1809; Lexington, Ky.'s *Reporter*, December 5, 1809; Pendleton, S.C.'s *Miller's Weekly Register*, March 17, 1810; Conn.'s *Windham Herald*, December 1, 1809; *New-Bedford Mercury*, December 1, 1809; Warren,

RI's *Bristol County Register*, December 2, 1809; Newark's *Centinel of Freedom*, December 5, 1809; Concord's *New-Hampshire Patriot*, November 28, 1809; Kennebunk's *Weekly Visiter*, December 2, 1809; Windsor's *Spooner's Vermont Journal*, December 4, 1809; Nashville's *Review*, December 15, 1809; New Bern's *Carolina Federal Republican*, February 12, 1810; Philadelphia's *Poulson's American Daily Advertiser*, March 7, 1810; Milledgeville's *Georgia Journal*, March 27, 1810; Wilmington, Del.'s *American Watchman*, March 14, 1809; *Hagers-Town Gazette*, April 17, 1810.

27   Whitaker, *United States and the Independence of Latin America*, 52–55, 87–93; Pompeian, "Spirited Enterprises," 273–357 (on merchant views and deeds).

28   Solnick, "American Opinion," 44, 55 (for the Baltimore *Whig* and *Louisiana Gazette*); Walpole, N.H.'s *Farmer's Museum*, September 24, 1810 (reprinted in Windsor, Vt.'s *Washingtonian*, September 24, 1810).

29   *Weekly Register*, September 14, 1811; *New-York Evening Post*, October 12, 1811; St. Louis's *Gazette*, July 19, 1810, as cited in Solnick, "American Opinion," 47. For more on views of Spanish-American Catholicism, see Mark G. Jaede, "Brothers at a Distance: Race, Religion, Culture, and U.S. Views of Spanish America, 1800–1830" (Ph.D. diss., State University of New York at Buffalo, 2001), 86–114.

30   Thomas Jefferson to William Short, January 3, 1793, Founders Online, National Archives, http://www.founders.archives.gov; Vajda, "Thomas Jefferson on the Character of an Unfree People," 272–292 (including remaining quotations). After Louisiana became a state in 1812, a group of Virginians drew an explicit connection to Spanish-American insurgents, proclaiming (in a July Fourth toast) that Louisiana had been "prove[n] . . . worthy of admittance into our great Republican sisterhood"; "May her edification be fruitful in proselytes on the Southern hemisphere." *Richmond Enquirer*, July 24, 1812.

31   *Weekly Register*, September 14, 1811; *Commercial Advertiser*, August 29, 1811; Norval Neil Luxon, *Niles' Weekly Register: News Magazine of the Nineteenth Century* (Baton Rouge, 1947), esp. 1–65, 194–222.

32   For muted partisan (and regional and commercial) takes on Latin American independence, also see Whitaker, *United States and the Independence of Latin America*, 39–99. For a concise summary of Federalist and Republican views of the U.S. Revolution, see Len Travers, *Celebrating the Fourth: Independence Day and the Rites of Nationalism in the Early Republic* (Amherst, Mass., 1997), 94–95.

33   *Richmond Enquirer*, July 9, 1822 (reprinting the *Norfolk Herald*); Travers, *Celebrating the Fourth*.

34   *Richmond Enquirer*, July 12, 1808; Travers, *Celebrating the Fourth*.

35   *Democratic Press*, July 24, 1813. On accidents, see Travers, *Celebrating the Fourth*, 128–135.

36 For the Declaration of Independence and its international logic, see David Armitage, *The Declaration of Independence: A Global History* (Cambridge, Mass., 2007), 1–102, 165–171; Eliga H. Gould, *Among the Powers of the Earth: The American Revolution and the Making of a New World Empire* (Cambridge, Mass., 2012). For patriotism and partisanship, see David Waldstreicher, *In the Midst of Perpetual Fetes: The Making of American Nationalism, 1776–1820* (Chapel Hill, 2004); Travers, *Celebrating the Fourth*; Pauline Maier, *American Scripture: Making the Declaration of Independence* (New York, 1997), 154–208.

37 *Columbian Centinel*, July 11, 1810; Gustavus Myers, *The History of Tammany Hall* (New York, 1917), 11, 31–34; Sean Wilentz, *The Rise of American Democracy: Jefferson to Lincoln* (New York, 2005), 86–87, 190. On Tammany's early garb, also see Philip J. Deloria, *Playing Indian* (New Haven, 1998), 10–58.

38 *Richmond Enquirer*, July 11, 1809; *Cooperstown Federalist*, June 9, 1810. The above statistics (like references to sampled toasts throughout the book) include reports of all parties for which more than one toast is listed. (For 1808 to 1815, N=225.) They do not include reports on out-of-state festivities, although they *do* include parties from out of town. For example, the *Richmond Enquirer* figures include parties in Harper's Ferry (then part of Virginia), but not those in Washington, D.C., or Maryland. In order to maintain consistency with statistics for 1820 and later, I have not counted the occasional toasts from Maine celebrations toward the Massachusetts figures, even though Maine was part of Massachusetts until 1820. For each year in question, I read all sampled newspapers from July through late August, counting only those toasts that explicitly referred to the rebel movements in Latin America; I did not count toasts to generalities like "liberty across the globe." I have not distinguished between "volunteer" and other toasts, nor have I included toasts that expressed skepticism toward Latin America (such toasts were exceedingly rare, totaling in the low single digits out of over 600 sampled toasts through 1825). I did not include toasts to the annexation of the Floridas, since not one sampled toast explicitly connected annexation to the idea of Spanish-American independence. (In any case, sampled toasts to Florida were rare.) I did not double-count parties on which both the Boston *Patriot* and the *Columbian Centinel* reported. Throughout this book, I have weighted the figures according to each state's white adult male population (as found in the 1820 federal census for white men aged twenty-six and above). The unweighted line differs little from the weighted one, however; see the Appendix. U.S. Department of State, *Census for 1820* (Washington, 1821).

39 Travers, *Celebrating the Fourth*, esp. 115; Joanne B. Freeman, *Affairs of Honor: National Politics in the New Republic* (New Haven, 2001), 98–99; Waldstreicher, *In the Midst of Perpetual Fetes.*

40 My view of July Fourth toasts' importance draws from Simon P. Newman,

Parades and the Politics of the Street: Festive Culture in the Early American Republic (Philadelphia, 1997); Waldstreicher, *In the Midst of Perpetual Fetes*, esp. 219−221; Travers, *Celebrating the Fourth*. I also follow Daniel Walker Howe's use of newspaper statistics on riots in the 1830s; as Howe writes, "the figures . . . give a sense of public perceptions and relative frequency," even though they were neither scientific nor comprehensive. See Howe, *What Hath God Wrought*, 431, using statistics from Leonard Richards, *Gentlemen of Property and Standing* (New York, 1970), 11−12. For a sample draft list of toasts, see the young Andrew Jackson's effort in "Toasts for Independence Day Celebration," [ca. July 1, 1805], in *The Papers of Andrew Jackson*, ed. Harold D. Moser and Sharon MacPherson (Knoxville, 1984), II:63−64.

41 *Richmond Enquirer*, July 10, 1818.

42 J. C. A. Stagg, *The War of 1812: Conflict for a Continent* (New York, 2012); Donald R. Hickey, *The War of 1812: A Forgotten Conflict* (Urbana, Ill., 1989); Alan Taylor, *The Civil War of 1812: American Citizens, British Subjects, Irish Rebels, and Indian Allies* (New York, 2010); Troy Bickham, *The Weight of Vengeance: The United States, the British Empire, and the War of 1812* (New York, 2012); Drew R. McCoy, *The Elusive Republic: Political Economy in Jeffersonian America* (Chapel Hill, 1980).

43 Elizabethtown's *New-Jersey Journal*, August 11, 1812; Newport's *Rhode-Island Republican*, January 15, 1812 (citing the Baltimore *Whig*); *Richmond Enquirer*, May 12, 1812; Walpole, New Hampshire's *Democratic Republican*, November 9, 1812 (citing Philadelphia's *Democratic Press*).

44 John Adams to Abigail Adams, January 14, 1793, Founders Online, National Archives, http://www.founders.archives.gov; David Hackett Fischer, *The Revolution of American Conservatism: The Federalist Party in the Era of Jeffersonian Democracy* (New York, 1965); Linda K. Kerber, *Federalists in Dissent: Imagery and Ideology in Jeffersonian America* (Ithaca, N.Y., 1970); James M. Banner, *To the Hartford Convention: The Federalists and the Origins of Party Politics in Massachusetts, 1789−1815* (New York, 1970); Rachel Hope Cleves, *The Reign of Terror in America: Visions of Violence from Anti-Jacobinism to Antislavery* (New York, 2009); Seth Cotlar, *Tom Paine's America: The Rise and Fall of Transatlantic Radicalism in the Early Republic* (Charlottesville, Va., 2011); Richard Buel, *America on the Brink: How the Political Struggle over the War of 1812 Almost Destroyed the Young Republic* (Gordonsville, Va., 2006), esp. 155−235. There are caveats and exceptions, of course: Federalists did not uniformly oppose Spanish-American independence and had in fact been some of Miranda's most prominent supporters in 1805 and 1806, evidently because of commercial ties; moreover, Federalists had directly aided black revolutionaries in Saint-Domingue (albeit in pursuit of economic and diplomatic objec-

tives as much as revolutionary ideals). Federalists may also have been inclined to sympathize with Spain's Regency and its British military backers because of financial investment in the Peninsular grain trade, though here, too, partisan lines were blurry; see Pompeian, "Spirited Enterprises," 333–338. For a bipartisan July Fourth celebration that toasted Spanish-American independence, see, for example, Salem, Mass.'s *Essex Register,* July 7, 1810.

45 Walpole, N.H.'s *Democratic Republican,* November 9, 1812 (citing the *Democratic Press* of October 8, 1812); *Aurora General Advertiser,* July 9, 1810. I address Republican support for Spanish-American independence in the early 1810s— and the War of 1812's hemispheric context more generally—in greater detail in Caitlin A. Fitz, "The Hemispheric Dimensions of Early U.S. Nationalism: The War of 1812, Its Aftermath, and Spanish American Independence," *Journal of American History* 102.2 (September, 2015), 356–379.

46 *Aurora General Advertiser,* July 15, 1812; *Federal Gazette and Baltimore Daily Advertiser,* July 2, 1812; *Alexandria Gazette,* July 19, 1821 (citing the *St. Louis Enquirer*); *Niles' Weekly Register* (Baltimore; March–September, 1816), X:ii. For maps and travel accounts, see, for example, John Melish, *Universal School Geography* (Philadelphia, 1818); Henry S. Tanner, *The New American Atlas,* published serially and repeatedly beginning in 1818 (Philadelphia, 1818, 1822– 23, 1825–27); Jedidiah Morse, *American Universal Geography* (Charlestown, Mass., 1819), esp. I:768; "Map of South America," in Henry M. Brackenridge, *Voyage to South America, Performed by Order of the American Government in the Years 1817 and 1818, in the Frigate Congress* (Baltimore, 1819), I: map (enclosed). The sample set (1810–1815) included eleven toasts to South America and six to Spanish America (note that some parties contained more than one inter-American toast). I discuss the emphasis on South America in greater detail—and with larger sample sizes and other, corroborative pools of data— in Chapters Two and Four.

47 *Enquirer,* July 9, 1811 (for Florida) and July 24, 1812 (for "Southern hemisphere"); Charles Carroll Griffin, *The United States and the Disruption of the Spanish Empire, 1810–1822* (New York, 1937), 15–68; Frank Lawrence Owsley, Jr., and Gene A. Smith, *Filibusters and Expansionists: Jeffersonian Manifest Destiny, 1800–1821* (Tuscaloosa, Ala., 1997), esp. 1–81, 103–117; David E. Narrett, "Liberation and Conquest: John Hamilton Robinson and U.S. Adventurism Toward Mexico, 1806–1819," *Western Historical Quarterly* 40.1 (Spring, 2009), 23–43; Chasteen, *Americanos,* 66–94. A handful of toasts referred to John Armstrong, the late U.S. minister to France, who had unsuccessfully attempted to facilitate Florida's annexation, but only one of these toasts referred to southwestern expansion, and that was merely implicit; see *Richmond Enquirer,* July 9, 1811. Whitaker also notes an empha-

sis on South America, not Mexico, in *United States and the Independence of Latin America*, 137–138.

48 *Carthage Gazette*, August 7, 1812, citing the *Nashville Clarion* and quoted in Sarah E. Cornell, "Americans in the U.S. South and Mexico: A Transnational History of Race, Slavery, and Freedom, 1810–1910" (Ph.D. diss., New York University, 2008), 20–48, quotation on 30–31; Whitaker, *United States and the Independence of Latin America*, 16–17, 24–27, 61, 101, 136–139; Griffin, *United States and the Disruption of the Spanish Empire*, 67; Solnick, "American Opinion," 51. By the early 1820s, trade with Mexico had increased, outweighing trade with the rest of mainland Spanish America; see Timothy Pitkin, *A Statistical View of the Commerce of the United States of America* (New Haven, 1835), 225–227; *Hazard's Register of Pennsylvania*, October 11, 1828. Mexican rebels' widespread native and mestizo ancestry does not seem to explain the lack of U.S. interest; newspaper reports on Mexico's rebellion were usually blithely unconcerned with race, as Cornell shows in "Americans in the U.S. South and Mexico," 20–48. U.S. audiences were similarly unconcerned about reports of people of color in South America, as Chapter Three will show.

49 *Niles' Weekly Register*, November 4, 1815, February 1, 1812; Jefferson to Humboldt, December 6, 1813, Founders Online, National Archives, http://www.founders.archives.gov.

50 Patricia Tyson Stroud, *The Man Who Had Been King: The American Exile of Napoleon's Brother Joseph* (Philadelphia, 2005), 35–36, 59.

CHAPTER TWO: Agents of Revolution

1 For French and Haitian arrivals, see François Furstenberg, *When the United States Spoke French: Five Refugees Who Shaped a Nation* (New York, 2014); Ashli White, *Encountering Revolution: Haiti and the Making of the Early Republic* (Baltimore, 2010); Rafe Blaufarb, *Bonapartists in the Borderlands: French Exiles and Refugees on the Gulf Coast, 1815–1835* (Tuscaloosa, Ala., 2005).

2 This section draws especially on Charles H. Bowman, Jr., "Manuel Torres, A Spanish American Patriot in Philadelphia, 1796–1822," *Pennsylvania Magazine of History and Biography* 94.1 (January, 1970), 26–53.

3 Orea to [unidentified], November 24, 1811; Juan Pedro de Aguirre and Diego de Saavedra to Telésforo de Orea, November 20, December 1, 6, and 9, 1811; Orea to Saavedra and Aguirre, February 12, 1812; all in Archivo General de la Nación (Buenos Aires; hereafter AGN), S1-A2-A4, No. 9 (also available as Photostat copies in the Library of Congress, Washington, D.C.). All translations are mine unless otherwise noted.

4 José Manuel Restrepo, "Diario de un viaje que hice de Kingston de Jamaica

a New York," July 14, 1817, available online through the Biblioteca Luis Ángel Arango (http://www.banrepcultural.org/blaavirtual/historia/manres /manres2b.htm). Previous examinations of South Americans in the early United States have focused mostly on individual agents or cities; none have attempted to collectively gauge the community's size and makeup, nor have any examined the manifold connections between Spanish-American and Brazilian agents. See, for example, Laura Bornholdt, *Baltimore and Early Pan-Americanism* (Northampton, Mass., 1949); Samuel Flagg Bemis, *Early Diplomatic Missions from Buenos Aires to the United States, 1811–1824* (Worcester, Mass., 1944); Charles Harwood Bowman, Jr., *Vicente Pazos Kanki: Un boliviano en la libertad de América*, trans. Raúl Mariaca G. and Samuel Mendoza (La Paz, 1975); Harold A. Bierck, *Vida pública de Don Pedro Gual* (Caracas, 1983); and, most comprehensively yet, Gordon S. Brown, *Latin American Rebels and the United States, 1806–1822* (Jefferson, N.C., 2015). The profile of the expatriate community that I develop in this section (regarding geographic breadth, education, race, language, and so forth) is based on the list that I compiled in Caitlin A. Fitz, "Our Sister Republics: The United States in an Age of American Revolutions" (Ph.D. diss., Yale University, 2010), Appendix I, 301–333, and from a reference to seventeen Caracas earthquake refugees that I subsequently located in *Poulson's American Daily Advertiser*, June 4, 1812. Taken together, these individuals comprise all South Americans in the United States of whom I am aware for the years 1810–1826. My research is not meant to be exhaustive, but it seems safe to say that South American expatriates numbered in the hundreds rather than the thousands. The figure does not include Mexicans, who, especially given their prominence in neighboring New Orleans and the Gulf Coast, would have rendered the numbers significantly higher.

5   Manuel Dorrego, "Al ciudadano P.O.L.G.B. y R.," November 15, 1816, in Bonifacio del Carril, *El destierro de Dorrego, 1816* (Buenos Aires, 1986), 170–171. For another exile-turned-activist, see Bowman, *Vicente Pazos Kanki.*

6   Bowman, *Vicente Pazos Kanki*, 28–35, 272 n. 42. Pazos did not use the name Kanki in his 1818 *Exposition, Remonstrance and Protest of Don Vincente Pazos* (Philadelphia, 1818) or in his *Letters on the United Provinces of South America, Addressed to the Hon. Henry Clay*, trans. Platt H. Crosby (New York, 1819), esp. 247–249. He added the name Kanki for his 1825 *Compendio de la historia de los Estados Unidos de América* (Paris, 1825). Not all expatriates were genteel, of course; some came as servants. Class distinctions likely set such individuals apart from more prominent expatriates, though the written record leaves scant if any account of their experiences. Perhaps Pazos declined to mention his native ancestry for fear of discrimination or distraction; for editors' depictions of indigenous and mestizo Mexicans, see Sarah E. Cornell, "Americans

in the U.S. South and Mexico: A Transnational History of Race, Slavery, and Freedom, 1810–1910" (Ph.D. diss., New York University, 2008), 20–91.

7   Bierck, "Pedro Gual and the Effort to Capture a Mexican Port, 1816"; *Baltimore Patriot & Mercantile Advertiser*, May 29, 1817; Bornholdt, *Baltimore and Early Pan-Americanism*; Carlos de Alvear to the government of Buenos Aires, September 30, 1824, Sala X, 1-5-2, AGN; Fitz, "Our Sister Republics," 63–64.

8   Manuel Torres to the Secretary of State of Colombia, December 26, 1820, in Francisco José Urrutia, ed., *Los Estados Unidos de América y las repúblicas hispano-americanas de 1810 á 1830* (Madrid, 1918), 210 (also see Torres to Roscio and Revenga, May 20, 1820, 199); *Niles' Weekly Register*, July 27, 1822 (citing the *Aurora*, July 16, 1822).

9   Gregorio Gómez to Juan Martín de Pueyrredón, November 13, 1817, S4-A2-A4, No. 9, AGN; *Aurora General Advertiser*, July 28, 1822; *Niles' Weekly Register*, July 27, 1822; *Richmond Enquirer*, July 23, 1822; *New-York Evening Post*, July 20, 1822.

10   Duane to Henry Clay, July 15, 1822, James F. Hopkins and Mary W. M. Hargreaves, eds., *Papers of Henry Clay* (Lexington, Ky., 1963), III:261; *Richmond Enquirer*, July 23, 1822.

11   On Torres's influence, see Bowman, "Manuel Torres."

12   Laurentino Gomes, *1808: The Flight of the Emperor*, trans. Andrew Nevins (2007; English ed., Guilford, Conn., 2013), 101–168.

13   Arnold Wiznitzer, "The Exodus from Brazil and Arrival in New Amsterdam of the Jewish Pilgrim Fathers, 1654," *Publication of the American Jewish Historical Society* 44 (May, 1954), 80–97; Stuart B. Schwartz, *Sugar Plantations in the Formation of Brazilian Society: Bahia, 1550–1835* (New York, 1985). Pernambuco was also growing cotton by the early nineteenth century, and coffee was becoming important to southern Brazil's economy as well.

14   Carlos Guilherme Mota, *Nordeste 1817: Estruturas e argumentos* (São Paulo, 1972); Evaldo Cabral de Mello, *A outra independência: O federalismo pernambucano de 1817 a 1824* (São Paulo, 2004); Jeffrey C. Mosher, *Political Struggle, Ideology, and State Building: Pernambuco and the Construction of Brazil, 1817–1850* (Lincoln, Nebr., 2008), 9–40; Roderick J. Barman, *Brazil: The Forging of a Nation, 1798–1852* (Stanford, Calif., 1988), 55–60; Gomes, *1808*, 115–123 (esp. 115, for "a crippling fear of crustaceans and thunder").

15   "Os Patriotas Governadores Provisórios da Província" to Monroe, March 12, 1817, in *Documentos Históricos* (Rio de Janeiro, 1953–1955; hereafter DH), 101:18–19; "Memórias históricas da Revolução de Pernambuco," DH 107:254; João Lopes Cardoso Machado, "Carta narrando os acontecimentos do dia 6 de março com pormenores," June 15, 1817, DH 102:8; "Defesa de José Pereira Caldas," DH 108: 278; Cabral de Mello, *A outra independência*, 46–48. For various foreign influences, see Mota, *Nordeste 1817*, 31–38, 261–262, 285; Luiz

Geraldo Santos da Silva, "O avesso da Independência: Pernambuco (1817–
1824)," in *A independência brasileira: Novas dimensões*, ed. Jurandir Malerba
(Rio de Janeiro, 2006), 365–369.

16   Provisional Government of Pernambuco to Castlereagh, March 12, 1817, DH
109: 260–261. For U.S. influence (and lack thereof) in Spanish America, also
see Merle E. Simmons, *La revolución norteamericana en la independencia de
hispanoamérica* (Madrid, 1922); Javier Ocampo López, *La independencia de los
Estados Unidos de America y su proyección en hispanoamerica: El modelo nor-
teamericano y su repercusión en la independencia de Colombia* (Caracas, 1979);
Jaime E. Rodríguez O., "Sobre la supuesta influencia de la independencia de
los Estados Unidos en las independencias hispanoamericanas," *Revista de
Indias* 70.250 (2010), 691–714; Karen Racine, "'This England and This Now':
British Cultural and Intellectual Influence in the Spanish American Indepen-
dence Era," *Hispanic American Historical Review* 90.3 (2010), 423–454.

17   *Daily National Intelligencer* of April 29, 1817 (reprinting the *Norfolk Herald* of
April 24, 1817). For reprintings in fourteen states, see Maysville, Ky.'s *Eagle*,
May 16, 1817; *Baltimore Patriot*, April 26, 1817; Brownsville, Pa.'s *American Telegraph*, May 14, 1817; Cooperstown, N.Y.'s *American Watch-Tower*, May 15, 1817;
Burlington, Vt.'s *Northern Sentinel*, May 9, 1817; Portsmouth, N.H.'s *Intelligencer*, May 1, 1817; Massachusetts's *Dedham Gazette*, May 9, 1817; Maine's *Hallowell Gazette*, May 7, 1816; New Bern, N.C.'s *Carolina Federal Republican*, May
10, 1817; *Newport Mercury*, May 3, 1817; Hartford's *Connecticut Courant*, May
6, 1817; Charles Town, Va.'s *Farmer's Repository*, May 7, 1817; *Trenton Federalist*, May 5, 1817; Chillicothe's *Weekly Recorder*, May 14, 1817; South Carolina's
Camden Gazette, May 12, 1817. On Bowen and his relationship with editors
and rebel leaders, also see José Antônio Gonsalves de Mello, *Ingleses em Pernambuco* (Recife, 1972), 42–43; Gláucio Veiga, "O Cônsul Joseph Ray, os Estados Unidos e a Revolução de 1817," *Revista do Instituto Arqueológico, Histórico
e Geográfico Pernambucano* 52 (1979), 271–272; Richard Rush to James Madison, June 14, 1817, in Léon Bourdon, ed., *José Corrêa da Serra: Ambassadeur
du Royaume-Uni de Portugal et Brésil a Washington, 1816–1820* (Paris, 1975),
304–307 (hereafter *JCS*); Corrêa da Serra to Barca, May 31, 1817, in Bourdon,
ed., *JCS*, 290–295.

18   *Baltimore Patriot & Evening Advertiser*, April 28 (quotations), 29, 30 and
May 1, 3, 1817 (title change); *Weekly Aurora*, May 5, 1817. For reprintings, see
Baltimore Patriot, April 28, 1817; Stockbridge, Mass.'s *Berkshire Star*, May
8, 1817; Goshen, N.Y.'s *Orange County Patriot, or, the Spirit of "Seventy Six,"*
May 6, 1817; Elizabethtown's *New-Jersey Journal*, May 6, 1817; Middletown,
Conn.'s *Middlesex Gazette*, May 8, 1817; Brattleboro, Vt.'s *Reporter*, May
16, 1817; Leesburg, Va.'s *Genius of Liberty*, May 6, 1817; N.H.'s *Dover Sun*,

May 6, 1817; Reading, Pa.'s *Berks and Schuylkill Journal*, May 10, 1817; Chillicothe, Ohio's *Weekly Recorder*, May 21, 1817; Wilmington, Del.'s *American Watchman*, May 3, 1817; Charleston, S.C.'s *Times*, May 5, 1817; Providence's *Rhode-Island American, and General Advertiser*, May 16, 1817; Maysville, Ky.'s *Eagle*, May 16, 1817; Hallowell, Maine's *American Advocate and Kennebec Advertiser*, May 10, 1817; *National Intelligencer*, May 1, 1817. According to Corrêa da Serra, Bowen arrived in Baltimore on the afternoon of April 28; the *Baltimore Patriot* broke the Seebohm reports that evening. The timing is not impossible: the printers may have had just enough time to set the type and pump out the papers. See Corrêa da Serra to Barca, May 31, 1817, in Bourdon, ed., *JCS*, 291; Jeffrey L. Pasley, *"The Tyranny of Printers": Newspaper Politics in the Early American Republic* (Charlottesville, Va., 2001), 16–26; W. J. Rorabaugh, *The Craft Apprentice: From Franklin to the Machine Age in America* (New York, 1986), 11–14.

19   John Quincy Adams, Diary 30, April 27, 1818, 340; Diary 31, April 8, 1819, 80; both in *The Diaries of John Quincy Adams: A Digital Collection* (Boston, 2004), https://www.masshist.org/jqadiaries; Richard Beale Davis, "The Abbé Correa in America, 1812–1820: The Contributions of the Diplomat and Natural Philosopher to the Foundations of our National Life," *Transactions of the American Philosophical Society* 45.2 (May, 1955), 89–197.

20   Monroe to Madison, May 16, 1817, and Robert Walsh to Jefferson, April 14, 1823, in Bourdon, ed., *JCS*, 270, 635. Davis explores additional reasons for Corrêa da Serra's alienation in "The Abbé Correa in America," 108–111.

21   Corrêa da Serra to Comte da Barca, May 31, June 20, 1817, in Bourdon, ed., *JCS*, 294, 308; Corrêa da Serra to Vilanova Portugal, June 25, 1819, in Bourdon, ed., *JCS*, 496–497.

22   *Baltimore Patriot & Mercantile Advertiser*, February 5, 1818; Corrêa da Serra to the Comte da Barca, May 31, 1817, and Rush to Madison, June 14, 1817, in Bourdon, ed., *JCS*, 290–295, 304–307.

23   Cleonir Xavier de Albuquerque da Graça e Costa, "Elementos para uma biografia de Antonio Gonçalves da Cruz, o Cabugá," *Revista do Instituto Arqueológico, Histórico, e Geográfico Pernambucano* 49 (1977), 95–111 (quotations on 102, 104); Bernardo Teixeira's questions of Jorge Fleming Holdt, DH 103:109–111.

24   JCS to Comte da Barca, July 25, 1817, in Bourdon, ed., *JCS*, 315; Gomes, *1808*, 203; Graça e Costa, "Elementos para uma biografia"; Caesar Rodney to Monroe, June 6, 1817, in Bourdon, ed., *JCS*, 298.

25   On Cruz's perceived racial background in Brazil, see Graça e Costa, "Elementos para uma biografia" (quotations on 98–99).

26   For military costume, see Governo Provisório de Pernambuco to Cruz, March

27, 1817, Arquivo Histórico do Palácio Itamaraty (Rio de Janeiro; hereafter Itamaraty), 195/4/4. For secretaries, see Adams to Jefferson, May 26, 1817, in Bourdon, ed., *JCS*, 285. For public figures, see Cruz, "Conferencia que tive com Mr. Cesar A. Rodeney ... e com Mr. W.m Jones ...," Itamaraty, 194/4/5; Rodney to Monroe, June 6, 1817, in Bourdon, ed., *JCS*, 297–299; *Baltimore Patriot & Mercantile Advertiser*, June 23, 1817. For outfitted privateers (which never successfully cruised) and for munitions, see correspondence of Antônio Simões Roussado e Freire, December 20, 1817, DH 102:181–2; "Memórias históricas da Revolução de Pernambuco," February 5, 1818, in DH 107:257; Corrêa da Serra to João Paulo Bezerra, February 5, 1818, in Bourdon, ed., *JCS*, 361–364; Luís do Rego Barreto, ofício, March 1, 1818, Biblioteca Nacional, Secção de Manuscritos (Rio de Janeiro), I-33, 26, 3; Luís do Rego Barreto, ofício, to Conde da Palma, March 2, 1818, in DH 104:1; Corrêa da Serra to Comte da Barca, July 25, 1817, August 30, 1817, in Bourdon, ed., *JCS*, 314–318, 329–331; Helio Vianna, "O 'Cabugá,' de revolucionário a diplomata (1817/1833)," *Vultos do império* (São Paulo, 1968), 6–30; Charles G. Fenwick, *The Neutrality Laws of the United States* (Washington, D.C., 1913). For Bonapartists, see J. A. Ferreira da Costa, "Napoleão I no Brasil," *Revista do Instituto Arqueológico, Histórico e Geográfico Pernambucano* 10.57 (March, 1903), 197–217; Caitlin A. Fitz, "A Stalwart Motor of Revolutions: An American Merchant in Pernambuco, 1817–1825," *The Americas* 65.1 (July, 2008), 39–43.

27   Governo Provisório to Cruz, March 27, 1817, Itamaraty, 195/4/5; Cruz to "Patrias Governadores," March [?], 1817, Itamaraty, 194/4/5; *Boston Patriot*, May 16, 1817.

28   *New-York Columbian*, December 19, 1817. For process and tactics, see *Boston Patriot*, May 21, 24, 28, 31, 1817; *Baltimore Patriot & Mercantile Advertiser*, May 27, 1817; *Boston Daily Advertiser*, May 15, 1817.

29   *Boston Patriot*, May 17, 1817; [Antônio Gonçalves da Cruz], *Correspondence Between Senhor Jose Silvestre Rebello, Chargé d'Affaires of H. M. the Emperor of Brazil, Resident at Washington, and Citizen Antonio Gonsalves da Cruz, Consul-General of the Same Empire* (Philadelphia, 1824), 18. Editors often published materials free of charge, but sometimes they received money; see Cruz, *Correspondence*, 18, as well as Charles Carroll Griffin, *The United States and the Disruption of the Spanish Empire, 1810–1822* (New York, 1937), 130; *New-York Columbian*, December 19, 1817; *Aurora General Advertiser*, July 28, 1817, July 24, 1820.

30   Corrêa da Serra to Comte da Barca, May 31, 1817, in Bourdon, ed., *JCS*, 294. For original articles that seem likely to have been authored or personally informed by Cruz, see *Boston Daily Advertiser*, May 15, 1817; *Boston Patriot*, May 17, 1817; *Boston Patriot*, May 21, 1817; *Boston Patriot*, May 24, 1817 (two arti-

cles); *Boston Patriot*, May 28, 1817 (two articles); *Boston Yankee*, May 30, 1817; *Boston Patriot*, May 31, 1817; *Baltimore Patriot & Mercantile Advertiser*, June 12, 1817; *Baltimore Patriot & Mercantile Advertiser*, June 23, 1817; *Philadelphia Aurora*, July 30, 1817; Philadelphia *Aurora*, August 12, 1817; *New-York Columbian*, December 19, 1817 (three articles); *Baltimore Patriot & Mercantile Advertiser*, February 3, 1818; also see *National Intelligencer*, June 18, 1817. This list does not include translated rebel proclamations that Cruz provided to editors, and nondigitized newspapers are underrepresented. For sample reprintings and responses, see Leesburg, Va.'s *Genius of Liberty*, June 24, 1817; Bridgeton, N.J.'s *Washington Whig*, June 2, 1817; Amherst, N.H.'s *Farmer's Cabinet*, May 17, 1817; Maysville, Ky.'s *Eagle*, June 6, 1817 (citing an unidentified Pittsburgh paper); Providence's *Rhode-Island American, and General Advertiser*, May 16, 1817; New Haven's *Columbian Register*, May 24, 1817; Chillicothe's *Weekly Recorder*, June 11, 1817; Windsor's *Vermont Republican*, May 26, 1817; New Bern, N.C.'s *Carolina Federal Republican*, May 31, 1817; Charleston's *Carolina Gazette*, June 7, 1817. For positive press corresponding with Cruz's movement along the coast, see (in addition to the Boston example) the aforementioned seventeen articles alongside Rodney to Monroe, June 6, 8, 1817, and Corrêa da Serra to Comte da Barca, July 25, 1817, in Bourdon, ed., *JCS*, 297–301, 314–318. For Brazilian newspapers, see Denis Antônio de Mendonça Bernardes, *O patriotismo constitucional: Pernambuco, 1820–1822* (São Paulo and Recife, 2006), 277, 305; Kirsten Schultz, *Tropical Versailles: Empire, Monarchy, and the Portuguese Royal Court in Rio de Janeiro, 1808–1821* (New York, 2001), 71.

31   My sample comprises the 169 English-language titles published in 1817 and available in series 1–5 of Readex's *America's Historical Newspapers* online database (Early American Newspapers) as of July 2008 (http://infoweb.newsbank.com); 134 of those papers, or 79 percent, covered the Pernambuco uprising. I have excluded titles that went out of print before news of the revolt arrived, as well as those that went into print only after definitive news of the revolt's collapse. Illustrative rather than exhaustive, the sample remains large enough to give a raw indication of circulation and distribution. For a full listing of newspapers included in the sample set, see Fitz, "Our Sister Republics," Appendix II, 339–344. Readership estimates do not account for the innumerable individuals who heard newspapers read aloud in public spaces, nor do they account for the over 300 newspapers that are not available in the aforementioned Readex database series. For newspapers and readership, see Pasley, *Tyranny of Printers*, 196–228, 403; Daniel Walker Howe, *What Hath God Wrought: The Transformation of America, 1815–1848* (New York, 2007), 227.

32   Norfolk's *American Beacon and Commercial Diary*, May 8, 1817 (citing New York's *Commercial Advertiser* and reprinted in Cooperstown's *Otsego Herald*,

May 8, 1817; Charleston's *Times*, May 9, 1817; Brattleboro's *Reporter*, May 6, 1817); Boston's *Columbian Centinel*, May 7, 1817 (reprinted in Amherst, N.H.'s *Farmer's Cabinet*, May 10, 1817; *Newport Mercury*, May 10, 1817; *Gazette of Maine*, May 13, 1817).

33 William Maclay, *Journal of William Maclay*, May 1, 1789, ed. Edgar S. Maclay (New York, 1890), 10–12; John Adams to James Lloyd, March 27, 1815, Founders Online, National Archives, http://founders.archives.gov.

34 Adams to Jefferson, May 26, 1817, in Founders Online, National Archives, http://founders.archives.gov; *Boston Patriot*, May 24, 1817; John Ferling, *John Adams: A Life* (New York, 1992), 229, 295–297; Corliss Knapp Engle, "John Adams, Farmer and Gardener," *Arnoldia* 61.4 (2002), 13–14.

35 *Boston Patriot*, May 24, 28, 17, 1817. For reprintings, see Chillicothe's *Weekly Recorder*, June 11, 1817; Newark's *Centinel of Freedom*, June 3, 1817; *Baltimore Patriot*, May 21, 1817; Washington's *National Intelligencer*, May 22, 1817; Windsor's *Vermont Republican*, May 26, 1817; Norfolk's *American Beacon*, May 27, 1817; *Providence Patriot*, May 24, 1817; Philadelphia's *Weekly Aurora*, May 26, 1817; New Bern, N.C.'s *Carolina Federal Republican*, May 31, 1817; *The Aeolian Harp, or Songster's Cabinet; Being a Selection of the Most Popular Songs and Recitations; Patriotic, Sentimental, Humorous, &c.* (2 vols.; New York, 1817), I:42–43.

36 *Boston Yankee*, May 30, 1817.

37 *Boston Patriot*, May 16, 1817 (reprinted in *Carthage Gazette, and Friend of the People*, July 1, 1817); *Poulson's American Daily Advertiser*, May 8, 1817, citing Boston's *Columbian Centinel*). For a similar observation about anti-Spanish sentiment, see Mark G. Jaede, "Brothers at a Distance: Race, Religion, Culture, and U.S. Views of Spanish America, 1800–1830" (Ph.D. diss., State University of New York at Buffalo, 2001), 104–105.

38 For Massachusetts responses to hemispheric independence, see Chapter Four. For fewer South Americans in Boston, see Fitz, "Our Sister Republics," Appendix I, 301–333.

39 *National Intelligencer*, May 12, 13 (citing the *Savannah Republican*), 1817; *Albany Argus*, May 6, 1817.

40 Corrêa da Serra to Comte da Barca, May 31, 1817, and Madison to Rush, June 27, 1817, in Bourdon, ed., *JCS*, 294, 311–312 (quotations). Also see Rush to Corrêa da Serra, May 24, 1817, Corrêa da Serra to Rush, May 25, 1817, Rush to Corrêa da Serra, May 28, 1817, and Rush to Madison, June 14, 1817, in Bourdon, ed., *JCS*, 283–284, 286–287, 304–307. For the blockade announcement, see *National Intelligencer*, May 12, 22, 1817. For setting the record straight, see, for example, *Boston Patriot*, May 17, 28, 1817; *Baltimore Patriot*, May 24, 1817; *National Intelligencer*, May 27, June 3, 1817. For closed purse strings, see Corrêa da Serra to Comte da Barca, June 20, 1817, in Bourdon, ed., *JCS*, 308.

41   Cruz to Rush, June 16, 18, 1817, in DH 109:262–266. I discuss Spanish-American
recognition and popular pressure in Chapter Five.

42   *North American Review*, July, 1825 (reprinted in Philadelphia's *National
Gazette and Literary Register*, July 30, 1826); also see *Charleston Mercury*, as
cited in the *Baltimore Patriot & Mercantile Advertiser*, November 29, 1822;
Christian Advocate, October, 1824. For toasts, see Philadelphia's *Aurora*, July 7
and 17, 1817; *New-York Columbian*, July 9, 1817; Jaede, "Brothers at a Distance,"
53. Twenty-eight percent of hemispheric toasts from 1810 to 1816 were to *Spanish* America (N=29, drawing from the same sample set used in Chapters One
and Four). For 1817 through 1820, that figure fell to 5 percent (N=101). Toasts
to South America, meanwhile, rose from 66 percent to 80 percent. Although
the sample set is too small to identify a precise year of terminological transition, the declining usage of *Spanish America* seems clear, and toasts to Spanish
America did not reemerge even after Mexicans established a new republican
government in 1824.

43   Corrêa da Serra to Vilanova Portugal, June 1, 1818, in Bourdon, ed., *JCS*,
395–396. For Roscio's pamphlet, see *Reply to the Author of the Letter on South
America and Mexico, by an American, Addressed to Mr. James Munroe* (Phil-
adelphia, 1817); for authorship, see *City of Washington Gazette*, May 21, 1821.
For lobbying, see Corrêa da Serra to João Paulo Bezerra, February 5, 1818, in
Bourdon, ed., *JCS*, 362. For seeing rebels off, see Corrêa da Serra to Vilanova
Portugal, September 16, 1818, in Bourdon, ed., *JCS*, 415–416. For Torres, see
Juan Germán Roccio to Cruz, December 31, 1818, 186/1/7-9, Itamaraty.

44   Instructions from the Government of the Provincias Unidas del Río de la
Plata to David Curtis DeForest, February 24, 1818, in S1-A2-A4, No. 8, AGN;
Government of the Provincias Unidas del Río de la Plata to Manuel Hermenegildo de Aguirre, January 31, 1818, in S4-A2-A4, No. 9, AGN; Rivadavia
to Alvear, February 26, 1824, in Emilio Ravignani, ed., *Documentos para la
historia argentina*, vol. XIV; *Correspondencias generales de la Provincia de Buenos Aires relativas a relaciones exteriores (1820–1824)* (Buenos Aires, 1921), 455;
Bierck, *Vida pública de Don Pedro Gual*, 62.

45   Boston's *Independent Chronicle*, July 5, 1810; *Connecticut Courant*, June 13, 1810
(citing the *Baltimore Evening Post*); [Manuel Palacio Fajardo], *Appeal to the
Government and People of the United States, in Behalf of the Independent South
American Provinces* (New York, 1818), 29, 31; Manuel Torres, *An Exposition of
the Commerce of Spanish America: With Some Observations upon Its Importance
to the United States* (Philadelphia, 1816), 10; Pazos, *Letters on the United Provinces of South America*, 121–122; Manuel Palacio Fajardo, *Outline of the Revolution in Spanish America, or, An Account of the Origin, Progress, and Actual State
of the War Carried on Between Spain and Spanish America* (New York, 1817).

46 John Stuart Skinner to José Miguel Carrera, n.d. [probably late November, 1817], Carrera Manuscripts, Archivo Nacional de Chile (Santiago), AcD.R. Σ 1338, accessed in Photostat form in the Library of Congress, Box 1; David Porter to Joel Roberts Poinsett, October 23, 1817, in the Joel Roberts Poinsett Papers, Historical Society of Pennsylvania (Philadelphia), Box 2, Folder 2. Skinner and his allies had a personal financial interest in the outcome; for this and for Carrera's English, see Bornholdt, *Baltimore and Early Pan-Americanism*, esp. 61.

47 Junta Provisional Guvernativa de las Provincias del Río de la Plata, instructions to Diego de Saavedra and Juan Pedro de Aguirre, June 5, 1811, in S1-A2-A4, No. 9, AGN (for fictitious names).

48 Cabral de Mello, *A outra independência*, 65–237; Bernardes, *Patriotismo constitucional*, 315–631; Amy Caldwell de Farias, *Mergulho no Letes: Uma reinterpretação político-histórica da Confederação do Equador* (Porto Alegre, 2006). For Cruz's subsequent U.S. citizenship and for his service as Brazil's consul general in the United States and Bolivia, see "Documento do distrito de Filadélfia, sobre a naturalização do brasileiro Antônio Gonçalves da Cruz . . . ," November 4–5, 1818, Itamaraty, 186/1/7-9; Vianna, "O Cabugá"; Cabral de Mello, *A outra independência*, 234–235; [Cruz], *Correspondence between Senhor Jose Silvestre Rebello . . . and Citizen Antonio Gonsalves da Cruz.*

49 Francisco Augusto Pereira da Costa, *Anais Pernambucanos* (Recife, 1951–1966), 9:60–61; Marcus Joaquim Maciel de Carvalho, "Hegemony and Rebellion in Pernambuco (Brazil), 1821–1835" (Ph.D. diss., University of Illinois, 1989), 67–69.

50 Francisco de Lima e Silva to Luiz José de Carvalho e Mello, April 12, 1825, Itamaraty 309/2/16; Mundrucu, "Manifiesto que Hace a la Nacion Colombiana Emiliano Felipe Benicio Mundrucu . . . dirijido al respetable publico y ejercito de la Republica de Colombia" (1826), in Vamireh Chacon, ed. and trans., *Da Confederação do Equador à Grã-Colômbia: Natividade Saldanha* (Brasília, 1983), 198–199; Caitlin A. Fitz, "A Stalwart Motor of Revolutions: An American Merchant in Pernambuco, 1817–1825," *The Americas* 65.1 (July, 2008), 35–62. For bayonets and cartouche boxes, see *Saratoga Sentinel*, December 1, 1824 (reprinting the *National Gazette*).

51 E. S. Abdy, *Journal of a Residence and Tour in the United States of North America, from April, 1833, to October, 1834* (London, 1835), I:136; Izidoro da Costa e Oliveira, "Relação nominal dos individuos que se tem evadido de varias provincias do Imperio do Brazil, e que tem aportado a estes estados," May 26, 1825, in Itamaraty, 233/2/21; José Silvestre Rebello to Luiz José Carvalho e Mello, August 26, 1825, in *Archivo Diplomático da Independencia* (Rio de Janeiro, 1923), V:157; Corrêa da Serra to Vilanova Portugal, September

16, 1818, December 6, 1820, in Bourdon, ed., *JCS*, 415–416, 608; Mundrucu, "Manifiesto." I have been able to trace the experiences of only one other Pernambuco *mulato* refugee in the United States; see Argeu Guimarães, *Vida e morte de Natividade Saldanha (1796–1832)* (Lisbon, 1932); Fitz, "Our Sister Republics," 98–100.

52   For this paragraph and the next, see Abdy, *Journal of a Residence and Tour*, I:136–140; Lydia Maria Child, *An Appeal in Favor of that Class of Americans Called Africans* (Boston, 1833), 219–223; David Lee Child, *The Despotism of Freedom; Or the Tyranny and Cruelty of American Republican Slave-Masters, Shown to be the Worst in the World* (Boston, 1833), esp. 8–9, 66; *The Boston Directory* (Boston, 1825–1830); *Baltimore Patriot & Mercantile Advertiser*, March 10, 1830. With support from his lawyers Daniel Webster and David Child, Mundrucu took the steamboat captain to court for breach of contract; he won before a packed audience in the court of common pleas but lost on appeal in the state supreme court, receiving nationwide attention. See, for example, *New-York Commercial Advertiser*, October 18, 1833; *Nantucket Inquirer*, October 26, 1833; *National Intelligencer*, October 22, 1833; *New-Bedford Mercury*, January 31, 1834.

53   Child, *Appeal*, 219–223; Abdy, *Journal of a Residence and Tour*, I:138; Child, *Despotism of Freedom*, 8, 66. For a background on the Childs, see Carolyn L. Karcher, *The First Woman in the Republic: A Cultural Biography of Lydia Maria Child* (Durham, 1994), esp. 48, 173–194. For Mundrucu's donations, see *The Liberator*, June 1, 1833, February 10, 1860, February 15, 1861.

54   For this paragraph and the next, see Sean Wilentz, ed., *David Walker's Appeal* (New York, 1995), esp. 5–7, 35–36, 49; Peter P. Hinks, *To Awaken My Afflicted Brethren: David Walker and the Problem of Antebellum Slave Resistance* (University Park, Pa., 1997). For Mundrucu's age, see the obituaries in *Boston Daily Advertiser*, September 22, 1863; *Frank Leslie's Illustrated Newspaper*, October 24, 1863. By 1833, Mundrucu was also an acquaintance of William Lloyd Garrison and a leader in Boston's free black community; see, for example, *The Liberator*, April 13, 1833; *Salem Observer*, January 3, 1863.

55   Wilentz, ed., *David Walker's Appeal*, xii–xix, 36 (the latter page noting that Walker also expressly cited Frederick Butler, *A Complete History of the United States of America, Embracing the Whole Period from the Discovery of North America, Down to the Year 1820* [3 vols., Hartford, 1821]); Hinks, ed., *David Walker's Appeal*, xliv. For the hemispheric perspectives of *Freedom's Journal*, see Chapter Four.

56   *National Intelligencer*, April 29, 1817 (citing the *Norfolk Herald* of April 24, 1817); *Baltimore Patriot & Mercantile Advertiser*, May 1, 1817; *Charleston's Times*, May 9, 1817. For retrospective criticism, see *New-York Daily Advertiser*, July 18, 1817.

CHAPTER THREE: The News, in Black and White

1   Jeffrey L. Pasley, *"The Tyranny of Printers": Newspaper Politics in the Early American Republic* (Charlottesville, Va., 2001); James C. Bonner, *Milledgeville, Georgia's Antebellum Capital* (Athens, Ga., 1978).

2   W. J. Rorabaugh, *The Craft Apprentice: From Franklin to the Machine Age in America* (New York, 1986), 11–14; Pasley, *Tyranny of Printers*, 16–26.

3   John Lynch, *Simón Bolívar: A Life* (New Haven, 2007), 88–102; Paul Verna, *Pétion y Bolívar: Una etapa decisiva en la emancipación de Hispanoamérica, 1790–1830* (Caracas, 1980); Sibylle Fischer, "Bolívar in Haiti: Republicanism in the Revolutionary Atlantic," in Carla Calargé, Raphael Dalleo, Luis Duno-Gottberg, and Clevis Headley, eds., *Haiti and the Americas* (Jackson, Miss., 2013), 25–53. On the printing shop location, see Bonner, *Milledgeville*, 22–61. Although U.S. newspapers seldom drew a distinction, there were actually two Haitis in 1816: Pétion's Republic of Haiti to the south and Henri Christophe's kingdom to the north. Bolívar fled to the former.

4   *Georgia Journal*, July 3, 10, 17, 24 (quotation), 31, 1816; 1820 census, Baldwin County, Georgia, 54, 62 (available at http://www.ancestrylibrary.com). On dirty work, see Rorabaugh, *Craft Apprentice*, 11–14; Pasley, *Tyranny of Printers*, 16–26. On another early-nineteenth-century Georgia print shop that likely relied in part on slave labor, see Susanna Ashton, "Slavery, Imprinted: The Life and Narrative of William Grimes," in Lara Langer Cohen and Jordan Alexander Stein, eds., *Early African American Print Culture* (Philadelphia, 2012), 136–138, 367–368 n. 16.

5   *Georgia Journal*, July 10 and 17, 1816; Bonner, *Milledgeville*, esp. 35, 60–78; U.S. Department of State, *Census for 1820* (Washington, D.C., 1821), 116.

6   Ohio's *Western American*, July 6, 1816; Charleston's *City Gazette and Daily Advertiser*, June 21, 1816; western Virginia's *Farmer's Repository*, June 26, 1816; Kentucky's *Union*, June 28, 1816.

7   Peter Blanchard, *Under the Flags of Freedom: Slave Soldiers and the Wars of Independence in Spanish South America* (Pittsburgh, 2008); Aline Helg, *Liberty and Equality in Caribbean Colombia, 1770–1835* (Chapel Hill, 2004); Marixa Lasso, *Myths of Harmony: Race and Republicanism During the Age of Revolution, Colombia 1795–1831* (Pittsburgh, 2007); Marcela Echeverri, "Popular Royalists and Revolution in Colombia: Nationalism and Empire, 1780–1820" (Ph.D. diss., New York University, 2008); Mark G. Jaede, "Brothers at a Distance: Race, Religion, Culture, and U.S. Views of Spanish America, 1800–1830" (Ph.D. diss., State University of New York at Buffalo, 2001), 122–126. For ends and means, see Robin Blackburn, *The Overthrow of Colonial Slavery, 1776–1848* (1988; New York, 2011), esp. 331–379, 526–527.

8   Leesburg's *Genius of Liberty*, June 3, 1817 (citing the *Boston Yankee*, May 16,

1817, and reprinted in Haverhill's *Essex Patriot*, May 31, 1817, among many others).

9   *New-York Columbian*, June 13, 29 (quotation), 1816.

10   John Quincy Adams, Diary 31, November 22, 1819, in *The Diaries of John Quincy Adams: A Digital Collection* (Boston, 2004), 210 (available at http://www.masshist .org/jqadiaries). Laura Bornholdt, *Baltimore and Early Pan-Americanism: A Study in the Background of the Monroe Doctrine* (Northampton, Mass., 1949), 64–66; Charles H. Bowman, Jr., "Manuel Torres, a Spanish American Patriot in Philadelphia, 1796–1822," *Pennsylvania Magazine of History and Biography* 94 (January, 1970), 26–53; Pasley, *Tyranny of Printers*, 284; *Niles' Weekly Register*, November 23, 1822; Lewis Hanke, "Baptis Irvine's Reports on Simón Bolívar," *Hispanic American Historical Review* 16 (August, 1936), 360–373. Not that Irvine sided blindly with Spanish-American insurgents: he clashed with Bolívar when in Venezuela and defended a royalist weapons shipment while serving the administration. See Marie Arana, *Bolívar: American Liberator* (New York, 2013), 215–216, 259–261.

11   *Shamrock*, June 15, 1816 (and June 22, 1816); John Quincy Adams, Diary 31, November 22, 1819, in *The Diaries of John Quincy Adams: A Digital Collection* (Boston, 2004), 210 (available at http://www.masshist.org/jqadiaries). For Irvine's reprinted commentary, see, for example, Chillicothe's *Weekly Recorder*, July 24, 1816; Bridgeport, Conn.'s *Republican Farmer*, July 23, 1816; Elizabethtown's *New-Jersey Journal*, July 2, 1816; Easton, Md.'s *Republican Star*, July 2, 1816; *Alexandria Gazette, Commercial and Political*, July 12, 1816. For "able and brave," see Boston's *New England Palladium*, September 3, 1816; *Baltimore Patriot & Evening Advertiser*, September 5, 1816; Wilmington's *Delaware Gazette and Peninsula Advertiser*, September 9, 1816; Norfolk's *American Beacon and Commercial Diary*, September 11, 1816; Charles Town, Va.'s *Farmer's Repository*, September 18, 1816. My newspaper sample for the 90 percent figure (N=128) represents roughly one-fourth to one-fifth of all the newspapers printed in the United States in 1816; it comprises the English-language newspapers available on series 1–5 of the America's Historical Newspapers online database (as of July 2008) for the period between May 1 and September 30, 1816—the period when news on Bolívar's Haitian alliance and anti-slavery proclamations was arriving. I have excluded all titles for which fewer than five issues are available in the appointed time period. For a full list of titles, see Caitlin A. Fitz, "Our Sister Republics: The United States in an Age of American Revolutions" (Ph.D. diss., Yale University, 2010), Appendix II, 334–338.

12   David Bushnell, *Simón Bolívar: Liberation and Disappointment* (New York, 2004), 76–78; Lynch, *Simón Bolívar*, 100–110, 151; Echeverri, "Popular Royalists and Revolution in Colombia."

13   Philadelphia's *Democratic Press*, August 17, 1816. For sample reprintings, see N.Y. *Columbian*, August 19, 1816; S.C. *Camden Gazette*, August 29, 1816; Middlebury,

Vt.'s *National Standard*, September 4, 1816; *Baltimore Patriot & Evening Advertiser*, August 19, 1816; Norfolk's *American Beacon and Commercial Diary*, August 22, 1816; Ballston Spa's *Independent American*, August 28, 1816; *Newburyport Herald*, August 23, 1816; *Providence Patriot*, August 24, 1816; Bridgeton, N.J.'s *Washington Whig*, August 26, 1816; Concord's *New-Hampshire Patriot*, August 27, 1816; Kennebunk, Maine's *Weekly Visiter*, August 28, 1816; Hartford's *Connecticut Mirror*, August 26, 1816; *Kline's Weekly Carlisle Gazette*, August 27, 1816; Wilmington, Del.'s *American Watchman*, August 28, 1816; *Georgia Journal*, September 4, 1816. For "complete success," see, for example, the *Chillicothe Weekly Recorder*, July 24, 1816; for reprints, see Salem, Mass.'s *Essex Register*, June 19, 1816; *Albany Advertiser*, June 19, 1816; New Haven's *Connecticut Herald*, June 18, 1816; *Daily National Intelligencer*, June 18, 1816; *Alexandria Herald*, June 19, 1816; Charleston's *City Gazette and Daily Advertiser*, June 21, 1816; Newport's *Rhode-Island Republican*, June 26, 1816; Chambersburg, Pa.'s *Democratic Republican*, June 24, 1816; Williamsburg, Ohio's *Western American*, July 6, 1816; Windsor's *Spooner's Vermont Journal*, June 24, 1816; Newark, N.J.'s *Centinel of Freedom*, June 25, 1816; Easton, Md.'s *Republican Star or General Advertiser*, June 25, 1816; Wilmington, Del.'s *American Watchman*, June 26, 1816; Charles Town, Va.'s *Farmer's Repository*, June 26, 1816; Washington, Ky.'s *Union*, June 28, 1816; *Georgia Journal*, July 3, 1816.

14 The mean number of days of Pernambuco coverage was 197; the median, 220. For Barbados statistics, see Edward Bartlett Rugemer's careful analysis in *The Problem of Emancipation: The Caribbean Roots of the American Civil War* (Baton Rouge, 2008), esp. 88–89; for Pernambuco coverage, see Chapter Two in this book. To the degree possible, I have studied coverage in the same newspapers that Rugemer did. *Niles' Weekly Register* covered Pernambuco for at least 246 days; the *Charleston City Gazette and Commercial Advertiser*, for 166; the *New-York Evening Post*, for 128; the *Richmond Enquirer*, for 220; the *Daily National Intelligencer*, for 225.

15 Rory T. Cornish, "Camden, South Carolina, Plot (1816), in Junius P. Rodriguez, ed., *Encyclopedia of Slave Resistance and Rebellion* (Westport, 2007), I:97–98.

16 *Camden Gazette*, August 29, 1816; Lacy K. Ford, *Deliver Us from Evil: The Slavery Question in the Old South* (New York, 2009), 173–190.

17 Ford, *Deliver Us from Evil*, 173–190 (quotations, 176); Rodriguez, *Encyclopedia of Slave Resistance and Rebellion*, 97–98. The author referencing "vigilance" was evidently quoting from George Colman, Jr., *The Surrender of Calais: A Play in Three Acts* (first performed in London in 1791; new ed., London, 1808).

18 *Richmond Enquirer*, August 31, 1816 and June 3, 1817 (quotation). In December of 1816, scared by the alleged conspiracy, Langley went on to advocate an end to the interstate slave trade and toyed with the idea of colonization. He emphatically denied that he favored emancipation, however, and his core audience remained staunch defenders of slavery. Ford, *Deliver Us from Evil*, 189–190.

19   *Vermont Gazette*, July 9, 1816 (also see *Pittsfield Sun*, August 29, 1816); *Boston Recorder*, July 24, 1816 (also in *Hallowell Gazette*, July 31, 1816). For indifference, see Ballston Spa's *Independent American*, August 28, 1816.

20   For *Phocion's* essays, see the *Daily National Intelligencer*, November 20, December 1, 8, 16, 1817 (quotations in the last two issues).

21   *City of Washington Gazette*, December 17, 1817; *Weekly Aurora*, December 29, 1817; *Daily National Intelligencer*, December 29, 1817. For other responses to *Phocion*, see the *Daily National Intelligencer*, December 1, 1817; Philadelphia's *Weekly Aurora*, December 8 and 22, 1817; January 26, February 23, March 2 and 23; April 6, 1818; *Baltimore Patriot & Mercantile Advertiser*, December 9 and 12, 1817; *City of Washington Gazette*, February 16 and March 28, 1818. For the pamphlet, see *The Essays of Phocion, on the Policy of the United States, in Relation to the War Between Spain and Her Colonies* (Washington City, 1818).

22   John Quincy Adams to John Adams, December 21, 1817, Founders Online, National Archives, http://founders.archives.gov. For the abbé and for authorship, see James E. Lewis, Jr.'s meticulous analysis in *The American Union and the Problem of Neighborhood: The United States and the Collapse of the Spanish Empire, 1783–1829* (Chapel Hill, 1998), 242 n. 36.

23   Fincastle's *Herald of the Valley*, November 5, 1821; *Carolina Centinel*, July 5, 1823 (quotations). For the legislation, see *Rhode-Island American, and General Advertiser*, October 19, 1821 (citing the *New-York Daily Advertiser*); *New-Bedford Mercury*, October 26, 1821; Ill.'s *Edwardsville Spectator*, November 13, 1821; Charleston's *City Gazette and Commercial Daily Advertiser*, October 23, 1821; New Haven's *Connecticut Herald*, October 23, 1821; *Richmond Enquirer*, October 23, 1821; Vermont's *Woodstock Observer*, January 28, 1821 (citing the *Philadelphia American*); Portsmouth's *New-Hampshire Gazette*, January 8, 1822. For the second account, in New England and the Mid-Atlantic see, for example, *Newburyport Herald*, October 23, 1821 (citing the New York [*National?*] *Advocate*). Also see Harold A. Bierck, Jr., "The Struggle for Abolition in Gran Colombia," *Hispanic American Historical Review* 33.3 (August, 1953), esp. 371; Lasso, *Myths of Harmony*, 58–59.

24   Thomas Jefferson to John Holmes, April 22, 1820, Founders Online, National Archives, http://founders.archives.gov; Robert Pierce Forbes, *The Missouri Compromise and its Aftermath: Slavery and the Meaning of America* (Chapel Hill, 2007). The 36°-30' line only applied to the rest of the Louisiana Purchase territory—not to future territorial acquisitions.

25   James F. Hopkins et al., *Papers of Henry Clay* (Lexington, Ky., 1959–1992), II: 858. For Clay on slavery more broadly, see Ford, *Deliver Us from Evil*, esp. 326–327; Daniel Walker Howe, *What Hath God Wrought: The Transformation of America, 1815–1848* (New York, 2007), 264.

26   For trade, see Timothy Pitkin, *A Statistical View of the Commerce of the United*

States of America (New Haven, 1835), 219–227; *Hazard's Register of Pennsylvania*, October 11, 1828. For demographics, see José Manuel Restrepo, *Historia de la Revolución de la República de Colombia en la América Meridional* (Besançon, 1858), I:xiv; Alfonso Múnera, *El Fracaso de la nación: Región, clase y raza en el Caribe colombiano (1717–1810)* (Bogotá, 1998), 40–41; Helg, *Liberty and Equality in Caribbean Colombia*; Blackburn, *Overthrow of Colonial Slavery*, 334–335. These demographic contours appeared widely in the United States; see, for example, the *Daily National Intelligencer*, May 24, 1816; *Weekly Aurora*, December 8, 1817, April 6, 1818; *Rhode-Island American, and General Advertiser*, January 1, 1819; *Boston Weekly Messenger*, July 1, 1824; *Boston Commercial Gazette*, July 23, 1826; [James Yard], *Spanish America and the United States; or, Views of the Actual Commerce with the United States and the Spanish Colonies* (Philadelphia, 1818), 40–44. For expatriates, see Vicente Pazos, *Letters on the United Provinces of South America, Addressed to the Hon. Henry Clay, Speaker of the House of Representatives of the U. States*, trans. Platt H. Crosby (New York, 1819), 55–56; Clay to Pazos, July 27, 1819, *Papers of Henry Clay*, II:701; [Manuel Palacio Fajardo], *Outline of the Revolution in Spanish America* (New York, 1817), 105–6. For responses to antislavery efforts in other parts of South America, see Fitz, "Our Sister Republics," 120–121.

27 Restrepo, *Historia de la Revolución de la República de Colombia*, I:xiv; Bureau of the Census, *Historical Statistics of the United States: Colonial Times to 1970* (Bicentennial ed., Washington, D.C., 1975), I:14, A 91–118, n. 1; Department of State, *Census for 1820* (Washington, D.C., 1821), 18.

28 Lynch, *Simón Bolívar*, 98, 114; *New Haven's Connecticut Herald*, January 18, 1820; An officer of the United States Army [Lieutenant Richard Bache], *Notes on Colombia, Taken in the Years 1822–3* (Philadelphia, 1827), 142–143. Ajax comparisons dated to Páez's own lifetime; see *City of Washington Gazette*, July 28, 1821.

29 *Democratic Press*, August 17, 1816; Pasley, *Tyranny of Printers*, 314–319.

30 *Democratic Press*, November 22, 1817.

31 *New-England Palladium and Commercial Advertiser*, November 28, 1817; *New-York Columbian*, November 26, 1817 (Irvine was no longer editor). For Páez, see Lynch, *Simón Bolívar*, 114; Chasteen, *Americanos*, 130. For reprintings of the *Democratic Press* article, see, for example, New York's *Plattsburgh Republican*, December 13, 1817; *Daily National Intelligencer*, November 25, 1817; *Vermont Intelligencer and Bellows' Falls Advertiser*, December 1, 1817; *Independent Chronicle and Boston Patriot*, November 29, 1817; New Haven's *Connecticut Herald*, December 2, 1817; Wilmington's *American Watchman*, December 3, 1817; Chillicothe's *Weekly Recorder*, December 3, 1817; Pennsylvania's *Washington Reporter*, December 8, 1817; Lexington's *Western Monitor*, December 13, 1817; St. Louis's *Missouri Gazette*, January 9, 1818. I have, with some hesitation, periodically followed Latin Americanists' practice in using the term "mulatto," recognizing that there is no

simple English equivalent for those whom many Latin Americans called *pardos* or *mulatos* (people of both African and European ancestry).

32   *City of Washington Gazette*, June 12, 1819. For reprintings, see, for example, Chillicothe's *Weekly Recorder*, July 2, 1819; New London's *Connecticut Gazette*, June 23, 1819; Clarksville's *Town Gazette and Farmer's Register*, August 2, 1819; Cooperstown's *Otsego Herald*, June 28, 1819; Gettysburg's *Adams Centinel*, June 30, 1819; Wilmington's *American Watchman*, June 19, 1819; Middlebury's *National Standard*, July 7, 1819; *South-Carolina State Gazette and Columbian Advertiser*, June 29, 1819; *Daily National Intelligencer*, June 15, 1819; *Alexandria Gazette and Daily Advertiser*, June 15, 1819; Stockbridge's *Berkshire Star*, June 24, 1819; *Providence Patriot*, June 23, 1819. For "chivalric exploit," see Goshen's *Orange County Patriot or the Spirit of 'Seventy Six*, July 6, 1819; *Plattsburg Republican*, July 10, 1819. Leading Spanish Americans of color had previously and sporadically appeared in the U.S. press without racial descriptors, such that readers probably understood them to be white. But the whitening seemingly began in Colombia itself, where the newspapers and government documents that informed U.S. reports themselves often declined to mention race, as a point of color-blind principle. It was only when Páez's unusual popularity attracted unusual scrutiny that U.S. editors learned of his ancestry. They thereafter reported on it openly without dwelling on it, much as they had done with Spanish-American antislavery efforts. For reports on these other Spanish Americans of color, including Judas Tadeo Piñango, José Prudencio Padilla, and Manuel Piar, see Fitz, "Our Sister Republics," 122–124.

33   *North American Review*, July, 1825. For sample reprintings, see Middletown's *American Sentinel*, August 17, 1825; *Providence Gazette*, August 13, 1825; *Boston Weekly Messenger*, July 7, 1825.

34   Norfolk's *American Beacon*, February 10, 1819; *City of Washington Gazette*, September 14, 1820 (reprinted in Arkansas Post's *Arkansas Gazette*, November 11, 1820; *Frankfort Argus*, October 5, 1820; Bellows Falls's *Vermont Intelligencer*, September 25, 1820; New Haven's *Connecticut Herald*, September 18, 1820; *Alexandria Gazette and Daily Advertiser*, September 18, 1820; *New-York Daily Advertiser*, September 15, 1820); New Haven's *Connecticut Herald*, July 17, 1821 (citing the Baltimore *Federal Gazette*; for sample reprintings, see Stockbridge's *Berkshire Star*, July 18, 1821; Danville's *North Star*, July 19, 1821; *Saratoga Sentinel*, July 18, 1821; *Richmond Enquirer*, July 13, 1821; Hartford's *American Mercury*, July 17, 1821); *Washington Gazette*, July 28, 1821; *Weekly Aurora*, October 18, 1819 ("gallant"); *New-York Evening Post*, June 16, 1819 ("immortal"); *Boston Weekly Messenger*, July 8, 1824 ("brave").

35   *Weekly Aurora*, December 8, 1817 (first quotation); "An American Citizen" [José Corrêa da Serra], *An Appeal to the Government and Congress of the United States, Against the Depredations Committed by American Privateers on*

the Commerce of Nations at Peace with Us (Philadelphia, 1819), 32–33 (second quotation); for authorship, see Léon Bourdon, ed., Corrêa da Serra to Tomás Antonio Vilanova Portugal, June 25, 1819, José Corrêa da Serra: Ambassadeur du Royaume-Uni de Portugal et Brésil a Washington, 1816–1820 (Paris, 1975), 497. The minister cited the Democratic Press of January, 1818, but I have found no such article in the newspaper that month. Royalists of color received more criticism; see, for example, Philadelphia's Weekly Aurora, December 29, 1817. Editors readily expressed racialized virulence toward rebels of color closer to home (as a subsequent section in this chapter shows), which only strengthens the case that they felt less racialized discomfort toward far-off South America.

36   Helg, Liberty and Equality in Caribbean Colombia; Lasso, Myths of Harmony; Blanchard, Under the Flags of Freedom; Echeverri, "Popular Royalists and Revolution in Colombia."

37   For contrasts between racial ideology in the United States and that in Spanish America, see, for example, Lasso, Myths of Harmony, 64, 153–157; Rodríguez O., Independence of Spanish America, esp. 239; Frank Tannenbaum, Slave and Citizen: The Negro in the Americas (New York, 1946).

38   Merton L. Dillon, Benjamin Lundy and the Struggle for Negro Freedom (Urbana, Ill., 1966), 1–10; [Thomas Earle], The Life, Travels and Opinions of Benjamin Lundy (Philadelphia, 1847), 12–19.

39   Dillon, Benjamin Lundy, 1–10; Earle, Life, Travels, and Opinions, esp. 15.

40   Earle, Life, Travels, and Opinions, 1–20; Dillon, Benjamin Lundy, 14–54.

41   Genius of Universal Emancipation, May, 1825; also see July 8, 1826; November, 1823. Northern Haiti was not a republic for most of this period, but southern Haiti was.

42   Genius of Universal Emancipation, July, 1821 (masthead); Genius of Universal Emancipation, July, 1822 (circulation). Statistics on Latin America come from the 204 issues published from July, 1821, through December, 1828 (I have included the Genius of Universal Emancipation, the Genius of Universal Emancipation and Baltimore Courier, and the other variations of Lundy's primary antislavery periodical). These articles focused on a wide variety of regions within Latin America, not just Mexico (which would become Lundy's chief concern by the 1830s).

43   Genius of Universal Emancipation, December, 1821; March, 1822; August, 1822; cf. Forbes, Missouri Compromise, 29, 144. On abolitionists' early interest in republican and constitutionalist uprisings elsewhere in the world, see W. Caleb McDaniel, The Problem of Democracy in the Age of Slavery: Garrisonian Abolitionists and Transatlantic Reform (Baton Rouge, 2013), 21–44.

44   Genius of Universal Emancipation, July, 1822; July 8, 1826; also see issues of November, 1823; June, 1825; October 27, 1827. For hemispheric slave popula-

tion, see Seymour Drescher, "The Limits of Example," in David Geggus, ed., *The Impact of the Haitian Revolution in the Atlantic World* (Columbia, S.C., 2001), 11.

45 *Genius of Universal Emancipation*, December, 1821 (also see September, 1823; May 1824; May 1825); *Abolition Intelligencer*, September, 1822.

46 Pauline Maier, *American Scripture: Making the Declaration of Independence* (New York, 1997), esp. 154–208; David Armitage, *The Declaration of Independence: A Global History* (Cambridge, Mass., 2007), 1–102, 165.

47 *Genius of Universal Emancipation*, July, 1822. Armitage, *Declaration of Independence*, 92–93; Maier, *American Scripture*, 196. Lundy was not the first to channel the Declaration against slavery; despite the overall trend, some people had done so since 1776. See Eric Slauter, "Rights," in *The Oxford Handbook of the American Revolution*, ed. Jane Kamensky and Edward G. Gray (New York, 2012), 447–464.

48 *Genius of Universal Emancipation*, June 5, 1823, April 29, 1826; Earle, *Life, Travels, and Opinions*, 20–21; Dillon, *Benjamin Lundy*, 49–54. For slaveholders' perspective on antislavery critiques, see esp. Erskine Clarke, *Dwelling-Place: A Plantation Epic* (New Haven, 2005).

49 New York's *Evening Post*, August 24, 1816; Bushnell, *Simón Bolívar*, 78–82; David Bushnell, *The Santander Regime in Gran Colombia* (Newark, Del., 1954), 6–8; Lester D. Langley, *The Americas in the Age of Revolution, 1750–1850* (New Haven, 1998), 175–190; Anthony McFarlane, "Building Political Order: The 'First Republic' in New Granada, 1810–1815," in Eduardo Posada-Carbó, ed., *In Search of a New Order: Essays on the Politics and Society of Nineteenth-Century Latin America* (London, 1998), 8; Lynch, *Simón Bolívar*, 81–83; Indalecio Liévano Aguirre, *Los grandes conflictos sociales y económicos de nuestra historia* (3d ed.; Bogotá, 1968), 617–670.

50 *Washington City Weekly Gazette*, September 7, 1816 (also see August 31, 1816; for sample reprintings, see *Albany Advertiser*, September 21, 1816; *New York Evening Post*, September 13, 1816; *Boston Gazette*, September 19, 1816). For fifteen state reprintings of the *New York Evening Post* article, see, for example, *Baltimore Patriot & Evening Advertiser*, August 26, 1816; *Nantucket Gazette*, August 31, 1816; *Alexandria Herald*, August 30, 1816; N.H.'s *Farmer's Cabinet*, September 7, 1816; S.C.'s *Camden Gazette*, September 12, 1816; Del.'s *American Watchman*, August 28, 1816; *Newport Mercury*, August 31, 1816; *Vermont Republican*, September 2, 1816; *Portland Gazette and Maine Advertiser*, September 3, 1816; *Georgia Journal*, September 11, 1816; *Norwich Courier*, August 28, 1816; *Daily National Intelligencer*, August 28, 1816; Ky.'s *Eagle*, September 13, 1816; Pa.'s *Berks and Schuylkill Journal*, August 31, 1816; N.J.'s *Washington Whig*, September 2, 1816; *Raleigh Register, and North-Carolina Gazette*, September 6, 1816. For final quotation, see Greenfield's

Franklin Herald, September 3, 1816. For newspapers that had not previously criticized the expedition, see, for example, *Baltimore Patriot & Evening Advertiser*, August 26 and September 5, 1816; *Washington City Weekly Gazette*, June 15 and 22 and July 13 and 20, 1816.

51 *New-York Courier*, August 24, 1816. For reprintings, see *Northern Whig*, September 3, 1816; *Hampshire Gazette*, September 11, 1816; *Camden Gazette*, September 19, 1816. For response, see Windsor's *Vermont Republican*, September 16, 1816; *New-York Courier*, September 26, 1816. For continued praise, see Chambersburg, Pa.'s *Democratic Republican*, September 2, 1816.

52 William Earl Weeks, *John Quincy Adams and American Global Empire* (Lexington, Ky., 1992); Jane Landers, *Black Society in Spanish Florida* (Urbana, 1999).

53 Jennifer L. Heckard, "The Crossroads of Empire: The 1817 Liberation and Occupation of Amelia Island, East Florida" (Ph.D. diss., University of Connecticut, 2004); Charles H. Bowman, Jr., "Vicente Pazos and the Amelia Island Affair, 1817," *Florida Historical Quarterly* 53.3 (January, 1975), 273–295; Charles H. Bowman, Jr., "Vicente Pazos, Agent for the Amelia Island Filibusters, 1818," *Florida Historical Quarterly* 53.4 (April, 1975), 429–442; José Corrêa da Serra to João Paulo Bezerra, February 5, 1818, in Bourdon, ed., *José Corrêa da Serra*, 362.

54 M. Rafter, *Memoirs of Gregor McGregor* (London, 1820), 20–92, 375–392; Heckard, "Crossroads of Empire"; David Sinclair, *The Land That Never Was: Sir Gregor MacGregor and the Most Audacious Fraud in History* (2003; Cambridge, Mass., 2004), 110–181; Matthew Brown, "Inca, Sailor, Soldier, King: Gregor MacGregor and the Early Nineteenth-Century Caribbean," *Bulletin of Latin American Research* 24 (2005), 44–70.

55 Brown, "Inca, Sailor, Soldier, King," 48; Heckard, "Crossroads of Empire," esp. 137, 158; Rafter, *Memoirs*, 97.

56 Adams, Diary 31, April 5, 1818, 331 (available at http://www.masshist.org/jqadiaries); Andrew Jackson to James Monroe, January 6, 1818, in Harold D. Moser, David R. Hoth, George H. Hoemann, eds., *The Papers of Andrew Jackson* (Knoxville, 1994), IV:167. Tulio Arends, *La República de las Floridas, 1817–1818* (Caracas, 1986); Frank Lawrence Owsley, Jr., and Gene A. Smith, *Filibusters and Expansionists: Jeffersonian Manifest Destiny, 1800–1821* (Tuscaloosa, Ala., 1997), 118–140; Heckard, "Crossroads of Empire," esp. 137, 158.

57 Cooperstown's *Otsego Herald*, November 13, 1817 (citing the *Charleston Courier*) (first quotation); Petersburg, Va.'s *American Star*, October 30, 1817 (citing Charleston's *City Gazette and Daily Advertiser*) (second quotation); *Georgia Journal*, December 16 (quotation), October 21 and 28, 1817. For early support, see Heckard, "Crossroads of Empire," esp. 150.

58   *Daily National Intelligencer*, October 17, 1817; *National Advocate*, November 25, 1817 (for reprintings, see, for example, Petersburg's *American Star*, November 29, 1817; Charles Town's *Farmer's Repository*, December 3, 1817); *Daily National Intelligencer*, December 22, 1817 (for a sample reprint, see Portsmouth's *New-Hampshire Gazette*, January 13, 1818).

59   *Weekly Aurora*, March 2, 1818 (first quotation); Milledgeville, Ga.'s *Reflector*, January 13, 1818 (citing the *Savannah Republican*) (second quotation). For reprints, see, for example, Stockbridge's *Berkshire Star*, January 22, 1818; Reading's *Berks and Schuylkill Journal*, January 17, 1818; New Bern's *Carolina Federal Republican*, January 17, 1818; Portland, Maine's *Eastern Argus*, January 20, 1818; *Newport Mercury*, January 17, 1818; *Richmond Enquirer*, January 13, 1818; *Palmyra Register*, January 28, 1818; Hartford's *Connecticut Mirror*, January 19, 1818; New Hampshire's *Portsmouth Oracle*, January 17, 1818.

60   For proximity's influence on high-level diplomacy, also see Lewis, *American Union*, 35–39, 78, 171–176. People of color in Mexico received more positive (if far more sporadic) reactions in the U.S. press than did their counterparts at Amelia Island. I suspect the main reason was that the rebellion in the heart of Mexico presented less of an immediate security threat than did Florida, with most people and policymakers seeing it as more remote (as noted in the conclusion). On coverage of Mexicans, see Sarah E. Cornell, "Americans in the U.S. South and Mexico: A Transnational History of Race, Slavery, and Freedom, 1810–1910" (Ph.D. diss., New York University, 2008), 20–91.

CHAPTER FOUR: Bolivar, U.S.A.

1   *New York Times*, July 8, 1864; Henry Inman, *George Pope Morris* (c. 1836), oil on canvas, National Gallery of Art; George P. Morris, *Poems by George P. Morris: With a Memoir of the Author* (17th ed.; New York, 1860).

2   G. P. Morris and T. W. H. B. B., *Bolivar. A Peruvian Battle Song* (Philadelphia, 1826[?]), Levy Sheet Music Collection, Johns Hopkins University, Box 011, Item 095 (accessed through the JScholarship database at https://jscholarship.library.jhu.edu/handle/1774.2/17506); T. Allston Brown, *A History of the New York Stage* (vol. 1; New York, 1903), 84–90.

3   Robert Stevenson, "Visión musical norteamericana de las otras Américas hacia 1900," *Revista Musical Chilena*, 31 (January–March, 1977), esp. 5–8; Richard J. Wolfe, *Secular Music in America, 1801–1825* (3 vols.; New York, 1964), esp. I:xv–xvi, 34–35 and II:832; *Aurora and Franklin Gazette*, July 6, 1826; *Democratic Press*, July 9, 13, 1825, July 13, 1826.

4   *Columbian Centinel*, July 13, 1822; *Democratic Press*, July 8, 1825.

5   *Richmond Enquirer*, July 9, 1822.

6   Ibid. Despite the toast to "South America," I suspect that the Mexican mon-

archy's flag was included in the display, given the recent U.S. recognition of mainland Spanish American independence.

7 *Richmond Enquirer*, July 16, 1819; *Daily National Intelligencer*, July 24, 1816.

8 A graph of year-by-year inter-American toasts appears in the Appendix (N=895, 1808–1830). As in Chapter One, figures include reports of all parties for which more than one toast is listed. They do not include reports on out-of-state festivities, although they do include parties from out of town. I have used the following newspapers: *Columbian Centinel* (Boston, 1808–1830); *Boston Patriot* (1809–1815); *Boston Patriot and Morning Advertiser* (1816); *Independent Chronicle and Boston Patriot* (1817); *Boston Patriot and Daily Chronicle* (1818); *Boston Patriot and Daily Mercantile Advertiser* (1819–1824); *Boston Patriot and Mercantile Advertiser* (1825–1829); *Aurora General Advertiser* (Philadelphia, 1808–1824); *Aurora and Franklin Gazette* (Philadelphia, 1825–1827); *Aurora and Pennsylvania Gazette* (Philadelphia, 1828–1829); *Democratic Press* (Philadelphia, 1823–1829, as the *Aurora* recorded too few July Fourth parties in these years to produce a reliable sample); *Arkansas Gazette* (Arkansas Post and Little Rock, 1820–1830); *Edwardsville Spectator* (Illinois, 1819–1826); *Enquirer* (Richmond, 1808–1830). As in Chapter One, the nationwide figures are weighted to reflect each state's and territory's adult white male population (age twenty-six and above) as found in U.S. Department of State, *Census for 1820* (Washington, D.C., 1821), though the difference between weighted and unweighted is marginal. The overall mean of 55 percent affords equal weight to each year; the median of 56.5 percent definitionally does the same. For editorial observations, see *Enquirer*, July 10 and 31, 1816; July 18, 1817; July 21, 1820; July 15, 1825; *Aurora General Advertiser*, July 18, 1821; *Columbian Centinel*, July 10, 1822.

9 "An American" [Henry Marie Brackenridge], *South America: A Letter on the Present State of that Country, to James Monroe* ... (Washington, D.C., 1817); *Baltimore Patriot*, May 6, 1817. On Brackenridge and the South American commission, see Laura Bornholdt, *Baltimore and Early Pan-Americanism: A Study in the Background of the Monroe Doctrine* (Northampton, Mass., 1949), 81–108. Bornholdt argues for an "eclipse of the patriot cause" in Baltimore starting in 1820; if that eclipse did occur in Baltimore (where financially interested partisans supported rival insurgent regimes), it did not occur more broadly. For a toast that referenced Catholicism and supported the rebels, see, for example, *Edwardsville Spectator*, July 10, 1819. Support for Greece appears to have been more religiously driven, perhaps because the Greeks' Muslim opponents were seen as beyond the pale (like Haiti when it came to race), or perhaps because (unlike in Latin America) the rebellion pitted two major religions against each other; see Charles L. Booth, "Let the American Flag Wave in the Aegean:

America Responds to the Greek War of Independence (1821–1824)," (Ph.D. diss., New York University, 2005).

10 *Register of Debates*, Senate, 19th Cong., 1st sess. (in conclave), 236; *Democratic Press*, July 15, 1823. On nationalism in the War of 1812 and its aftermath, see Alan Taylor, *The Internal Enemy: Slavery and War in Virginia, 1772–1832* (New York, 2013), 395–98; David Waldstreicher, *In the Midst of Perpetual Fetes: The Making of American Nationalism, 1776–1820* (Chapel Hill, 2004), 246–93; Caitlin A. Fitz, "The Hemispheric Dimensions of Early U.S. Nationalism: The War of 1812, Its Aftermath, and Spanish American Independence," *Journal of American History* 102.2 (September, 2015), 356–379. On Independence Day celebrations, see Pauline Maier, *American Scripture: Making the Declaration of Independence* (New York, 1997), esp. 154–208; David Armitage, *The Declaration of Independence: A Global History* (Cambridge, Mass., 2007), 1–102.

11 *Columbian Centinel*, July 13, 1822.

12 *Charleston Mercury*, as cited in the *Baltimore Patriot & Mercantile Advertiser*, November 29, 1822; *Christian Advocate*, October, 1824.

13 For debates about the Monroe Doctrine's relevance to Greece; other reasons that Congress voted against Greek recognition; and Greece's relation to Spanish-American policy more generally, see Arthur Preston Whitaker, *The United States and the Independence of Latin America, 1800–1830* (Baltimore, 1941), 540–543; Ernest R. May, *The Making of the Monroe Doctrine* (Cambridge, Mass., 1975), esp. 11.

14 *Aurora General Advertiser*, July 19, 1822 (Fredericktown); *Edwardsville Spectator*, July 19, 1823 (Manchester, Mo.); *Richmond Enquirer*, July 23, 1822 (Charlestown); *Edwardsville Spectator*, July 13, 1822 (Vandalia); *Aurora General Advertiser*, July 15, 1822 (Harrisburg); *Boston Patriot and Daily Mercantile Advertiser*, August 7, 1822 (Natchez). Family metaphors surged in 1822, when the United States formally recognized Spanish-American independence, but they started as early as 1810; see, for example, *Richmond Enquirer*, July 10, 1810. As a crude measuring stick, I searched America's Historical Newspapers (Early American Newspapers, series 1, 6, and 7, news/opinion only) for references to "sister republic*" and "greek*" from 1821 to 1824 (the asterisks denote "wildcard" search terms); these terms resulted in seventeen hits, none of which ultimately referred to the Greeks as family. The same search for "sister republic*" and "south america*" resulted in 37 hits, 31 of which referred to South Americans as family. Toasts exhibit the same trend (though for an exception—Greece as "the first-born of the family of Free Nations"— see *Richmond Enquirer*, July 12, 1825). Much the same might be said of toasts to Spain's insurgent liberal constitutionalists: although revelers frequently toasted both Spanish-American insurgents and Spanish peninsular liberals

in the early 1820s, they rarely if ever referred to the latter as family. Toasts routinely reconciled the apparent discrepancy of cheering both Spain and Spanish America by suggesting that liberal constitutionalists in Spain would recognize Spanish-American independence. See, for example, three separate parties listed in the *Richmond Enquirer*, July 8, 1823.

15 *Aurora and Franklin Gazette*, July 19, 1826.

16 Arndt M. Stickles, *Simon Bolivar Buckner: Borderland Knight* (Chapel Hill, 1940), 3; Donald R. Hickey, *The War of 1812: A Forgotten Conflict* (Bicentennial ed., Urbana, Ill., 2012), 132.

17 Constantine Rafinesque, *New Flora and Botany of North America* (Philadelphia, 1836), 12–13; 1820 federal census, Munfordville, Hart County, Kentucky, accessed through ancestrylibrary.com; Stickles, *Simon Bolivar Buckner*, 3–4; William Armstrong Crozier, *The Buckners of Virginia* (New York, 1907), 43–44, 66.

18 Stickles, *Simon Bolivar Buckner*, 4–5.

19 Hardy Murfree Cryer to Andrew Jackson, December 26, 1829, in Daniel Feller et al., eds., *Papers of Andrew Jackson* (Knoxville, 2007), VII:647–649; Robert Desha to Jackson, January 21, 1828, in Harold D. Moser and J. Clint Clifft, eds., *Papers of Andrew Jackson* (Knoxville, 2002), VI:412 n. 6; Stickles, *Simon Bolivar Buckner*, 3–4.

20 John Lynch, *Simón Bolívar: A Life* (New Haven, 2007), 122, 190. I searched online U.S. census records from 1810 through 1880 at www.ancestrylibrary.com and at www.heritagequest.com (as of July 2010); drawing on Mark G. Jaede's meticulous "Brothers at a Distance: Race, Religion, Culture, and U.S. Views of Spanish America, 1800–1830" (Ph.D. diss., State University of New York at Buffalo, 2001), 48, I have also included several individuals who had Bolivar as a middle name and are harder to find in census reports. On the rare occasions when different censuses indicate different birth years for the same individual, I have used the data from the earliest census. Comparative scale for other names derives from initial federal census record searches at www.ancestrylibrary .com. Baby Ipsilantis, of whom there were evidently fewer than a dozen, did not appear until later in the 1820s and early 1830s. For the Nabb and Johnson families, see 1850 federal census for Lawrence County, Illinois, and Bennington, New York, respectively (accessed on ancestrylibrary.com).

21 Alexander Bölöni Farkas, *Journey in North America*, trans. and ed. Theodore Schoenman and Helen Benedek Schoenman (Philadelphia, 1977), 151–152; Jeffrey L. Pasley, *"The Tyranny of Printers": Newspaper Politics in the Early American Republic* (Charlottesville, Va., 2001), esp. 7–9.

22 On hearing news alongside other people, see esp. Timothy Mason Roberts, *Distant Revolutions: 1848 and the Challenge to American Exceptionalism* (Charlottesville, Va., 2009), 43.

23   For Cooper, see 1850 federal census for Cherry Valley, New York; for Laugh-
     lin, see 1850 federal census for Bracken County, Ky.; for Horton, see 1850 fed-
     eral census for Colchester, N.Y. (all accessed at ancestrylibrary.com).

24   Per capita naming statistics are calculated based on 1830 census figures for
     white males under age ten. Because early census reports do not always list
     parental birthplaces, I have geographically classified parents according to the
     state in which their children were born. In my calculations, New England
     includes Maine, New Hampshire, Vermont, Massachusetts, Rhode Island,
     and Connecticut (.004% of white males under ten named Bolivar); the
     Mid-Atlantic includes New York, Pennsylvania, New Jersey, and Delaware
     (.007%); the Southeast includes Maryland, Virginia, North Carolina, South
     Carolina, and Georgia (.012%); the Southwest includes Alabama, Missis-
     sippi, Louisiana, Tennessee, Kentucky, Missouri, and Arkansas (.015%); and
     the Midwest includes Michigan, Ohio, Indiana, Illinois, and Iowa (.016%).
     For congressional votes, see n. 32, below, and Chapter Five. These regional
     groupings are of course imperfect, as they tend to conceal diversity within
     each region. I employ them periodically in order to gauge and assess general
     nationwide patterns, confident that what I lose in precision (especially in
     border regions) is gained in the broader trends and national scope that I am
     thereby able to consider.

25   William Earl Weeks, *John Quincy Adams and American Global Empire* (Lex-
     ington, Ky., 1992), 91–94; Linda K. Salvucci, "Supply, Demand, and the Mak-
     ing of a Market: Philadelphia and Havana at the Beginning of the Nineteenth
     Century," in Franklin W. Knight and Peggy K. Liss, eds., *Atlantic Port Cit-
     ies: Economy, Culture, and Society in the Atlantic World, 1650–1850* (Knoxville,
     1991), 40–57; A Merchant of Philadelphia [James Yard], *Spanish America and
     the United States; Or, Views of the Actual Commerce of the United States with the
     Spanish Colonies* (Philadelphia, 1818); remarks of William Smith, *Annals of
     Congress*, 14th Cong., 2nd sess., January 24, 1817, 738; Stephen Chambers, "At
     Home Among the Dead: North Americans and the 1825 Guamacaro Slave
     Insurrection," *Journal of the Early Republic* 33.1 (Spring, 2013), 61–86; Stephen
     Chambers, *No God but Gain: The Untold Story of Cuban Slavery, the Monroe
     Doctrine, and the Making of the United States* (New York, 2015); Edward P.
     Pompeian, "Spirited Enterprises: Venezuela, the United States, and the Inde-
     pendence of Spanish America, 1789–1823" (Ph.D. diss., College of William
     and Mary, 2014). For votes from Pennsylvania's congressional delegation, see
     n. 32, below.

26   *Columbian Centinel*, July 12, 1817; Pasley, *Tyranny of Printers*, esp. 40, 232–233.
     For the purpose of calculating partisan differences, the *Boston Patriot* (N=81)
     and *Columbian Centinel* (N=35) figures double-count the scattered parties on

which both papers reported. For the purpose of gauging nationwide hemispheric toast frequency, the N=895 figure (and the accompanying graph in the Appendix) does not double-count these parties. These figures represent a modest correction to my *Journal of American History* article (which listed 38 percent for the *Boston Patriot* and "fewer than 14 percent" for the *Centinel*); that article neglected to double-count July Fourth parties when assessing partisan trends. The difference, fortunately, is inconsequential to the argument. See Fitz, "The Hemispheric Dimensions of Early U.S. Nationalism," 366. For congressional votes, see n. 32, below.

27   *North American Review*, April 1821, 433–438; May, *Making of the Monroe Doctrine*, 189. On Federalist views, see Chapter One.

28   *North American Review*, April 1821, 433–438; May, *Making of the Monroe Doctrine*, 189; Paul Revere Frothingham, *Edward Everett: Orator and Statesman* (Boston, 1925), esp. 30; Michael G. Kammen, *A Season of Youth: The American Revolution and the Historical Imagination* (New York, 1978), 47. For a precedent in Federalists' attitudes toward formerly French and Spanish Louisiana, see Peter J. Kastor, *The Nation's Crucible: The Louisiana Purchase and the Creation of America* (New Haven, 2004), 50, 194.

29   *Newburyport Herald*, May 21, 1822; W. Caleb McDaniel, *The Problem of Democracy in the Age of Slavery: Garrisonian Abolitionists and Transatlantic Reform* (Baton Rouge, 2013), 21–44; Henry Mayer, *All on Fire: William Lloyd Garrison and the Abolition of Slavery* (New York, 1998), esp. 29.

30   *Newburyport Herald*, July 16, 19, 26, 1822; McDaniel, *The Problem of Democracy*, 21–44.

31   *New-York Courier*, September 26, 1816; *Columbian Centinel*, May 27, 1817, July 10, 1822.

32   In identifying former Federalists, I have relied on the *Biographical Directory of the United States Congress* (http://bioguide.congress.gov), and "Congress Profiles" (http://history.house/gov/Congressional-Overview/Profiles/14th) for the fourteenth, fifteenth, and sixteenth Congresses. For breaking ranks, I have studied the following votes: the vote on engrossing the neutrality bill, in *Annals of Congress*, 14th Cong., 2nd sess., Jan. 28, 1817, 767; the vote on a petition from Vicente Pazos, in *Annals of Congress*, 15th Cong., 1st sess., March 11, 1818, 1268; a vote on appropriating $18,000 for a minister to Buenos Aires, in *Annals of Congress*, 15th Cong., 1st sess., March 30, 1818, 1655; a vote on appropriating funds for whatever new ministers the president saw fit, in *Annals of Congress*, 16th Cong., 1st sess., May 10, 1820, 2229–2230; a similar vote in *Annals of Congress*, 16th Cong., 2nd sess., Feb. 9, 1821, 1077; a vote on resolving that the House joined the people in sympathizing with the rebels, in *Annals of Congress*, 16th Cong., 2nd sess., Feb. 10, 1821, 1091; and the vote

on explaining that the House of Representatives would support the president if he came out in favor of recognition, ibid., 1091–1092. For Federalist and Republican convergence more generally, also see Lindsay Schakenbach, "From Discontented Bostonians to Patriotic Industrialists," esp. 388–392; Chambers, *No God but Gain*, esp. 27–62.

33   *Daily National Intelligencer*, May 24, 1816 (for the Louisiana correspondent); Robert V. Remini, *Andrew Jackson* (1977; 2nd ed., Baltimore, 1998), I:131–149 (incl. quotation); Weeks, *John Quincy Adams and American Global Empire*, 91–94. On eastern merchants' eagerness to protect trade with the remaining Spanish Empire, also see Pompeian, "Spirited Enterprises."

34   Jay Sexton, *The Monroe Doctrine: Empire and Nation in Nineteenth-Century America* (New York, 2011); William Appleman Williams, *The Tragedy of American Diplomacy* (1959; New York, 1972), 18–58; Jack P. Greene, "Colonial History and National History: Reflections on a Continuing Problem," and responses from David Armitage, Eliga H. Gould, Michael Zuckerman, Kariann Yokota, Adam Rothman, and Robin Einhorn, *William and Mary Quarterly* 64 (April 2007), 235–286; Kariann Akemi Yokota, *Unbecoming British: How Revolutionary America Became a Postcolonial Nation* (New York, 2011). For southwestern expansion, see Frank Lawrence Owsley, Jr., and Gene A. Smith, *Filibusters and Expansionists: Jeffersonian Manifest Destiny, 1800–1821* (Tuscaloosa, Ala., 1997), 7–9; Andrew McMichael, *Atlantic Loyalties: Americans in Spanish West Florida, 1785–1810* (Athens, Ga., 2008); J. C. A. Stagg, *Borderlines in Borderlands: James Madison and the Spanish-American Frontier, 1776–1821* (New Haven, 2009); Weeks, *John Quincy Adams and American Global Empire*; James G. Cusick, *The Other War of 1812: The Patriot War and the American Invasion of Spanish East Florida* (Gainesville, 2003).

35   On Robinson, see David E. Narrett's excellent "Liberation and Conquest: John Hamilton Robinson and U.S. Adventurism Toward Mexico, 1806–1819," *Western Historical Quarterly* 40 (Spring 2009), 23–50.

36   *Carthage Gazette*, July 8, 1812 (citing Nashville's *Clarion*).

37   *Richmond Enquirer*, July 9, 1811 (toasting West Florida's "peacefull sucession[?] to the federal Union," also cited in Chapter One) and May 2, 1817 (quotation); also see *Georgia Journal*, September 30, 1817. West Florida's annexation did not involve filibusters, properly speaking; see Robert May, *Manifest Destiny's Underworld: Filibustering in Antebellum America* (Chapel Hill, 2002), xv.

38   *Aurora General Advertiser*, July 6, 9, 11, 1818, July 16, 1819 (San Martín, Artigas, Páez); *Richmond Enquirer*, July 15, 1825 (Sucre).

39   The 85 percent figure derives from the same sample set analyzed earlier in the chapter, covering the period from 1816 to 1825. It double-counts toasts that fit more than one category—so a toast to "the Patriots of Mexico and South

America" would count toward both geographic regions. Most remaining toasts went to geographically indeterminate groups like "the patriots of the South" (N=293). For Mexican-inspired displays, see Stickles, *Simon Bolivar Buckner*, 3–6; Stevenson, "Visión musical norteamericana de las otras Américas hacia 1900," 7. For newspaper coverage of Mexico, see Sarah E. Cornell, "Americans in the U.S. South and Mexico: A Transnational History of Race, Slavery, and Freedom, 1810–1910" (Ph.D. diss., New York University, 2008), 20–91. For other studies that look far beyond the border, see Charles Carroll Griffin, *The United States and the Disruption of the Spanish Empire, 1810–1822* (New York, 1937), 5; and esp. Whitaker, *United States and the Independence of Latin America*, 137–138.

40 John Quincy Adams, Diary 31, March 29, 1820, in *The Diaries of John Quincy Adams: A Digital Collection* (Boston, 2004), 298 (available at http://www.masshist.org/jqadiaries); Weeks, *John Quincy Adams and American Global Empire*; Griffin, *United States and the Disruption of the Spanish Empire*, 161–276.

41 Adams to Richard C. Anderson, May 27, 1823, in Worthington Chauncey Ford, ed., *Writings of John Quincy Adams* (New York, 1917), VII:469. One reason for Adams's sense of optimistic engagement here was that (as the following chapter will show) the United States had netted Florida two years before.

42 "Motion and Speech on Recognition of the Independent Provinces of the River Plata," March 24–25, 1818, in *The Papers of Henry Clay*, ed. James F. Hopkins et al. (Lexington, Ky., 1961), II:519; "Speech on South American Independence," May 10, 1820, in *Papers of Henry Clay*, II:856; Trimble, *Annals of Congress*, 17th Cong., 1st sess., March 28, 1822, 1386; Randolph B. Campbell, "The Spanish American Aspect of Henry Clay's American System," *The Americas* 24.1 (July 1967), 3–17; Jay Sexton, *Monroe Doctrine*, 74–75. Clay did, of course, see a connection between territorial expansion, Latin American independence, and trade—see James E. Lewis, Jr., *The American Union and the Problem of Neighborhood: The United States and the Collapse of the Spanish Empire, 1783–1829* (Chapel Hill, 1998), 96–177—but in his speeches about the hemispheric American System he clearly emphasized the latter. For towhaired, see David S. Heidler and Jeanne T. Heidler, *Henry Clay: The Essential American* (New York, 2010), 24.

43 *National Register*, August 10, 1816; also see Weeks, *John Quincy Adams and American Global Empire*, 91–94; Vicente Pazos, *Letters on the United Provinces of South America*, trans. Platt H. Crosby (New York, 1819), 240–42; Alejandra Irigoin, "The End of a Silver Era: The Consequences of the Breakdown of the Spanish Peso Standard in China and the United States, 1780s–1850s," *Journal*

of World History 20.2 (June, 2009), 207–243; Javier Cuenca Esteban, "Trends and Cycles in U.S. Trade with Spain and the Spanish Empire, 1790–1817," *Journal of Economic History* 44.2 (June, 1984), 521–543.

44 Samuel C. Williams, ed., "Journal of Events (1825–1873) of David Anderson Deaderick," *East Tennessee Historical Society's Publications* 8 (1936), 130–131; *Tennessee: A Guide to the State, Compiled and Written by the Federal Writers' Project of the Works Projects Administration for the State of Tennessee* (New York, 1939), 490.

45 Ibid.

46 U.S. Geological Survey, Geographic Names Information System (http://geonames.usgs.gov/pls/gnispublic/); J. B. Mansfield, ed., *History of Tuscarawas County, Ohio* (Chicago, 1884), 568–569; Georgia Drew Merrill, ed., *Allegany County and Its People: A Centennial Memorial History of Allegany County, N.Y.* (Alfred, N.Y., 1896); Mildred Kessler Bushong, *Historic Jefferson County* (Boyce, Va., 1972), 121–127. The one possible exception to the 1825 founding date was Bolivar, Pennsylvania, a town so tiny that it seems to have left no clear documentation of the exact year of its naming, though the mid-1820s seems likely; see George Dallas Albert, *History of the County of Westmoreland, Pennsylvania, with Biographical Sketches of Many of its Pioneers and Prominent Men* (Philadelphia, 1882), 400–401, 576. Other Bolivar towns emerged around this period, although I am less certain about the precise dates. For a Bolivar, Alabama, founded sometime before 1834, see John R. Kennamer, *History of Jackson County* (Winchester, Tenn., 1935), 149, 169; other Bolivar locales emerged sporadically throughout the 1830s, as noted in Chapter Six. I have been unable to find an approximate founding date for Bolivar, Maryland. For Mexico, Maine (founded in 1818), Peru, Maine (in 1821), and Cuba, New York (in 1822), see Theresa Thomas, "The Town of Mexico: A Brief Summary of Historical Growth," in Ruby Bragdon and Theresa Thomas, eds., *A Story of the Town of Mexico, 1818–1968* (no publisher, 1968); Mary Searles Vaughn, *A History of the Town of Peru, Maine* (Rumford, Maine, 1971), 18; Merrill, *Allegany County and Its People*; Jaede, "Brothers at a Distance," 48–49 (including other hemispherically inspired names, most of them evidently founded after the independence era).

47 Mansfield, ed., *History of Tuscarawas County, Ohio*, 568; Bushong, *Historic Jefferson County*, 121–127; Howe, *What Hath God Wrought*, 254–255; Buffalo Historical Society, *Canal Enlargements in New York State: Papers on the Barge Campaign and Related Topics* (Buffalo, 1909), 383–384; Noble E. Whitford, *History of the Canal System of the State of New York* (Albany, 1906), I:708–727; Albert, *History of the County of Westmoreland*, 400–401, 576. I have not found evidence of canal fever in the two Maine towns, though for other infrastructural improvements, see Vaughn, *History of the Town of Peru*, 14–63.

48 A Merchant of Philadelphia [James Yard], *Spanish America and the United*

States, 56. For publicity, see comments of Henry Clay, *Annals of Congress*, 15th Cong., 1st sess., March 28, 1818, 1610; *Weekly Aurora*, March 30, April 6, and May 25, 1818; *City of Washington Gazette*, April 2, 4, 6, and 13, 1818; *Boston Daily Advertiser*, April 22, 1818 (also in Boston's *Repertory*, April 25, 1818); Weeks, *John Quincy Adams and American Global Empire*, 89–90. For the commercially minded hemispheric toast, see *Aurora General Advertiser*, July 7, 1820. For congressional and editorial appeals to money, see, for example, *Daily National Intelligencer*, May 24, 1816; *City of Washington Gazette*, April 4, 1818; Charleston's *City Gazette and Commercial Daily Advertiser*, April 12, 1820; comments of Thomas Robertson and John Floyd, *Annals of Congress*, 15th Cong., 1st sess., March 26, 1818, 1534–1535, 1553. On economic rivalry, also see Pompeian, "Spirited Enterprises," 14–15, 347–357. For a similar assessment of economics and enthusiasm, see Jaede, "Brothers at a Distance," 75.

49 Griswold to Carrera, September 16, 1816, Box 1, Ac. D. R. E 1338, Archivo Carrera, Archivo Nacional de Chile (Santiago; Photostats accessed in the Library of Congress, Washington, D.C.); also transcribed under September 18, 1816, in *Archivo del General José Miguel Carrera*, ed. Armando Moreno Martín (Santiago de Chile, 1999), XVII:130–131.

50 Griswold to Carrera, April 3, 1816, in Moreno Martín, ed., *Archivo del General José Miguel Carrera*, XVII:174; "Diario," February 18, 1816, in Moreno Martín, ed., *Archivo del General José Miguel Carrera*, XVI:66.

51 Griswold to Carrera, September 18, 1816, XVII:130–131 (anxiety); Griswold to Carrera, April 6, 1816, XVI:245 (pain); Griswold to Carrera, n.d., "Substance of a Letter," XVII:134, all in Moreno Martín, ed., *Archivo del General José Miguel Carrera*.

52 Griswold to Carrera, November 7, 1816, XVII:234–235; "Diario de Viaje a los Estados Unidos de Norte América," October 11, 1816, XVII:155; Griswold to Carrera, August 5, 1816, XVII:48–49; Griswold to [Carrera?], September 5, 1817, XVII:74, all in Moreno Martín, ed., *Archivo del General José Miguel Carrera*.

53 Griswold to Carrera, September 5, 1817 [*sic*, though the letter appears amid other 1816 correspondence], in Archivo Carrera.

54 *Ladies' Weekly Museum, or Polite Repository of Amusement and Instruction*, May 3, 1817, August 1, 1818; Linda Kerber, "The Republican Mother: Women and the Enlightenment—An American Perspective," *American Quarterly* 28.2 (Summer, 1976), 187–205; Jan Lewis, "The Republican Wife: Virtue and Seduction in the Early Republic," *William and Mary Quarterly* 44.4 (October, 1987), 689–721.

55 For the *"Female patriots"* article, see, for example, New York's *Weekly Visitor, and Ladies' Museum* (title changed), September 18, 1819; Washington, Pa.'s *Reporter*, September 20, 1819; Leesburg, Va.'s *Genius of Liberty*, September 21, 1819; Connecticut's *Norwich Courier*, September 22, 1819; Concord's *New-Hampshire Patriot*,

September 14, 1819; Hallowell's *American Advocate, and Kennebec Advertiser*, September 25, 1819; Claiborne's *Alabama Courier*, October 15, 1819; Bellows Falls's *Vermont Intelligencer*, September 20, 1819; *City of Washington Gazette*, September 1, 1819; Wilmington, Del.'s *American Watchman*, September 8, 1819; *St. Louis Enquirer*, September 29, 1819; *Independent Chronicle and Boston Patriot*, August 31 and September 1, 1819; Georgetown, S.C.'s *Winyaw Intelligencer*, October 2, 1819; New Bern's *Carolina Centinel*, October 16, 1819; *Rochester Telegraph*, October 5, 1819; Fredericktown, Md.'s *Bartgis's Republican Gazette, and General Advertiser*, September 18, 1819; *Augusta Chronicle & Georgia Gazette*, September 20, 1819.

56   *New-York Evening Post*, June 28, 1825 (also in *The American*, June 29, 1825); *Nor-wich Courier*, July 30, 1823; Hartford's *American Mercury*, November 18, 1823; Chillicothe's *Supporter and Scioto Gazette*, November 22, 1823; *Albany Argus*, July 23, 1824; *Georgian*, October 26, 1824; *Independent Chronicle and Boston Patriot*, April 10, 1824. Bolivar hats, at least some of which were imported, also seem to have been popular in Haiti, France, and perhaps England: the cause of liberty transcended the United States, even if the July Fourth advertiser suggested otherwise. See Sibylle Fischer, "Bolívar in Haiti: Republicanism in the Revolutionary Atlantic," in Carla Calargé et al., eds., *Haiti and the Americas* (Jackson, Miss., 2013), 26; "French Female Fashions," London's *Repository of Arts, Literature, Fashions, Etc.* 6.32 (August 1, 1825), 122. Women's interest in revolutionary France served as a precedent for women's interest in Latin America several decades later; on France, see Susan Branson, *Those Fiery Frenchified Dames: Women and Political Culture in Early National Philadelphia* (Philadelphia, 2001); Rosemarie Zagarri, *Revolutionary Backlash: Women and Politics in the Early American Republic* (Philadelphia, 2007).

57   *Aurora General Advertiser*, July 12, 1820 (quotation); July 24, 1819; July 20, 1818; July 19, 1820; *Edwardsville Spectator*, July 10, 1819; McDaniel, *Problem of Slavery*, 30–36.

58   *Genius of Universal Emancipation*, September 12, 1825; Seth Rockman, *Scraping By: Wage Labor, Slavery, and Survival in Early Baltimore* (Baltimore, 2009), 1–44; Charles H. Wesley, "The Struggle for the Recognition of Haiti and Liberia as Independent Republics," *Journal of Negro History* 2.4 (October, 1917), 376; Don E. Fehrenbacher, *The Slaveholding Republic: An Account of the United States Government's Relations to Slavery*, ed. Ward M. McAfee (New York, 2001), 111–118.

59   Winston James, *The Struggles of John Brown Russwurm: The Life and Writings of a Pan-Africanist Pioneer, 1799–1851* (New York, 2010), esp. 5–43 (quotation on 24).

60   *Freedom's Journal*, March 16, 1827.

61   *Freedom's Journal*, June 1, 1827. Of the 41 issues of *Freedom's Journal* published in 1827, at least 23 mentioned Spanish America or Brazil. For Haiti, see Julie Winch, *Philadelphia's Black Elite: Activism, Accommodation, and the Struggle*

for Autonomy, 1787–1848 (Philadelphia, 1988), 49–66; James and Lois Horton, *In Hope of Liberty: Culture, Community, and Protest Among Northern Free Blacks, 1700–1860* (New York, 1997), 177–202; Charlton W. Yingling, "No One Who Reads the History of Hayti Can Doubt the Capacity of Colored Men: Racial Formation and Atlantic Rehabilitation in New York City's Early Black Press, 1827–1841," *Early American Studies* 11.2 (Spring, 2013), 314–348; Sara Fanning, *Caribbean Crossing: African Americans and the Haitian Emigration Movement* (New York, 2015). African Americans' positive associations with Spanish America had a precedent among enslaved people in Georgia and South Carolina who pondered escaping to freedom in Spain's nearby colonies. See Jane Landers, *Black Society in Spanish Florida* (Urbana, Ill., 1999); Jane Landers, *Atlantic Creoles in the Age of Revolutions* (Cambridge, Mass., 2010).

62 For black Bolivars, I searched U.S. federal census reports through 1880 on ancestrylibrary.com, as well as Freedmen's Bank records (accessed through HeritageQuest at www.heritagequestonline.com). For Hawkins, see 1870 federal census, Leon County, Florida; for Harris, see 1880 federal census, Sumter County, Alabama.

63 Ira Berlin, *Many Thousands Gone: The First Two Centuries of Slavery in North America* (Cambridge, Mass., 1998), 112, 188, 240, 285; Julius S. Scott, "The Common Wind: Currents of Afro-American Communication in the Era of the Haitian Revolution" (Ph.D. diss., Duke University, 1986); Daniel J. Sharfstein, *The Invisible Line: Three American Families and the Secret Journey from Black to White* (New York, 2011).

64 Federal census, 1850, Washington County, Pennsylvania, accessed through ancestrylibrary.com; *Abstract of the Returns of the Fifth Census* (Washington, D.C., 1832), 13; Richard S. Newman, *The Transformation of American Abolitionism: Fighting Slavery in the Early Republic* (Chapel Hill, 2002), 60–84.

65 Federal censuses for 1790 (Rowan County, N.C.), 1850 (Philadelphia, Pa.), 1860 (Philadelphia, Pa.), and "Proofs of Citizenship Used to Apply for Seamen's Certificates for the Port of Philadelphia" (all accessed on ancestrylibrary.com). The two men do not appear in pre-1850 census reports—further evidence that they or their parents were born into slavery. George Bolivar worked as a sailmaker for the prominent black leader James Forten and eventually prospered in the tobacco business, perhaps thanks to his North Carolina connections; he and his pregnant wife Elizabeth LeCount Proctor Bolivar hosted Frederick Douglass for two months in the 1840s, as they awaited the arrival of their first child. See *North Star*, March 9, 1849; William C. Welburn, "To 'Keep the Past in Lively Memory': William Carl Bolivar's Efforts to Preserve African American Cultural Heritage," *Libraries and the Cultural Record* 42.2 (2007), 169–170.

CHAPTER FIVE: A Genuine American Policy

1   Harry Ammon, *James Monroe: The Quest for National Identity* (New York, 1971); Daniel Walker Howe, *What Hath God Wrought: The Transformation of America, 1815–1848* (New York, 2007), 91; Philipp Ziesche, *Cosmopolitan Patriots: Americans in Paris in the Age of Revolution* (Charlottesville, Va., 2010), 88–110.

2   [William Wirt], *The British Spy* (Newburyport, 1804), 96; Ammon, *James Monroe*, 369 (quoting Calhoun); Jefferson to Madison, April 27, 1809, in *Papers of Thomas Jefferson*, Retirement Series, vol. 1, ed. J. Jefferson Looney (Princeton, 2004), 168–170. Material on the Monroe Doctrine in this section draws especially from Jay Sexton, *The Monroe Doctrine: Empire and Nation in Nineteenth-Century America* (New York, 2011); Ernest R. May, *The Making of the Monroe Doctrine* (Cambridge, Mass., 1992); Dexter Perkins, *The Monroe Doctrine, 1823–1826* (Cambridge, Mass., 1932); Samuel Flagg Bemis, *John Quincy Adams and the Foundations of American Foreign Policy* (New York, 1973), 341–408.

3   The United States and Britain had already reached a postwar rapprochement in the 1817 Rush-Bagot Treaty and the 1818 Commercial Convention; Canning's 1823 proposal, with its broader global implications, would have built on those developments.

4   Jefferson to Monroe, October 24, 1823, Founders Online, National Archives (http://founders.archives.gov).

5   John Quincy Adams, Diary 34, November 15 and 7, 1823, in *The Diaries of John Quincy Adams: A Digital Collection* (Boston, 2005), http://www.masshist.org/jqadiaries, 157–158, 149. Another drawback to Canning's proposal was that it would have required the United States to join Britain in disavowing future expansion into Spain's disintegrating empire. For an important new argument about Cuba's role in the Monroe Doctrine, also see Stephen Chambers, *No God but Gain: The Untold Story of Cuban Slavery, the Monroe Doctrine, and The Making of the United States* (New York, 2015).

6   On imperialism and anticolonialism, see Sexton, *Monroe Doctrine*; William Appleman Williams, *The Tragedy of American Diplomacy* (1959; New York, 1972), 18–58.

7   James E. Lewis, Jr., *The American Union and the Problem of Neighborhood: The United States and the Collapse of the Spanish Empire, 1783–1829* (Chapel Hill, 1998).

8   May, *Making of the Monroe Doctrine*; cf. Harry Ammon, "The Monroe Doctrine: Domestic Politics or National Decision?" *Diplomatic History* 5.1 (1981), 53–70.

9   La Junta Provisional Guvernativa de las Provincias del Río de la Plata to Saavedra and Aguirre, June 5, 1811, Archivo General de la Nación (Buenos

Aires, hereafter AGN; Photostats also available in the Library of Congress), S1-A2-A4, No. 9.

10   Ibid.; Samuel Flagg Bemis, *Early Diplomatic Missions from Buenos Aires to the United States, 1811–1824* (Worcester, Mass., 1944), 10–15; John C. Chasteen, *Americanos: Latin America's Struggle for Independence* (New York, 2008), 58–61.

11   S. G. Goodrich, *Recollections of a Lifetime* (New York, 1856), II:402; Aguirre and Saavedra to Telésforo de Orea, December 9, 1811, and to the Junta Provisional Guvernativa, November 11, 1811, AGN, S1-A2-A4, No. 9; La Junta Provisional to James Madison, June 6, 1811, S1-A2-A4, No. 9.

12   Manuel Hermenegildo de Aguirre to Juan Martín de Pueyrredón, August 30, 1817, in Sala X 1-5-1, AGN; Antônio Gonçalves da Cruz, "Conferencia que tive com Mr. Cesar A. Rodeney . . ." [June 1817?], Arquivo Histórico do Palácio Itamaraty (Rio de Janeiro; hereafter Itamaraty), 194/4/pasta 5; "Conferencia, á que se refire la Nota No. 10, entre S.E. el S.or Presid.te de los E.U. y el Min.o Plenip.o que subscrive," October 14, 1824, Sala X, 1-5-2, AGN; Charles G. Fenwick, *The Neutrality Laws of the United States* (Washington, D.C., 1913), 32–43, 103–124.

13   Luiz do Rego Barreto, Ofício, October 3, 1817, *Documentos Históricos* (Rio de Janeiro, 1953–1955; hereafter DH), 102:126 (also available in Biblioteca Nacional, Rio de Janeiro, Sala de Manuscritos, I-33, 26, 39); Fenwick, *Neutrality Laws of the United States*, 32–43, 103–124; Miguel Varas Velásquez, *Don José Miguel Carrera en Estados Unidos: Apuntes para un estudio tomados de su diario* (Santiago de Chile, 1912) (for a self-appointed emissary); mission of Juan Pedro de Aguirre and Diego de Saavedra, in AGN, S1-A2-A4, No. 9 (for official emissaries).

14   Vicente Lecuna and Harold A. Bierck, eds., Lewis Bertrand, trans., *Selected Writings of Bolívar* (New York, 1951), I:124; Charles Carroll Griffin, *The United States and the Disruption of the Spanish Empire, 1810–1822* (New York, 1937), 115 (for the Spanish minister). For muskets and flints, see Aguirre and Saavedra to ? [Junta del Poder Executivo de las Provincias del Río de la Plata?], May 14, 1812, AGN, S1-A2-A4, No. 9. For the 1810 shipment see Robert K. Lowry to Robert Smith, July 10, 1810, in William R. Manning, ed., *Diplomatic Correspondence of the United States Concerning the Independence of the Latin-American Nations* (New York, 1925), II:1144.

15   For the gunpowder, see Adams, Diary 31, March 29, 1820, 298–299 (http://www.masshist.org/jqadiaries); for the government declining similar transactions, see John Bach McMaster, *The Life and Times of Stephen Girard, Mariner and Merchant* (2 vols.; Philadelphia, 1918), II:163–171; and Charles H. Bowman, "The Activities of Manuel Torres as Purchasing Agent, 1820–1821," *Hispanic American Historical Review* 48.2 (May, 1968), 241–243. The figures on weapon and supply shipments are my own rough estimates, patched together from a variety of dis-

parate sources in domestic and foreign archives. They are illustrative, not comprehensive, and scholars more strictly devoted to the weapons trade will surely find other transactions. I identified 94,386 firearms shipped to South America in *specified* quantities from 1810 to 1825. The mean shipment size was 4,389 firearms; the median, 3,000. I also located references to 17 other shipments of *unspecified* numbers of firearms. My estimate results from multiplying those 17 shipments by the 3,000 estimated firearms per shipment for a total of 51,000 firearms sent in *unspecified* quantities; this is a conservative estimate, in part because it relies on the median rather than on the significantly higher mean. For other details and for a full listing of the rebel and royalist shipments on which my estimates and assessment are based, see Caitlin A. Fitz, "Our Sister Republics: The United States in an Age of American Revolutions" (Ph.D. diss., Yale University, 2010), Appendix III, 345–354. As recognized nation-states, Portugal and Spain had perhaps less need for weapons from the United States, which would help explain the apparently lower number of shipments to their representatives. On the other hand, Spain and Portugal themselves had weak domestic arms industries (compared to production centers in France, England, and modern-day Belgium), and their representatives in the Americas relied at least partly on imported weapons. The point, in any case, is not that principle routinely trumped profit for U.S. merchants; rather, as I argue below, it is simply that merchants took extra pride when the two coincided. On European arms production, see Ken Alder, *Engineering the Revolution: Arms and Enlightenment in France, 1763–1815* (Chicago, 1997).

16   For secrecy and code, see, for example, Henry Hill to Palmer and Hamilton, August 18, September 27, 1817, Henry Hill Papers, Box 1, Folder 5, Yale University Manuscripts and Archives (New Haven). On British weapons to Spanish America, see Rafe Blaufarb's illuminating "Arms for Revolutions: Military Demobilization After the Napoleonic Wars and Latin American Independence," in Alan Forrest, Karen Hagemann, Michael Rowe, eds., *War, Demobilization, and Memory: The Legacy of War in the Era of Atlantic Revolutions* (Basingstoke, 2016); I am grateful to the author for sharing his manuscript with me in advance. Blaufarb likewise senses that post-Napoleonic North Atlantic sales to Spanish-American rebels significantly outweighed those to Spanish royalists, and he shows that Britain exported few weapons directly to Spanish-American insurgents; instead, it seems to have directed weapons through merchants in the United States, the Caribbean, and Brazil. Britain sent more weapons directly to South America than to Mexico, Blaufarb writes, while Brazil received the greatest number of direct British exports; Blaufarb hypothesizes that many of the Brazil-bound arms went toward the transatlantic slave trade

as well as toward crushing the dual rebellions in Pernambuco. My impressionistic sense is that weapons exported (and reexported) from the United States were more commonly destined for Spanish-American and Pernambucan insurgents. Lindsay Schakenbach Regele observes that many of the U.S.-produced weapons came from federal armories; see "Manufacturing Advantage: War, the State, and the Origins of American Industry, 1790–1840" (Ph.D. diss., Brown University, 2015), 145–185.

17 Luis Brión to Simón Bolívar, January 4, 1820, *Memorias del General O'Leary publicadas por su hijo Simon B. O'Leary* (Caracas, 1881), XII:10; Torres to Roscio and Revenga, May 20, 1820, in Francisco José Urrutia, ed., *Los Estados Unidos de América y las repúblicas hispano-americanas de 1810 á 1830* (Madrid, 1918), 199–200; Chasteen, *Americanos*, 101, 157; Edward P. Pompeian, "Spirited Enterprises: Venezuela, the United States, and the Independence of Spanish America, 1789–1823" (Ph.D. diss., College of William and Mary, 2014), 309. In "Arms for Revolutions," Blaufarb argues that foreign weapons were one decisive factor in Spanish-American independence.

18 McMaster, *Life and Times of Stephen Girard*, esp. II:163–171; Stephen Simpson, *Biography of Stephen Girard* (Philadelphia, 1832); Bemis, *Early Diplomatic Missions*, 13–15.

19 McMaster, *Life and Times of Stephen Girard*, II: 171 (quotation); Simpson, *Biography of Stephen Girard*; Bemis, *Early Diplomatic Missions*, 13–15; Saavedra and Aguirre to the Junta of the United Provinces, February 16, 1812, and Saavedra and Aguirre to William Miller and Abraham Van Beuren, November 11, 1811, both in AGN, S1-A2-A4, No. 9.

20 Varas Velásquez, *Don José Miguel Carrera en Estados Unidos*, 11, 29, 59–71; José Corrêa da Serra to the Conde da Barca, May 31, 1817, in Léon Bourdon, ed., *José Corrêa da Serra: Ambassadeur du Royaume-Uni de Portugal et Brésil a Washington, 1816–1820* (Paris, 1975), 293.

21 Henry Lee to James Mackillop, August 11, 1817, and Lee to Alexander and Company, June 12, 1817, both in Lee Family Papers, vol. 45, Massachusetts Historical Society (Boston); *City Gazette and Commercial Daily Advertiser*, April 12, 1820 (reprinted in the *Nashville Gazette*, May 6, 1820; Charles Town, Va.'s *Farmers' Repository*, April 26, 1820; Ithaca, N.Y.'s *American Journal*, May 3, 1820; *Boston Daily Advertiser*, April 22, 1820; *Providence Patriot*, April 26, 1820; New Bern's *Carolina Centinel*, April 29, 1820; Windsor's *Vermont Journal*, May 1, 1820; Philadelphia's *Franklin Gazette*, April 20, 1820; Wilmington, Del.'s *American Watchman*, April 22, 1820).

22 This paragraph and the next two draw collectively on Box 1, Folder 5, of the Henry Hill Papers; quotations are from Hill to Palmer and Hamilton, October 22 and July 21, 1817; Hill to Perry, August 8 and June 18, 1817; Hill to D'Arcy,

Didier, and Sheppard, August 19, 1817. For the *Savage* and for Bibles, see Henry Hill, *Recollections of an Octogenarian* (Boston, 1884), 78–86. For French, also see Henry Hill, "Incidencias en Chile, Sud-América," in *Revista Chilena de Historia y Geografía* 87 (July–December, 1939), 37. For opium, see Marie Arana, *Bolívar: American Liberator* (New York, 2013), 275–276. The banished rebel leader was none other than José Miguel Carrera, who fled to New York and tried to stir up support from people like the Griswolds (as mentioned in Chapter Four).

23 Hill to D'Arcy, Didier, and Sheppard, September 1, 1817, and Hill to O'Higgins, August 8, 1817, Henry Hill Papers, Box 1, Folder 5; Eugenio Pereira Salas, "Henry Hill: Negociante, vice-cónsul, y misionero," *Revista Chilena de Historia y Geografía* 87 (July–December, 1939), 5–30.

24 Benjamin Keen, *David Curtis DeForest and the Revolution of Buenos Aires* (New Haven, 1947), esp. 9, 159 (quotations), 38–39, 145 ("millionaire"); David Curtis DeForest to John DeForest, August 12, 1809, Letterbook 4, David Curtis DeForest Papers, Yale University Manuscripts and Archives (New Haven). On the broader economic context, see Pompeian, "Spirited Enterprises"; Chambers, *No God but Gain*. "Dual citizen" is an anachronism, but DeForest did simultaneously profess U.S. and Buenos Aires citizenship; see Bemis, *Early Diplomatic Missions*, 80–95.

25 Philadelphia *Weekly Aurora*, March 2, 1818.

26 Ibid.; Jeffrey L. Pasley, *"The Tyranny of Printers": Newspaper Politics in the Early American Republic* (Charlottesville, Va., 2001), 174; Charles H. Bowman, Jr., "Manuel Torres, A Spanish American Patriot in Philadelphia, 1796–1822," *Pennsylvania Magazine of History and Biography* 94.1 (January 1970), 26–53; Charles Harwood Bowman, Jr., *Vicente Pazos Kanki: Un boliviano en la libertad de América* (La Paz, Bolivia, 1975), trans. Raúl Mariaca G. and Samuel Mendoza. Duane was not as piously hands-off as he suggested; see Bowman, "Manuel Torres," 46–47; Robert Pierce Forbes, *The Missouri Compromise and Its Aftermath: Slavery and the Meaning of America* (Chapel Hill, 2007), 89. Before 1815, at least, he had also published occasional columns from royalist perspectives; see Pompeian, "Spirited Enterprises," 144, 254, 331. For Torres's acquaintance with Cruz, see Juan G. Roscio to Cruz, December 31, 1818, in Itamaraty, 186/1/7-9.

27 Porter to Poinsett, March 19, 1816, Box 1, Folder 19, Poinsett Papers, Historical Society of Pennsylvania (Philadelphia); *Weekly Aurora*, March 2, 1818; Chasteen, *Americanos*, 137.

28 For arthropod metaphors, see *Annals of Congress*, 14th Cong., 2nd sess., January 24, 1817, 736; *Baltimore Patriot & Evening Advertiser*, February 5, 1817; *Daily National Intelligencer*, December 1, 1817; Corrêa da Serra to Thomas Mann Randolph, February 4, 1820, Bourdon, ed., *JCS*, 529. For neutrality legislation, this paragraph and the next two draw on Lewis, *American Union*, 69–143; Arthur

Preston Whitaker, *The United States and the Independence of Latin America, 1800–1830* (Baltimore, 1941), 189–222, 275–316; Griffin, *United States and the Disruption of the Spanish Empire*; Charles Edel, *Nation Builder: John Quincy Adams and the Grand Strategy of the Republic* (Cambridge, Mass., 2014); David Head, *Privateers of the Americas: Spanish American Privateering from the United States in the Early Republic* (Athens, Ga., 2015); Pompeian, "Spirited Enterprises," 273–357.

29   *Annals of Congress*, 14th Cong., 2nd sess., January 24, 1817, 732; José Corrêa da Serra to the Marquis de Aguiar, December 28, 1816, in Bourdon, ed., *JCS*, 247; Corrêa da Serra to Adams, March 17, 1819, in Bourdon, ed., *JCS*, 469.

30   Adams to William Johnson, September 5, 1820, quoted in Lewis, *American Union*, 162; Jefferson to Albert Gallatin, June 16, 1817, in *Writings of Thomas Jefferson*, ed. H. A. Washington, VII (Washington, D.C., 1854), 78. Jefferson supported the neutrality legislation, urging "Right to both parties, innocent favor to the juster cause."

31   Griffin, *United States and the Disruption of the Spanish Empire*, 102 (and also 116–120, 244–247); Head, *Privateers of the Americas*, esp. 4. For Britons, see Matthew Brown, *Adventuring Through Spanish Colonies: Simón Bolívar, Foreign Mercenaries, and the Birth of New Nations* (Liverpool, 2006); Eric Lambert, "Los Legionarios Britanicos," in *Bello y Londres: Segundo Congreso del Bicentenario* (Caracas, 1980), I:360, 364; D. A. G. Waddell, "British Neutrality and Spanish American Independence: The Problem of Foreign Enlistment," *Journal of Latin American Studies* 19.1 (May, 1987), 17. U.S. foreign enlistment continued after 1821, perhaps because it was harder to regulate the actions of overseas sailors and because foreign enlistment represented a quantitatively smaller phenomenon. For numbers, see Fitz, "Our Sister Republics," 205, n. 13. Neutrality laws also outlawed filibustering, but for reasons outlined in Chapter Four, I have not counted filibusters among those fighting for Latin American independence.

32   Henry Koster, *Travels in Brazil* (London, 1817), 1:3–8; Caitlin A. Fitz, "A Stalwart Motor of Revolutions: An American Merchant in Pernambuco, 1817–1825," *The Americas* 65.1 (July, 2008), 35–62; "Original do prócesso militar a que respondran Lazaro de Souza Fonte e James H. Rodgers," January 8, 1825, Instituto Arqueológico, Histórico, e Geográfico Pernambucano (Recife), 106/3.

33   "Original do prócesso militar."

34   Ibid.; Francisco Augusto Pereira da Costa, *Anais Pernambucanos* (Recife, 1951–1966), 9:147–156; New York's *Evening Post*, June 2, 1825; Portland, Maine's *Eastern Argus*, June 13, 1825.

35   "Original do prócesso militar"; Condy Raguet to Luiz José de Carvalho e Mello, February 11, 1825, Despatches from United States consuls in Rio de Janeiro, U.S. Department of State; New York *Evening Post*, June 2, 1825.

36   J. Fisher, Jr. to ?, April 18, 1823, Diversos Consules (Agentes Consulares em Pernambuco), vol. 1, 1822–1826, Arquivo Público Estadual Jordão Emerenciano (Recife); Daniel Griswold to José Miguel Carrera, August 14, 1816, Archivo Carrera, in Archivo Nacional de Chile, Ac. D.R.E 1338 [Santiago; Photostats in Library of Congress; transcribed in Armando Moreno Martín, ed., *Archivo del General José Miguel Carrera* (Santiago de Chile, 1999), XVII:57]; *Washington City Weekly Gazette*, February 16, 1818. David Head deftly chronicles privateers' varied motives in *Privateers of the Americas*, 122–148.

37   This paragraph and the next draw from Robert V. Remini, *Henry Clay: Statesman for the Union* (New York, 1991), esp. 150–151 (quotation); David S. Heidler and Jeanne T. Heidler, *Henry Clay: The Essential American* (New York, 2010), esp. 45 (tabletop dance), 136 (retirement).

38   "Speech on South American Independence," May 10, 1820, James F. Hopkins and Mary W. M. Hargreaves, eds., *Papers of Henry Clay* (Lexington, Ky., 1961), II:856; Remini, *Henry Clay*, esp. 65, 134–135, 181–182 (final quotation); Randolph B. Campbell, "The Spanish American Aspect of Henry Clay's American System," *The Americas* 24.1 (July, 1967), 3–17; May, *Making of the Monroe Doctrine*, 50–57, 173–181.

39   The scholarship here is extensive; this chapter draws especially on Edel, *Nation Builder*, 107–184; Bemis, *John Quincy Adams*; Whitaker, *United States and the Independence of Latin America*; Lewis, *American Union*; May, *Making of the Monroe Doctrine*; William Earl Weeks, *John Quincy Adams and American Global Empire* (Lexington, Ky., 1992); Remini, *Henry Clay*, 154–177; Pompeian, "Spirited Enterprises." There is no apparent correlation between foreign policy positions in the postwar decade on one hand and future political affiliations on the other; see Fitz, "Our Sister Republics," 193 n. 1. As I note in Chapter Four, though, Congress's diminishing pool of erstwhile Federalists opposed greater hemispheric engagement.

40   For the only three toasts that even vaguely seemed to prescribe a policy, see Philadelphia's *Aurora*, July 10, 1816; Boston's *Patriot*, July 6, 1818; Richmond's *Enquirer*, July 11, 1823. Scattered others offered after-the-fact endorsements.

41   *Aurora General Advertiser*, July 8, 1813; *Newburyport Herald*, July 26, 1822; *Richmond Enquirer*, July 15, 1823.

42   *Richmond Enquirer*, July 29, 1825 (in Ohio and thus not included in the sample set); Henry Howe, *Historical Collections of Ohio* (3 vols., Columbus, 1891), II:323–324.

43   Susan Watkins et al. to Henry Clay, July 12, 1825 (and accompanying editorial notes), *Papers of Henry Clay*, ed. James F. Hopkins and Mary W. M. Hargreaves (Lexington, Ky., 1972), IV:526; Archibald Shaw, *History of Dearborn County, Indiana: Her People, Industries, and Institutions* (Indianapolis, 1915), 230–243.

44 For the one sampled toast that explicitly hailed Clay's inter-American advocacy, see *Richmond Enquirer*, July 15, 1825. For Kentucky and New York, see *Aurora General Advertiser*, August 11, 1818, and July 20, 1819.

45 John Quincy Adams to Thomas Boylston Adams, April 14, 1818, Founders Online, National Archives, http://founders.archives.gov; Clay to Henry M. Brackenridge, August 4, 1818, *Papers of Henry Clay* II:590; *Annals of Congress*, 16th Cong., 1st sess., May 10, 1820, 2225; *Annals of Congress*, 15th Cong., 1st sess., March 28, 1818, 1613. As to how the enthusiasm empowered Clay even though it was vague on specifics, I am especially influenced by John Kingdon's framework in *Agendas, Alternatives, and Public Policies* (Boston, 1984).

46 *Annals of Congress*, 16th Cong., 1st sess., May 10, 1820, 2228; Clay to Charles Wilkins et al., June 3, 1820, *Papers of Henry Clay*, II:867; "Toast and Speech at Lexington Public Dinner," June 7, 1820, *Papers of Henry Clay*, II:869.

47 *Annals of Congress*, 15th Cong., 1st sess., March 28, 1818, 1646–1647; Fitz, "Our Sister Republics," 218–224. On Nelson, also see Fillmore Norfleet, *Saint-Memin in Virginia: Portraits and Biographies* (Richmond, 1942), 81, 191–192.

48 Adams, Diary 31, March 9, 1821, and November 22, 1819, 551, 210 (http://www .masshist.org/jqadiaries); John Adams to John Quincy Adams, January 8, 1818, and John Quincy Adams to Thomas Boylston Adams, April 14, 1818, both available on Founders Online, National Archives (http://founders.archives .gov); Adams, *Address, Delivered at the Request of a Committee of the Citizens of Washington* (Washington, D.C., 1821), 32; Bemis, *John Quincy Adams*, 356.

49 *Annals of Congress*, 15th Cong., 1st sess., March 25, 28, 1818, 1511–1512, 1635; *Annals of Congress*, 14th Cong., 2nd sess., January 25, 1817, 747; Alvin Laroy Duckett, *John Forsyth: Political Tactician* (Athens, Ga., 1962), 12–13. For a similar statement of Latin American political difference, see John Randolph's comments in *Annals of Congress*, 14th Cong., 2nd sess., January 24, 1817, 732–733.

50 Adams, Diary 30, January 13, 1818, 295 (http://www.masshist.org/jqadiaries); Remini, *Henry Clay*, 156.

51 Weeks, *John Quincy Adams*, 56–57; Remini, *Henry Clay*, 154–177; Heidler and Heidler, *Henry Clay*, 66.

52 *United States' Telegraph*, April 7, 1826; Remini, *Henry Clay*, 154.

53 John Solomon Otto, *The Southern Frontiers, 1607–1860: The Agricultural Evolution of the Colonial and Antebellum South* (New York, 1989), 111–112; Weeks, *John Quincy Adams*, 27–29.

54 Adams, Diary 30, May 3, 1817, 181. For recognition, see May, *Making of the Monroe Doctrine*; Griffin, *United States and the Disruption of the Spanish Empire*; Whitaker, *United States and the Independence of Latin America*; Lewis, *American Union*; Edel, *Nation Builder*, 138–184.

55 *Annals of Congress*, 15th Cong., 1st sess., March 30, 1818, 1655; F. L. Paxson, *Independence of the South American Republics: A Study in Recognition and Foreign Policy* (Philadelphia, 1916), 134; Pompeian, "Spirited Enterprises," 273–357.

56 Robertson to Clay, January 19, 1826, *Papers of Henry Clay*, ed. James F. Hopkins and Mary W. M. Hargreaves (Lexington, Ky., 1973), V:48; Whitaker, *United States and the Independence of Latin America*, 214 n. 43 (quoting King); Pompeian, "Spirited Enterprises," 223–272.

57 In a state-by-state assessment of legislative votes and baby names, $R^2 = .2825$ (drawing on the same congressional votes and regional definitions as detailed in Chapter Four, n. 24, n. 32). For Bolivar naming patterns studied in reference to Congress's 1826 Panama debates, see Chapter Six.

58 Congress had previously debated hemispheric policy questions (such as whether to extend aid to earthquake-stricken Caracas), of course, but earlier debates were far shorter and received accordingly less editorial attention; they were also overshadowed by the War of 1812.

59 Adams, Diary 30, March 28, 1818, 327 (http://www.masshist.org/jqadiaries); Bemis, *John Quincy Adams*, 251–255; Lee H. Burke and Richard S. Patterson, *Homes of the Department of State, 1774–1976: The Buildings Occupied by the Department of State and its Predecessors* (Washington, D.C., 1977), 35–36; Griffin, *United States and the Independence of the Spanish Empire*, 270–271.

60 Adams, Diary 31, May 10, 1820, 336 (http://www.masshist.org/jqadiaries); Carlos de Alvear, "Conferencia, á que se refire la Nota No. 10 . . . ," October 14, 1824, Sala X, 1-5-2, AGN.

61 See esp. May, *Making of the Monroe Doctrine*, 35, 182 (on Adams's electoral incentives); and also Burke and Patterson, *Homes of the Department of State*, 37–40; Lewis, *American Union*, esp. 136–187; Sexton, *Monroe Doctrine*, 39–45; Edel, *Nation Builder*, 107–184. Though his assessment stops around 1818, Edward Pompeian has strongly argued that commercial ties to Cuba and the rest of Spain's remaining American empire also explain why recognition didn't happen sooner. That would provide further testament to the influence of popular enthuasism, which was evidently strong enough by 1822 to help override policymakers' and merchants' economic misgivings. See Pompeian, "Spirited Enterprises," 223–357.

62 Griffin, *United States and the Disruption of the Spanish Empire*, 273–274; *Annals of Congress*, 17th Cong., 1st sess., April 29, 1822, 430–431. On losing reelection, see the account of William Smith at the end of this chapter.

63 *Richmond Enquirer*, July 9, 1822; *Aurora General Advertiser*, July 16, 1822; *Arkansas Gazette*, July 9, 1822; *Edwardsville Spectator*, July 6, 1822. The Monroe Doctrine was in December of 1823; the 34 percent figure references celebrations on the ensuing July Fourth in 1824. The 75 percent figure is (like the

others) weighted according to each state's adult white male population; the unweighted figure of 69 percent would still have been a record. I join scholars who downplay the Monroe Doctrine relative to other policy developments; see esp. Lewis, *American Union*, 156, 177–187.

64 Lacy K. Ford, *Deliver Us from Evil: The Slavery Question in the Old South* (New York, 2009), esp. 202; Forbes, *Missouri Crisis and Its Aftermath*, 144–149; William W. Freehling, *The Road to Disunion: Secessionists at Bay, 1776–1854* (New York, 1990), 150.

65 Charleston's *Carolina Gazette*, February 15, March 1, esp. March 15, 1823 (also in *Richmond Enquirer*, February 11, 1823; Camden's *Southern Chronicle*, February 26, March 12, 19, 26, 1823, citing Washington's *National Intelligencer*).

66 *Carolina Gazette*, March 15, 1823.

67 Ibid.

68 *Annals of Congress*, 14th Cong., 2nd sess., January 4, 1817, 733; *Carolina Gazette*, March 15, 1823; May, *Making of the Monroe Doctrine*, esp. 17–65; Bowman, "Activities of Manuel Torres as Purchasing Agent," 241–245; Adams, Diary 31, March 29, 1820, (http://www.masshist.org/jqadiaries), 298; Sexton, *Monroe Doctrine*, 76. The preservation of Cuban slavery perhaps offered further reason for the Monroe Doctrine, as Stephen Chambers insightfully argues in *No God but Gain*, though the evidence remains circumstantial; if Cabinet members did voice explicit concerns on the issue, they declined to commit those views to print and in public. On Amelia Island, see *Annals of Congress*, 15th Cong., 1st sess., December 8, 1817–January 10, 1818, 409–416, 646–650 (quotations on 647, 411), and March 11, 1818, 1251–1268, as well as *Annals of Congress*, 15th Cong., 1st sess., appendix, 1785–1813.

CHAPTER SIX: An Imaginary Kindred

1 For this paragraph and the next, see esp. Robert V. Remini, *Henry Clay: Statesman for the Union* (New York, 1991), 234–272. For a revised examination of the popular vote, also see Donald Ratcliffe, "Popular Preferences in the Presidential Election of 1824," *Journal of the Early Republic* 34.1 (Spring, 2014), 45–77.

2 Adams's First Annual Message to Congress, December 6, 1825, University of Virginia's Miller Center for Public Affairs, (http://millercenter.org/scripps/archive/speeches/detail/3514); "Swearing-In Ceremony for President John Quincy Adams," March 4, 1825, http://www.inaugural.senate.gov/swearing-in/event/john-quincy-adams-1825. For unexpectedness of the opposition and, subsequently, expected votes, see esp. John Quincy Adams, Diary 37, November 23–December 1, 1825, January 9, 31, February 13, 1826, in *The Diaries of John Quincy Adams: A Digital Collection* (Boston, 2004), 14–19, 62, 81, 92 (http://

www.masshist.org/jqadiaries); Clay to Richard C. Anderson, November 25, 1825, Clay to Lafayette, December 13, 1825, Clay to John J. Crittenden, March 10, 1826, in James F. Hopkins and Mary W. M. Hargreaves, eds., *Papers of Henry Clay* (Lexington, Ky., 1972–1973) IV:851, 905, V:158; Samuel Flagg Bemis, *John Quincy Adams and the Foundations of American Foreign Policy* (New York, 1973), 551; Daniel Webster to Joseph Hopkinson, January 8, 1826, in Charles M. Wiltse and Harold D. Moser, eds., *Papers of Daniel Webster: Correspondence* (vol. II, 1825–1829) (Hanover, N.H., 1976, hereafter *PDW*), II:76; James Buchanan to Andrew Jackson, March 8, 1826, in Harold D. Moser, J. Clint Clifft, eds., *Papers of Andrew Jackson* (Knoxville, 2002, hereafter *PAJ*), VI:147. At least some opposition members initially hoped for victory, but the attacks (racialized and other) continued well after that hope had subsided.

3   *Gazette of Maine*, March 28, 1826; *Register of Debates*, 19th Cong., 1st sess., April 4, 1826, 2023; Martin Van Buren, *Autobiography of Martin Van Buren*, ed. J. C. Fitzpatrick (Washington, D.C., 1919), 199. All subsequent *Register of Debates* citations in this chapter refer to the 19th Cong., 1st sess. Many historians have addressed the Panama debates, though few of them at length. My assessment builds on their work in several ways. By emphasizing (in earlier chapters) the universalist lens through which U.S. observers over the previous decade viewed South American race relations, my assessment of the Panama debates highlights the magnitude of the rhetorical change that opposition southerners proposed in 1826. It also demonstrates how opposition southerners' initiative in pressing the slavery issue rendered the Panama debates a noteworthy moment in U.S. political history, and it explores editorial and popular reactions. I have been especially informed by Robert Forbes's account, which notes the "new narrative" that opposition southerners offered in 1826 (though Forbes necessarily addresses the debate only in passing). See Robert Pierce Forbes, *The Missouri Compromise and Its Aftermath: Slavery and the Meaning of America* (Chapel Hill, 2007), 207–209.

4   For slavery's spread, see esp. Adam Rothman, *Slave Country: American Expansion and the Origins of the Deep South* (Cambridge, Mass., 2005); Walter Johnson, *River of Dark Dreams: Slavery and Empire in the Cotton Kingdom* (Cambridge, Mass., 2013); Edward E. Baptist, *The Half Has Never Been Told: Slavery and the Making of American Capitalism* (New York, 2014).

5   Details in this paragraph and the next draw from Marie Arana's remarkable *Bolívar: American Liberator* (New York, 2013), esp. 208, 231, 315, 327, 337.

6   Ibid., esp. 243–355 (quotation on 341); John C. Chasteen, *Americanos: Latin America's Struggle for Independence* (New York, 2008), 169.

7   Bolívar, "Reply of a South American to a Gentleman of this Island [Jamaica],"

September 6, 1815, in Vicente Lecuna and Harold A. Bierck, eds., *Lewis Bertrand*, trans., *Selected Writings of Bolívar* (New York, 1951), I:118; Arana, *Bolívar*, 243. This paragraph and the rest of the section also draw on John Lynch, *Simón Bolívar: A Life* (New Haven, 2007), 39, 212–216; David Bushnell, *Simón Bolívar: Liberation and Disappointment* (New York, 2004), 150–154.

8 Bolívar's Angostura address, February 15, 1819, in Lecuna and Bierck, *Selected Writings of Bolívar*, I:179–181; Lynch, *Simón Bolívar*, esp. 261.

9 Haverhill's *Gazette and Patriot*, November 26, 1825 (citing New York's *National Advocate*); *Gazette of Maine*, June 27, 1826; *Portland Advertiser*, May 16, 1826.

10 Adams, First Annual Message to Congress.

11 Bemis, *John Quincy Adams and the Foundations of American Foreign Policy*, 543–555; James E. Lewis, Jr., *The American Union and the Problem of Neighborhood: The United States and the Collapse of the Spanish Empire, 1783–1829* (Chapel Hill, 1998), 188–214; Daniel Walker Howe, *What Hath God Wrought: The Transformation of America, 1815–1848* (New York, 2007), 243–284; John Quincy Adams, Message to the Senate, December 26, 1825, *Register of Debates*, appendix, 43. For Cabinet discussions and diary routine, see Adams, Diary 37, November 23–December 31, 1825, 13–51 (http://www.masshist.org/jqadiaries, and quotation on February 13, 1826, 92); Charles Edel, *Nation Builder: John Quincy Adams and the Grand Strategy of the Republic* (Cambridge, Mass., 2014), 111–113.

12 *Register of Debates*, April 17, 1826, 2324, and January 31, 1826, 1214; Edel, *Nation Builder*, 214 (for twenty-seven uses of "improvement").

13 *Register of Debates*, in conclave, 338, and March 30, 1826, 402; Jackson to James Knox Polk, May 3, 1826, *PAJ*, VI:166; Andrew R. L. Cayton, "The Debate over the Panama Congress and the Origins of the Second American Party System," *The Historian* 47.2 (February, 1985), 219–238; Forbes, *Missouri Compromise*, 121–237, esp. 204–208. For the era's politics more generally, see esp. Sean Wilentz, *The Rise of American Democracy: Jefferson to Lincoln* (New York, 2005), 242–311; Howe, *What Hath God Wrought*, 158–159, 203–222, 243–284, 330. Congress had met in special session during the first days of Adams's presidency, when, led by future opposition members, it rejected a treaty with Colombia for the suppression of the Atlantic slave trade. The vote perhaps retrospectively served as an early test of political strength, but the debate was not evidently recorded; the few newspapers that discussed it did not invoke partisan assessments; and Adams himself didn't bother to mention the vote among the day's events in his diary that evening, perhaps because the treaty had originated in Monroe's administration. Moreover, although the rejected treaty's U.S. signatory (Richard Anderson) was one of the proposed

ministers to Panama, he was not criticized in the Panama debates, even as the other proposed minister, John Sergeant, faced criticism for his antislavery principles. See *Senate Executive Journal*, 19th Cong., special sess., March 8–9, 1825, 444–447; Adams, Diary 33, March 8 and 9, 1825, 110–113 (http://www.masshist.org/jqadiaries); New York's *American*, March 14, 1825; *Daily National Intelligencer*, March 11, 18, 1825.

14   Constance McLaughlin Green, *Washington: Village and Capital, 1800–1878* (Princeton, 1962), I:67–107. Green's chapter title also employs a phoenix metaphor.

15   Adams, First Annual Message to Congress; *Register of Debates*, April 20, 1826, 2455. Washington hadn't actually offered a blanket warning against all future foreign alliances; he warned specifically against permanent alliances with European powers, as Jeffrey J. Malanson notes in "The Congressional Debate over U.S. Participation in the Congress of Panama, 1825–1826: Washington's Farewell Address, Monroe's Doctrine, and the Fundamental Principles of U.S. Foreign Policy," *Diplomatic History* 30.5 (November, 2006), 813–838. For perceptive overviews of the Panama debates, also see Mark G. Jaede, "Brothers at a Distance: Race, Religion, Culture, and U.S. Views of Spanish America, 1800–1830" (Ph.D. diss., State University of New York at Buffalo, 2001), 156–193, 205; and Paul D. Naish, "Safe Distance: U.S. Slavery, Latin America, and American Culture, 1826–1861 (Ph.D. diss., City University of New York, 2011), 21–80.

16   *Register of Debates*, esp. February 3, 1826, 1294, and April 11, 1826, 2178 (quotation).

17   *Register of Debates*, 330–331, 338 (in conclave); Benton, *Speech of Mr. Benton, (of Missouri), delivered in the Senate of the United States (in Secret Session), March 13, 1826* (Washington City, 1826), cited in *United States' Telegraph*, May 18, 1826; Charleston's *City Gazette and Commercial Daily Advertiser*, November 16, 1826; *United States' Telegraph*, April 15–19, 1826; Robert V. Remini, *Andrew Jackson: The Course of American Empire, 1767–1821* (1977; paperback ed., Baltimore, 1998), I:180–186; Elbert B. Smith, *Magnificent Missourian: The Life of Thomas Hart Benton* (Philadelphia and New York, 1957), 16–101.

18   *Register of Debates*, 166, 207 (both in conclave), and April 10, 1826, 2150. For reprintings, see *Richmond Enquirer*, March 29, 30, 31, 1826 and the *Gazette of Maine*, April 4, 1826 (citing the *National Intelligencer*); *United States' Telegraph*, March 30, 1826; *National Gazette and Literary Register*, March 30, 1826.

19   Bemis, *John Quincy Adams and the Foundations of American Foreign Policy*, 538–543; Aline Helg, *Liberty and Equality in Caribbean Colombia, 1770–1835* (Chapel Hill, 2004), 196; Germán A. de la Reza, *El Congreso de Panamá y otros ensayos de integración latinoamericana del siglo XIX* (Mexico City, 2006), 42, 81–89.

20 *Register of Debates*, April 10, 1826, 2153–2154, March 1, 1826, 114; Matt Childs, *The 1812 Aponte Rebellion in Cuba and the Struggle Against Atlantic Slavery* (Chapel Hill, 2006), 9–70.

21 *Register of Debates*, in conclave, 330; de la Reza, *Congreso de Panamá*, 93–107; Jay Sexton, *The Monroe Doctrine: Empire and Nation in Nineteenth-Century America* (New York, 2011), 70–84. Haiti was neither invited to nor repre-sented at the Panama Congress, despite what several scholars have said.

22 *Register of Debates*, April 19, 1826, 2405, and April 5, 1826, 2030.

23 Jackson to John Branch, March 3, 1826, *PAJ*, VI:142; Jackson to Samuel Hous-ton, March 8, 1826, *PAJ*, VI:144. For Jackson's relationship with Randolph, see, for example, Jackson to Houston, November 22 and December 15, 1826, January 5, February 4, and February 15, 1827, *PAJ*, VI:235, 244, 254, 275, 292; John Henry Eaton to Jackson, May 5, 1826, *PAJ*, VI:169; Jackson to John Caldwell Calhoun, July 18, 1826, *PAJ*, VI:187; Samuel Houston to Jackson, December 13, 1826, January 5, January 28, 1827, *PAJ*, VI:242, 256, 270; Forbes, *Missouri Compromise*, 117, 175, 215, 228; Howe, *What Hath God Wrought*, 279–284, 330.

24 In the Senate, Randolph, White, Berrien, Benton, and Hayne all used scorn-ful, racialized rhetoric; Tazewell authored (and Macon endorsed) the January 16 Foreign Relations Committee report, which emphasized the dangers of an unstable Caribbean. The exception was North Carolina's John Branch. I have not included rising Democrats Richard Mentor Johnson and Thomas Reed because both eventually voted *for* the mission—after all, party lines were still developing—and because their speeches do not easily align with their final votes. Reed's speech emphasized slavery but was undecided on both the mis-sion and on its implications for U.S. slavery; Johnson openly questioned the mission by arguing that Adams lacked the power to appoint delegates to Pan-ama. Other opposition southerners cast silent votes or else let their speeches go unrecorded. Votes in the House are harder to parse because some oppo-sition members ultimately supported a watered-down version of the mission as amended by Louis McLane, but see, for example, speeches by Hamilton, Weems, and Floyd. For the Senate committee report, see *Register of Debates*, appendix, 92–100 (followed by other official documents regarding Panama).

25 William Cabell Bruce, *John Randolph of Roanoke, 1773–1833* (New York, 1922), I:249–40, 565–650, esp. 568 (quotation), II:184–189; David S. Heidler and Jeanne T. Heidler, *Henry Clay: The Essential American* (New York, 2010), 87–88. Saber reference inspired by David Johnson, *John Randolph of Roanoke* (Baton Rouge, 2012), 3 (for "Excalibur"; also first quotation).

26 Alan Taylor, *The Internal Enemy: Slavery and War in Virginia, 1772–1832* (New York, 2013), esp. 132; Bruce, *John Randolph*.

27   *Register of Debates*, February 28, March 2, 1826, 112–131. The phrase "all men are born free and equal" appears in the 1780 Massachusetts Declaration of Rights, drafted by John Adams, senior; perhaps Randolph intended the reference as an insult to the son. For authorship, see John Ferling, *John Adams: A Life* (1992; 2nd ed., New York, 2010), 214–215.

28   *Raleigh Register*, April 28, 1826; *Register of Debates*, January 31, 1826, 1215. For sample reprintings, citations, and commentary on Randolph's speech, see *Niles' Weekly Register*, March 4, 1826; *Richmond Enquirer*, March 4, 14, 1826; *New-York Spectator*, March 7, 1826; *Rhode-Island Republican*, March 9, 1826; *Eastern Argus*, March 10, 1826; *Vermont Gazette*, March 14, 1826; *Norwich Courier*, March 15, 1826; *Berkshire Star*, March 16, 1826; *National Gazette and Literary Register*, March 7 and, 9, 1826; *Augusta Chronicle and Georgia Advertiser*, March 15, 1826; *Edwardsville Spectator*, April 1, 1826; South Carolina's *Georgetown Gazette*, March 24, 1826; *Farmer's Cabinet*, March 11, 1826; *Pensacola Gazette and West Florida Advertiser*, April 8, 1826 (citing the *Petersburg Intelligencer*). For sample discussions of Floyd's speech, see *National Gazette and Literary Register*, February 4, 1826; *Richmond Enquirer*, February 4, 1826; *Vermont Journal*, February 13, 1826; *Connecticut Courant*, February 14, 1826; *New-Hampshire Sentinel*, March 10, 1826; *Rhode-Island American, and Providence Gazette*, February 7, 1826.

29   On slavery's spread, see Rothman, *Slave Country*; Johnson, *River of Dark Dreams*; Baptist, *The Half Has Never Been Told*.

30   *Genius of Universal Emancipation*, July, 1821; Michael P. Johnson, "The Making of a Slave Conspiracy: Denmark Vesey and His Co-Conspirators," *William and Mary Quarterly* 58.4 (October, 2001), 913–976; Pauline Maier, *American Scripture: Making the Declaration of Independence* (New York, 1997), esp. 154–208; David Armitage, *The Declaration of Independence: A Global History* (Cambridge, Mass., 2007), 1–102.

31   For the justification of long-existing prejudice in the 1820s, see the evocative assessment in Forbes, *Missouri Compromise*, esp. 10, 120, 207; Howe, *What Hath God Wrought*, 279–284.

32   For slavery's role in congressional politics before 1826, see Matthew Mason, *Slavery and Politics in the Early American Republic* (Chapel Hill, 2006); Matthew Mason and John Craig Hammond, eds., *Contesting Slavery: The Politics of Bondage and Freedom in the New American Nation* (Charlottesville, Va., 2011); Bemis, *John Quincy Adams and the Foundations of American Foreign Policy*, 552; Lacy K. Ford, *Deliver Us from Evil: The Slavery Question in the Old South* (New York, 2009), 200–202 (and 279–296 for earlier moves away from universalism at the state level); Wilentz, *Rise of American Democracy*, 222–231. For slaveholders' often tentative and exploratory arguments in the

Missouri debates, and for the observation that the "speeches against the Panama mission represented a new level of skepticism regarding the possibility
of progress" and a new level of "gloom about flawed human nature," also see
Forbes, *Missouri Compromise*, 39–41, 105–8, 147, 163, and esp. 206–208. The
line between attack and counterattack is necessarily blurred in the tit-for-tat
nature of politics; I mean simply to call attention to rhetorical positioning as
well as to the issue of choice—that is, to the fact that opposition members not
only chose to oppose the Panama mission in the first place (when there were
other issues at play), but that they chose slavery as one of their prominent
objections (when they could more exclusively have emphasized constitutional,
diplomatic, political, and religious concerns). Slaveholders were neither passive nor defensive in the federal government more generally. See, for example,
Don E. Fehrenbacher, completed and edited by Ward M. McAfee, *The Slaveholding Republic: An Account of the United States Government's Relations to
Slavery* (New York, 2001); Rothman, *Slave Country*.

33 Adams, Diary 37, February 13, 1826, 92 (http://www.masshist.org/jqadiaries).
For publicizing speeches after defeat was clear, see, for example, *United States'
Telegraph*, March 30, 1826 (Hayne's speech), April 19, 1826 (Benton's), and esp.
May 18, 1826 (advertising Benton's speech, "as corrected by himself," in pam-
phlet form).

34 For earlier proslavery articulations, see Padraig Riley, "Slavery and the
Problem of Democracy in Jeffersonian America," in Hammond and Mason,
Contesting Slavery, 227–246; Ford, *Deliver Us from Evil*. Randolph had advocated against the Atlantic slave trade and he opposed slavery's extension into
the Indiana Territory in 1803, although he vociferously supported slavery's
extension in Missouri sixteen years later. In fact, Randolph's ambivalence was
evident in his Panama speech itself; he called slavery a "cancer," but (in addition to indicting the Declaration's egalitarian rhetoric) he added that he had
"read myself into this [antislavery] madness" and then "worked myself out of
it." He also proffered a related, economic solution to slavery, arguing that it
would fade away in areas where it was "unprofitabl[e]." *Register of Debates*,
March 2, 1826, 117–119, 130; Henry Adams, *John Randolph*, ed. Robert McCo-
lley (Armonk, N.Y., 1996), 1–16, 203; Taylor, *Internal Enemy*, 345–408; Ford,
Deliver Us from Evil, 125–126; Nicholas Wood, "John Randolph of Roanoke
and the Politics of Slavery in the Early Republic," *Virginia Magazine of History
and Biography* 120 (Summer, 2012), 106–143; also see n. 37, below. On Floyd,
see, for example, Ford, *Deliver Us from Evil*, 361–369, 629–630 n. 8; Alison
Goodyear Freehling, *Drift Toward Dissolution: The Virginia Slavery Debate
of 1831–1832* (Baton Rouge, 1982). Regardless of their views on slavery at other
places and times, opposition southerners in 1826 were also innovating, Robert

Forbes suggests, in the degree to which they celebrated racial inequality more generally; see Forbes, *Missouri Compromise*, 206–7.

35 Merrill D. Peterson, *The Great Triumvirate: Webster, Clay, and Calhoun* (New York, 1987), 141 (quotations); Howe, *What Hath God Wrought*, 248; Bruce, *John Randolph*, I:510–525.

36 *Baltimore Gazette and Daily Advertiser*, September 19, 1826 (citing the *Richmond Enquirer*); *Richmond Enquirer*, September 19, 22, 1826.

37 *Register of Debates*, April 6, 1826, 2063; Howe, *What Hath God Wrought*, 264; Heidler and Heidler, *Henry Clay*, 445–452. Randolph had also supported colonization, but mainly as a way to protect slavery by expelling free black people, who might otherwise set a dangerous example to their enslaved friends and families. He withdrew his earlier support for the American Colonization Society just weeks before the Panama debates began, saying he was "for the good old plan of making the negroes *work*," and many opposition members voiced similar concerns. See Taylor, *Internal Enemy*, 401–404 (quotation); Ford, *Deliver Us from Evil*, 298–328; *Register of Debates*, March 2, 1826, 118–119.

38 *Register of Debates*, in conclave, 233; Adams to the House of Representatives, March 15, 1826, in *Register of Debates*, appendix, esp. 71 (on preserving "tranquillity" in Cuba). Adams's thinking about slavery shifted from pragmatically minded complicity and even support in the 1810s and 1820s to a crusade against it in the 1830s and 1840s. See esp. Lindsay Schakenbach, "From Discontented Bostonians to Patriotic Industrialists: The Boston Associates and the Transcontinental Treaty, 1790–1825," *New England Quarterly* 84.3 (September, 2011), 377–401; Stephen Chambers, *No God but Gain: The Untold Story of Cuban Slavery, the Monroe Doctrine, and the Making of the United States* (New York, 2015); Edel, *Nation Builder*, 155–159, 249–289.

39 "Toasts and Speech at Public Dinner, Lewisburg, Virginia," August 30, 1826, *Papers of Henry Clay*, V:659–660; for sample reprintings, see *Baltimore Patriot*, September 15, 1826; Fredericksburg's *Virginia Herald*, September 20, 1826; Salem's *Essex Register*, September 21, 1826; Philadelphia's *National Gazette*, September 21, 1826; Maine's *Eastern Argus*, September 22, 1826; *Rhode-Island American, and Providence Gazette*, September 22, 1826; Middletown, Conn.'s *Middlesex Gazette*, September 27, 1826; Bridgeton, N.J.'s *Washington Whig*, September 30, 1826; New Hampshire's *Portsmouth Journal of Literature and Politics*, October 7, 1826; *Augusta Chronicle and Georgia Advertiser*, October 14, 1826; Bennington's *Vermont Gazette*, October 17, 1826; *Daily National Journal*, September 15, 1826; *City Gazette and Commercial Daily Advertiser*, October 23, 1826 (citing Columbus's *Ohio State Journal*). For Johnston, see *Register of Debates*, in conclave, 224, reprinted in the *Portsmouth Journal of Literature and Politics*, April 8, 1826. For other quotations, see Webster to Jeremiah Mason,

March 27, 1826, *PDW*, II:99; *New-Hampshire Sentinel*, March 17, 1826 (citing a Providence paper).

40 Van Buren, *Autobiography*, 200; *Register of Debates*, in conclave, 331–332. Benton's talk of a united South (which may itself have been an effort to shore up regional unity) evolved; in the 1840s, he was ambivalent about slavery and Texas annexation. The Missouri slaveholder was in many ways more a "westerner" than a "southerner," but his Panama speech (like most speeches on slavery during the Panama debates) emphasized northern and southern identities, and Benton aligned himself clearly with the latter (and with Kentucky's Anderson, whom he tellingly called "a Southern man"). I therefore treat him as a southerner in this context, and certainly as a slaveholder, on his own terms. For Benton's career as related to slavery, see William W. Freehling's *The Road to Disunion: Secessionists at Bay, 1776–1854* (New York, 1990), esp. 432, 541–546; Adam Arenson, *The Great Heart of the Republic: St. Louis and the Cultural Civil War* (Cambridge, Mass., 2011), 28–46. For Calhoun's role in opposition leadership, see esp. John Niven, *John C. Calhoun and the Price of Union* (Baton Rouge, 1993), 113–118.

41 Richard H. Brown, "The Missouri Crisis, Slavery, and the Politics of Jacksonianism," *South Atlantic Quarterly* 65 (1966), 55–72 (including quotation); Adams, Diary 37, February 11, 1826, 91. For coalition building, see esp. Robert V. Remini, *Martin Van Buren and the Making of the Democratic Party* (New York, 1959), 105–113; Forbes, *Missouri Compromise and its Aftermath*, 179–237; George Dangerfield, *The Awakening of American Nationalism, 1815–1828* (New York, 1965), 249–255; Bemis, *John Quincy Adams and the Foundations of American Foreign Policy*, 552–555.

42 *Register of Debates*, February 28–March 2, 1826, and in conclave, 112–132 (quotations on 115, 132), 152–175.

43 *Register of Debates*, in conclave and on April 11, 1826, 236, 2179–2180. For commercial arguments in favor of the mission, and for opposition legislators who had emphasized trade in previous debates only to emphasize other issues (including race) in 1826, see Arthur Preston Whitaker, *The United States and the Independence of Latin America, 1800–1830* (Baltimore, 1941), 577; Hayne and Berrien, *Register of Debates* (in conclave), 152–175, 285; Frances L. Reinhold, "New Research on the First Pan-American Congress Held at Panama in 1826," *Hispanic American Historical Review* 18.3 (August, 1938), 342–363; Cayton, "The Debate over the Panama Congress," 232–237. Although several historians have identified Van Buren as the opposition's chief organizer in the Panama debates (and as a backer of the accompanying racial rhetoric), I have found no direct evidence of Van Buren's opinions on the racialized barbs. See, for example, Forbes, *Missouri Compromise*, 204–205; Remini, *Martin Van Buren*, 106–109.

44 *United States' Telegraph*, March 9, 1826; *Register of Debates*, April 11, 1826, 2180–2181, and March 14 and May 4, 1826, 150, 671 (votes). On Democrats' evolving web of issues, see Forbes, *Missouri Compromise and Its Aftermath*, 179–237; Wilentz, *Rise of American Democracy*, 294–311; Howe, *What Hath God Wrought*, 243–284.

45 *Register of Debates*, April 20, 1826, 2449–2450, and remarks in conclave, 285; also see Howe, *What Hath God Wrought*, 510; Donald J. Ratcliffe, "The Decline of Antislavery Politics, 1815–1840," in Hammond and Mason, eds., *Contesting Slavery*, 267–290; Forbes, *Missouri Compromise*, 204. Opposition members were building here on John Randolph and Nathaniel Macon's earlier warnings about a connection between emancipation and federally funded internal improvements. Sergeant's nomination itself offers further evidence that Adams did not anticipate much objection to the Panama mission, especially not on the grounds of slavery: why else nominate someone who would be such easy bait?

46 *Register of Debates* (in conclave), 274; Ratcliffe, "Decline of Antislavery Politics," and James Oakes, "Conflict vs. Racial Consensus in the History of Antislavery Politics," both in Mason and Hammond, eds., *Contesting Slavery*, esp. 278–279, 293–294. For a helpful distinction between Democrats' northern and southern wings, and for Democrats' efforts to keep slavery out of federal politics, also see Wilentz, *Rise of American Democracy*, 117–125, 186–201. But to keep slavery out of federal politics was simultaneously to preserve the slaveholding status quo, regardless of party leaders' attitudes toward southern radicals. For Democrats' racialized policies (and the Whigs' slightly less racialized ones), see Howe, *What Hath God Wrought*, esp. 279–284, 330, 497–498.

47 *City Gazette*, November 16, 1826 (citing the *Missouri Republican*).

48 *Richmond Enquirer*, April 29, May 6, October 21, November 15, 28, December 8, 1825; *National Gazette and Literary Register*, November 24, 1825 (reprinted without comment in *Richmond Enquirer*, December 2, 1825); *Ballston Spa Gazette*, May 24, 1825, citing New York's *Statesman* (also in the *Ithaca Journal*, May 25, 1825); for other reports on Cuba and Panama, see Fitz, "Our Sister Republics," 264–265.

49 *Easton Gazette*, December 2, 1826 (citing the *National Journal*); *Richmond Enquirer*, April 4, March 9, 1826; *United States' Telegraph*, April 6 (final quotation), 8, 1826 (citing the *Charleston Mercury*); *Louisiana State Gazette*, July 10, 1826.

50 *Baltimore Gazette and Daily Advertiser*, March 3, 1826; *United States' Telegraph*, March 14, 1826; Jared Sparks to Joel Roberts Poinsett, March 10, 1826, Papers of Jared Sparks, MS Sparks 147b (Houghton Library, Harvard University, Cambridge, Mass.).

51 *Rhode-Island American, and Providence Gazette*, March 10, 1826 (reprinted in *Connecticut Courant*, March 13, 1826; *Newport Mercury*, March 11, 1826; *Essex Register*, March 13, 1826; *New-Hampshire Sentinel*, March 17, 1826; *Haverhill Gazette and Essex Patriot*, March 18, 1826); Salem's *Essex Register*, March 20, 1826 (citing, in part, a Boston paper); *Albany Argus*, May 2, 1826 (also March 17, April 11, 28, 1826).

52 *Carolina Observer*, March 15, 1826; *Natchez Gazette*, May 6, 1826 (citing the *Kentucky Reporter*); *Niles' Weekly Register*, March 4, 1826; Norval Neil Luxon, *Niles' Weekly Register: News Magazine of the Nineteenth Century* (Baton Rouge, 1947), 130–139, 212–213.

53 *Genius of Universal Emancipation*, March 18, April 29, 1826.

54 Salem's *Essex Register*, March 16, 1826 (citing the *New-York Observer*); Providence's *Literary Cadet, and Saturday Evening Bulletin*, September 30, 1826. For precedents in northern antislavery politics, see Mason, *Slavery and Politics in the Early American Republic*.

55 Herbert B. Adams, *The Life and Writings of Jared Sparks* (Boston, 1893), I:96–258; Thomas Sully, *Jared Sparks*, 1831, Reynolda House Museum of American Art (oil on canvas mounted on panel).

56 Sparks to José Manuel Restrepo, February 13, 1826, Papers of Jared Sparks, MS Sparks 147b, and Manuel Moreno to Sparks, January 11, 1826, Papers of Jared Sparks, MS Sparks 153 (for language abilities).

57 *Baltimore Patriot & Mercantile Advertiser*, May 29, 1826; Dangerfield, *Awakening of American Nationalism*, 253; *Register of Debates*, Senate, 19th Cong., 1st sess., May 3, 1826, 671; Arana, *Bolívar*, 354–355. Attempts at a follow-up congress in Tacubaya, Mexico, were similarly disappointing and confirmed the negative U.S. reaction.

58 Lynch, *Simón Bolívar*, 224 (quotation); Jared Sparks to Alexander H. Everett, May 14, 1827, Papers of Jared Sparks, MS Sparks 147d. For Britain's observer, see Whitaker, *United States and the Independence of Latin America*, 582–584.

59 Lynch, *Simón Bolívar*, 201–211; Arana, *Bolívar*, 344–355 (quotation on 351).

60 Jaime E. Rodríguez O., *The Independence of Spanish America* (New York, 1998), 235–236 (quotation); Lynch, *Simón Bolívar*, 218–276; Arana, *Bolívar*, 366–368.

61 *Portland Advertiser*, December 8, 1826 (reprinted in *Gazette of Maine*, December 12, 1826); *National Gazette and Literary Register*, December 14, 1826. For sample coverage of the conflict in Colombia, see *National Gazette and Literary Register*, June 3, 1826; *Richmond Enquirer*, June 6 and 7, 1826; *Providence Patriot and Columbian Phenix*, June 7, 1826. For Chile, see New Orleans' *Louisiana State Gazette*, July 1, 1826; *Baltimore Gazette and Daily Advertiser*, July 22, 1826 (citing a "Providence Journal" of July 17; reprinted in the *National Gazette*, July 22, 1826; *Times and Hartford Advertiser*, July 25, 1826; *Richmond Enquirer*, July

28, 1826). For the La Plata basin, see *Baltimore Gazette and Daily Advertiser*, July 24, 1826 (also in the *Baltimore Patriot*, July 24, 1826; Connecticut's *Middlesex Gazette*, July 26, 1826; Hagerstown's *Torch Light and Public Advertiser*, July 27, 1826).

62 *Boston Commercial Gazette*, August 3, 1826 (citing a "Louisiana Gazette").

63 *Richmond Enquirer*, October 31, 1826; William R. Shepherd, "Bolivar and the United States," *Hispanic American Historical Review* 1.3 (August, 1918), 281. Haiti's 1816 constitution was perhaps still more important as a model; see Sibylle Fischer, "Bolívar in Haiti: Republicanism in the Revolutionary Atlantic," in Carla Calargé et al., eds., *Haiti and the Americas* (Jackson, Miss., 2013), 25–53.

64 *Literary Cadet, and Saturday Evening Bulletin*, November 18, 1826.

65 *United States' Telegraph*, April 5, 1826 (letter dated March 18).

66 *City Gazette and Commercial Daily Advertiser*, August 18, 1826 (New Jersey); *New-Hampshire Gazette*, September 19, 1826; *Richmond Enquirer*, September 29, 1826; *Louisiana State Gazette*, October 16, 1826; Newport's *Rhode-Island Republican*, October 19, 1826. N=38 for the *Enquirer*.

67 *Richmond Enquirer*, July 11, 14, 1826. Statistics on July Fourth toasts and on baby Bolivars (below) draw from the same sample sets used in Chapter Four. Because my data sets have defined "hemispheric toasts" as those that *supported* Latin America, the aforementioned critical or ambivalent toasts do not count toward the percentages of "hemispheric toasts." For increased doubts in 1826, also see Jaede, "Brothers at a Distance," 188.

68 *Register of Debates*, April 6, 1826, 2078.

69 For 1815 to 1825, N=45. For 1827 to 1830, N=102. I did not include the boom year of 1826 in these particular calculations because the census does not specify exact birthdates, leaving it impossible to know which babies were born before the debates and which were born after. (The smaller pre-1826 N value results from the fact that the baby Bolivar boom didn't take off until Bolívar skyrocketed to fame in 1825.) My figures exclude the handful of Bolivars for whom no birthplace is listed. The line between slave states and free states was of course hazy, but for analytical purposes I have considered Maine, New Hampshire, Massachusetts, Connecticut, New York, Pennsylvania, New Jersey, Ohio, Illinois, Indiana, Iowa, and Michigan free states and territories, and Virginia, Maryland, North Carolina, South Carolina, Georgia, Tennessee, Kentucky, Louisiana, Alabama, and Mississippi slave states and territories. Other states had no baby Bolivars.

70 For Virginia toasts in 1825 and 1826, N=75; for Pennsylvania, N=42. Massachusetts (N=24) saw a 20 percent rise in hemispheric toasts, although here, too, the small sample size prevents one from making much of the change. The

Arkansas and Illinois data is still more sparse. The *Aurora* had proposed Jackson as a presidential candidate as early as 1822, but in 1825 and 1826 it published only five toasts total (versus thirty-seven toasts for the pro-administration *Democratic Press*). See Jeffrey L. Pasley, *"The Tyranny of Printers": Newspaper Politics in the Early American Republic* (Charlottesville, Va., 2001), 356; Wilentz, *Rise of American Democracy*, 245; John Binns to Henry Clay, May 10, 1826, *Papers of Henry Clay*, V:352. For antebellum politics, see esp. Howe, *What Hath God Wrought*, 243–284, 586; Ratcliffe, "Decline of Antislavery Politics," and James Oakes, "Conflict vs. Racial Consensus in the History of Antislavery Politics," esp. 278–279, 293–294. Naish compellingly argues that Panama was a harbinger of antebellum discussions of race in "Safe Distance," 26, 44.

71 Bruce, *John Randolph*, I:537–538. Southern Bolivar towns and counties subsequently emerged in Georgia, Arkansas, Mississippi, and Missouri (although local lore in Bolivar, Missouri, at least, suggests that these later towns were sometimes named after earlier Bolivar communities rather than after the famous Venezuelan). To the north emerged Peru, Illinois; Mexico, Indiana; Peru, Indiana; Lima, Ohio; a "Bolivar Hall" in Philadelphia by 1832; and a Bolivar Pond in Massachusetts, evidently named in the 1830s or perhaps in the 1820s. The founding date for Bolivar, Indiana, remains unclear. See Jaede, "Brothers at a Distance," 48–49; J. Thomas Scharf and Thompson Westcott, *History of Philadelphia, 1609–1884* (Philadelphia, 1884), esp. 635; Henry S. Beebe, *The History of Peru* (Peru, Ill., 1858); Massachusetts Historical Commission, "Reconnaissance Survey Town Report: Canton" (n.p., 1979), online at http://www.sec.state.ma.us/mhc/mhcpdf/townreports/Eastern/can.pdf; "The City of Bolivar" (citing the *Bolivar Herald-Free Press* and available online at http://www.bolivarmo.com/).

72 Bruce, *John Randolph*, I:542–543. Aside from Randolph, who moved from the Senate to the House, I have not found any opposition southerners who used racialized rhetoric and then lost in the 1826–1827 midterm elections. Reelection information is summarized in the *Biographical Directory of the United States Congress*, http://bioguide.congress.gov.

73 Charles Hammond to Clay, April 7, 1826, *Papers of Henry Clay* V:220; Alexander Keyssar, *The Right to Vote* (New York, 2000), 43–47; James Brewer Stewart, "The Emergence of Racial Modernity and the Rise of the White North, 1790–1840," *Journal of the Early Republic* 18 (Summer, 1998), 181–217; Chambers, *No God but Gain*; Schakenbach, "From Discontented Bostonians to Patriotic Industrialists"; David Roediger, *The Wages of Whiteness: Race and the Making of the American Working Class* (New York, 1991); Noel Ignatiev, *How the Irish Became White* (New York, 1995); Howe, *What Hath God Wrought*, esp. 586.

74   Maria W. Stewart, "An Address, Delivered Before the Afric-American Female Intelligence Society, of Boston" (1832), in *Productions of Mrs. Maria W. Stewart, Presented to the First African Baptist Church and Society of the City of Boston* (Boston, 1835), 56–63.

75   Robert S. Levine, ed., *Martin R. Delany: A Documentary Reader* (Chapel Hill, 2003), esp. 25–29, 69 (quotation), 325; Tunde Adeleke, *Without Regard to Race: The Other Martin Robison Delany* (Jackson, Miss., 2003).

76   Martin Robison Delany, *Condition, Elevation, Emigration, and Destiny of the Colored People of the United States: Politically Considered* (Philadelphia, 1852), 184; Levine, *Martin R. Delany,* 325; Howe, *What Hath God Wrought,* 262; Julie Winch, *Philadelphia's Black Elite: Activism, Accommodation, and the Struggle for Autonomy, 1787–1848* (Philadelphia, 1988), 49–66; James Horton and Lois Horton, *In Hope of Liberty: Culture, Community, and Protest Among Northern Free Blacks, 1700–1860* (New York, 1997), 177–202; Sara Fanning, *Caribbean Crossing: African Americans and the Haitian Emigration Movement* (New York, 2014).

77   Francis Jackson Garrison, *William Lloyd Garrison, 1805–1879* (New York, 1885), I:220–221 (quotation); Henry Mayer, *All on Fire: William Lloyd Garrison and the Abolition of Slavery* (New York, 1998), 71–94. Garrison's global sympathies did not disappear; they just shifted away from South America. For his continued interest in Europe, see W. Caleb McDaniel, *The Problem of Democracy in the Age of Slavery: Garrisonian Abolitionists and Transatlantic Reform* (Baton Rouge, 2013).

78   Lydia Maria Child, *An Appeal in Favor of that Class of Americans Called Africans* (Boston, 1833), 223; "The President and his Speeches," *Douglass' Monthly,* September, 1862.

79   Len Travers, *Celebrating the Fourth: Independence Day and the Rites of Nationalism in the Early Republic* (Amherst, 1997), 218–227; Andrew Burstein, *America's Jubilee: How in 1826 a Generation Remembered Fifty Years of Independence* (New York, 2001); Michael Kammen, *A Season of Youth: The American Revolution and the Historical Imagination* (Ithaca, N.Y., 1978), 43–49.

CONCLUSION: Destined by Providence

1   Manuel de Mier y Terán to President Guadalupe Victoria, June 30, 1828, excerpted at length in Alleine Howren, "Causes and Origin of the Decree of April 6, 1830," *Southwestern Historical Quarterly* 16.4 (April, 1913), 395–398; Mier y Terán to the Minister of War, November 14, 1829, reprinted in Ohland Morton, *Terán and Texas: A Chapter in Texas-Mexican Relations* (Austin, 1948), 99–103; Mier y Terán to Lucas Alamán, March 6, 1831, quoted in David J. Weber, *The Mexican Frontier, 1821–1846* (Albuquerque, 1983), 171; Mier y

Terán to Alamán, July 2, 1832, reprinted in Morton, *Terán and Texas*, esp. 182–183 (also for Terán's background and suicide).

2   For population, see Pekka Hämäläinen, *The Comanche Empire* (New Haven, 2008), 179; Weber, *Mexican Frontier*, 4. For attitudes toward Mexico, see Sarah E. Cornell, "Americans in the U.S. South and Mexico: A Transnational History of Race, Slavery, and Freedom, 1810–1910" (Ph.D. diss., New York University, 2008).

3   James Monroe to Thomas Jefferson, May 27, 1820, Founders Online, National Archives, http://founders.archives.gov/. On Clay's protests, see Robert V. Remini, *Henry Clay: Statesman for the Union* (New York, 1991), 171–176. Andrew Jackson would later charge that Congress's disavowal of a Texas claim in the Transcontinental Treaty was a deliberate effort to "cripple the rising greatness of the west." See Andrew Jackson to John Overton, June 8, 1829, in Daniel Feller et al., eds., *The Papers of Andrew Jackson, Volume VII: 1829* (Knoxville, 2007), 270. Despite the final terms of the treaty, Secretary of State John Quincy Adams had initially pushed for further expansion into Mexico—ironic, given that he spent much of his later career opposing annexation. See, for example, Samuel Flagg Bemis, *John Quincy Adams and the Foundations of American Foreign Policy* (New York, 1949), 561–565. J. C. A. Stagg likewise notes ambivalence toward Texas in "The Political Essays of William Shaler," *William and Mary Quarterly*, web supplement, 59.2 (April, 2002; https://oieahc.wm.edu/wmq /Apr02/stagg.pdf), 9; in "The Madison Administration and Mexico: Reinterpreting the Gutiérrez-Magee Raid of 1812–1813," *William and Mary Quarterly* 59.2 (April, 2002), 449–480; and in *Borderlines in Borderlands: James Madison and the Spanish-American Frontier, 1776–1821* (New Haven, 2009), 203–205. For an overview of the treaty, see esp. William Earl Weeks, *John Quincy Adams and American Global Empire* (Lexington, Ky., 1992).

4   Weber, *Mexican Frontier*, esp. 129, 160–177; Andrés Reséndez, *Changing National Identities at the Frontier: Texas and New Mexico, 1800–1850* (New York, 2005), esp. 93, 162.

5   Pablo Obregón (paraphrasing U.S. editors) to Mexico's Secretary of State, November 12, 1825, quoted in Weber, *Mexican Frontier*, 166 (first quotation); Lucas Alamán, cited in Weber, *Mexican Frontier*, 158 (second quotation); Stephen Austin to S. M. Williams, August 28, 1833, cited in Weber, *Mexican Frontier*, 175 (final quotation). For Austin, see Gregg Cantrell, *Stephen F. Austin: Empresario of Texas* (New Haven, 1999), 4–9, 115–116; for *anglo* settlement more generally, see esp. Weber, *Mexican Frontier*; Reséndez, *Changing National Identities*. None of this is to say that U.S. expansion actually was inevitable; for one thing, it was inadvertently but dramatically helped by Apaches and especially Comanches, whose disruptive raids had rendered

northern Mexico easy prey; see Brian DeLay, *War of a Thousand Deserts: Indian Raids and the U.S.-Mexican War* (New Haven, 2008), esp. xv–xxi; Hämäläinen, *Comanche Empire*, esp. 232–235.

6   William Carroll to Joel Roberts Poinsett, August 27, 1825, in Joel Roberts Poinsett Papers, 1785–1851, Historical Society of Pennsylvania (Philadelphia), Box 3, Folder 2; Austin's *Texas Gazette*, June 26, 1830.

7   Polk, First Annual Message to Congress, December 2, 1845, American Presidency Project, University of California at Santa Barbara, http://www .presidency.ucsb.edu/sou.php; James Monroe, Message to Congress, December 2, 1823, the University of Virginia's Miller Center for Public Affairs (http:// millercenter.org/scripps/archive/speeches/detail/3604). For Polk's narrowing horizons, also see Frederick Merk, *The Monroe Doctrine and American Expansionism, 1843–1849* (New York, 1966), 5–6, 281; Jay Sexton, *The Monroe Doctrine: Empire and Nation in Nineteenth-Century America* (New York, 2011), 102–111. For early mapmakers, see Jedidiah Morse, *Geography Made Easy* (New Haven, 1784), 14, 17–142; John Melish, *Universal School Geography, Being a Companion for his Universal School Atlas, and Intended as a Class Book for his Map of the World and Map of the United States* (Philadelphia, 1818); Henry S. Tanner, *New American Atlas* (Philadelphia, 1818, 1822–1823, 1825–1827); for an overview, also see Mark G. Jaede, "Brothers at a Distance: Race, Religion, Culture, and U.S. Views of Spanish America, 1800–1830" (Ph.D. diss., State University of New York at Buffalo, 2001) 62–65. For two continents in the antebellum era, see Martin W. Lewis and Kären E. Wigen, *The Myth of Continents: A Critique of Metageography* (Berkeley, 1997), 30, 219–220 n. 75.

8   Focusing on intellectuals and politicians, Reginald Horsman argues for a similar change in *Race and Manifest Destiny: The Origins of American Racial Anglo-Saxonism* (Cambridge, Mass., 1981). In the minds of many antebellum expansionists, of course, the more idealistic storyline about spreading republicanism abroad overlapped with the storyline about white men's democracy, as the next several paragraphs suggest. For a concise statement of this point, see Wilentz, *Rise of American Democracy*, 562–563.

9   There is an enormous body of work about manifest destiny. Among the most important studies are Merk, *The Monroe Doctrine and American Expansionism*; Frederick Merk, *Manifest Destiny and Mission in American History: A Reinterpretation* (Cambridge, Mass., 1963); Anders K. Stephanson, *Manifest Destiny: American Expansion and the Empire of Right* (New York, 1995); Albert K. Weinberg, *Manifest Destiny: A Study of Nationalist Exceptionalism in American History* (Baltimore, 1935); Thomas R. Hietala, *Manifest Design: Anxious Aggrandizement in Late Jacksonian America* (Ithaca, N.Y., 1985); Horsman, *Race and Manifest Destiny*; Robert E. May, *Manifest Destiny's Underworld: Fil-*

ibustering in Antebellum America (Chapel Hill, 2002). For white southerners' increasingly racialized views of Mexico by the 1830s, see Cornell, "Americans in the U.S. South and Mexico," 85–187. For a thoughtful distinction between early-nineteenth-century expansion and antebellum manifest destiny, see Stagg, *Borderlines in Borderlands*, esp. 5–6.

10 John Quincy Adams, Diary 45, February 19, 1845, in *The Diaries of John Quincy Adams: A Digital Collection* (Boston, 2004), http://www.masshist .org/jqadiaries, 50 (with noticeably shaky handwriting). For annexation and war, see Sean Wilentz, *The Rise of American Democracy: Jefferson to Lincoln* (New York, 2005), 561–632; Daniel Walker Howe, *What Hath God Wrought: The Transformation of America, 1815–1848* (New York, 2007), 658–791; Amy S. Greenberg, *A Wicked War: Polk, Clay, Lincoln, and the 1846 U.S. Invasion of Mexico* (New York, 2012); DeLay, *War of a Thousand Deserts*; Robert W. Johannson, *To the Halls of the Montezumas: The Mexican War in the American Imagination* (New York, 1985); Timothy J. Henderson, *A Glorious Defeat: Mexico and Its War with the United States* (New York, 2007). For continued postwar expansion efforts, see Amy Greenberg, *Manifest Manhood and the Antebellum American Empire* (New York, 2005).

11 Bolívar to Santander, December 23, 1822, in Piero Gleijeses, "The Limits of Sympathy: The United States and the Independence of Spanish America," *Journal of Latin American Studies* 24.3 (October, 1992), 489; Bolívar to Patrick Campbell, August 5, 1829, in John Lynch, *Simón Bolívar: A Life* (New Haven, 2006), 264.

12 Timothy Mason Roberts, *Distant Revolutions: 1848 and the Challenge to American Exceptionalism* (Charlottesville, Va., 2009); Yonatan Eyal, *The Young America Movement and the Transformation of the Democratic Party, 1828–1861* (New York, 2007); Edward L. Widmer, *Young America: The Flowering of Democracy in New York City* (New York, 2009); David E. Narrett, "Liberation and Conquest: John Hamilton Robinson and U.S. Adventurism Toward Mexico, 1806–1819," *Western Historical Quarterly* 40.1 (Spring, 2009), 23–43. U.S. responses to Europe's 1830 revolts are understudied (and seemingly less marked than responses to Europe's 1848 revolts); so are responses to Canada's 1837–1838 uprisings. But because these insurgents were evidently understood to be predominantly white, U.S. support for them did not clearly represent the same kind of universalism as did earlier support for Latin America.

13 Ralph Waldo Emerson, 1846, in Edward Waldo Emerson and Waldo Emerson Forbes, eds., *Journals of Ralph Waldo Emerson* (Boston, 1913), VII:206. Even southward-looking antebellum slaveholders regularly asserted their own superiority to Latin American slaveholders. See Matthew Pratt Guterl, *American Mediterranean: Southern Slaveholders in the Age of Emancipa-*

tion (Cambridge, Mass., 2008), 9, 48; and esp. Paul D. Naish, "Safe Distance: U.S. Slavery, Latin America, and American Culture, 1826–1861" (Ph.D. diss., City University of New York, 2011), 284–340. On antebellum slaveholders' inter-American interests, also see Gerald Horne, *The Deepest South: The United States, Brazil, and the African Slave Trade* (New York, 2007); Robert E. May, *The Southern Dream of a Caribbean Empire, 1854–1861* (Baton Rouge, 1973); May, *Manifest Destiny's Underworld*; Walter Johnson, *River of Dark Dreams: Slavery and Empire in the Cotton Kingdom* (Cambridge, Mass., 2013). The relationship between the Mexican War and the Civil War is well established, but see, for example, Greenberg, *Wicked War*; Wilentz, *Rise of American Democracy*, 594–796.

14   Alexander Stephens, "Speech Delivered on the 21st March, 1861, in Savannah, Known as 'the Corner Stone Speech,' Reported in the *Savannah Republican*," in Henry Cleveland, ed., *Alexander H. Stephens, in Public and Private* (Philadelphia, 1866), 721; *New York Times*, February 23, 1861 (citing Atlanta's *Gate City Guardian*); Douglas R. Egerton, *Year of Meteors: Stephen Douglas, Abraham Lincoln, and the Election that Brought on the Civil War* (New York, 2010), 281–282; James M. McPherson, *Battle Cry of Freedom: The Civil War Era* (New York, 1988), 59–74, 237–259.

CREDITS

Portions of this book appeared previously in Caitlin A. Fitz, "'A Stalwart Motor of Revolutions': An American Merchant in Pernambuco, 1817–1825," *The Americas* 65.1 (July 2008), 35–62, and in Caitlin A. Fitz, "The Hemispheric Dimensions of Early U.S. Nationalism: The War of 1812, Its Aftermath, and Spanish American Independence," *Journal of American History* 102.2 (September, 2015), 356–379. They are gratefully reprinted here with the permission of Cambridge University Press and Oxford University Press.

The Execution of Ten of Miranda's Officers, in Moses Smith, *History of the Adventures and Sufferings of Moses Smith* (Brooklyn, 1812), following p. 48. Engraving with hand coloring. Courtesy of the John Carter Brown Library at Brown University.

Francisco de Goya y Lucientes, *The Third of May 1808 in Madrid* (1814). Oil on canvas. Copyright of the image Museo Nacional del Prado / Art Resource, NY.

bpk, Berlin / Art Resource, NY. Original portrait located in the Fundación Boulton, Colección Bolivariana, Caracas.

Alexandre Sabés Pétion (Paris?, 1807–1818?). Lithograph. Courtesy of the John Carter Brown Library at Brown University.

Ramage Printing Press. Collection of Old Salem Museums & Gardens.

Lancers of the Plains of Apuré, Attacking Spanish Troops, 1827, engraving in J. P. Hamilton, *Travels through the Interior Provinces of Columbia* (London, 1827), I:168. Courtesy of the John Carter Brown Library at Brown University.

1822 engraving by Peter Maverick after the original portrait by Charles Bird King. Courtesy of the Pennsylvania Academy of the Fine Arts, Philadelphia. John S. Phillips Collection.

Engraving by L. H. Everts after the original painting by John Lewis Krimmel, *Fourth of July Celebration in Centre Square*, 1819. The Art Archive at Art Resource, NY.

Gate & Slave Market at Pernambuco, engraved by Edward Finden, in Maria Graham, *Journal of a Voyage to Brazil, and Residence There, During Part of the Years 1821, 1822, 1823* (London, 1824), following p. 106. Courtesy of the John Carter Brown Library at Brown University.

Lydia Maria Francis (Child), engraving after the Francis Alexander portrait in the Medford (Massachusetts) Historical Society. Lydia Maria Child / Encyclopaedia Britannica / UIG / Bridgeman Images.

Engraving by unidentified artist after portrait by A. Dickinson, in Francis Jackson Garrison's "Portraits of American Abolitionists." Collection of the Massachusetts Historical Society.

Anonymous, *John B. Russwurm*, c.1850. Oil on canvas. National Portrait Gallery, Smithsonian Institution / Art Resource, NY.

Gilbert Stuart, *John Quincy Adams* (1818). Oil on panel. The White House Historical Association (White House Collection).

G. P. Morris and T. W. H. B. B., *Bolivar. A Peruvian Battle Song* (Philadelphia, 1826[?]), Levy Sheet Music Collection, Johns Hopkins University. Sheridan Libraries / Levy Sheet Music Collection / Gado / Getty Images.

The House of Representatives (c. 1822). Oil on canvas. Morse, Samuel Finley Breese (1791–1872) / Corcoran Collection, National Gallery of Art, Washington D.C., USA / Bridgeman Images.

John Wesley Jarvis, *John Randolph (of Roanoke) (1773–1833), American Statesman* (1811). Oil on panel. National Portrait Gallery, Smithsonian Institution / Art Resource, NY.

INDEX

Page numbers beginning with 257 refer to endnotes.